UNITED STATES NAVY & MARINE CORPS

Aviation Squadron Lineage, Insignia and History

Volume 2

Marine Scout Bomber, Torpedo Bomber, Bombing & Attack Squadrons

Michael J. Crowder

Schiffer Publishing Ltd

4880 Lower Valley Road • Atglen, PA 19310

Designed by Molly Shields
Cover designed by Justin Watkinson
Type set in ITC Bodoni BdCn BT/Times New Roman

Printed in China.
ISBN: 978-0-7643-4755-9

We are interested in hearing from authors with book ideas on related topics.

Published by Schiffer Publishing Ltd.
4880 Lower Valley Road
Atglen, PA 19310
Phone: (610) 593-1777
FAX: (610) 593-2002
E-mail: Info@schifferbooks.com.
Visit our web site at: www.schifferbooks.com
Please write for a free catalog.
This book may be purchased
from the publisher.
Try your bookstore first.

Contents

PREFACE

This manuscript represents my second attempt to document the insignia, lineage and history of the various squadrons of the aviation arm of the United States Marine Corps. This volume follows the same format as the earlier work on the fighter squadrons. As opposed to the other excellent efforts by a number of authors who have taken, for a lack of a better term, a "horizontal" approach to the subject matter in that their works, whether single or multiple volumes, covered a specific time period.

This volume and the others in the series take a "vertical" approach to the subject matter. The decision to include a given squadron in this volume is based on either its current or, in the case of squadrons on the inactive list, its last mission designation of attack, scout-bomber, torpedo, or bombing at the time of its deactivation. The range of squadrons and units in a given volume is narrower than would be the case with a "horizontal" presentation of the subject matter. But, they are covered from the date of their activation through the date of their deactivation or until the present day, as well as what for some were several changes of designations and missions. This has led to questions regarding why a specific squadron was included in a particular volume.

For example, the current attack squadrons VMA-211, the "Wake Avengers" and VMA-214, the "Black Sheep," are included in this volume instead of the previous volume on fighter squadrons. Both these squadrons originally were fighter, or "fighting" squadrons in the proper terminology of the period, and their service during World War II could be said to represent the "highlight" of their respective histories. While this may or may not be the case, the fact remains that for a majority of their history both these squadrons have been designated attack squadrons, and they are so designated today. For this reason, they are included in this volume as opposed to the volume on fighter squadrons. It also would be well for those who may choose to disagree with this decision to remember that there are squadrons serving today which began life as fighting squadrons during World War II, but they served for only a few months before they were deactivated. Some of those same squadrons serve today as rotary wing squadrons and have served as such for far longer than they did as fighting squadrons. The reader is more than welcome to agree or disagree with this line of reasoning as they may see fit.

Also, it should be noted that a certain amount of literary license has been taken with the term "attack squadron." The mission designation "attack" came into use in the Navy with the complete reorganization of its aviation assets in November 1946. The old mission designations of "bombing" and "torpedo" squadrons were dropped and merged into the attack designation. As a consequence, the carrier-based bombing and torpedo squadrons that survived the massive wave of disestablishments in the months immediately following the Japanese surrender on 2 September 1945 were redesignated attack squadrons. With regard to the bombing, scout bombing, and torpedo squadrons in the Marine Corps, all of them were deactivated in the months immediately following the end of World War II.

As far as the Marine Corps is concerned, the attack designation was adopted at the same time as was the case in the Navy, 1947, but it was not applied to an actual squadron until the Korean War of 1950-1953, when several existing fighter squadrons were redesignated as attack squadrons. There are a number of reasons for the late coming of the attack designation to the Marine Corps. The first was the deactivation of all the Marine squadrons that would have filled this role in the manner of their Navy brethren during the post-war force reductions. Secondly, the vast majority of Marine bombing missions flown during World War II were more the "light" type with the exception of those flown by the B-25-equipped VMB squadrons, and the rugged, fast F4U Corsair had proven the equal of the specialized dive bomber in this role. And, when the attack designation was applied to existing squadrons, it was taken in recognition of the actual combat situation that existed at the time. Marine squadrons, with a few exceptions, did not engage in air-to-air combat in Korea, and the fighter squadrons spent most of their combat tours engaged in the delivery of air-to-ground ordnance while engaged in interdiction or close air support missions.

Hence, the reasoning behind the decision to organize the material to include those squadrons whose primary mission was the delivery of air-to-surface ordnance from fixed-wing aircraft in this volume. This encompasses the horizontal bombing squadrons, the VMBs, the scout bombing squadrons, the VMSBs, the torpedo bombing squadrons, the VMTBs, and the attack squadrons, the VMAs.

INTRODUCTION

It did not take the armed services of the world long to see the potential military applications for aircraft in the wake of the Wright brothers' epic achievement on 17 December 1903 among the wind-swept sand dunes of North Carolina's Kill Devil Hills. As the reliability and range of an ever increasing flow of new aircraft grew by leaps and bounds, some of the more farsighted officers in the United States realized that they would greatly increase the ability of fleet commanders to "see" what lay over the horizon and confer a considerable advantage to the fleet able to sight its opponent first. In pursuit of this goal, Lieutenant Theodore G. "Spud" Ellyson, USN, was ordered to flight training under the tutelage of the aviation pioneer Glenn Curtis. Ellyson completed or survived his training and was designated Naval Aviator No. 1 in 1911, and the Marines were not far behind. First Lieutenant Alfred A. Cunningham received his wings of gold on 20 August 1912 and was designated Naval Aviator No. 5.

The coming of World War I spurred the already rapid pace of aviation development, but due to its fervent desire to avoid involvement in the European war, the United States began to lag in military preparations in the face of the conflagration that was rapidly consuming a generation on the other side of the Atlantic. All the while, few in the military doubted America's eventual involvement, which came to pass in April 1917.

Among history's first Marine aviators to see combat were those assigned to the Northern Bombing Group and attached to an Allied force under the command of Billy Mitchell in 1918. The First Marine Aviation Force arrived in Brest, France on 30 July 1918. Led by Captain Alfred A. Cunningham, the Marines were to be based at Calais, but while the force had arrived safely in France, no arrangements had been made to get them from Brest to Calais a distance of some 400 miles. However, despite this and other obstacles, the ever-resourceful Cunningham managed to secure train transportation to Calais. In some respects, however, the battle to get into battle had just begun, when, upon arrival in Calais, the Marines discovered that they lacked flyable aircraft. The American-made versions of the British-designed DeHavilland DH-4 bomber that was to equip the Marines had been shipped to France but were still unassembled in their shipping crates. Lacking both the time and the infrastructure required to get these aircraft into service in a timely manner, the captain

The First Marine Aircraft to See Combat
The aircraft depicted is an American-built example of the British designed DeHavilland two-place day bomber. It was in aircraft such as this one that Marine Aviators entered combat for the first time. Note the twin Lewis machine guns on a mount in the rear cockpit and the single gun mounted for the pilot. Aircraft of this type would continue to serve with Marine squadrons until 1929. [U.S. Navy]

The First Director
Lieutenant Colonel Alfred A. Cunningham posed for this photograph on the occasion of his appointment as the first Director of Aviation for the Marine Corps. [U.S. Navy Photo]

managed to entice the British to come to his aid. A number of spare Liberty aircraft engines also had been shipped to France, and Cunningham arranged to swap some of the excess power plants for complete aircraft.

His horse-trading completed, Cunningham's aviators prepared to enter combat. Initially, each of the Marine aircrews were to fly three missions with Royal Air Force squadrons to gain combat experience prior to commencing operations on their own, and it was during these missions that the first aerial victory ever credited to the Marine Corps was recorded. On 28 September 1918, German fighters attacked a formation of aircraft from 218 Squadron, R.A.F., which included the bomber crewed by First Lieutenant E.S. Brewer and Gunnery Sergeant H.B. Wersheiner. Although both of the Marines were wounded in the ensuing dogfight, they managed to destroy one of their attackers.

In addition to the bombing missions, the flying Marines accomplished other firsts. A week after the first kill was recorded, the first aerial re-supply operation in Marine history took place. Three DH-4s dropped 2,600 pounds of food and supplies to a French regiment that had been cut off and surrounded by German forces. In recognition of this successful operation, the three officer pilots were awarded the Distinguished Service Medal, and their three enlisted aircrewmen were awarded the Navy Cross.

By mid-October, the Marines were deemed to have accumulated sufficient combat experience while operating with the R.A.F. to begin offensive missions on their own. On 14 October, a mixed formation of five DH-4s and three DH-9As, a derivative version of the DH-4, were sent against a German rail yard in occupied Belgium. The attack was unopposed until the Marines were returning to their base. The formation then was set upon by a formation of German fighters that seemed to single out the aircraft crewed by Second Lieutenant Ralph Talbot and his gunner, Corporal Robert G. Robinson. A trio of fighters attacked from the rear. Robinson shot down one of the attackers but was severely wounded by the fire of the other two. Despite his wounds, the determined gunner continued to defend his aircraft as other Germans bored in to gain firing positions against the wildly maneuvering bomber. Robinson received two more wounds and collapsed over his guns. Talbot hauled the lumbering bomber around to bring his gun to bear on the enemy. He succeeded in shooting down one of the attackers and dived for the ground to escape. Talbot eluded the remaining enemy fighters and landed at a Belgian airfield near a hospital. Robinson was pulled from the bloody rear cockpit of the DeHavilland and rushed to the hospital where the medical personnel were successful in saving the intrepid gunner. Both Talbot and Robinson received the Medal of Honor for their heroism that day.

The Marine contingent of the Northern Bombing Group lacked any organic fighter component and as a result, most of the Marines' attacks were carried out without the benefit of fighter escort. These unescorted bombers made attractive targets for the German *jadgstafflen*, and the first Marine aircraft lost in aerial combat was shot down by enemy fighters on 22 October.

The attacks by the Northern Bombing Group continued until the armistice was signed and went into effect on 11 November. By the end of hostilities, the Marines had flown forty-three missions with the R.A.F. and fourteen more all-Marine missions. They had destroyed four confirmed enemy aircraft and claimed eight others that could not be verified. These successes had cost the lives of four Marines in action. It had been a short but active introduction into combat for Marine aviation.

The First Marine Aviation Force, composed of 282 officers and 2,180 enlisted men, was returned to the United States in December. Despite its impressive record of service in the World War, the Force was disbanded in September 1919, and its personnel and aircraft dispersed to various installations on the East Coast. Immediately, an intense lobbying effort was undertaken to convince Congress and others that the Marines should retain their aviation forces separate from Naval Aviation and, more importantly, separate from the Army Air Service. Somewhat surprisingly, some of the opposition to this proposal came from within the Marine Corps itself. This lack of internal support came from those who were angry that the First Marine Aviation Force did not provide support to the Marine Brigade while it was engaged in combat on the Western Front. This was not the fault of the aviators themselves, and Cunningham was wholehearted in his agreement with this frustration, stating that "the only excuse for aviation in any service is its usefulness in assisting the troops on the ground to successfully carry out their operations." On this basis, the lobbying paid dividends when, eighteen months later, Congress authorized that overall manning of the Marine Corps aviation component at twenty percent of

Naval Aviation as a whole and, in addition, allocation was made for a permanent Marine aviation force. Further, Marine air stations were established at Quantico, Virginia, San Diego, California and Parris Island, South Carolina.

Thus, a significant milestone was passed in the history of Marine aviation, and with that behind them, the Marine aviators prepared for what lay ahead. Soon aviation units became a fixture in the various Marine expeditionary forces that would be deployed to China, Central America and the Caribbean over the next decade and more. Many of those officers who would rise to high rank or who would win enduring fame during World War II learned much about their trade in these seemingly endless expeditionary actions. Also, the various tactical techniques that would be forged and tempered in the fire of battle across the length and breadth of the vast Pacific in the years to come saw their initial use during these actions. Chief among these were dive-bombing and close air support of troops in contact with the enemy. First Lieutenant Christian F. Schilt was awarded the Medal of Honor for his efforts on behalf of a Marine unit surrounded by Sandinista rebels during the United States' intervention in Nicaragua when he flew supplies into perimeter held by the Marines and evacuated their wounded on the outbound leg of the mission.

The Depression-plagued decade of the 1930s saw all the armed services of the United States wither away to hardly more than a police force, and due to its smaller size in the first place, the Marines perhaps suffered more than the others did. However, despite the overall bleakness of these years, the foundations were laid that would see the Marine Corps through the Second World War and remain largely in place to this day. The mission of the seizure of advanced naval bases to enable the Navy to advance westward toward a climactic battle against the Imperial Japanese Navy in accordance with the existing pre-war doctrine became the primary reason for the Marines' existence. In support of such expeditionary operations, it was realized that dedicated air support would be required, thus, informally at least, codifying the place of Marine aviation.

As the clouds of war began to gather in the latter years of the decade, the purse strings gradually began to loosen, and a slow expansion began, but to describe the pace of this expansion as glacial would not be far off the mark. However, considering the general state of the military of the United States in the mid-1930s, anything was certainly far in advance of nothing. The first squadron to carry a designation that would be considered to be within the "attack" classification came into existence on 1 July 1933, when Marine Fighting Plane squadron Ten, VF-10M, the famed "Red Devils," were redesignated Marine Bombing Plane Squadron Four, VB-4M and then VB-2M. Approximately two years later, Marine Observation Squadron Nine, VO-9M, was redesignated Marine Bombing Plane Squadron Six, VB-6M. (The "M" suffix was applied to the designation to indicate a Marine squadron.)

On 1 July 1941, two Marine Scout Bombing Squadrons came into existence at MCAS, Quantico, Virginia, when Marine Scouting Squadron 1 was redesignated Marine Scout-Bombing Squadron 131, VMSB-131, and Marine Bombing Squadron 1 was redesignated VMSB-132. On the same date, at MCAS, Ewa, Territory of Hawaii, VMS-2 and VMB-2 were redesignated VMSB-231 and VMSB-232, respectively. Despite the initial

First Medal of Honor
This photograph of Captain Christian F. Schilt was taken at the White House, seen in the background, on the occasion of his receipt of the Medal of Honor from President Calvin Coolidge in 1928. [USMC Photo]

efforts to expand the military power of the United States prior to 7 December 1941, growth remained slow until the attack on Pearl Harbor. The coming of World War II found the aviation strength of the Marine Corps to consist of a total of two aircraft wings, two aircraft groups, thirteen squadrons of something on the order of 250 or fewer aircraft. Despite the expansion of the late 1930s and early 1940s, to use the adjective "obsolescent" to describe the majority of these 250 aircraft would be a far more kind description than they deserved.

In contrast to this pitifully small beginning, by the time of the Japanese surrender less than four years later, five aircraft wings, approximately thirty aircraft groups and 128 squadrons had seen service. Included in this number were fifty-five "attack" squadrons divided among VMB (horizontal) bombing squadrons, scout bombing, VMSB, and torpedo bombing VMTB, squadrons. As impressive as these numbers may be, they can be somewhat deceiving. While all the VMB squadrons that served during World War II were newly activated units, some of the scout bombing squadrons were pre-war scouting and bombing squadrons, others saw service for the first time after the attack on Pearl Harbor. With regard to the VMTB squadrons, redesignating existing VMSB squadrons created some, while the remainder were newly activated units.

It has been said that timing is everything, and in the case of the Marines' torpedo squadrons, this certainly was the case. With the exception of a relative handful of torpedo actions in the Solomons, the VMTB squadrons seldom went into battle armed with their primary weapon. The reasons for this are twofold. First, by the time most of the VMTB squadrons were in service, the Imperial Japanese Navy had been driven from the Solomons, and the Japanese fleet lay beyond the reach of the Marines. Secondly, to describe the performance of the Mk. XIII aerial torpedo as miserable largely would be an understatement of considerable magnitude. It was perhaps the worst excuse for a weapon ever to come out of the Navy's Bureau of Ordnance. It was full of bugs, often running deeper that its actual depth setting, and hampered by an exploder that was completely unreliable under certain circumstances. Added to these defects was its delicacy, which required the aircraft to release the weapon from an altitude of not more than 100 feet and a maximum speed of approximately 100 knots. If either of these parameters were exceeded, it would probably fail to run properly if it did not break apart upon hitting the water. Should it manage to enter the water and actually run toward its intended target, it did so at a slow speed of less than 40 knots. It possessed a speed advantage of less than 10 knots over most Japanese warships! When it did manage to strike its target and detonate, its warhead was smaller than those in contemporary weapons in service with other navies and inflicted less damage per hit on its victims. These limitations greatly complicated the tactical employment of the weapon. The torpedo design problems largely were cured by the start of the Central Pacific Campaign of 1944, but by this time, the chances for the Marines to employ a torpedo had evaporated, and the torpedo squadrons flew the vast majority of their combat sorties armed with bombs.

With regard to the scout-bomber squadrons, some were redesignated as torpedo squadrons during the war, while the mission of the remainder was gradually usurped by fighting squadrons equipped with the superlative F4U Corsair. The F4U proved to be virtually the equal of the pure scout-bomber in the bombing role in accuracy and carried a larger bomb load. Added to these advantages were its inherent qualities as a fighter.

The horizontal bombing mission of the VMB squadrons was largely a wartime expedient. It seems the B-25 Mitchell medium bomber was rolling off the assembly lines faster than the Army Air Forces could absorb them, and the Marines agreed to take on the new role of horizontal bombing. The VMB squadrons went on to compile an excellent record of service, but little real justification can be found for their relatively short existence in the first place. In many ways, these squadrons suffered from "being neither fish nor fowl." Their only advantage over the fighter, scout-bomber and torpedo bomber squadrons was in range, and as a result, they did long survive the war's end.

By the end of 1946, the bombing, scout bombing and torpedo bombing missions and their squadrons had been deactivated, and it would be seven years before the attack designation came into use in the Marine Corps. The first would be reserve fighter squadron VMF-121 when it was recalled to active duty for service in Korea and was redesignated VMA-121 on 15 May 1951. Over the next two years, several more fighter squadrons were redesignated as attack squadrons. Some of these squadrons merely

drew a sufficient amount of insignia white paint from stores and changed the fighter designation on the fuselage of their Corsairs from VMF to VMA and carried on with their missions. Others, such as VMA-121 and VMA-251 were re-equipped with the AD Skyraider, the first purpose-built dedicated attack aircraft in the Marines' inventory.

Many of the Marine attack squadrons entered the era of jet aircraft operations when they began to be re-equipped with the fighter-bomber versions of the North American FJ-3 and –4 Fury. A cousin to that company's superb F-86 Sabrejet of Korean War fame, the Fury was a stable, comfortable aircraft, but it was clearly one of the many stopgap "attack" aircraft operated by the Marine Corps during those post-Korean War years.

By 1960, Marine attack squadrons began to be re-equipped with the Douglas A4D Skyhawk series. For some of these units the arrival of the A4D marked their entry into the era of jet aircraft for the first time, while others traded their aging North American FJ-3 and –4 fighter-bombers for the nimble little Skyhawk. By the middle of the decade, the number of A-4 squadrons, both regular and reserve, had peaked at more than a dozen, most of which would soon begin to participate in the apparently endless war in Southeast Asia. However, almost as soon as the peak was reached, a new aircraft began to join the ranks of Navy and Marine Corps attack aircraft, and some of the A-4 squadrons began to exchange their Skyhawks for this new warplane.

The newcomer was the magnificent Grumman A-6 Intruder. The result of a post-Korean War Navy Request for Proposals for a carrier-based, all-weather attack aircraft, the A-6 was beginning to enter squadron service with the Navy as the U.S. involvement in the Vietnam War started to increase significantly. It would become a workhorse for the Marines in the near future. The A-6 represented a quantum leap forward in capability and in complexity when compared to anything that had preceded it in the inventory of the Marines' attack squadrons. From an aesthetic viewpoint, it was anything but a "pretty" aircraft, and over the years, it became even less so as various lumps, bumps and antenna were added. However, if one measures beauty by the ability of a given aircraft to perform its mission, few will ever surpass the A-6 Intruder. Its digital integrated attack and navigation equipment, known as DIANE for short, bestowed upon the A-6 the ability to place an ordnance load equal to its weight on any target within range in virtually any weather. This capability did not come without a price, however, at least at first. The very systems that made the A-6 what it was represented an order of magnitude increase in complexity over any aircraft the Marines had operated previously. As a result, the learning curve for the first squadrons to receive the aircraft was quite long, both as a result of the bugs that will exist in any new system and the general inexperience of those struggling to maintain a system of this complexity while preparing to enter combat. Despite the early problems, the A-6 made an immediate impact in combat in Vietnam, and by the end of the Marines' peak commitment to the war, most of the problems had been solved.

Nothing lasts forever, however, and despite its unquestioned prowess in the all-weather attack role, the A-6 no longer flies in Marine or Navy colors. By Operation *Desert Storm*, the days of the Intruder were rapidly drawing to a close. Several replacements and upgrades were proposed and discarded for various reasons. The former all-weather attack squadrons have been re-

Starting Its Roll
An AV-8B of VMA-214
is about to begin its
takeoff from USS Makin
Island (LHD-8) during
twilight operations in
2011. [USMC Photo]

designated all-weather fighter/attack squadrons and re-equipped with the F/A-18D Hornet.

The days of the much-loved A-4 Skyhawk came to an end even before those of the Intruder. The A-4 replacement in the Marine Corps came in the form of an aircraft unique in U.S. service, the AV-8 Harrier. The vertical/short take-off and landing capabilities of the Harrier make it an ideal weapon for employment in the expeditionary force mission of the Marine Corps. The aircraft is capable of operations from virtually any area slightly larger than the wingspan and length of the airframe, whether afloat or ashore, and this ability to operate quite close to the battlefield acts as a "force multiplier" in that a particular aircraft can theoretically complete more sorties in a given period of time than a more conventional aircraft based some distance away from the battlefield. Although operated by a relatively small number of squadrons, the impact of each is increased by this ability to fly more sorties within a given timeframe than one equipped with a conventional aircraft. The most recent variant of the Harrier, the AV-8B Night Attack aircraft, has been upgraded from the original design to a more powerful engine, a larger wing with additional stores stations, and night/all-weather avionics make the AV-8B a quantum leap forward over the initial versions of the Harrier, the AV-8A. These changes will insure the Harrier remains a viable attack platform well into the new decade. The AV-8B squadrons remain the only fixed-wing squadrons in today's Marine Corps that retain the pure attack designation.

Another factor in the extremely successful marriage of the Harrier to the Marines is the inclusion of detachments from the attack squadrons to medium helicopter and tilt-rotor squadrons during deployments, or "floats," aboard the many modern, extremely capable amphibious warfare platforms during the last two decades.

What the future holds for attack aviation in the Marine Corps is an open question at the moment. A great deal of hope and no small amount of ever more scarce funding have been invested in the F-35 Joint Strike Fighter, or JSF. If all goes as planned, at least three versions of the aircraft will eventually see service in the U.S. armed forces, a conventional, land-based version for the Air Force, a carrier-capable version for the Navy, and V/STOL version for the Marines. However, the first prototype has only recently taken flight, and recent attempts at attack aircraft procurement have met with something less than resounding success, the aborted A-12 Avenger II, for example. For the time being, we are left in a position of wait and see. However, recent budgetary reductions have called for the procurement of the F-35 to be slowed, which will inevitably increase the unit cost, endangering the entire program.

With regard to the lineage of the units included in this volume, the treatment of the subject matter is made easier by the fact that the Marine Corps, as opposed to their Navy brethren, is far more aware of and concerned with a unit's lineage and history. Take, for example, what may arguably maybe the most recognizable and famous of all Navy squadron insignia, the stark, black and white skull and crossbones. This insignia was worn first by Fighting 17 in 1943. VF-17 was the first Navy fighting squadron to take the remarkable Chance Vought F4U Corsair into combat, and it is the most successful in terms of enemy aircraft destroyed in aerial combat. The squadron was credited with the destruction of 154½ enemy aircraft in seventy-six days of combat during its first tour of duty in the South Pacific. After the end of this, its first and only combat tour, it returned to the United States and was disestablished in 1944. (There is, however, some dispute regarding the disestablishment of the squadron. According to the Naval History Center, the squadron was not disestablished, but in his book entitled *The Jolly Rogers*, Captain J.T. Blackburn, U.S.N. (Ret), the squadron's first commanding officer, states flatly that he "tearfully read the official orders decommissioning [*sic*] Fighting Squadron Seventeen" on 10 April 1944.) Regardless, the lineage of the skull and crossbones is a tangled one.

Within weeks, another squadron was established and designated VF-17. It served as a component squadron of Air Group 17 aboard USS *Hornet* (CV-12) and deployed to the Pacific in early 1945. This squadron survived the reductions of the aftermath of World War II and was redesignated VF-5B in 1946 and then VF-61 in 1948. This squadron was disestablished in 1959, bringing to an end the lineage of a squadron designated VF-17.

Regarding the famous skull and crossbones insignia, however, it continues to live on. After the disestablishment of VF-61, the commanding officer of VF-84, whose lineage is traced to the establishment of VA-86 on 1 July 1955 and redesignated VF-84 on the same day and was known then as the "Vagabonds," and of no lineal connection to the VF-84 of World War II, requested and received permission to adopt the nickname and insignia of VF-61. The "Jolly Rogers" of VF-84 were disestablished on 31 October 1995. Now, the "Sluggers" of VF-103 have adopted the skull and crossbones and nickname of VF-17/VF-5B/VF-61 and VF-84. With the exception of the "second" VF-17, VF-5B and VF-61, none of the squadrons to wear the skull and crossbones have any lineal relationship to one another.

This is but one of a host of examples almost too numerous to count of the Navy's former practice of what appears to be a plot to confuse unit lineage to such a degree as to make it a Gordian knot. Squadrons were established, disestablished ,and redesignated in what appeared to be an almost random manner. Squadron designations were used many times for different squadrons with no lineal connections to one another. Furthermore, a given insignia design cannot be used as an indicator to trace unit lineage because, with permission from the office of the Chief of Naval Operations, a squadron may choose to adopt the insignia of an old, disestablished squadron to which the current squadron has no lineal connection. The example of the skull and crossbones cited above is just one example of this practice. This continued until as recently as the late 1990s, when the Navy adopted the practice of activation and deactivation of squadrons in order to preserve their lineage.

In stark contrast to this welter of confusion stands the Marines' strict adherence to unit lineage, history, and tradition. With regard to an aviation unit, once a squadron is activated and given a numerical designation, no other unit will receive that same number. Should the squadron bearing that numerical designation be deactivated at some point, its colors are cased and returned to the Headquarters, Marine Corps. Should any squadron with that same numerical designation ever be activated again, the colors of the previous squadron are dusted off and presented to the "new" squadron and the lineage of that numerical unit continues unbroken, regardless of its alphabetical mission designation as illustrated by the fact there are several rotary wing squadrons in service today that began life as World War II fighting squadrons.

Also, as far as is known, once a squadron insignia is approved by the Headquarters, Marine Corps, it forever is the property of that squadron and will never be worn by any other squadron. A given squadron may submit a new insignia design for approval and change its insignia, but once a particular insignia design or variations of it fall into disuse, the design can be resurrected only by the squadron to which it belonged originally.

This does not appear to be the result of any regulation that prohibits this practice but one of tradition.

From the standpoint of some, there are both good and bad aspects to this. The "good" is that it removes the stumbling block of attempting to use an insignia to trace a portion of a squadron's lineage, something that can never be done with a Navy squadron insignia. The "bad" is that many famous, well-known Marine squadron insignia have disappeared from the view of all but collectors, historians and museum curators.

Two examples of this are the insignia of the "Fighting Falcons" of VMF-221. This squadron was activated in July 1941 and deactivated in September 1945. During its relatively short service, the squadron fought at Midway, in the Solomons and from the deck of USS *Bunker Hill* (CV-17). VMF-221 ranks second only to VMF-121 in terms of enemy aircraft destroyed in combat. However, despite the squadron's outstanding record of service, its insignia of a flaming falcon with the inverted gull wings of an F4U Corsair has not been used since 1945.

The second example is the historic old gray ghost of the recently deactivated VMFA-531. Activated on 16 November 1942 as the Marines' first night fighting squadron, VMF(N)-531, the squadron subsequently was designated in turn, VMF-531, VMF(N)-531 again, VMF(AW)-531 and VMFA-531 and was in continuous service for more than half a century until it was deactivated on 27 April 1992. It is likely that this insignia design that served the squadron with virtually no alteration from 1942 until 1992 will never again see service.

In contrast to the disappearance of these insignia is the figure of a leaping red lion that is central to the insignia of today's Marine Attack Squadron 211, the "Wake Avengers." The squadron was activated on 1 January 1937 as Marine Fighting Squadron 4, VF-4M. The squadron adopted a figure of a leaping red lion on a red-bordered, green disk as its insignia. It was later redesignated VMF-2 and VMF-211 during World War II. After the squadron's heroic but futile efforts in defense of Wake Island in the two weeks immediately following the attack on Pearl Harbor, a red outline of the V-shaped island of Wake was added to the insignia below the figure of the lion and the background color was changed from green to white, bordered in green. In the years following World War II, the background color was changed from white to orange, but the design itself has remained virtually the same since the addition of the outline of the island in 1943. The red lion has served the squadron since 1937, and any insignia with the leaping lion as its central figure is the property of VF-4M/VMF-2/VMF-211/VMA-211.

Throughout all of this, the squadrons of the Marine Corps that have served in the "attack" role, whether equipped with the DeHavilland DH-4, the AV-8B night attack Harrier or the Joint Strike Fighter, have compiled an enviable record of service to this nation and to their Corps. They will continue to do so, regardless of aircraft and mission designation, and when sipping the occasional adult beverage with their fighter pilot brethren are quick to remind the fighter jocks of the fact that "fighter pilots make movies, but attack pilots make history."

MARINE AVIATION INSIGNIA

From the dawn of organized military forces, units have selected and used symbols or insignia to serve as rallying points and to bolster individual and unit *esprit de corps*. Almost from the moment that aircraft donned military colors, the individual units or squadrons began to apply markings to their aircraft as an aid to recognition when airborne. These markings have run the full gamut from official to unofficial and from orderly and fairly restrained systems of combinations of letters of the alphabet and numbers to geometric symbols that were utilized uniformly throughout a branch of service to just about anything imaginable in which individual units appeared to vie with other to approach or to exceed the limits prescribed by the ever-present regulations that govern virtually every aspect of military life.

A natural extension of these markings has been individual squadron or unit insignia. Whether applied to the unit's aircraft, to the flight suits and flight jackets of the squadron members or even to items owned by the squadron, from hangers to coffee cups, these insignia serve the same function today that they have served since their earliest use – they mark the individuals who wear them as members of a particular unit. They are a source of individual and unit pride and a sense of community and of belonging to something greater than one's self. Many a fist has flown as the result of a disparaging remark about an insignia over the years.

In the earliest days of military aviation, there seemed to be little interest among the higher echelons of command in regulating the design and content of unit insignia. As time passed and aviation grew in importance and influence within a given military service, this attitude of "live and let live" still seemed to prevail as long as the insignia in question was within the contemporary bounds of good taste. The social mores of the time seemed to be the only, and, perhaps, the most appropriate guidelines. If the symbolism of a given insignia was rather risqué in nature, it was considered to be somewhat of an inside joke among the squadron members.

With regard to insignia design, whatever constraints previously in existence went by the wayside with the coming of the Second World War. The authorities were faced with far higher priorities, and they seemed to take little or no notice of the insignia that grew in numbers consistent with the proliferation of units that were created by the dictates of a global conflict. Insignia designs that ranged from the whimsical to the overtly profane seemed to sprout like mushrooms were produced by all manner of artists from the highly skilled professional to those of, at best, only marginal talent.

One of the phenomena in insignia design that marked the World War II era as unique appears to have escaped the Marine Corps to a greater degree than the other armed forces is the tremendous number of designs created by the extremely talented artists of the Walt Disney Studios. The work entitled *DISNEY DONS DOG TAGS* published in 1992 describes the efforts of these individuals in response to the vast number of requests received from various units of the armed forces for insignia designs. During the war years, the Disney Studios produced more than 1,200 designs for all of the armed forces of the United States as well as those of our Allies. It seems that most of these designs were created as the result of requests received from the Army Air Forces, and the majority featured cartoon characters from Disney's stable of "actors." However, many featured characters were created from the fertile minds of the cartoonists that had never appeared before, and some of these have lasted for more than half a century. Perhaps the most recognized of all these insignia is that of the Construction Battalions of the United States Navy, the famous Seabees. But, despite the almost universal popularity of Disney's work, it seems that the Marine Corps called upon the work of these artists least of all the Armed Services, both American and Allied. Also, while more than a few Marine squadrons requested the Disney studios to create insignia designs for them, several chose to substitute insignia of their own creation in place of the Disney products. Perhaps this is due, in part at least, to the apparent Marine preference for insignia designs that appear more overtly war-like and sinister and those that deal with death and the supernatural. Even at their most war-like, the Disney designs consistently display a certain amount of whimsy about them – a word that seldom, if ever, appears in the lexicon of the United States Marine Corps. These unused designs reside in the Studio's archives and make a fascinating subject for study on their own merits.

Whatever the source of the idea for the original design, the insignia of Marine aviation represent a colorful and historic series of designs that parallel the history of the organizations that wear them. Some are completely original upon the date of the activation of the squadron or unit, and some have been carried on from the earliest days of Marine aviation. An example of the latter is the Ace of Spades, the traditional playing card symbol for death. Today, it is the property of Marine Attack Squadron 231. However, it was also worn by Marine Observation Squadron 1, the lineal predecessor of VMA-231, and its use dates back to the early 1920s.

Regarding the insignia depicted in this work, the majority of them are originals that either were obtained directly from the squadrons or were purchased or traded with insignia dealers and other collectors. In the case of any insignia obtained directly from a squadron, obviously these must be considered to be authentic and "official." Any insignia obtained from a dealer or other collector has been authenticated through multiple sources and references.

Some of the insignia shown are, however, reproductions. In the case of the reproductions, every effort has been made to verify the accuracy of the design and its colors. The reproductions were made from artwork that was created using a sample of the original as the model. Again, multiple sources have been utilized to verify the authenticity of the original or of the artwork. Many purists decry the fact that these reproductions exist in any form, and to some extent, they do have a legitimate point. That said, however, it should remembered that many of the insignia from the 1942/43 period were made in Australia or New Zealand during a squadron's R&R. They may have been made in numbers of fifty or fewer, and many of them have been lost or fallen victim to the ravages of time and moths over the intervening seven decades. When one finds one of these for sale, the prices are well beyond most would-be collectors. As long as a reproduction is clearly marked as such or can easily be differentiated from an original, it seems that little harm is done by them.

That said, it brings up a subject to which insignia collectors have devoted countless hours of discussion, if not argument, in the past and will continue to debate at length in the future, sort of the insignia collectors' equivalent to baseball's "hot stove league." The question under discussion is what is an authentic insignia and what is not authentic. These differences of opinion usually center upon minor variations in size, color or in some detail of the central design of the insignia in question. As mentioned earlier, one of the sources of the insignia depicted in this work has been the squadrons themselves. Most, if not all, of the squadrons have various items of unit memorabilia, including their insignia, for sale, and the proceeds go into the squadron's recreation [party] fund. I doubt that few would argue the authenticity of an insignia obtained from the actual squadron. Since the sale of these items is motivated by the best of capitalistic ideals, profit, the squadrons from time to time will obtain these items from different suppliers or manufacturers. When this occurs, there are often minor variations in the insignia. When I have had occasion to purchase multiple insignia or to place repeat orders, the items received have frequently differed to some extent in detail and colors. These represent points that should be borne in mind among those of you who collect these insignia.

Also, squadron insignia will change from time to time due to changes in the regulations regarding design, size or content. All new squadron insignia designs and changes to existing ones must be submitted to and approved by the Department of the Navy to be regarded as "official." [It must be remembered that the Navy officially "owns" the Marine Corps, but there are many Marines would claim the situation is actually the reverse.] In brief summary, these regulations require a design to be round, approximately 4 inches in diameter, in "good taste," etc., and designs that depict significant events in the squadron's history are favored. Those that feature a specific type of aircraft with which the squadron has been or is currently equipped are frowned upon. Exceptions may be made for old designs of "historical significance," but it is difficult to imagine that a desire of today's VMFA-122 to revert to the original World War II design of a wolf piloting an aircraft made of a poison bottle while holding his middle digit aloft would be approved despite the historical significance of the design!

The squadron members may choose to change their insignia entirely to commemorate a significant event, such as the receipt of a new aircraft type or a change in designation/mission. Commanding officers will, from time to time, suggest [order] a change for some reason or another. Usually, but not always, such weighty matters are put before the squadron members for a vote, but it should be kept in mind that, should the C.O. choose to make it so, his [or, at some point in the future, her] vote counts 51%!

There exists an almost unlimited number of unofficial and commemorative insignia. In the case of unofficial versions of the squadron's unit insignia, since they are unofficial to begin with, they are not submitted for approval. This skirting of regulations has led virtually endless variations on any given theme. These unofficial designs range from minor differences between the official and the unofficial to items that bear little or no resemblance to the official design. An example of the latter is the insignia of VMAQ-2. For many years, its official insignia consisted of a rampant gold griffin on a red-bordered, light blue background. However, for almost an equal number of years the squadron called themselves the Playboys, and the white Playboy rabbit on a red-bordered black background all but supplanted the official design. The "dark forces" of political correctness descended in its full weight on the squadron over the bunny design, and the squadron's insignia was changed to a black panther's head outlined in blue and silver that was taken from the logo of the Carolina Panthers of the National Football League, a logical selection in view of the squadron's home station at Cherry Point, North Carolina. This design existed for several years and was superceded by the current official insignia of a red-eyed white skull wearing a jester's headdress and a new squadron nickname, the "Death Jesters" in another example of the apparent Marine preference for insignia design denoting the supernatural and death.

Squadrons have adopted the practice of designing a commemorative insignia for almost every occasion. The most common of these is what is commonly referred to as a "cruise" patch, often referred to as a "float" patch by the Marines. These can feature almost any variation of the central design of the official insignia to something really best described as "off the wall" and any variation between these two extremes. They will usually, but not always, bear the dates of the deployment somewhere on the insignia.

Squadrons subject to service in detachments, as opposed to entire unit deployments, frequently design an insignia that signifies these periods of detached duty.

Recently, it seems that the Marines have adopted a common Air Force practice of wearing a smaller version of their squadron insignia on their flight suits. These are usually an inch or so smaller than the more common version that is usually worn on the right breast of the flight jacket.

It is appropriate to mention the materials from which the insignia are made as this also has been a source of "discussion" among collectors. Many of the earliest examples of squadron/unit insignia were hand embroidered on felt. Some were made by cutting pieces from different colored material and stitching them on the desired background. Later examples were hand or machine embroidered on a twill background of the appropriate color while on others, the embroidery covers the entire front of the insignia.

As can be readily discerned from the foregoing, the subject of squadron insignia is an ever-changing kaleidoscope of color and theme. It is a fascinating field for the collector, who may choose to collect the full spectrum of Marine aviation insignia or specialize in a more narrow aspect of the subject. Whatever an individual's preference, these are symbols rich in a heritage of service and valor.

Sadly, some old and historic units, many with a half-century of proud service to this nation, have been deactivated in recent years, and many more will undoubtedly follow their predecessors into limbo in the days to come. Such are the facts of life in today's post-Cold War world, but, the events following 11 September 2001 will likely postpone any unit deactivations. However, rather than to reflect upon their passing with sadness, we should remember what they represented to this nation with a deep sense of pride and humility. A squadron or unit is composed of individuals brought together by common circumstance, and it is neither better nor worse than those individuals. Their accomplishments in peace and in war represent a legacy upon which each of us should reflect from time to time. We should be thankful that they were able to put aside their individual differences and to unite for a common purpose of service, fidelity and sacrifice. Each of us should pray that those who will follow will do as well and surely they will.

Author's Collection

ORGANIZATION & MISSIONS

As is the case with their Navy counterparts, the organization of Marine aviation is that of a flexible force which can be quickly tailored to meet the requirements of a given situation. The framework around which this organization is built is its mission of support of the Fleet Marine Forces that compose the primary operational commands of the entire Corps. If it were a separate air force, today's Marine aviation would constitute one of the world's largest air forces in terms of aircraft and personnel.

This flexible, powerful structure has been in a state of near-constant evolution since Lieutenant Cunningham won his aviator's certification on 12 May 1912. Over the ensuing 100 years, Marine aviation has expanded, contracted and adapted to meet the needs of the nation and of the Marine Corps. In the discussion that follows, we will concentrate on the theoretical structure with comments where appropriate to differentiate between theory and practice.

The current organizational structure has its roots in the Second World War and in the post-war unification of America's armed forces under the National Defense Act that created the Department of Defense from the separate Departments of War and Navy. At the head of Marine aviation is the Deputy Chief of Staff for Aviation. In addition to serving under the Commandant of the Corps, this officer is the Marines' representative in the office of the Deputy Chief of Naval Operations (Air Warfare), designated OP-05, on the staff of the Chief of Naval Operations. The Deputy Chief of Staff has responsibility for all matters relating to the aviation requirements of the Marine Corps from aircraft procurement to personnel.

At the apex of the operational forces are four Marine Aircraft Wings (MAWs), numbered 1 through 4. (It should be noted that the usual written designation for a MAW is to identify it numerically with a Roman numeral, followed by a lower case "d", e.g., IId MAW.) In theory, each Marine division would have its associated air wing of the same number, that is, the First Marine Division would be supported by Id MAW and so on. Today, this organizational structure is more closely followed than it has been at other times. Id MAW is based on the West Coast with the First Marine Division, IId MAW is based on the East Coast with the Second Marine Division, IIId MAW is based in the Far East and IVd MAW is the air wing of the Marine Reserves with its headquarters in New Orleans.

This organizational scheme came about during World War II, but it was never fully put into practice. During the war years,

the Marine Corps grew to a peak strength of six divisions, but the maximum number of Marine Air Wings was five, MAWs I, II, III, IV and IX, with the latter being activated on 1 April 1944 and serving the remainder of the war as a training organization. It was deactivated shortly after the war's end.

Next in the pecking order of Marine Aviation is the Marine Aircraft Group or MAG. Each MAG is designated by a two-digit Arabic numeral, e.g., MAG-11, MAG-26, etc. Again, in theory, each Marine Aircraft Wing would be composed of MAGs numbered 11, 12 and so forth in the case of Id MAW and 21, 22, etc., in IId MAW. It must be remembered that this is a theoretical organization because, in fact, today's IId MAW is composed of MAGs 14, 26, 29, 31, and 32!

In addition to the Marine Air Groups, a Marine Air Wing will have a Marine Wing Headquarters Squadron, MWHS, assigned whose function is that of command, control and logistics support. There is also a Marine Air Control Group, MAGC, which controls its assigned anti-aircraft missile squadrons, which are individually assigned to the component Marine Air Groups of the Wing.

Each MAW has a Marine Wing Support Group, MWSG, responsible for the providing of command, control, supply and logistics support for the Wing's component squadrons. In this manner, the MWSG is the squadron-level equivalent of the Wing's Headquarters Squadron.

Although the composition of each of the Marine Air Wings is slightly different, all are made up of one each of the organizations mentioned in the preceding paragraph and three or more Marine Aircraft Groups or MAG's.

While the Marine Air Wing is primarily an administrative command organization, it is the Marine Air Group that is the fighting "sharp end" of the aviation assets of the Corps. It is the MAG that is organized to deploy to whatever location worldwide and to control the day-to-day operations of its component squadrons. It is also at this level within the organizational structure that one finds the required supporting units necessary for operations, such as Marine Air Traffic Control Squadrons, Marine Air Logistics Squadrons, Light Anti-Aircraft Battalions, and the like.

Generally, but not always, while at its home base, a MAG will be composed of the same type or closely related types of squadrons, i.e., fixed-wing squadrons are assigned a particular MAG and rotary wing squadrons are assigned to another within their parent MAW. It is also usually the case to find squadrons

Hard Work and Hot Sun
"Somewhere in the South Pacific," Marine ground crewmen performing maintenance on an F4U-1A
Corsair of an unidentified squadron. The large rectangular object just forward of the windscreen that
is receiving so much attention from the crewmen is the main fuel cell of an F4U. (Northrop-Grumman)

equipped with a particular type of fixed-wing aircraft or heli-copter to be grouped together in the same MAG. This serves to streamline the support and administrative functions and lower costs, always an increasingly important consideration as defense allocations continue to shrink. However, there are exceptions that prove the rule, as they say. The most notable exception to this is MAG-24, based at MCAS, Kaneohe, Hawaii. In late 1991 and early 1992, MAG-24 was composed of four medium helicopter squadrons, a single heavy helicopter squadron, three fighter/attack squadrons, and the various support squadrons of the MAG. In this respect, MAG-24 more closely resembles a wartime organization than does any other of the current MAGs, but more on that subject later.

Fixed-wing aircraft MAGs are also the parent organizations of the Marine Refueller Transport Squadrons, VMGRs,

while Marine Observation Squadrons, VMOs, were generally assigned to the groups composed primarily of helicopter squadrons. Other types of squadrons, such as training squadrons, tactical electronic warfare squadrons and photographic reconnaissance squadrons are assigned to various MAGs as required for operational efficiency.

During stateside peacetime operations, squadrons are assigned to their parent MAGs on a semi-permanent basis. Periodically, on a rotational basis, the squadrons are subject to deployment to one of the Marine Corps Air Stations in the Far East, MCAS, Iwakuni, Japan or MCAS, Futenma on the island of Okinawa or to European stations in support of NATO operations, etc. Sometimes squadrons deploy as part of a Navy Carrier Air Wing, a CVW, for an at-sea deployment where they function as an integral part of the air wing. (No doubt the Marines consider themselves to be an integral but superior part of the carrier's air wing during these blue water deployments.) Less frequently, they may deploy to a Naval Air Station or other air base overseas, but deployments such as thse are usually made on a temporary basis during a squadron's overseas deployment. Also, it should be noted that with the reductions ordered in the defense budget and the resulting reduction in the number of aviation units in all the armed services, the Marine Corps and the Navy have been ordered to further integrate Marine squadrons into Carrier Air Wings. To what extent this will be done remains to be seen at this time, however. Some have expressed the concern that, as the integration of Marine squadrons into the Navy's CVWs increases due to the continuing reductions among Navy squadrons, it will become increasingly more difficult for the Marine aviation units to continue to carry out their primary mission of support of the Marine Corps.

Unfortunately, this concern may prove to be all too valid. The world of today may be more unstable and dangerous than at any other time in recent memory. The collapse of the Soviet Union has removed a sinister but stabilizing force from those portions of the world that fell under its baleful influence. Events in the dismembered remains of Yugoslavia and in some of the southern republics of what was the Soviet Union provide ample proof of this fact. The only aviation assets that can be deployed reliably prior to a potential crisis erupting into an actual crisis are those based aboard a carrier. This serves to avoid the potentially very real stumbling block of the requirement to obtain permission to base aircraft in a friendly nation close enough to the scene to be effective and/or the question of overflight rights regarding the territory of a sovereign nation. The vast majority of the world's population resides within range of aircraft operating from a carrier at sea in international waters. All this adds up to an increasing need for carrier air power at a time when the number of active carriers and air wings is being reduced. If Marine squadrons continue to be called upon to fill some of the gaps in the carrier air wings, there simply may not be enough of them to go around.

When a squadron deploys to an overseas installation or as a component of a carrier air wing, operational control of the squadron passes from its semi-permanent parent Group to the MAG assigned to the squadron's destination or to the Carrier Air Wing to which it is assigned for the duration of its deployment. These deployments average approximately a year in duration when the squadron moves to an overseas MCAS while those aboard a carrier average something on the order of six to nine months. However, carrier deployments have exceeded 12 months in recent years. [Your author can testify that these extended at-sea deployments can rate very low on the fun meter.]

In times of conflict, Marine Air Groups are tailored to meet the requirements of a particular circumstance or mission. For example, during Operations *Desert Shield* and *Desert Storm*, a total of six MAG's were to see service in the zone of operations, and of these six, four were deployed from their bases in the United States to the combat zone. These were MAG-11 from MCAS, El Toro, California; MAG-13 from MCAS, Yuma, Arizona; MAG-16 from MCAS, Tustin, California and MAG-26 from MCAS, New River, North Carolina.

In addition, two provisional units, MAGs 40 and 50 were established for the duration of the operations in Southwest Asia.

MAG-40 flew in support of the Fourth Marine Expeditionary Brigade, and MAG-50 supported the Fifth Marine Expeditionary Brigade. These provisional air groups were composed of helicopter squadrons, with the exception of VMA-311, which served in MAG-40. All ten of the squadrons of these units operated from naval vessels as part of the amphibious forces that were poised to strike into either Kuwait or into Iraq. Shortly after the end of hostilities, both the provisional air groups were deactivated, and the squadrons that composed them were returned to the operational control of their various parent organizations in both the regular and the reserve forces.

At various times, Marine Air Groups have been activated with the performance of a specific mission in mind. Such was the case of MAG-51, which was activated at MCAAF, Oak Grove, North Carolina on 1 January 1944. Its mission was the destruction of the German V-1 rocket sites along the Channel Coast of Europe. The group's operational squadrons were equipped with the F4U Corsair, and its pilots were trained in the delivery of the 11.75-inch "Tiny Tim" rocket against the German launch sites. For various reasons that will be discussed later, no Marine squadrons saw service in Europe, and on 5 November 1944, MAG-51 was redesignated Marine Aircraft Service Group 51 (MASG-51), and its component squadrons were reassigned to other groups.

The final organizational level to be discussed is that of the individual squadrons themselves. Each of the aircraft squadrons, both fixed-wing and rotary-wing, is composed of approximately a dozen aircraft of the same type. (It should be noted most squadrons, particularly fixed-wing squadrons, also will have one or two aircraft assigned that are used for administrative or utility functions and are known as "hacks." Perhaps the most common "hack" found in the squadrons equipped with jet aircraft was a two-seat version of the A-4 SkyHawk, either the TA4-F or the TA4-J. Among the duties for which the hacks are utilized are instrument training, VIP orientation, maintaining flight status for squadron personnel such as flight surgeons, etc.)

On an as required basis, squadrons are subject to division into detachments, or "Dets" on a temporary basis for special duties. Upon completion of the special duties, the Det is dissolved and the aircraft and personnel assigned to it are returned to their parent squadron.

Due to technological innovations, funding considerations or political decisions, the passage of time has brought forth additions, deletions and restructuring to the unit structure of Marine aviation. As an example, progress in the miniaturization of electronic components and the advancement of the science of aeronautical engineering have made it possible to eliminate the pure fighter, night fighter and all-weather fighter squadrons from the current unit structure. The fighter/attack and all-weather fighter/attack squadrons of today are more capable in those missions than were the dedicated squadrons that preceded them.

In the wake of World War II, the Navy rightly decided to do away with the specialized carrier-based bombing and torpedo squadrons and to combine this mission in the attack mission. The ability of the F4U Corsair and the AD Skyraider made this possible. However, a combination of funding restrictions and political decisions saw to the elimination of the all-weather attack missions that, as far as the Marine Corps was concerned, was fulfilled by the superb Grumman A-6 Intruder for almost three decades. Nothing before or since matches the ability of the

A-6 to place a heavy load of ordnance on target virtually without consideration of the weather. However, age caught up with the Intruder, and it has passed from the current inventory, and its planned successor, the stealthy A-12 Avenger II, was cancelled when it was found to be badly over budget and unlikely to meet the performance criteria set forth in its development contract.

In the period following the successful conclusion of Operation *Desert Storm,* the original military aviation mission, observation, passed from the mission structure of Marine aviation. It was determined that the modern battlefield was no place for an aircraft such as the OV-10 Bronco, and with the A-4 already gone from the inventory of the active forces, it made little sense from a funding standpoint to keep the two-seat versions of this aircraft in service. In place of the observation squadrons, the all-weather fighter/attack squadrons have assumed this mission. It remains to be seen, however, how well these aircraft will be able to perform this mission.

Perhaps the most glaring omission from the current force structure is the absence of any dedicated light photographic reconnaissance capability. This mission, vital though it may be with regard to tactical battlefield considerations, had passed not only from the force structure of the Marine Corps, but also from that of the entire U.S. military force as well. The Air Force made the decision to retire the superb SR-71 prior to the war in Southwest Asia. The Navy disestablished the last of its light photo squadrons with the retirement of the remainder of its small fleet of RF-8G Crusaders from the Reserves, and the last Marine photo squadron, VMFP-3, languishes on the inactive list.

These decisions were not made in a vacuum or with anything but the best of intentions, but "the best laid plans," as they say, have encountered more than a few problems that run the gamut from technological to the ever-present turf battles that have been part and parcel of this nation's history since the founding of the Republic. The Navy planned to fulfill this role with the T.A.R.P.S., tactical air reconnaissance pod system, fitted to the aircraft of one of the two F-14 squadrons in each carrier wing. While it works, two factors have mitigated against its total success. *Desert Storm* was the first combat use of the system, and its imagery, while useful, was not the highest of quality. Improvements subsequently have been made to the system that has corrected the technical problems, but another has raised its ugly head that may be beyond resolution. Again, due to politics and dollars, the decision was made to cut the number of F-14 squadrons in half, with only one per air wing, and to increase the number of strike fighter squadrons per CVW from two to three. At the same time, the retirement of the A-6 brought about the inclusion of all-weather strike to the mission of the VF squadrons. Now, our erstwhile Tomcat driver must be equally proficient in all the aspects of the fighter squadron mission, all-weather strike and aerial photography. As good as these crews may be, that is a tall order for anyone. (The F-14 has since been retired as well.) They have been subsumed into the strike fighter mission, the VFAs, and are analogous to the Marine fighter/attack squadrons, the VMFAs.

Included in the development of the F/A-18 Hornet was a self-contained camera/sensor pallet that is fitted in the nose of the aircraft in place of its internal cannon. It was planned to replace the retired RF-8s with this system, but for whatever reason, it was never adopted.

Another source of the required photo imagery are the various "national intelligence assets," read satellites, that orbit the Earth. In many ways, their capabilities are superb but are optimized to meet strategic, as opposed to tactical, reconnaissance requirements. Three other quite real limitations have been imposed on satellite photography as a substitute for aircraft based systems. First, quite rightly, the capabilities of these "birds" are among this nation's most closely held secrets, and they are controlled by a separate agency that appears loathe to be subjected to military control. As a result, there usually seems to be a considerable time lag between the time the images are captured on film and the time the pictures are in the hands of those on the battlefield. Secondly, as good as the satellites are, photography is still photography, and space-based systems are even more limited by conditions of poor visibility than aircraft based systems. Third, should a situation arise that requires satellite imagery that is not in the orbital path of any of the photo birds, an existing one must be maneuvered into position to photograph the area in question, and the maneuver capability of any satellite is finite.

Another partial solution to the need for tactical aerial reconnaissance is the unmanned aerial vehicle, or U.A.V, that received its baptism of fire in Southwest Asia. They worked quite well, but a question remains regarding their survivability against an enemy whose "head work" is better that the bewildered mob that was the Iraqi army in the latter stages of *Desert Storm.* While small and fairly stealthy, they are extremely vulnerable to ground fire if they are discovered. Further, they can only "see" what the remote operator sees from the sensors aboard the vehicle. They lack the ability to scan all quadrants that an on board human operator possesses.

The various types of current squadrons and the aircraft assigned to them are as follows:

Author's Collection

FIGHTER/ATTACK, VMFA

The fighter/attack squadrons are equipped with single-seat models of the McDonnell Douglas F/A-18 Hornet, which replaced the F-4 and are tasked equally with fulfilling the traditional fighter role as well as the air-to-ground fighter-bomber role. While the terms "fighter" and "fighter-bomber" may sound relatively simple, there are many variations upon each theme. "Fighter" may encompass everything from strike escort to "counter air," the denial of friendly airspace to the enemy, and "fighter-bomber" can range from close air support and interdiction employing both "dumb" and precision-guided munitions and "Iron Hand" anti-SAM missions employing various anti-radiation missiles.

ALL-WEATHER FIGHTER/ATTACK, VMFA(AW)

These squadrons are equipped with two-seat versions of the Hornet, currently the F/A-18D, and are the replacements for the earlier all-weather attack squadrons that were equipped with various models of the Grumman A-6 Intruder. While their designation would indicate equal capabilities in the delivery of both air-to-air and air-to-ground ordnance, in practice they concentrate in the night/adverse weather strike (air-to-ground) role. Furthermore, despite several improvements since the F/A-18 entered service, it has yet to equal the A-6 in the all-weather strike role. Its weapons load and range are less than that of the earlier aircraft. The Hornet is an excellent aircraft in many respects, but it appears that it may be, perhaps, being called upon to do too many things, and by the time it is loaded with all the equipment and design compromises required for this multitude of roles, it is incapable of doing an outstanding job at any of them.

A post-*Desert Storm* addition to the mission of the all-weather fighter/attack squadrons has been the assumption of the forward air control mission from the observation squadrons. This is an excellent example of too many roles for a single aircraft type. The F/A-18 typically operates at a speed and altitude that may preclude it performing the observation mission in a satisfactory manner. Should it descend to the usual altitude at which the OV-10A operated, it becomes just as vulnerable as the Bronco.

ALL-WEATHER ATTACK, VMA(AW) & LIGHT ATTACK, VMA

The attack squadrons of the Regular forces are equipped with the unique and flexible McDonnell Douglas AV-8B Harrier II in place of the earlier A-4 series. The Harrier's ability to take off and land vertically or with an extremely short take off roll has added tremendous flexibility to these squadrons. All are in the process of converting to the night attack capable version of the AV-8B, which adds even further to the effectiveness of these squadrons.

The Reserve attack squadrons are a thing of the past. Previously equipped with the McDonnell/Douglas A-4M SkyHawk, an aircraft with a record of service that goes back nearly four decades, the A-4 has reached the end of its service life. What the future holds in store for the Reserve attack squadrons is not completely clear at this time. At least three of these squadrons have been deactivated in recent years, while others have been redesignated as VMFAs and re-equipped with the F/A-18A or C-models of the Hornet. Apparently, the remainder will follow their recently deactivated sisters into limbo. It does not appear that any will be re-equipped with the Harrier, due to cost considerations. A squadron equipped with an aircraft that is, at best, obsolescent is a prime candidate to be deactivated as a quick, relatively easy way to reduce expenditures in the face of defense budgets that continue to decline.

The all-weather attack squadrons have also passed into history. All of these squadrons have been redesignated all-weather fighter/attack squadrons and re-equipped with the F/A-18D. In view of the Marines' decision to forego the Super Hornets, the E and F models, in favor of the Joint Strike Fighter, they may choose to revisit this decision because of the delays recently imposed on that procurement program.

Author's Collection

Author's Collection

TACTICAL ELECTRONIC WARFARE, VMAQ

While it has been recognized for quite some time that electronic warfare was the key to survival in a modern air battle, the impact of electronic warfare aircraft during Operation *Desert Storm* has led to an increase in the number of VMAQ's. Prior to *Desert Shield/ Desert Storm*, there was one VMAQ in the Regular forces and one in the Reserve forces. After the end of the operations in Southwest Asia, the single Regular squadron has been split into three squadrons and the Reserve squadron stood down as a reserve unit and was immediately activated as a regular unit. All are equipped with the Grumman EA-6B Prowler, a four-seat variant of the A-6 Intruder airframe, which is no longer in production The EA-6B is being replaced with yet another variant of the F/A-18 airframe. While virtually all of us are aware of the continuing advances in electronic miniaturization and automation, the occupant of the back seat of the electronic F/A-18F is very likely to be quite busy as he/she fulfills the functional duties of three flight officers. In view of the critical contributions of electronic warfare in today's aerial combat environment, we can only sincerely hope this can be done effectively. If not, the combat aircrews will pay the price in blood.

Since the decision was made to take the Air Force's EF-111A electronic warfare aircraft out of service and to make electronic warfare a truly joint service function, several joint VAQ squadrons have been established under Navy control in recent months. Personnel for these squadrons are both Navy and Air Force, with the squadrons themselves organized and administered in a manner comparable to all-Navy units. Whether this will lead to an increase in the number of VMAQ squadrons is unknown. Since the new Navy squadrons are supposed to be "expeditionary" in mission, it would have seemed more logical to activate additional Marine squadrons in the first place. After all, the Marine Corps is supposed to be the nation's expeditionary force, but strange are the ways of "joint" operations.

OBSERVATION, VMO

Despite the fact that observation is the original role fulfilled by all military aviation organizations, the life span of the VMO squadrons is at an end. The last VMO squadron in the Regular forces was deactivated recently, and the days of those in the Reserves are numbered. The VMOs, both Regular and Reserve, are/were equipped most recently with various models of the Rockwell OV-10 Bronco. The primary mission of these squadrons has been forward air control of strike aircraft in the close air support and battlefield interdiction roles. While *Desert Storm* provided the needed impetus to expand the number of electronic warfare squadrons, it has proved the undoing of the observation squadrons. The skies above the modern battlefield are extremely dangerous at best, and a propeller-driven aircraft like the OV-10 is faced with a difficult enough task in merely surviving. This mission has been assigned to the VMFA(AW) squadrons. No doubt the fast movers will do their best to fulfill this mission, but experience has shown that this role is made more difficult by the speeds at which jet aircraft operate.

Author's Collection

REFUELER/TRANSPORT, VMGR

The refueler/transport squadrons fill the dual role of intra-theater logistics support and tanker support. Inter-theater transport and logistical support for Marine units are supplied by either the Navy's VR squadrons or by the Air Force. These units are equipped with various models of the ubiquitous Lockheed C-130 Hercules. An interesting side note to the function of the VMGR squadrons is that one of their C-130s is assigned to the support of the Navy flight demonstration squadron, the famous Blue Angels. In its brilliant Navy blue, white and gold paint scheme, it stands quite apart from its brothers in the drab tactical paint schemes that adorn the vast majority of the Marines' other aircraft. Known as "Fat Albert," it is almost always flown during a Blue Angels' performance to highlight the capabilities of this outstanding and long-lived aircraft.

LIGHT HELICOPTER & LIGHT ATTACK HELICOPTER, HML & HMLA

There are a number of light helicopter and light attack helicopter squadrons in both the Regular forces and in the Reserve forces. The exact differentiation between the two, aside from their respective designations, is somewhat less than clear. Both are equipped with a mixture of models of the Bell AH-1 Sea Cobra and the UH-1 Iroquois, better known as the "Huey." These machines are good examples of the Marines' "make do" attitude regarding aircraft. The Army replaced their AH-1 Cobra gunships with the AH-64 Apache several years ago. While the Apache is certainly a newer, faster machine, there is little to choose between it and the latest models of the Marines' Sea Cobras, the AH-1W. However, it may come to pass that the Bell product is eventually replaced by the AH-64. Most of the AH-1Ws currently in service are upgrades of older aircraft, and even helicopters reach the end of their service lives eventually.

MEDIUM HELICOPTER, HMM/TILTROTOR, VMM

The medium helicopter squadrons are found in both the Regular and the Reserve forces. They form the backbone of the Marines' helicopter lift capability. The twin-engine/rotor Boeing-Vertol CH-46 Sea Knight, known as the "Frog," has served the Marines faithfully since the Vietnam War in both the troop and cargo transport role, but it, too, is approaching the end of its service life. It were planned to replace the CH-46 with versions of the Bell tiltrotor MV-22 Osprey, but the former Secretary of Defense Richard Cheney ordered funding cut off for this extraordinary design. Subsequently, the Clinton Administration restored funding to the V-22, and it has progressed successfully through the initial phases of its test regime. Currently, a test and evaluation squadron and a training squadron have been activated, and re-equipment of the medium helicopter squadrons is under way. It is also planned to introduce the MV-22 into the executive transport function of HMX-1, but not as a VIP (Presidential) transport. The Osprey is proving itself in the harsh environment of combat, and while the Marine Corps has stated the procurement of a replacement for the CH-46 is its number one aircraft priority, it remains to be seen whether this revolutionary design will be procured in the desired numbers.

An interesting variation/addition to the HMM/VMM squadrons are their temporary designations as HMM/VMM-XXX(REIN). The "REIN" suffix designated "Reinforced" and indicates a short-term augmentation of the squadron with a detachment of AV-8B Harriers from one of the attack squadrons for the duration of the current deployment. One of the factors that makes this concept extremely workable is the proliferation of the Navy's amphibious platforms, such as the LHA, and it is largely driven by the continuing combat requirements of the global war on terrorism. Also, the detachment of Harriers is always on hand to provide air support to the embarked Marines, and the AV-8B has a respectable air-to-air capability, reducing the requirement to have a CV nearby.

HEAVY HELICOPTER, HMH

The Sikorsky CH-53 helicopter and the squadrons equipped with it form the heavy-lift arm of Marine rotary-wing aviation. The lifting capability of this machine is exceeded by but a few others in the world today. Used primarily as a cargo lifter, as opposed to a troop transport, the CH-53 is capable of the rapid movement of artillery pieces and the like. The CH-53 is another helicopter that has been in service for a number of years, but no replacement is currently planned.

Regarding the medium and heavy helo squadrons, when deployed as a part of a Marine expeditionary unit, detachments of light helicopters and AV-8B Harriers are attached to them, resulting in a "composite" squadron. These detachments are attached for the duration of the deployment, and when it ends, the Dets. are released to return to their parent units.

At the present time, there is a glaring omission from the ranks of Marine aviation missions. There is no photo-reconnaissance capability. The last Marine photo squadron, VMFP-3, has been deactivated, and for the present, at least, no unit has taken

Author's Collection

the photo mission in its place. A palletized camera installation has been developed that is installed in the nose section of the Hornet, but at the present time, it has not been procured.

In addition to the types of squadrons listed here, there are training squadrons associated with the fighter/attack and helicopter squadrons that will be dealt with in the appropriate volume of this work.

With regard to the overall training functions, such as flight training, carrier qualification, etc., the Marine Corps utilizes the standard Naval Aviation training pipeline.

It should be readily apparent from the preceding discussion that Marine aviation is organized as a highly flexible and capable force that can deploy to any point on the globe on short notice and is prepared to fight almost from the moment of its arrival. Its primary mission is the support of the Marine Air-Ground Task Force, and its capabilities toward that end are exceeded by only a very few of the world's air forces, regardless of their size.

It should be noted that these are the squadron designations that were in use at the conclusion of *Operation Desert Storm*. As noted earlier, the last of the Marines' observation squadrons has been deactivated, and the original mission of military aviation no longer has units dedicated to it. Further, there are some missions and several mission designators that are no longer current. The pure horizontal "bombing" mission came to an end in the Marine Corps with the deactivation of the last of the VMB squadrons shortly after the end of World War II. Likewise, the mission designator for a transport squadron, "D," has been changed to "R."

THE MARINE ATTACK SQUADRONS
VMA, VMA(AW), VMSB, VMTB & VMB

MARINE AVIATION WEAPONS AND TACTICS SQUADRON 1

Author's Collection

MAWTS-1 was activated on 1 June 1978 at MCAS, Yuma, Arizona. The squadron is under the operational control of the Deputy Chief of Staff for Training, Headquarters Marine Corps, and its stated mission is "to increase the combat readiness of aviation units." It is somewhat unique in that the squadron has no organic aircraft assigned but utilizes those from the units that send personnel to the courses conducted by MAWTS-1.

The primary course of instruction conducted by the squadron is the Weapons and Tactics Instructor Course. Conducted for both Marine air and ground officers, selected members of Army, Navy and Air Force also attend the WTI course. It is held in three phases: the first is the ground phase devoted to threats and contingencies, command, control and communications, and specific warfare studies for the fixed- and rotary-wing units.

The second phase is devoted to actual flight operations within the arenas stated above.

The final week is the planning and conduct of actual strike operations based upon the materials covered earlier in the course of instruction. In many ways, the WTI course parallels the Navy's Strike Warfare course conducted at NAS, Fallon, Nevada and the Air Forces' various "Flag" courses held at Nellis AFB.

As its name implies, graduates of the WTI course are then qualified to return to their parent units to conduct specialized variants of the course tailored to the specific needs of their squadron, e.g., the customized course for a fighter/attack squadron will differ significantly from those for a refueler/transport squadron or a rotary-wing squadron.

A second, very important mission of the squadron is the work of its Aviation Development, Tactics, and Evaluation Department, which is somewhat analogous to the Navy's Test and Evaluation [VX] squadrons.

The insignia depicted is the only one to have been worn by MAWTS-1 since its activation.

MARINE ATTACK TRAINING SQUADRON 102
THE SKY HAWKS

via Holmberg

VMAT-102 was activated on 1 January 1969 at MCAS, Yuma, Arizona, under the command of Major J. W. Sanders. The squadron's parent organization was Marine Combat Crew Readiness Training Group 10 of IIId MAW, and it was tasked with training aviators in the A-4 pipeline in the day and night delivery of conventional ordnance. In short, it was to function as the "finishing school" for the Marines' Skyhawk pilots and could be considered the light attack equivalent of VMFAT-101 in the fighter/attack community.

The squadron's first students were on board by 23 April training with the older models of the A-4, utilizing the A-4C, and Major T.D. Cooney assumed command on 27 May.

Lieutenant Colonel D.A. Schaeffer relieved Major Cooney on 15 November, and the following spring, the aging -C models of the Skyhawk were replaced with the A-4E, which was more closely representative of the aircraft with which the tactical light attack squadrons of the Marine Corps were equipped. For a time, the two models were operated side by side to avoid interrupting the flow of trained aviators that reached the operational squadrons. No doubt, this was, at least in part, due to the continuing war in Southeast Asia.

The newer aircraft obviously were not as "tired" as the older models and allowed many more flying hours per month, as the squadron averaged a steady increase in monthly flight hours. As its operational tempo continued to rise, VMAT-102 soon began to amass the highest total hours in IIId MAW, topping 1,000 hours per month in 1971. In the midst of this activity, Lieutenant Colonel R.D. Reid assumed command on 19 September 1970.

In June 1971, a new training syllabus was implemented, and this expanded training program placed increased emphasis on air combat maneuvering and air-to-air gunnery, in addition to air-to-ground ordnance delivery. The expanded syllabus was initiated shortly after the Navy began its Fighter Weapons School, i.e. Top Gun, course and was indicative of naval aviation's rediscovery of the need for air combat training. The Navy was employing various models of the A-4 as adversary aircraft at the Fighter Weapons School, and the little Scooter was proving itself to be a worthy opponent in the rough and tumble world of fighter vs. fighter combat. This served to produce more of a well-rounded aviator upon his arrival at his operational assignment.

In November of that same year, Lieutenant Colonel John J. Cahill assumed command of VMAT-102.

On 31 May 1972, VMT-103 was deactivated, and VMAT-102 assumed the duties of the deactivated squadron, type training in the A-4. Prior to this date, VMT-103 had introduced an aviator into the skills required to fly the A-4, while VMAT-102 served to instruct a graduate of -103 how to translate his newly found skills into something that would support the mission of an operational squadron.

Initially, this additional responsibility created some maintenance difficulties in that the TA-4F and -4J aircraft differed substantially in equipment from the A-4E. Also, the needed expansion of the training syllabus to include an instructor in the rear seat to guide the student as he acquired proficiency in the Skyhawk required a few weeks to accomplish smoothly. In recognition of the outstanding job the squadron did in assuming these additional duties while carrying on its original training missions, VMAT-102 was awarded the Meritorious Unit Commendation in May 1972.

On 2 February 1973, Lieutenant Colonel D.E. Kirby assumed command of the squadron and the following month, it reached another milestone when it completed 46 sorties for a total of 124.6 flight hours on 20 March.

On 18 September, Lieutenant Colonel Kirby flew the squadron's 40,000th accident-free flight hour to set another record for VMAT-102. This was followed by receipt of the Chief of Naval Operation's Aviation Safety Award on 19 October.

On 8 March 1974, Lieutenant Colonel Kirby turned command of the squadron over to Lieutenant Colonel Henry L. Searle, and VMAT-102 continued to compile an enviable record. It surpassed 45,000 accident-free flight hours on 20 May. For this record-setting flight, Major General R.W. Taylor, Commanding Officer of IIId MAW and the squadron's Operations Officer, Captain E.E. Hastings, flew the mission in one of the two-seat training versions of the A-4.

The squadron's impressive safety record continued to grow when it surpassed 49,000 accident-free hours on 26 November, and barely six weeks later, 50,000 hours. Also, it received its second consecutive CNO Safety Award. By 30 June 1975, this total had grown to 54,096.5 hours. A second Meritorious Unit Commendation came on 26 February 1976. This was followed by the milestone of 60,000 safe flight hours on 6 April. By March 1977, the squadron had reached 66,000 hours without an accident, but this record came to an end on 15 April when one of the squadron's aircraft was involved in landing accident in severe cross winds at Luke Air Force Base, Arizona.

Bomb Away!
This A-4M of VMAT-102 has just released a pair of Napalm canisters over one of the ranges near the squadron's home station at Yuma, Arizona. [USMC Photo]

The squadron continued to carry out its training duties with the A-4 until that aircraft's days in the active inventory of the Marine Corps came to an end, but as the Skyhawk was replaced by the AV-8B Harrier or the F/A-18 Hornet in the Corps' attack squadrons, VMAT-102 was deactivated in 1988.

The first two insignia of VMAT-102 depicted are two slightly different versions of the only officially approved design to be attributed to the squadron during its service. On this particular example, the hawk, sword, and star are embroidered on a black twill background.

The third design is a unofficial patch worn by the squadron during the early 1970s and served to remind one of the desert environment and the emphasis on air-to-ground ordnance delivery.

[The author would like to express his appreciation to Mr. Mike Wilson of Marquette, Michigan, who kindly provided much of the information upon which this account of VMAT-102 was based. Mr. Wilson's father served in the squadron.]

via Holmberg

MARINE ATTACK SQUADRON 131, THE DIAMONDBACKS

Author's Collection

The lineage of VMA-131 marks it among the most senior squadrons in the Marine Corps in terms of its date of activation. It was activated in the mid-1920s as Marine Observation Squadron 4, VO-4M. It was redesignated Marine Observation Squadron 7, VO-7M on 1 July 1927. During this early period of the squadron's history, it was a part of the Marine Expeditionary Force, Nicaragua.

The following year, still in Nicaragua, it was assigned to the Marines' Second Brigade, and it continued to serve in this Central American nation until early 1933. It then was withdrawn and assigned to the East Coast Expeditionary Force based at Quantico, Virginia, and with the organization of the Fleet Marine Force, VO-7M became a component squadron of Aircraft One, Fleet Marine Force, Quantico in 1935. Two years later, on 1 July 1937, the Chief of Naval Operations ordered a complete reorganization of the aviation assets of the Navy and Marine Corps. One result of this reorganization was a change in designation for virtually all of the existing squadrons, and as a result, VO-7M was redesignated Marine Scouting Squadron 1, VMS-1, on this date although its parent organization did not change.

After Europe erupted into World War II on 1 September 1939, the United States realized that it must begin to expand its armed forces from the near-pitiful levels to which they had fallen during the depths of the 1930s Great Depression. Despite the obvious urgency brought about by events in Europe, however, this expansion took place slowly as Congress continued to place a low priority on military budget matters, and it was nearly two years before Marine aviation saw much in the way of this growth. As a result of this expansion, however slow it may have been, VMS-1 was redesignated Marine Scout-Bomber Squadron 131, VMSB-131, the first squadron of Marine Air Group 31, on 1 July 1941, and Captain Paul Moret assumed command on 7 July.

Immediately after the Japanese attack on Pearl Harbor, the squadron was transferred from Quantico to San Diego where it continued its retraining as scout-bomber squadron. It was re-equipped with the obsolescent Vought SB2U-3 Vindicator dive-bomber, and Major Nathaniel S. Clifford relieved Captain Moret on 1 March 1942. Major Clifford's tenure was short, and the newly promoted Major Moret assumed command of the squadron again on 24 March. While these command changes were taking place, the squadron continued its hectic preparations for eventual deployment to the South Pacific. VMSB-131 was alerted to prepare for movement overseas in late August. By this time, America's first amphibious assault of the war had taken place in the Solomons, and the airfield on Guadalcanal was rapidly prepared to receive aircraft. The crude airstrip, named Henderson Field in honor of a Marine squadron commander lost at Midway, was the key to the success or failure of the operations in the lower Solomons. In the wake of the Allied naval defeat in the Battle of Savo Island, a strange "change of command" took place with the rising and setting of the sun. During daylight hours, the aircraft based at Henderson Field commanded the sea approaches to the island to the extent of their range. With the coming of darkness, however, the Imperial Japanese Navy ruled the waters around the island during the campaign's initial stages. Any attempt by either party to alter this situation was sure to result in a bloody naval engagement.

The squadron departed the West Coast on 6 September 1942 en route to the South Pacific with the sure knowledge that its eventual destination would be Guadalcanal where the battle for control of the island was in full swing. It arrived at MCAS, Ewa, Territory of Hawaii in mid-September. There, despite its scout-bomber designation, the squadron was retrained as a torpedo bomber unit, the first of its kind in the Marine Corps, and re-equipped with the Grumman TBF-1 Avenger. The primary reason for this change of equipment was that events during the Battle of Midway had proven the Vindicator to be obsolete and practically useless as a weapon. The Navy's first-line dive-bomber, the soon-to-be legendary Douglas SBD Dauntless, was in short supply, and those that were available were urgently needed for the carriers' scouting and bombing squadrons that

A Vindicator in Living Color
A fine period color photograph of one of the SB2Us assigned to VMSB-131 in flight over the coast of Southern California, it illustrates many of the features of Marine aircraft of the period. Note the overall light gray color scheme and the squadron markings, painted in white on the fuselage side forward of the national markings. In this case the legend "131-S-11" indicates that this particular aircraft is number 11 of Scout-Bombing Squadron 131. [USMC Photo]

had suffered heavily at Midway. In addition to its obsolescence as a weapon, the version of the Vindicator that equipped the Marine scout-bomber squadrons, the -3, was virtually a flying fuel tank, bestowing upon it almost unprecedented range in the scouting role but severely hampering its performance in other areas. To make matters worse, these fuel tanks were unprotected by any armor or self-sealing liners. A single bullet in any of these vulnerable areas could turn the Vindicator into a torch. No doubt, few, if any, members of the squadron were sad to see the departure of the vulnerable, obsolescent SB2U-3. However, despite the change in mission and equipment, the squadron's designation remained unchanged as such administrative matters rightfully took a back seat to more pressing needs.

After the squadron's hurried retraining in torpedo tactics, it was dispatched to the South Pacific, and in early November 1942, the first of its aircraft and aircrews reached Guadalcanal. Shortly after the squadron's arrival on the island, the bloody and pivotal Naval Battle of Guadalcanal was contested, and the big, tough and relatively fast Avenger immediately made its presence felt. On 14 November, the morning following the savage night action that opened the battle, four of the squadron's Avengers under Captain George E. Dooley attacked an enemy battleship that was found limping homeward in the waters northwest of Savo Island. Severely damaged in the previous night's action, the battleship was unable to make good its escape outside the range of the aircraft based at Henderson Field. With an assist from Navy aircraft from Torpedo 10 of USS *Enterprise* (CV-6), VMSB-131 delivered the final blows to the cripple, H.I.J.M.S. *Hiei*, the first Japanese dreadnought to be sunk in World War II. For his leadership during this strike, Captain Dooley was

awarded the Distinguished Flying Cross. Other members of the squadron would receive their share of decorations for valor in the merciless destruction of the large enemy reinforcement convoy that precipitated the entire engagement. Shortly after this action, Major Moret was ordered to the staff of the Id MAW, and Captain Jens C. Aggerbeck, Jr. assumed command on 21 November. Major Moret would die in an aircraft crash on New Caledonia in 1943, and Moret Field at Zamboanga, Mindanao, the Philippines, was named in his honor in 1945.

After the Japanese defeat in the Naval Battle of Guadalcanal, the aircraft of VMSB-131 continued search and strike missions from Henderson Field until it was relieved from combat on 18 February 1943. Organized resistance on Guadalcanal ended during the night of 7/8 February when a force of Japanese destroyers succeeded in removing the final members of their diseased, starving garrison. The Japanese were so successful in their evacuation efforts that almost two days would pass before the Americans realized they were gone. It was one of the most successful maritime evacuations in history, and a brief lull descended on the area as both sides paused to catch their breaths in the wake of the bloody, savage campaign for control of the island. The squadron was ordered to Allied bases in the rear area for a brief period of rest and retraining, and on 15 March 1943, Captain George E. Dooley assumed command of the squadron.

Returning to combat and Henderson Field once again in April 1943, VMSB-131 took part in the initial strikes flown against Japanese positions in the islands north of Guadalcanal as the American forces began their 18-month climb up the ladder of the Solomons toward the Japanese bastion of Rabaul. After three months of these strikes, the squadron was relieved from

The "Flying Fuel Tank"
Another of the squadron's SB2U-3s is captured in flight over the California coastline while engaged in training exercises. It appears the occupant of the rear cockpit is enjoying the view. [USMC photograph]

combat operations in June, and it returned to the United States. The same month, it was redesignated VMTB-131, a somewhat belated official recognition of the squadron's change of mission prior to its departure for Guadalcanal, but better late than never. Upon its return, VMTB-131 began an extended period of rest and retraining at various bases on the West Coast. Most of the squadron's veterans were detached shortly after it arrived in the United States and ordered to other duty, and the new members of VMTB-131 were able to take advantage of the time in the U.S. to fully prepare for what lay ahead.

The squadron again departed the West Coast for the Pacific on 29 March 1944. On 15 April, it had arrived at Espritu Santo in the New Hebrides. By this period of the war, Espritu Santo was a quiet backwater, and its stay there was relatively short because the squadron was scheduled for further transfer to its new base of operations in the Marianas where VMTB-131 would be assigned to islands' aerial garrison forces in the wake of their planned capture beginning on 15 June. Its ground echelon departed for the Marianas by ship on 12 June, where it arrived on 13 August after an intermediate stopover at Eniwetok. The flight echelon deployed to its Marianas base by a transoceanic flight of 3,400 miles. The squadron was reunited at its new base on Guam, where it was assigned anti-submarine patrols and strike missions against the bypassed Japanese garrisons in the area. Major Douglas A. Bangert assumed command of VMTB-131 on 2 November 1944 while the squadron was engaged in its eight months of duty in the Marinanas.

[Editor's Note: An interesting piece of memorabilia of VMTB-131 from this period recently came into the author's possession. It is a bomb data case from aircraft number 796. In it are many aerial maps, strike photos and other assorted items including a copy of the squadron's newspaper, "The Antenna," dated 13 August 1944. The study of materials such as these is like taking a step back in time of more than a half-century.]

On 27 April 1945, VMTB-131 departed Guam for the Okinawa area. It began operations from the island of Ie Shima on 29 May. Upon its arrival there, it was once again assigned to anti-submarine patrol and support missions for the American troops engaged on Okinawa. Every weapon in the squadron's arsenal except the aerial torpedo was utilized at one time or another during these close support flown missions in behalf of the beleaguered ground troops. Among other things, the standard 325 lb. depth charge was found to be an extremely effective weapon amid the often broken, jumbled terrain of the island. The blast and concussion of one of these anti-submarine weapons was fearsome to behold when dropped into one of the many deep draws or caves in which the enemy sought concealment. As the battle for the island ground toward its inevitable conclusion, the squadron began to take part in strikes against the islands in the Ryukyus remaining under enemy control and against Kyushu, the southernmost of the Japanese Home Islands. The squadron remained in the Okinawa area until after the Japanese surrender.

Major Thomas E. Reese relieved Major Bangert on 11 July 1945 and led the squadron until his relief on 10 August by Major Wilbert H. Fuller, Jr.

In addition to recording five kills in aerial combat in the Solomons, VMSB/VMTB-131 was twice awarded the Presidential Unit Citation for its service in the Pacific. The first award was for its service during the Guadalcanal campaign and cov-

Guadalcanal
One of the squadron's TBFs was captured by the camera as it prepares for a flight from Henderson Field while another of its aircraft is undergoing maintenance in the background. While not of the best quality, this photo provides a good illustration of the primitive conditions that existed on Guadalcanal throughout the campaign. [USMC Photograph]

A Beautiful Day to Fly
This upgraded A-4E of VMA-131 was captured in flight in 1984. [USMC Photo]

ered the period 7 August through 9 December 1942. The second award was for service during the Okinawa-Ryukyus campaign for the period 29 May through 14 July 1945.

Shortly after the end of the hostilities in the Pacific, VMTB-131 returned to the United States, where it was deactivated on 16 November 1945.

In the late-1940s, the former VMTB-131 was one of several World War II squadrons to be reactivated as components of the Marine Corps Reserves. When the squadron was activated in the Reserves, it was redesignated VMF-131.

On 11 January 1951, VMF-131 was recalled to active duty as a result of the requirements for an increase in force levels due to the Korean War. Despite its recall, however, the squadron remained in the United States where it fulfilled the role of an organized replacement pool for pilots and ground crews for the units engaged in combat in the Far East.

After the end of the fighting in Korea on 27 July 1953, the squadron was released from active duty and returned to the Reserves at NAS, Willow Grove, Pennsylvania. It continued to serve as VMA-131, one of the components of MAG-49, and it was equipped with the A-4M Skyhawk. Its ultimate fate was determined as the force levels of America's armed forces, both Regular and Reserve, were reduced due to budget constraints in the wake of the Gulf War and as the A-4 reached the end of their service life. VMA-131 found itself not among the squadrons that was not re-equipped with the F/A-18 Hornet and was deactivated at MCAS, Cherry Point, North Carolina, on 5 December 1998.

The first two examples of the squadron's insignia in the plate dates from its service as a Reserve attack squadron. The design's central figure, the coiled diamondback rattler, has remained basically unchanged since the squadron's World War II service. The insignia on the left is a flight suit-size example that measures 3½ inches from top to bottom, and the one on the right is full-size and is almost 4½ inches in height. The third insignia is an example of one of a group made for a squadron reunion. Major Alvin J. Clark, USMC (Ret), who served in the squadron during World War II, designed the original version of the insignia.

via Holmberg

MARINE TORPEDO BOMBER SQUADRON 132, THE CRYING RED ASSES

Author's Collection

The lineal roots of VMTB-132 can be traced to the period between mid-1935 and February 1936 when the reports of aircraft dispositions among Marine squadrons note the assignment of a dozen of the big, lumbering Great Lakes BG-1 dive/horizontal bombers to Marine Bombing Squadron 6, VB-6M. As of February 1936, the squadron was assigned to Aircraft One, Fleet Marine Force, MCAS, Quantico, Virginia. It was redesignated VMB-1 as a result of the general reorganization of the aviation assets of the United States Navy and Marine Corps which became effective 1 July 1937. The squadron continued to perform its assigned duties from its home at Quantico throughout the remainder of the lean years of the Depression-ridden decade.

As the new decade of the 1940s dawned, the world situation had undergone radical change. On 1 September 1939, Hitler's legions had opened the Second World War with their attack on Poland, and the declaration of war by Great Britain and France came three days later. Across the Pacific, the Sino-Japanese War, begun by the sham of the "incident" at the Marco Polo Bridge, raged, and American-Japanese relations continued to deteriorate alarmingly.

These and other events led to a gradual rise in defense expenditures, which were aimed at two goals. The first was to increase American military preparedness in the face of the worsening world situation. This was coupled with an attempt to spend our way out of the Great Depression by providing sorely needed jobs in the factories and shipyards that received the armaments contracts. Despite this, however, the increased availability of more modern weapons had no immediate impact of the fortunes of VMB-1. While other squadrons benefited from the production of new aircraft, VMB-1 continued to operate the obsolete BG-1. A large, heavy biplane, it had been superseded by more modern monoplanes in most of the Navy's carrier squadrons, which had priority for re-equipment, but, as was the norm, the Marines soldiered on with the Navy's cast-offs for months or years.

As the armed forces of the United States continued to expand at a slowly increasing rate, the aviation assets of the fleet and the Marine Corps were reorganized again on 1 July 1941. On that date, VMB-1 was redesignated Marine Scout Bombing Squadron 132, VMSB-132, and Major Albert D. Cooley assumed command on that same date. Concurrently, the squadron began to exchange its hopelessly obsolete BG-1s for more modern aircraft, the SBD-1 Dauntless. Cooley welcomed the SBD-1, which was quite an improvement because it was merely obsolescent, as opposed to obsolete. The rugged little Douglas product would be the squadron's weapon throughout most of the coming war, but, as usual, despite the quantum leap forward over the BG-1 represented by the SBD-1, it was another Navy hand-me-down, having been superseded in fleet squadrons by the -3 model in late 1940. The SBD-1 lacked armor and self-sealing fuel tanks that combat experience in Europe had shown to be an absolute requirement for an aircraft to survive in a modern air battle.

The trauma of Pearl Harbor increased the squadron's preparations for combat from a hectic pace to one that bordered on the frantic. The combat-capable -3 model replaced the SBD-1's, and one of the great names from the ranks of the Marine scout bomber squadrons, Captain Joseph Sailer, Jr., assumed command of VMSB-132 on 1 March 1942. The squadron continued to operate from bases on the East Coast throughout the spring and summer of 1942.

Gradually, American spirits rose, along with the nation's military fortunes, from the depths of the unbroken string of defeats that followed Pearl Harbor and reached their nadir with the fall of Bataan and Corregidor in April and May, respectively. Events began to brighten within days of Corregidor's surrender when word was received of the check administered to the Japanese by the Navy's carriers in the Battle of the Coral Sea on 7 and 8 May. A month later, the Imperial Japanese Navy suffered its first major defeat in almost 500 years at Midway in which the Marines of VMF-221 and VMSB-241 played a gallant, if largely futile, part.

7 August 1942 saw the opening of America's offensive moves against Japan with the landing of the 1st Marine Division (Reinforced) on Guadalcanal and the surrounding islands in the lower Solomons. The primary tactical objective of the landing was the capture of the nearly completed airfield located on the broad coastal plain on Guadalcanal's north shore. Utilizing captured Japanese equipment the runway was lengthened and prepared to receive aircraft, a vital necessity if the Americans were to stand any chance of maintaining their toehold on the island. The first Marine aviation units arrived at the newly christened Henderson Field on 20 August, and the long, grinding battles of attrition that would mark the campaign for the next six months began.

Shortly after the landing in the Solomons, VMSB-132 was alerted for movement to the West Coast and then to the South Pacific. In early October, the squadron was ordered to San Di-

rapidly deteriorating weather in the area. Violent thunderstorms began to rage in the path of the three SBDs, and all three were lost in the heavy weather. Later, the bodies of Eldridge, Nawman, and their gunners were discovered in the wreckage of their aircraft on Santa Isabel Island. Gentry and his gunner were never found. Apparently, they fell victim to the same weather that claimed the others but crashed into the sea. Four members of the squadron were dead, and the enemy had suffered not at all in return. It was a bitter and painful initiation into combat.

The Japanese continued to rush troops and supplies to Guadalcanal aboard their hard-working destroyers, and more often than not, these supply runs, timed to reach the island under the cover of darkness, were opposed only by whatever aircraft the Americans were able to get into the air and to their intended targets before darkness made them virtually immune to attack from above. Frequently, the ships, if they succeeded in reaching the island to off-load their cargoes, would treat the American perimeter to a shelling as they departed the area. These destroyer bombardments were usually of short duration and caused little in the way of material damage. However, they served to rob the island's defenders of much needed rest as the ships rapidly departed the area to get beyond the range of the American strike aircraft based at Henderson Field before dawn.

On 7 November, a strike of ten Marine aircraft, including seven SBDs under Major Sailer, attacked an enemy force of eleven destroyers bearing some 1,300 reinforcements. One of the destroyers was incorrectly identified as a cruiser and received a disproportionate share of the attackers' attention. Two torpedo and one heavy bomb hits were claimed as a result, and claims were made for a torpedo and two bomb hits against another vessel. While these claims may have left something to be desired with regard to accuracy, two destroyers, H.I.J.M.S. *Takanami* and *Naganami*, were sufficiently damaged to force their premature return to Japanese bases in the Shortlands. Despite the best efforts of the aviators on Guadalcanal, however, the vast majority of the enemy supply runs were completed successfully. Clearly, the Japanese were preparing for a major attempt to recapture the island in the coming weeks.

The Japanese plans culminated in the bitter, bloody three-day Naval Battle of Guadalcanal, fought on 13-15 November 1942. The battle opened during the midwatch of Friday, the 13th, known thereafter as "Black Friday" in the annals of the United States Navy, when an American cruiser-destroyer force nearly collided head-on with a Japanese force of two battleships, a heavy cruiser and eleven destroyers in the waters to the east of Savo Island. The mission of this force was to bombard Henderson Field into submission, as well as to cover a force of eleven transports and a dozen destroyers bearing 14,500 reinforcements for the Japanese garrison. The action that followed was in the words of one of the participants "a knife fight in a telephone booth" and was one of the most bitter and confused surface engagements in American naval history. It is virtually unmatched in terms of concentrated bloodshed and in many ways resembled a fleet action from the age of sail than a modern naval engagement. The unexpected head-on meeting of the two forces destroyed any tactical cohesion that either side might have enjoyed. In the confusion that followed, Japanese fired on Japanese and Americans fired on Americans at ranges so close that some American destroyermen saw their torpedoes strike home and fail to detonate because they had not run the

Squadron Commander and Dive Bomber Pilot Extraordinaire Major Joseph J. Sailer, Jr., the commanding officer of VMSB-132 was awarded the Navy Cross for his actions during the period 10-15 November 1942. Tragically the Major did not survive to receive the award. [USMC photo]

ego, and it departed the United States on the 15th of the month. After almost two weeks at sea, it arrived at Noumea, New Caledonia on 28 October. The next day, the squadron was ordered to Guadalcanal. By 1 November, Major Sailer and the rest of the squadron were in place and ready for operations. In the aftermath of the bitter and costly Battle of Santa Cruz, fought between the respective carriers of the U.S. and Japanese fleets in late October, both sides rushed to increase their land-based aerial strength for the next round of combat.

The squadron's initial operations ended in tragedy when Lieutenants Melvin R. Nawman and Wayne R. Gentry, along with Lieutenant Commander John Eldridge, Jr. of the Navy's VS-71 departed Henderson Field in the gathering dusk of 2 November in an attempt to strike an estimated 21 Japanese destroyers. These ships were bound for the island with large numbers of troops and supplies to reinforce the Japanese garrison on Guadalcanal. In addition to the coming of darkness, the attempted attack faced

Slow But Deadly
Two of the squadron's ground crewman are hard at work on one of the squadron's
Dauntlesses on Henderson Field, Guadalcanal. Note the rather informal modes of
dress, a concession to the island's unremitting heat and humidity. Just barely visible on
the extreme right of the photo in the field's control tower. [USMC photo]

400 yards needed to arm their exploders. The Americans lost four destroyers outright and two cruisers, one scuttled to battle damage and a second to the torpedoes of a Japanese submarine the next day. A Japanese destroyer was sunk, and the battleship H.I.J.M.S. *Hiei* staggered out of the fight, her steering gear wrecked and her scuppers running red with the blood of slain crewmen. *Hiei* was originally conceived and constructed as a battlecruiser, and as a result of several modernizations prior to the coming of the war, she was armored on a scale that fell in between that of a battlecruiser and a dreadnought battleship. In a more normal action this would have been more than sufficient to protect her vitals from the 8-inch guns of the American heavy cruisers she faced. However, the battle was contested at such short ranges that the armor-piercing 8-inch rounds from the guns of USS *San Francisco* (CA-38) and *Portland* (CA-33) had little difficulty penetrating her armor. Despite the barbarous nature of the engagement and heavy losses, the Americans gained their objective. The action was confined to the waters of Savo Sound, and not a single Japanese shell fell on the vital airfield.

The coming of daylight revealed a desolate scene of battered, dying ships occasionally punctuated by the thunder of naval gunfire. Damaged and unable to steer but with her main battery intact, *Portland*'s guns broke the morning silence to fire several salvos at a drifting, burning Japanese destroyer. Hit by "Sweet P's" shells, the hapless tin can exploded and sank. Here and there, small boats from Guadalcanal and nearby Tulagi scurried across the oil stained waters to rescue any survivors of the sunken ships. Ashore, the rumble of aircraft engines marked the beginning of a long day for the American aviators on Guadalcanal. The first aircraft aloft were scouts to locate the oncoming en-

emy convoy and to pinpoint the locations of the ships damaged in the night action. These missions bore fruit almost before they departed the immediate vicinity of Henderson Field when battered *Hiei* was sighted in the waters north of Savo Island. Anxious to extract revenge for the losses of the previous night and for the numerous terror-filled nights spent at the mercy of Japanese ships, the aerial hounds were let off their leashes. As soon as her location was reported to Henderson Field, SBDs and TBFs swarmed after the crippled battleship. Major Sailer of VMSB-132 led most of the strikes against the battered dreadnought.

Hiei was in a terrible plight. Her armor had been pierced by numerous shells from the American heavy cruisers, which destroyed her ability to steer away from the scene of the action. Her anti-aircraft batteries had been greatly reduced by the rain of hits from the American destroyers and light cruisers. Unable to defend herself against the air attacks or to steam out of range of the vengeful aircraft, she was doomed. Major Sailer led a strike of six SBDs of VMSB-132 that arrived shortly after 1100. The aircraft were armed with 1,000-pound armor piercing bombs, and Sailer and two others scored direct hits. The other three bombs were near misses that crushed plating and added to the flooding that was slowly claiming *Hiei*. After Sailer's aircraft departed, two all-Navy strikes of Avengers put six torpedoes into the battleship's hull. Just before dusk, Sailer led the last strike against *Hiei*, but bad weather prevented any additional hits. As darkness fell, the survivors of the battleship's crew scuttled her. Gone was the first Japanese battleship to be sunk in action during World War II.

Despite the unwelcome attention she received, *Hiei* posed little danger to Henderson Field, but soon reports of numerous sightings of other Japanese forces headed toward Guadalcanal

Battered but Not Broken
*This SBD served with VMSB-132 on Guadalcanal and was later re-
turned to the Douglas Aircraft plant in El Segundo, California for repair.
In addition to the obvious damage to the elevators and the rudder, it is
missing its engine and cowling. The round opening visible in the national star insignia on the fuselage is the life raft storage compartment.
[U.S. Navy Photo]*

Squadron Exec
*Major Louis B. Robertshaw, USMC, succeeded Major Sailer as the
commanding officer of VMSB-132 in the wake of the latter's loss.
[USMC photo]*

began to reach the island. A force of four heavy cruisers and six
destroyers was sighted in the Slot, the nickname bestowed on
the New Georgia Sound, 140 miles to the northwest and closing.
Before he turned his attention to the crippled, dying battleship,
Major Sailer led his first mission of the day against this force.
Five SBDs and six TBFs found the enemy just before 0800.
Sailer led the dive-bombers against H.I.J.M.S. *Maya* while the
torpedo aircraft singled out another heavy cruiser, H.I.J.M.S.
Kinugasa. The SBDs failed to score any direct hits, but several
near misses started fires and leaks which reduced *Maya's* speed.
Kinugasa, on the other hand, was not so fortunate. Despite her
radical maneuvers, four torpedoes ripped into her hull, the first
of many hits that would put her on the bottom before day's end.

The third enemy force to receive the unwelcome attention of
the American strikes from Guadalcanal that day was the Japanese
reinforcement convoy. Again, it was Major Sailer that began the
action when he led a strike by the SBDs of VMSB-132 and -141
against the transports and destroyers. Several Avengers of Torpedo
10, led by the squadron's commanding officer, Lieutenant Albert
"Scoofer" Coffin, USN, completed the strike, which was escorted
by fighters to prevent any interference from enemy fighters. The
strike found the enemy in the middle of the forenoon watch. The
dive-bombers of the two Marine squadrons picked their targets
as the Avengers circled to attain the most favorable position from
which to attack. Marine Wildcats tangled with several enemy
fighters in the area as the death dance of the dive-bombers began.
The SBDs split their dive brakes and rolled into their near-vertical
dives. Below them, the transports increased speed and zigzagged
as the destroyers vainly attempted to lay a smoke screen to hide
their vulnerable charges. Aboard the transports, jammed with

troops packed shoulder-to-shoulder, the hapless soldiers could
do nothing but watch the approach of death borne aloft on blue
wings. VMSB-132 scored six hits against two of the transports,
and VMSB-141 got six more against another. The TBFs finished
off two ships crippled by the dive-bombers and damaged a third
so badly she turned back toward the Shortlands. The Marine fighters prevented interception of the strike aircraft by the enemy and
claimed several kills in the resulting fights. The battle against the
convoy, which would last throughout the day, was off to an auspi-
cious start for the defenders of Guadalcanal.

Aboard the targets, the carnage created by the instantaneously
fused 1,000-pounders was nothing short of horrific. Many of the
troops and crewmen simply disappeared in the incandescent white-
hot bomb detonations. Others were hurled overboard by the blasts
and sank like stones from the weight of the equipment they carried.
More were reduced to bloody tatters by the clouds of steel splinters from shattered plating as the bombs found their targets. Before
darkness mercifully ended the slaughter, many more of the enemy
would meet a similar fate. And so it went for the remainder of the
day. Later, the Americans would call the near-continuous stream
of attacks against the convoy the "buzzard patrol" as the strike aircraft picked the bones of the transports. Some pilots reported ships'
decks literally ran red with the blood of the slain and maimed. Others were physically ill at the carnage they created, but despite the
ghastly scene, they went back again and again as soon as their aircraft were refueled and rearmed. Fittingly, Major Sailer led the last

strike of the day against the shattered convoy when a mixed bag of twenty SBDs and TBFs, escorted by seven F4Fs attacked late in the afternoon. This time, Japanese fighters, perhaps stung by the mauling of the convoy they had so far done little to prevent, struck hard at the Americans. Despite the best efforts of the defending fighters, Major Sailer and the others of VMSB-132 scored two direct hits and some near misses on the remaining transports. The other strike aircraft made equally punishing attacks, but several American aircraft were shot down, including the Wildcat flown by Major Joseph Bauer, the former commanding officer of VMF-212, who was serving as the commander of all the fighters based on Guadalcanal. As the coming of darkness ended the slaughter of the convoy, six of the original eleven lay on the bottom. Another, *Sado Maru*, turned back after being heavily damaged, but the remaining four, also all damaged were abandoned by their escorting destroyers, were ordered to beach themselves on Guadalcanal.

That night, the dark waters of Savo Sound were the scene of yet another bitter naval action. The Japanese were determined to bombard Henderson Field into impotence, and a force built around the sister of the dead *Hiei*, H.I.J.M.S. *Kirishima*, accompanied by the requisite cruisers and destroyers steamed past the sinister cone of Savo Island, bent on its mission of destruction. Again, the Americans were prepared to meet the enemy force with force. Four destroyers escorted the battleships USS *Washington* (BB-56) and *South Dakota* (BB-57), commanded by Rear Admiral Willis A. Lee, who flew his flag in *Washington*. As was usually the case in these night actions, the fighting was confused, brief and costly to those engaged. Two American destroyers were torpedoed and sunk, and a third reeled out of action severely damaged. *South Dakota* suffered a complete electrical failure at a critical time, and as she steamed blindly onward, she was heavily damaged by enemy fire but was saved by her heavy armor.

As the enemy's attention was drawn to the destroyers and *South Dakota*, *Washington* closed undetected on the scene of the action. Just before midnight, the darkness was shattered by the first full salvos from her nine 16-inch rifles. At point blank range, the 2,700-pound projectiles from *Washington's* guns pierced *Kirishima's* armor as if it were paper. Shattered by nine 16-inch hits and numerous others from the American secondary batteries, the Japanese battleship was quickly reduced to a floating wreck, her interior ablaze almost throughout her length. Surprised and confused by the sudden appearance of a second American dreadnought, the Japanese withdrew, pursued for a short time by *Washington*. Behind them, shattered *Kirishima* drifted slowly through the darkness, a dying, blazing catafalque for most of her crew. At 0320, she was abandoned and scuttled. So thorough had been the destruction wrought by American gunnery that witnesses later reported that her hull literally was glowing red hot as she slipped beneath the gentle seas, the second Japanese battleship to die off Guadalcanal in as many nights.

The coming of daylight on 15 November revealed the somewhat astonishing sight of four beached Japanese transports in Doma Cove and at Tassafaronga Point to the west of the American perimeter. Quickly recovering from their surprise, the Americans turned every available weapon against the ships. They were taken under fire by the long-ranged 155-mm guns of the Marine defense battalion ashore and a destroyer steamed along the beach methodically taking under fire every target she could find. And,

as soon as they could be readied, the "buzzards" swarmed aloft from the airfield to scavenge the enemy's remains.

Appropriately, the SBDs of VMSB-132, led by Major Sailer and VMSB-141, led by its commanding officer, Major Robert Richard made the first air strikes of the day. Included in the strike was a pair of SBDs from the Navy's Scouting 10. Despite including elements of three squadrons, the strike totaled only nine aircraft, an indication of the conditions that prevailed on Guadalcanal at the time despite the valiant efforts of the ground crews. But, despite the paucity of numbers, the nine scored four direct hits on one ship with 1,000-pounders and put another of the big bombs into a supply dump, starting a spectacular fire. This strike marked the final Marine attack of the battle. Navy aircraft accomplished the remainder of the destruction of the beached enemy ships, whose rusting remains lie there today, more than seventy years after their death.

The mid-November Naval Battle of Guadalcanal marked the high water mark of Japanese attempts to recapture the island, and in the wake of the shattering of the convoy, the Japanese made the decision to abandon their attempts to regain the island, although it would not be until the last days of January and first days of February 1943 that the Japanese withdrew the skeletal remains of their forces. Over the remaining ten weeks of the battle for the island, many hard actions would be fought that would result in painful losses on both sides. Among these was the redoubtable Major Sailer.

One of Sailer's Victims
This photograph shows one of the four Japanese transports that survived the gauntlet of air strikes that gutted the final enemy attempt to reinforce its garrison on Guadalcanal. This ship and three others were ordered to beach themselves and land whatever supplies and troops they could. It is shown after the attention it received from the Marine dive bombers on 15 November 1942. [USMC photo]

On 7 December, the Major led a strike against eleven destroyers located some 200 miles to the northwest of Guadalcanal. Attacking just before sunset, the SBDs heavily damaged one of the destroyers and inflicted lighter damage on two others. Sailer's aircraft was damaged by anti-aircraft fire during his dive, but he pressed his attack and dropped his bomb. On recovery from his dive, he found that he was unable to close his dive brakes, severely reducing the speed of his SBD, and he was shot down by a Zero as he struggled toward Guadalcanal. Lost with Major Sailer was his gunner, PFC James W. Alexander. During the five weeks he led VMSB-132 from Henderson Field, Major Sailer established himself as a leader almost without peer. He flew 25 missions and made contact with enemy ships nineteen times. He bombed the enemy twelve times and compiled a remarkable record of six direct hits and three near misses. His successor in command of the squadron, Major Louis B. Robertshaw, a holder of the Distinguished Flying Cross for his service with the squadron, spoke a simple, very suitable epitaph for Sailer when he described the fallen Major thusly, "Joe was the best dive-bomber pilot in the Pacific." Sailer was awarded the Navy Cross posthumously for his actions during the period 10 through 15 November 1942.

[The records pertaining to Major Sailer's final mission are somewhat less than clear. In his work *Dauntless Marine,* a biography of Sailer by Alexander White, the author states that Sailer had already been officially relieved of command of VMSB-132 by Major Robertshaw, but that Sailer insisted that he be allowed to lead this final mission in order to fulfill his desire to hit a Japanese destroyer, the only enemy ship type he had bombed but missed. White also states that it was one of the nearly ubiquitous Mitsubishi FM-2 Pete biplanes that claimed the Major's SBD, not a Zero. Lastly, White states that Sailer's regular radioman/gunner, Howard Stanley, was grounded on Sailer's expressed orders, which resulted in Private Alexander's presence in the rear cockpit that day. Regardless of the exact circumstances, Sailer and Alexander were lost on that mission.]

In late December, the flight echelon of VMSB-132 was withdrawn from Guadalcanal and ordered to Espiritu Santo in the New Hebrides. The ground echelon arrived in the rear area in January, and from there, the squadron was sent off to Sydney, Australia for a well-deserved period of rest and recreation. After its Australian fling, the squadron returned to Espiritu Santo, where it absorbed replacements for its losses at Guadalcanal and those transferred to other duties. At full strength once again, it honed its skills in dive-bombing, a highly perishable commodity that will erode quickly without constant practice. On 27 May, Major Russell D. Rupp assumed command of the squadron.

Ready to enter combat again, VMSB-132 departed the New Hebrides in June and returned to Guadalcanal. By this time, the once bitterly contested island had become a relatively quiet rear area. Unmolested by enemy attacks since April, many permanent facilities had sprouted in place of the tents and holes in the soggy ground that had characterized the American perimeter during the squadron's previous visit to the tortured island.

The first action of the second tour of VMSB-132 was in support of the Marine Raiders on New Georgia. Their pinpoint attacks proved very helpful as the Raiders battled the mud as much as the Japanese. Throughout the fighting on New Georgia, the squadron's SBDs hammered enemy strong points in advance of the Americans' ground attacks, and it was on this island that the full effect of precision close air support placed mere yards in advance of friendly troops was felt for the first time.

With New Georgia secured, the Americans turned their sights on Bougainville, the last major steppingstone before Rabaul. In their first opportunity to attack enemy ships since the previous December, VMSB-132 furnished half of the 36 dive-bombers taking part in a major anti-shipping strike off Kahili on 17 July. Apparently, the dive-bombing practice prior to returning to combat paid big dividends as the squadron claimed eleven hits: three on a large destroyer or cruiser; two on an oiler; four on a second destroyer and a single hit apiece on two more destroyers. Five days later, the squadron took part in another big strike in the same area against an enemy vessel initially identified as a cruiser, escorted by a pair of destroyers. The cruiser was actually the 9,000-ton seaplane tender H.I.J.M.S. *Nisshin,* which sank half an hour after the attack.

The island of Vella Lavella is located just across a narrow channel from the primary objective and was captured as a preliminary to the main event at Bougainville, and VMSB-132 lent an able hand to operations throughout the remainder of the summer and into the early fall. Enemy shipping south of the New Britain area became a scarce commodity as the American advance continued, and as a result, the most frequent missions flown by the squadron were close air support sorties against strong points in advance of friendly ground troops or those targeted against bypassed enemy garrisons located on islands throughout the Central and Northern Solomons.

As fall neared, VMSB-132 was alerted of its pending relief and return to the United States for an extended period of rest and reorganization. Major Rupp left the squadron on 26 September, and Lieutenant William H. Cohron was in command for three days, pending the arrival of Major Claude J. Carlson on 1 October. He led the squadron until Major Otis V. Calhoun, Jr., assumed command on 22 October. Finally, the squadron was relieved from combat duty and returned to the West Coast, arriving first at San Diego and immediately moved on to El Toro. The majority of those who served throughout the combat tours in the South Pacific were transferred to training commands and other non-combat duty upon arrival in the United States. As replacements reported aboard, VMSB-132 was a squadron of strangers as it began to train for its eventual return to combat, which, due to a combination of circumstances, lay more than a year in the future.

The squadron was redesignated VMTB-132 on 14 October 1944, and Captain Henry W. Hise assumed command on 27 October. Shortly thereafter, the new torpedo squadron was alerted of a pending change of station. It was ordered northward from El Toro to MCAS, Santa Barbara, where it joined the Marine squadrons earmarked for carrier training as a part of the program to assign all-Marine air groups to a number of escort carriers. These "green" carriers were to be employed in the specialized close air support role in amphibious operations, especially the expected invasion of the Japanese Home Islands.

Its carrier qualifications completed, other necessary training regimes, including close air support training under the guidance of the Navy's Amphibious Command at Coronado occupied the remainder of the squadron's time at Santa Barbara. VMTB-132 was then paired with VMF-351 in MCVG-4 under the command of Lieutenant Colonel Donald K. Yost, an ace with previous service in VMF-121 and VMF-111, and assigned to USS *Cape Gloucester* (CVE-109).

By the summer of 1945, all the Japanese bastions in the Pacific were either in American hands or had been bypassed and left to starve on a host of islands deemed not to be worth spilling Allied blood to capture. The sole exception was Okinawa, which had been assaulted on 1 April and would prove to be the scene of the last major battle of the war in the Pacific.

Cape Gloucester sailed for the western Pacific in late May. It stopped briefly at Leyte Gulf and then arrived off Okinawa just before the Japanese surrender. It spent a few days providing air cover for minesweepers operating off the island's southern coast. On 1 August, *Cape Gloucester*, in company with three Navy-manned escort carriers were released from the relative boredom off Okinawa and sent in search of targets off the coast of Mainland China. The aircraft ranged along the coast almost as far north as Shanghai but found no worthwhile targets. VMF-351 recorded a pair of kills, including the eighth and final one by Lieutenant Colonel Yost. But for VMTB-132, the cruise proved nothing short of boring. The squadron had been allowed to fly a small number of bombing missions against suspected enemy targets on Okinawa, but aside from that, the cruise was hardly more than a sight seeing tour of the western Pacific and coastal China.

After the Japanese surrender, the carrier was ordered to the West Coast. Upon arrival, MCVG-4 was ordered to Santa Barbara. VMTB-132 was deactivated on 9 November 1945.

During its service in the Pacific, VMSB-132 was credited with the destruction of nine Japanese aircraft in aerial combat. It was awarded the Presidential Unit Citation for its service in the Guadalcanal area during the period 7 August through 9 December 1942.

In the years following World War II, the squadron received a second life in the Reserves. It was reactivated and redesignated VMF-132 and based at NAS, New York, the historic old Floyd Bennett Field in Brooklyn. It continued to serve throughout the decade of the 1950s and was deactivated in one of the periodic reductions in the Reserves.

The first is the insignia of VMTB-132, known as the "Crying Red Asses." Captain Byron M. "Rip" Radcliffe designed this insignia. "Red-assed" is a term frequently used to express various levels of dissatisfaction with things during military service. Apparently, many members of the squadron were unhappy with their deployment aboard *Cape Gloucester* so late in the war. Adding to this feeling was the fact that, by the time the squadron deployed, several of those who had joined after its return from the South Pacific had been transferred and were replaced by men who had served more than one combat tour earlier in the war. One gets the impression that squadron morale was not extremely high during the latter months of 1945.

The second insignia is that of VMSB-132 and was designed by Lieutenant Colonel John H. Stock, USMC (Ret.). The bulldog wearing a flight helmet and goggles is emblematic of a Marine squadron, the golden-yellow bomb represents the squadron's mission, while the saguaro cactus represents the squadron's service at Guadalcanal, code-named "Cactus."

A third and final insignia design was proposed for VMSB-132 and was drawn by the Walt Disney Studios for the squadron. It was of a monkey dressed in the garb of a Japanese aviator being struck in the belly by a large-caliber shell. It is believed that no insignia were ever produced from this design but the original drawings for this design can be found in the Disney studio archives.

No record has been located regarding what, if any, insignia design was worn by the squadron during its service in the Reserves as a fighter squadron.

Marine "Green" Carrier
USS Cape Gloucester (CVE-109) was photographed shortly after her commissioning as she steamed through some light chop. [U.S. Navy Photo]

MARINE ATTACK SQUADRON 133, THE DRAGONS
A.K.A., THE FLYING EGGBEATERS, WW II

via Holmberg

The squadron was activated as VMSB-133 under the command of Captain Julian F. Acers on 1 May 1943 at MCAS, El Toro, California, but after only four months there, the squadron departed the West Coast for duty in the Pacific Theater. It arrived at MCAS, Ewa, Territory of Hawaii, on 9 September for additional training before its commitment to combat operations. This training period was marred by the loss of one of the squadron's SBDs in a collision with an F4U Corsair during inter-type tactics training. Lost with the aircraft were their crews.

Its stay in Hawaii, however, was brief. Shortly after its arrival, the squadron was divided into two echelons, each composed of equal numbers of aircraft, aircrews and ground personnel. Each then left Hawaii for separate locations in the South Pacific. One half was sent to Johnston Island, and the other was sent to Palmyra. After their arrival at their destinations, each was assigned local anti-submarine patrol duty and additional training before it would be committed to active combat.

After six months of searching millions of square miles of ocean from both locations for an enemy that was not there, the two halves of the squadron returned to Ewa, where they were reunited into a single entity once again. Shortly after its return to Ewa, Major Harrison Brent, Jr. assumed command from 1 July 1943 until 28 April 1944, when he was replaced by Major Lee A. Christoffersen, and after more training, VMSB-133 departed Ewa again, bound for Espiritu Santo, where it arrived on 6 July 1944. The squadron spent six weeks at Espiritu after which it then moved up the Solomons to the Allied base at Cape Torokina on Bougainville. After setting up shop at the Piva 1 airstrip on

Cape Torokina, VMSB-133 began to participate in the continuing series of air attacks against bypassed Japanese garrisons on Bougainville and the island of New Britain. By this period, the war had passed this part of the South Pacific, and these missions took on a rather boring, but necessary, character.

It was during its stay on Bougainville that the squadron began to experiment with the close air support techniques that would prove so valuable in the campaigns to come. While the Army Air Forces engaged in what they termed "close air support," in actual practice it proved quite different from the support provided by Marine and later, Navy, aircraft. Army aircraft did not employ the steep, 70-degree dives of the Dauntless, choosing instead to employ more shallow dives of approximately 45-degrees. The steeper dive preferred by the Marine Corps and Navy made for greater accuracy in the delivery of ordnance by significantly reducing range errors, "shorts" and "overs." The steeper dives also made for less exposure to anti-aircraft fire, a fact sincerely appreciated by the aircrews. The greater accuracy allowed ordnance to be employed in much closer proximity to friendly forces than would otherwise be the case. At first, the ground troops were somewhat leery of the prospect of "friendly" bombs being dropped within a few yards of their location, but they soon came to appreciate the fact that a single bomb on the target is far more effective than a number of bombs "near" the target. [Despite the fact that the receipt of more than 100 examples of both the SBD and the later SB2C, designated the A-24 and A-25, respectively, the Army Air Forces, steadfastly refused to employ the much steeped diving attacks practiced by the Navy and Marine Corps. This obstinate refusal to accept the obvious on the part of the Army made the few attacks they made with these aircraft far less effective than they otherwise would have been.]

Another Marine innovation involved using an aviator on the ground with a radio-equipped jeep to control the strikes. Used to viewing the ground from a cockpit, the aviator was better able to convey information to the aircraft regarding targets more easily in terms of its appearance from the air. To better mark the location of friendly troops on the ground, the infantry units were issued white towels to be laid on the ground in such a manner that they would be visible from the air. These initially primitive procedures marked the beginnings of Marine precision close air support that have become a feature of every battle in which the Corps has been engaged from Bougainville to the Persian Gulf, Iraq and Afghanistan, and VMSB-133 was among the pioneers of this tactic.

After three months spent engaged in these missions, the squadron was on the move again. On 12 December 1944, the squadron departed the Solomons area for the Philippines. The squadron arrived at the base at Mangaladan, in the vicinity of Lingayen Gulf on Luzon, and it flew its first strike missions in support of Army troops on 27 January 1945. It did not take long for the Army to develop an appreciation for the type of precision close air support of which VMSB-133 and the other Marine dive-bomber squadrons were capable. (Army Air Forces fighter and fighter-bomber squadrons in action in the Philippines greatly outnumbered the Marine squadrons. However, none of the AAF squadrons were equipped with dive-bombers. The accuracy achieved by the Marines as they rolled their SBDs into their precise, near-vertical dives was nothing short of phenomenal, and there were few, if any, Japanese strong points that were capable of withstanding 1,000-pound bomb hits. Unfortunately,

via Holmberg

VMSB-133 achieved an unwelcome first on 28 January when the Dauntless flown by Lieutenant Gordon L. Lewis with Corporal Samuel P. Melish in the rear cockpit was shot down by anti-aircraft fire over Tarlac Province. Both men were killed, the first Marines to die in the conquest of the Philippines. A second Dauntless was lost during an anti-shipping strike in Manila Bay on 19 February, and Lieutenant Donald M. Johnson and Private, First Class Vincent W. Hagalish were listed as missing in action.

Major Floyd Cummings assumed command of the squadron on 9 March 1945, and VMSB-133 moved from Luzon to the southernmost island of Mindanao on 21 April. Most of its early missions on this island were flown in support of the Army's 24th and 31st Infantry Divisions. On 26 April, the squadron suffered the loss of another aircraft and its crew when the SBD flown by Lieutenant Sidney Dallaway, Jr. and Private Charles A. Corrao failed to recover from its dive while engaged in a ground support mission against the town of Tagloan.

In addition to supporting the Army infantry units on the island, VMSB-133 was heavily engaged in support of the friendly guerrilla forces, which virtually controlled large portions of Mindanao. These guerrillas actively battled the Japanese alongside the American forces. Lacking weapons larger than mortars, close air support aircraft served as flying artillery support to

these allies. Two aircraft and two crewmen were lost in crashes on 2 May. The other two crewmen survived and were later rescued. VMSB-133 spent the remainder of the war in the Philippines where it was engaged in close support missions there until its deactivation on Mindanao on 1 August 1945.

For its service in the Philippines, VMSB-133 received two awards of the Navy Unit Commendation. The first award was in recognition for its services in the Lingayen Gulf-Manila area and covered the period 23 January through 10 April 1945. The second award was for the squadron's service in the Southern Philippines during the period 11 April through 30 June 1945.

On 14 April 1958, the squadron was reactivated as a component of the Marine Corps Reserves and based at NAS, Oakland, California under the command of Lieutenant Colonel D. Watts. Upon its reactivation, it was redesignated VMF-133 and equipped with the McDonnell F2H-2 Banshee. On 1 July 1961, the squadron was relocated to NAS, Alameda, when the base at Oakland was closed.

On 1 July 1962, VMF-133 was redesignated VMA-133 and surrendered its fighter aircraft in favor of the Douglas A-4 Skyhawk. It continued to serve as a Reserve unit until it was again deactivated on 30 September 1992 – a victim of a decreasing defense budget.

via Col .R.L. Carlsen, USMC (Ret)   *via Col .R.L. Carlsen, USMC (Ret)*   *Author's Collection*

During its service in the Marine Corps Reserves, sixteen officers commanded the squadron. It received the Pete Ross Aviation Safety Trophy for three different years – 1969, 1975 and 1979. VMA-133 received the Herman Ritter Marine Air Reserve Trophy in 1981 and 1986, and the Aviation Safety Unit Award for 10,000 accident-free flight hours in 1988.

Regarding the squadron insignia depicted, the first two date from the squadron's second life as a Reserve attack squadron. The first version was adopted by VMA-133 in the 1980s and was worn from the date of its adoption until the squadron's deactivation. The second and third insignia are examples of a design that was adopted shortly after the squadron was redesignated an attack squadron and was worn until the squadron changed its insignia to that of the dragon on the red background. Unfortunately, no example of the insignia of VMF-133 could be found for inclusion here, but it was identical in design to the VMA-133 insignia that featured the blue dragon. The background was lighter in color and the designation in the bottom ribbon was, of course, "VMF-133."

The fourth insignia depicted is an original decal-on-leather example of the squadron's World War II insignia, and the fifth is that of a hand-painted version on a leather disk that adorns the flight jacket of Colonel R.L. Carlsen, USMC (Ret), who served in VMSB-133 during its service in the Pacific. The last insignia is one of the reproductions one commonly finds today. While well made, it is a rather poor rendition of the squadron's World War II insignia.

The insignia of VMSB-133 was designed by Sergeant Andrew J. Clements, and before his enlistment, Clements worked as a commercial artist in Philadelphia. The symbolism of the design of the bulldog is known the world over as the mascot of the Marine Corps. The buckskins, coonskin cap and tomahawk represent the scouting portion of the squadron's mission. The gun and bomb represent the bombing portion of the squadron's mission and were included in the design by Sergeant Clements, who served as an ordnanceman in the squadron.

The poem represents an accurate description of the attitude of VMSB-133 toward the boring duty on Oahu, Johnston and Palmyra Islands, which the squadron was forced to endure during much of its active service.

HO HUM
Our ferocious squadron bulldog
Was overheard to say,
"This damn gun's getting heavy
Just waiting for the day!"
"They make me out a killer,
And I try to look my part,
But I think I'll go Hawaiian,
Before they ever start."
"My buckskin coat is heavy,
It's like a flannel shirt,
I think I'll get it surveyed
And wear a hula skirt."
"These guys don't need a killer
As my picture represents.
Their future combat duty
Consists of BASE DEFENSE!"

Much of the information upon which this section was based and the poem and the drawing were received from Mr. Curtis L. Ellison of Nixa, Missouri, who served in VMSB-133 from its activation until March 1945. His assistance with this project is sincerely appreciated. Special thanks are also due Colonel Carlsen.

MARINE ATTACK SQUADRON 141

Author's Collection

The squadron was activated on 1 March 1942 at Camp Kearney, California as VMSB-141 under the command of Captain George A. Sarles, who led the squadron for the first ninety days of its existence until he was succeeded in command by Major Gordon A. Bell on 1 July. After a training period lasting six months, VMSB-141 was deemed combat ready, and it departed the West Coast for the South Pacific on 30 August bound for New Caledonia.

Earlier that same month, the first American counteroffensive of World War II had begun with the assault landing by the 1st Marine Division (Reinforced) on the north shore of Guadalcanal and the smaller islands of Tulagi, Gavutu and Tanambogo which lay across Seelark Channel in the lower Solomons Islands. The initial American objective was the capture of the nearly completed Japanese airfield located on Guadalcanal, just inland from the invasion beaches. The Marines' 7 August assault was the opening move of the battle for possession of the island and its vital airfield that would last for six months. It also served as the beginning of a campaign that would last for the next eighteen months and climax with the neutralization of the Japanese fortress of Rabaul on the island of New Britain northwest of the Solomons.

With the aid of captured Japanese construction equipment, the airfield was hurried to completion, and the first American aircraft, in the form of the Wildcat fighters of VMF-223 and the Dauntless dive-bombers of VMSB-232, arrived at Henderson Field on 20 August. The field was named in honor of Major Lofton R. Henderson, the commanding officer of VMSB-241, who fell at Midway. It quickly became apparent to all that a key to success with regard to which side ultimately held the island and, therefore, controlled the surrounding seas and skies was the relative ability of each side to reinforce its garrison on Guadalcanal. To this end, the first two Marine squadrons, VMF-223 and

VMSB-232, were followed as quickly as possible by additional combat aviation units. VMSB-141 was among the second wave of American squadrons to take up residence at Henderson Field when five of the squadron's aircraft and aircrews arrived there on 23 September to begin the squadron's time in the purgatory of Guadalcanal. The remainder arrived four, five or six at a time during the next two weeks until Major Bell brought the squadron's largest contingent ashore when he led a total of 21 SBDs to Henderson on 5 October. Ultimately, VMSB-141 would be the largest Marine squadron committed to the island with a total of 39 aircrews.

The squadron immediately joined in the American efforts to stop the Japanese air and sea activity around the island. Enemy air raids were part and parcel of the daily scene, generally arriving shortly after the noon hour, and many nights found enemy ships attempting to land reinforcements and supplies for their garrison on Guadalcanal. It was the scout bombers and torpedo aircraft that were the key to halting the enemy reinforcements. Aided by intelligence from coast watchers, long-range search aircraft from a variety of Allied commands and searches flown from Henderson Field itself, no effort was spared to locate the enemy convoys.

An effort would then be made to strike them before they found shelter in the tropical darkness to complete the last leg of their voyages to Guadalcanal. The most frequent Japanese attempts at getting additional troops and supplies to the Japanese ashore came in the form of a few of the Imperial Japanese Navy's superb destroyers. Loaded with relatively small numbers of soldiers and bundles of supplies, they would endeavor to arrive in darkness, quickly unload their cargoes and hurry northward out of range of the aircraft at Henderson Field before the coming of dawn. Many nights the destroyers of the "Tokyo Express," as the supply runs became known, would pause long enough to hurl a few shells at the airfield. These destroyer shellings usually failed to inflict much in the way of material damage on the vital facilities, but they served to keep the defenders in their shelters and wide awake.

On other less frequent occasions, the enemy would make a major attempt at large-scale reinforcement involving substantial numbers of transports covered by battleships, cruisers and destroyers and by the carriers that came southward from the large enemy base at Truk in the Eastern Carolines. These attempts at large-scale reinforcement inevitably led to major naval engagements as the Americans reacted to the movements of the Japanese fleet.

The arrival of the first American aircraft at Henderson Field brought about a somewhat strange state of naval equilibrium to the waters around the island. Aided by American aircraft, the U.S. Navy ruled the waters of the lower Solomons as long as the sun was above the horizon. With the coming of darkness, however, the situation was reversed. Night flight operations were in their infancy, and Henderson Field enjoyed none of the crucial navigational aids required so when the sun dipped below the horizon, it was replaced by the Rising Sun battle flag of the Imperial Japanese Navy. But, before the first hint of the new day streaked the eastern sky, the Japanese warships scurried northward like frightened children to be out of range of the American search/strike missions that would rise from the airfield like angry hornets with the coming of dawn. Furthermore, any attempt to alter this state of affairs was sure to bring about a sharply contested naval engagement.

Frequently, either by design or by accident, opposing warships clashed in the foreboding, confined waters of Savo Sound. When these ships did meet, troops of both sides watched nervously as the sea battles that largely controlled their ultimate fate, but that they could do nothing to effect, were fought to their bloody conclusions. Generally, those ashore had no warning of a pending engagement. Their first awareness would come with the rumble of naval gunfire as it rolled across the waters of the Sound. Often, they would crowd any available vantage point to watch, fascinated, as tracers arched across the dark surface of the Sound followed by the thunder of the guns. Here and there, the darkness would be sundered by the flash of a detonating shell or by the flare of a torpedo warhead. When the weapons found their mark, a mortally wounded ship often would lie blazing like a bonfire until she slipped mercifully beneath the waves on her final voyage to the bottom, her agony ended.

After the man-made thunder died away, those ashore, whether American or Japanese, did not know who emerged victorious until some minutes after the battle ended. If no shells from the remaining ships were directed at Henderson Field, the Americans had driven their Japanese counterparts from the field. However, a shelling of the airfield usually followed a Japanese victory. Regardless of the victor in one of these night engagements, the first aviators to take to the air the following morning frequently bore witness to the final agonies of dying ships of both sides.

At first, the dead or dying ships were, more often than not, American. The U.S. Navy had spent little time in training for night actions in the years prior to the war, and when suddenly thrust into combat in the waters off Guadalcanal, they were handicapped by a lack of experience, faulty tactics and wretched torpedo performance. This was especially crucial in that the torpedo was the preferred weapon for destroyers in a surface engagement. On the other hand, their Japanese opponents had spent countless hours and no small amount of blood in pre-war training that produced ships and crews schooled to near-perfection in the difficult and often confusing arena of night naval combat. Moreover, they were equipped with a superb Type 93 torpedo, the deadly 24-inch oxygen fueled "Long Lance" of the Imperial Japanese Navy. It ran at double the speed of its American counterpart to twice the range, and its warhead had double the killing power. And, of even greater importance, when it found its target, it detonated with telling effect. Even today, more than seventy years after it entered service, it remains the finest non-guided torpedo ever produced.

Gradually, those American captains and crews who were good enough or lucky enough to survive these initial engagements learned their lessons well. While the performance of their torpedoes never reached the level of those of the enemy, they learned to use the priceless advantage conferred by radar to fight with their guns at long range and were often able to hammer their enemy to pieces long before he reached effective torpedo range. Also, dramatic improvements were made in American torpedo performance and tactics during the course of the campaign although it never reached parity with the Japanese with regard to weapons performance. By the end of battle for the island, however, the Americans won more often than they lost and, in so

doing, stopped many reinforcements from reaching the enemy and prevented many bombardments of the vital airfield.

On the same day that Major Bell led the bulk of VMSB-141 to Guadalcanal, Lieutenant Joseph M. Waterman opened the squadron's scorebook against the enemy. The destroyers H.I.J.M.S. *Minegumo* and *Murasame* were sighted some 150 miles northwest of the island in the Slot, as the body of water, the New Georgia Sound that divided the two parallel strings of islands that compose the Solomons was known. Waterman, in company with two other SBDs with Navy crews, attacked the two ships. The Navy aircraft struck *Minegumo*, and Waterman dove on *Murasame*. The Americans claimed one of the destroyers as definitely sunk and the other as probably sunk. In truth, neither received fatal damage, but the concussion from the near misses of heavy bombs close alongside caused major damage to both, putting them out of action and sent them limping northward trailing long ribbons of oil behind them. Waterman was awarded the Distinguished Flying Cross for his courage and accuracy.

The next morning, aircraft of VMSB-141 sighted and attacked an enemy force composed of two light cruisers and four destroyers. Lieutenant Wilbert H. Fuller, Jr., claimed a direct hit on one of the cruisers, and the others claimed a destroyer as damaged. He also received the Distinguished Flying Cross for his bomb hit.

During the night of 11-12 October, one of the numerous surface engagements fought off the island took place, the Battle of Cape Esperance. The Americans emerged victorious, but their margin of victory was not nearly as great as was first thought. Early the next morning, the American aircraft went hunting enemy cripples from the previous night's naval duel. Approximately 30 miles from the scene of the mayhem off Cape Esperance, near the Russells Islands, two undamaged Japanese destroyers were found tending to one of their crippled sisters. The scouting aircraft attacked, and their bombs were near misses for moderate damage to the enemy.

The day's second strike, which included aircraft of VMSB-141, arrived shortly after the departure of the first attackers and was composed of fighters, dive-bombers and torpedo bombers. They executed a near-perfect, coordinated attack against the enemy ships. Damaged by the first strike, H.I.J.M.S. *Murakumo* suffered three damaging near misses from the SBDs, which started leaks and damaged her steering. The crippled destroyer was an easy target for the Avenger torpedo bombers. She took a "fish" in her side and slid to a halt, mortally wounded. She wallowed in the gentle swells until she sank shortly after the noon hour.

The enemy activity of the previous days represented a major attempt on the part of the Japanese to drive the Americans from Guadalcanal. Undeterred by their losses off Cape Esperance and at the hands of the American aircraft, they kept coming. Another large force of enemy ships bore down on the island, and there were no American warships available to meet them. Several U.S. ships had been damaged the previous night, and the others were in need of fuel and ammunition or were required to escort a convoy of troopships carrying the first contingent of U.S. Army troops to the island as reinforcements. When the last of the troopships completed unloading, the convoy withdrew behind the shield of its escorts. For the time being at least, the Americans on Guadalcanal were without naval support.

Aside from the successful arrival of the Army troops, 13 October was one of those days during which virtually nothing went

The Hunters
Armed with 1,000lb. bombs, this section of SBDs of VMSB-141 is after Japanese ships in the waters off Guadalcanal. Note the considerable number of mission marks beneath the windscreen of the lead Dauntless. [USMC photo]

right for the American defenders. Two air raids reached the island without being detected until it was too late to position the defending fighters for an effective interception. Fortunately, the damage inflicted was relatively light despite a hit on a fuel dump that cost the Americans 5,000 gallons of aviation gasoline. Strangely, despite the presence of the unloading troopships, the enemy made no attempt to strike them. As an already long day began to draw to a close, enemy artillery fire began to fall near the western end of the runway. Two nights earlier, the Japanese had succeeded in bringing ashore a regiment-plus of heavy artillery, but the enemy had not been able to get the majority of these guns into range simultaneously. Due to the sporadic nature of the shelling, the Americans believed that only one gun was firing on them. The Marines were quick to dub the enemy artillery "Pistol Pete."

Despite the artillery fire, the Americans attempted to steal what rest they could before the start of the next day in "paradise." For the first few hours of darkness, all was relatively quiet, and the newly arrived officers and men of the Army's 164th Infantry Regiment restlessly began to endure their first night ashore. But, for those who survived it, the night of 13-14 October 1942 would be remembered forever after as the night of "The Bombardment." In the blackness of Savo Sound lurked a powerful Japanese task force. Built around a pair of battleships, the twins H.I.J.M.S. *Haruna* and *Kongo*, their mission was the utter destruction of Henderson Field. At 0140, the darkness was ripped open by a string of red, white and green parachute flares laid from east to west above the center of the runway by a floatplane from one of the ships. Almost before the last flare bloomed into its full brightness, the first salvoes were on their way. The Americans ashore were alerted to what was in the offing by the first flares. They scrambled into whatever shelter they could find as the battleships' heavy-caliber shells passed overhead with a terrifying roar before detonating with a force that made the earth writhe like a living creature in torment. Unmolested by opposing naval forces, aside from the nuisance created by the presence of a handful of PT boats newly arrived at Tulagi, the Japanese carried out their mission of destruction at their leisure. Salvo

after salvo marched and counter-marched throughout the area of Henderson Field.

Less than an hour later it was all over, but in that short period, more than nine hundred 14-inch projectiles and uncounted numbers of smaller caliber rounds had fallen within the American perimeter, most in the immediate vicinity of the airfield. In the words of one Japanese observer, the airfield was turned into "a sea of flame." As the ships ceased firing and withdrew, their shells were replaced by bombs from a few bombers that cruised above the American positions to rob the defenders of whatever rest the remaining hours of darkness might afford. In the immediate area of the main runway, material damage was extremely heavy. Of the 39 SBDs on hand when darkness fell on 13 October, only four remained at dawn on the 14th. The steel matting that covered the main runway was gouged and twisted into grotesque sculptures, and the underlying fill, the taxiways and aircraft revetments were gouged with giant shell craters. The supply of aviation gasoline, already short due to the fuel dump lost earlier in the day to enemy bombers, was further reduced by the bombardment.

Despite the amount of destruction, it could have been worse, much worse. Of the 918 main battery rounds fired by the enemy battleships, 68% had been armor piercing. With delayed-action fuses and thick shell casings that were designed to penetrate deep into heavily armored targets before detonating, their bursting charges were smaller than those of high-explosive bombardment rounds and did relatively less damage to the "soft" targets ashore. Also, although the enemy was aware of its existence, the recently completed second runway, known as Fighter One, where the majority of the fighter aircraft were located, escaped major damage. Most important of all, casualties among the Americans were mercifully light – the physical damage notwithstanding, only fofty-one men lost their lives. However, the description of "light" casualties was a relative one. VMSB-141 literally was decimated. Dead were Major Bell, Captains Edward F. Miller and Robert A. Abbott and Lieutenants Henry F. Chaney, Jr. and George L. Haley. The squadron's senior surviving officer was a second lieutenant. Seldom has any aviation unit suffered so terribly in a non-aviation action.

At first light, the island's defenders began to repair the damage and prepare for whatever lay ahead despite the fearful battering they had received the previous night. The ground crews readied the aircraft that had survived the shelling for search and strike missions against whatever enemy ships that were sure to attempt to follow in the battleships' wake. Others began to work something akin to miracles as they pieced aircraft together from the jigsaw puzzles of wreckage the enemy's salvoes left behind. This feverish activity began to produce results as more and more dive and torpedo bombers reached a state in which they could be considered to be more of a danger to the enemy than to their crews.

While none was needed, the initial reports from the scouts dispatched at first light added impetus to the urgency of the work as two groups of enemy ships were sighted on southward courses for the island. The first was a troop convoy of six transports and escorting destroyers. The second force was composed of two heavy cruisers and a pair of destroyers. Clearly, the enemy intended to bombard the airfield again during the night and to land large numbers of troops and supplies under the cover provided by the cruisers' guns. Throughout the morning and into the afternoon, and despite two enemy air raids, the ground crews continued to patch aircraft together sufficiently for them to be dispatched against the enemy.

By late afternoon, a strike of thirteen dive-bombers, escorted by seven fighters of the Army's 67th Fighter Squadron, was dispatched. By this time, the enemy troopships were only some seventy miles north of the island, and the SBDs hardly reached the altitude required for them to begin their dives before they sighted their targets. As they reached attack positions, each pilot in turn patted the top of his head to signal the next aircraft that he was about to attack, opened his dive brakes and rolled into his dive. The pilots' hands and feet manipulated the controls of their aircraft as they aligned their sights on their intended targets. The ships' anti-aircraft fire was heavy and accurate, and this, coupled with nerves stretched to the breaking point by the previous night's bombardment, caused many of the bombs to fall wide of their marks. Despite this, several hits were claimed, and reports received later from Allied coast watchers reported one of the transports sunk in the attack.

The coming of darkness brought the American attacks to a halt, and the island's defenders prepared to spend another night under the guns of the Imperial Japanese Navy. The heavy cruisers H.I.J.M.S. *Chokai* and *Kinugasa* fired 752 8-inch shells into the American perimeter. Again, the airfield was the primary target. Their night's work finished, the cruisers withdrew from the area. The cruisers' fire had again reduced the number of flyable aircraft at Henderson to practically nil. Only three SBDs remained undamaged, and the tireless ground crews began the laborious task of trying to make airworthy what remained.

Dawn revealed an insulting sight to the Americans. The enemy was so sure the pounding delivered on two consecutive nights had reduced the defenders to impotence that five transports lay at anchor off Tassafaronga unloading troops and supplies in full view of the defenders. These ships and their cargoes posed a mortal threat to the Americans who immediately began to arm what remained of their air power to attack the enemy.

The three undamaged SBDs were hurriedly loaded with bombs and sent against the Japanese. One fell into a shell crater as it taxied toward the runway, and another was wrecked when it hit a crater during its takeoff roll. Lieutenant Robert M. Patterson of VMSB-141 managed to get the last Dauntless airborne, but his bomb missed its target.

By 0700, four more single-plane attacks were made against the transports, which accounted for two hits, both by pilots of VMSB-141 – Lieutenants Waterman and Ashcroft. As the SBDs continued their solitary attacks, Navy and Marine fighters strove mightily to protect them from enemy fighters and to strafe the ships as the dive-bombers attacked, hoping to distract the ships' gunners. But, despite the fighters' efforts, the day proved to be almost as costly to the squadron as had been "the Bombardment." Three SBDs and their crews were lost to enemy fighters and to anti-aircraft fire. Lieutenant Ashcroft was awarded the Distinguished Flying Cross for his attack that morning.

Rather than continue to dissipate his remaining striking power in these costly, single-plane attacks, Marine Brigadier General Roy S. Geiger, who commanded the American aviation assets on the island, ordered them stopped until something resembling a coordinated strike could be launched. The ground crews continued to work miracles, and at 1000, twelve patched-up SBDs went hunting for Japanese scalps. The American fighters waded into the estimated 30 Japanese fighters that prowled above the ships as the dive-bombers went to work. After releasing their bombs, the SBDs pulled out of their dives at low altitude to rake the ships with their forward-firing twin .50-caliber guns. The gunners in the rear cockpits then hammered the enemy with their paired .30-caliber guns as the bombers passed their targets. The results of these attacks were immediate and dramatic as towering columns of flame and smoke from the stricken ships began to rise into the morning air.

The American attacks continued throughout the morning and into the afternoon as the ground crews patched, fueled and armed more of the aircraft damaged the previous night. Even General Geiger's personal aircraft, a PBY Catalina, was pressed into duty as a jury-rigged torpedo bomber. At 1550 that afternoon, the enemy transports upped anchor and retreated in the face of the continuous American attacks, but the survivors left behind three of their number, *Kyushu Maru*, *Sasako Maru* and *Azumasan Maru*, beached and burning. The enemy also lost most of the supplies that he managed to get ashore as the aircraft struck the temporary dumps holding them before they could be moved into the surrounding jungle. The Japanese did get some 4,500 troops ashore, but they were considerably the worse for wear.

The coming of darkness brought a lull to the combat, but later that night, Japanese warships again entered the lists as the heavy cruisers H.I.J.M.S. *Maya* and *Myoko* hurled 1,500 8-inch shells at defenders between 0025 and 0125 of 16 October. Again, American air power on the island took a beating, but as soon as it was light enough to do so, reinforcements began to move forward from Efate in the New Hebrides to bring the island's aerial striking power back to something approaching a respectable level.

Although they were unaware of it at the time, the island's defenders had successfully passed a major crisis. The enemy air attacks continued their normal pattern and were met by the recently arrived fighter reinforcements. Major naval activity shifted from the waters of the lower Solomons eastward to the vicinity of the Santa Cruz Islands, where the opposing fleets clashed in the bloody but inclusive Battle of Santa Cruz on 27 October. Ashore the enemy painfully made his way through the jungle to gain positions from which to launch his ground offensive against the American perimeter, but the enemy seriously underestimated the effects of the island's terrain on his plans. Instead of a massive, coordinated assault by three columns to drive the defenders into the sea and capture Henderson Field, the enemy attacks came piecemeal between 23 and 28 October. These assaults were driven back into the jungle with fearful losses. Much of the American success must be attributed to the efforts of VMSB-141 and the other squadrons of the Cactus Air Force. This support contributed mightily to the success of the Marine Raiders in holding the crucial "Bloody Ridge," the loss of which would have opened the door to Henderson Field to the Japanese. A great deal of difficult, bloody combat lay ahead, and many more men, ships and aircraft, Allied and Japanese, would die in the weeks to come. However, the enemy would never come as close to their goal of driving the defenders of Guadalcanal into the sea as they did during those crucial days in the latter half of October.

When the weather and their air strength permitted, the Japanese air attacks continued a more or less regular routine, but ashore and at sea, there was a lull in the fierce fighting that had marked October. Both sides welcomed the time to lick their wounds, to rebuild their tattered strength and to prepare for the next round. For VMSB-141, now commanded by Lieutenant W.S. Ashcroft, their daily diet of search and strike missions continued, and the Japanese continued their "Tokyo Express" runs of troops and supplies to the island.

On 7 November, an enemy force of one cruiser and nine destroyers was sighted 100 miles up the Slot on a course for Guadalcanal. In response, Major Joseph Sailer of the newly arrived VMSB-132 led a combined Navy and Marine strike against the ships. Lieutenant A. Sandretto of VMSB-141 got a hit on the cruiser, but despite their rough handling from the strike aircraft, the enemy succeeded in landing more reinforcements for its garrison on the island. Scarcely a night passed without additional enemy forces reaching the island. Clearly, something was in the wind.

That "something" would prove to be Japan's last throw of the dice with regard to their repeated attempts to recapture Henderson Field. In many ways, it was a repeat of their earlier attempts. The near nightly runs of the Tokyo Express continued to land troops and supplies in preparation for the coming assault. To prepare the way for the attack, the enemy stepped up his bombing raids to reduce American aerial strength on the island, and, prior to the actual assault, the Japanese navy was to administer the *coupe de grace* with another shattering series of naval bombardments.

The Americans had not been idle while the enemy's plans were set into motion. Additional squadrons and replacement aircraft were staged forward into the battle area, and the day prior to the commencement of the enemy attack, another regiment of U.S. Army infantry came ashore, along with additional supplies. The warships escorting this convoy would remain in the area to meet the enemy in the opening round of the coming battle, while additional ships were on their way to the scene.

Unfortunately, VMSB-141 continued to suffer additional casualties. Lieutenant Ashcroft was killed in action when his SBD was shot down on 8 November, and Lieutenant Robert M. Patterson assumed command of the squadron.

The Naval Battle of Guadalcanal, as the engagement become known, began in the second hour of the midwatch of Friday, 13 November 1942. At 0124, a force of U.S. cruisers and destroyers under Rear Admirals Daniel J. Callaghan and Norman Scott ran head-on into an enemy force of 17 ships built around the battleships H.I.J.M.S. *Hiei* and *Kirishima*. Radar detected the enemy at a range of 27,000 yards, but the disposition of the American ships was faulty – those with the most modern, effective radar were positioned near the rear of the column. By the time radar contact was made the leading U.S. destroyer was forced to maneuver violently to avoid literally colliding with the oncoming Japanese. The end result was one of history's most confused naval engagements. Both sides were guilty of firing at their own ships. Fought at ranges that were reminiscent of the days of sail, weapons ranged from destroyer torpedoes and the 14-inch guns of the Japanese battleships to the .45-caliber pistol of an officer aboard one of the American destroyers. The battle was as brief as it was bloody, lasting only 24 minutes, and when the firing stopped, the remaining ships of both sides withdrew to wonder at their survival.

If victory is determined by which side attained its objective, then the Americans clearly emerged victorious. The Japanese had set out to bombard Henderson Field into submission, but not a single shell had fallen within the American perimeter. However, the price of victory had been heavy. Both Admirals Callaghan and Scott lay dead amid the wreckage of their flag bridges. Callaghan's flagship, the heavy cruiser USS *San Francisco* (CA-38), had received a fearful battering at the hands of the enemy's battleships, but she had struck some heavy blows in return and would survive to fight again. Scott's flagship, the light anti-aircraft cruiser USS *Atlanta* (CL-51) was so heavily damaged she would be scuttled the next day. USS *Portland* (CA-33) lost a screw and much of her fantail to a torpedo and steered erratically, but her guns were undamaged and continued to hurl 8-inch salvoes at the retiring enemy. Four American destroyers were sunk or sinking, and all but two other U.S. ships, USS *Helena* (CL-50) and USS *Fletcher* (DD-445) had been damaged to a greater or lesser degree.

On the Japanese side, several destroyers were sunk outright, and *Hiei*'s decks and superstructure had been turned into a slaughterhouse. Originally built as a 27,500-ton battlecruiser prior to World War I, she had been rebuilt and reclassified as a battleship the year prior to the attack on Pearl Harbor. Despite her extensive reconstruction, however, her armor was not increased to match that of a battleship, and she suffered accordingly. The 8-inch guns of the American heavy cruisers had penetrated her armor to damage her steering and to reduce her speed. In total, she received more than 50 hits from all calibers of American guns, and her anti-aircraft batteries and other topside positions ran red with the blood of their dead and dying crews. Slowly, painfully, she crawled away from the battle area into the waters northwest of Savo Island. There, she would meet her fate the next day. Throughout the remaining hours of darkness, those watching the aftermath of the battle from positions ashore were witness to the terrible spectacle of blazing ships as their crews, if they were able, battled to quench their fires and to stem the floods. Some were successful, but others were not. Aboard some of the damaged ships the flooding gradually overcame what remained of their buoyancy, and their fires winked out as they slipped beneath the black waters of Savo Sound. To others, their end came in a far more spectacular fash-

The Campaign's Climax
An SBD of an unidentified squadron heads homeward after a long three days during the Naval Battle of Guadalcanal as the late afternoon sun lights the scene, 15 November 1942. In the background are the smoke spires from the beached Japanese transports at Doma Cove and Tassaforonga. [USMC photo]

ion when the flames reached a magazine, and they disappeared in a brilliant flash followed by a thunderous detonation that rolled across the gentle swells to assault the ears of those watching.

After its stinging defeat in the Battle of Savo Island two nights after the initial assault on Guadalcanal, the Navy withdrew its ships from the area, and many of those ashore felt they had been abandoned and left to their fate in unseemly haste. More than a few of those left behind on the island cursed the U.S. Navy and the Japanese with equal fervor, but whatever feelings had been held previously became ones of admiration and deep respect. Not only had the ships of Callaghan and Scott prevented a potentially devastating bombardment of the American positions, more than 1,600 officers and men of the United States Navy had given their lives to do so.

Before dawn, the ground crews of Henderson Field and Fighter One set about preparing their aircraft for their missions of the coming day. Some would be tasked with searching the waters of Savo Sound for survivors from both navies of the previous night's battle, reporting their positions to waiting rescue craft and offering whatever aid they could. Others would be sent in search of enemy ships retiring from the scene of battle, as well as those sure to be moving toward Guadalcanal for the second act of the drama begun the night before.

Almost as soon as the first searchers cleared the trees surrounding the airstrips, they began to sight the aftermath of the naval engagement. A total of seven ships, some American and some Japanese, struggled for survival or drifted, abandoned and sinking, within a 20 square mile area of Savo Sound. Those observing the scene soon had a renewed appreciation of their navy brethren when they watched a few, well-aimed salvoes from *Portland* tear apart a damaged Japanese destroyer unlucky enough to stagger within range of her guns.

Soon reports of bigger game began to reach the ears of the American commanders. An enemy battleship had been sighted

northwest of Savo Island. She was moving slowly and erratically, trying to escape the vengeful aircraft. As soon as the enemy's position could be relayed to the flight crews, they were airborne on a course to the enemy's reported position. Squadron integrity was nonexistent as dive-bombers were dispatched as soon as sufficient numbers could be made ready to attack. A division of three aircraft might be composed of a lead aircraft from VMSB-141 with one wingman from one of the other Marine scout bomber squadrons on the island and the other a Navy-manned aircraft.

As the first attackers arrived above the enemy dreadnought and prepared to attack, they reported her anti-aircraft fire to be weak and inaccurate, a strange happenstance for a type of ship normally capable of a withering barrage against aerial foes. The Dauntlesses were unmolested by enemy fighters as they released their bombs and recovered from their 70-degree dive at low altitude to observe the results of their work. Their intended victim was *Hiei,* and her attackers soon saw the reason for her weak defensive effort. Her upper works were twisted and blackened from the pounding she received the previous night, and those guns that fired on the SBDs did so at a slower than normal rate due to the slaughter of their crews. This strike was the first in a long and painful day for the Japanese.

A total of at least seven strikes were sent against *Hiei* that day. Several were led by Major Joseph E. Sailer, the commanding officer of the newly arrived VMSB-132, and each added more damage to that inflicted on the monster in the naval duel and by the preceding strikes. Due to the feeble opposition offered, the percentage of hits were very high, as much as 50% in some attacks, and the half-ton, armor-piercing bombs bored deep into her hull before they detonated. Each hit felled more of her crew and wrecked more of her vital equipment, adding to the conflagrations already raging or starting additional ones. The majority of the bombs that failed to strike her were near-misses close alongside. Due to the incompressibility of liquids, the concussion of these bombs stove in hull plating and started numerous leaks. Several of the strikes counted Avenger torpedo bombers among their numbers, and several torpedoes found their marks, further reducing her speed and admitting new torrents into her torn hull. The crews of VMSB-141 attacked with an especial desire for revenge, for in their sights lay a ship of the type that had inflicted such grievous losses on the squadron the previous month. [They had no knowledge of it at the time, but *Hiei* was one of a class of four ships including *Haruna* and *Kongo*, the perpetrators of the Bombardment.]

The final strike of the day, composed of SBDs of VMSBs -132 and -141, came at dusk and contributed its share to the carnage. After dark, the Japanese, realizing the hopelessness of their task, removed the surviving members of *Hiei's* crew and scuttled her.

During the night of 13-14 November, the heavy cruisers H.I.J.M.S. *Suzuya* and *Maya* fired more than 1,000 8-inch shells in a half-hour bombardment beginning at 0130. Fortunately, most of the projectiles missed their targets. Henderson Field was untouched, and only a handful fell on Fighter One, where they destroyed two fighters. Other aircraft received light damage that was repaired by daybreak. Harassed by PT boats, the cruisers withdrew northward to join the enemy force bearing down on Guadalcanal.

Composed of eleven large transports carrying a full division of infantry and escorted by battleships, cruisers and destroyers, this force represented Japan's strongest attempt to overwhelm the defenders of Guadalcanal. Those aboard these ships were aware of the cruisers' bombardment and had no knowledge of the results of the first act of the battle. They fully expected that American aerial strength had received a mortal blow so it must have been a truly unpleasant surprise when the first probing scouts from Henderson Field were sighted by those on the ships.

The sighting reports of the Japanese force stirred furious activity around the airfields. Straining ground crews struggled to position quarter- and half-ton bombs to the shackles beneath the bellies of the SBDs, while others winched one-ton torpedoes into the bomb bays of the TBFs. Still others fueled the aircraft, fed long belts of ammunition into the gun bays and cockpits and checked engines, radios and navigational equipment. The first strike was on its way before noon on 14 November and reached its targets at 1215. The proximity of the enemy to Guadalcanal permitted each strike to be escorted by the notoriously short-legged Wildcat fighters, which allowed the bombers to go about their deadly work largely unhindered by enemy fighters. Throughout the remaining hours of daylight the aerial *Danse Macabre* continued above the Japanese convoy. Strike after strike pounded the enemy without mercy. Here, a transport was torn in half by a bomb or a torpedo, spilling her human cargo into the waters of the Slot. There, another drifted helplessly, burning from stem to stern. The near-monotonous series of relentless attacks became known to the Americans as the "buzzard patrol" and counted among the "buzzards" were the dwindling numbers of SBDs and crews of VMSB-141.

American losses had been light, amounting to only six dive-bombers and two fighters, but among those who failed to return was Lieutenant Sandretto and his gunner, Corporal X.L. Fulton, of VMSB-141. The squadron was nearing the end of its tether. In the nearly eight weeks since the arrival of its first elements

on Guadalcanal, VMSB-141 had suffered staggering casualties – twenty-six killed, one wounded and five missing. For those members of VMSB-141 who survived it, Guadalcanal would forever remain an emotion than a name.

When darkness brought the day's slaughter to a halt, seven transports had been sunk or forced to withdraw northward out of range of the vengeful American aircraft, and several of their warship escorts had been disabled. But, despite their fearful battering, the four remaining ships of the convoy continued to stagger southward in a grim display of the suicidal determination so typical of the Japanese in battle. To aid the remnants of the convoy in its painful journey and to remove the thorn of Henderson Field from the Imperial side, another surface force was sent to bombard the American positions.

The Japanese force was composed of two heavy cruisers, two light cruisers, nine destroyers and the battleship H.I.J.M.S. *Kirishima*. Reports of an American force of two "large cruisers" and four destroyers moving toward Guadalcanal alerted the Japanese to the probability of another surface engagement. Scouts also warned the Americans of the approaching enemy force, so both sides entered the foreboding waters of Savo Sound expecting to meet the enemy. The action that followed would usher in the final acts of the three-day battle.

In typical Japanese fashion, their forces were divided into two groups, each with a separate mission. One of the light cruisers and six destroyers were to act as a "sweeping force" to deal with the expected American warships. The heavy cruisers, the battleship and three other destroyers then would be left free to deal with the pesky enemy ashore.

While their scouting aircraft provided ample warning of the pending surface engagement and was correct in his count of American ships, the Japanese pilot was in need of additional training in the subject of ship recognition. The reported "cruisers" were, in fact, the battleships USS *Washington* (BB-56) and *South Dakota* (BB-57), under the command of Rear Admiral Willis A. Lee, dispatched to the waters off Guadalcanal by Vice Admiral Halsey for the specific purpose of dealing with the enemy force now bearing down on the island. Admiral Lee differed from other officers who had commanded U.S. forces in the previous surface engagements in these waters. He understood the capabilities of the radar with which his ships were equipped, and he intended to use it to its full advantage. As it developed, however, the action that followed did much to undo the American advantage in electronics. Just before the battle opened, the Japanese further divided their forces when a light cruiser and some of the destroyers were detached from the bombardment force to serve as a screening force. Nonetheless, at 2200, some of the American radars began to register the flickering returns of the approaching enemy, and at the same time, Japanese lookouts caught their first glimpses of Lee's force.

When the battle action actually began, it quickly became the naval equivalent of a barroom brawl. Both sides opened fire almost simultaneously, but excellent Japanese gunnery and their superb torpedoes created havoc among the American destroyers, sinking two and severely damaging a third. Twice during the action, complete electrical failures rendered *South Dakota* "deaf, dumb and blind" for critical periods, and after the demise of the destroyers, she drew Japanese gunfire like a magnet. But, despite her personnel losses, the physical damage was largely superficial, and she remained in action.

Despite their visual sightings of both American battleships, the Japanese persisted in their belief they were engaging a cruiser-destroyer force. Even when main battery shells from the American battleships surrounded their opponents in a forest of shell splashes rising hundreds of feet into the air, they believed they had engaged nothing larger than a heavy cruiser. They had been warned of the likely presence of cruisers, therefore they had, by their reckoning, engaged cruisers, despite ample evidence to the contrary.

The Japanese concentration on the American destroyers and on *South Dakota* allowed *Washington* to close to within point-blank range of *Kirishima*. When *Washington's* main battery took her opposite number under fire, the effect was immediate and catastrophic. From a range of only 8,400 yards, the American 16-inch projectiles pierced *Kirishima's* armor as if it was cardboard before they detonated with murderous results deep within her hull. Within minutes, a deluge of more than fifty hits from *Washington's* main and secondary batteries reduced once-proud *Kirishima* to a staggering, gutted wreck. Despite efforts to save her, she rolled to starboard and sank at 0325, reunited forever with her sister *Hiei* beneath the waters of Ironbottom Sound. [*Kirishima's* capsized wreck was discovered recently by Dr. Robert Ballard's expedition to the waters off Guadalcanal.]

After the destruction of *Kirishima*, the battle petered out, and the Japanese withdrew from the lists, their mission of destruction of the American positions on the island unfulfilled. As their surviving warships turned northward, the remnants of the enemy convoy continued its painful journey to the south. The four remaining transports were under orders to beach themselves at Tassaforonga and Doma Cove. They did so shortly after 0400. As soon as the ships came to rest on the island, efforts to off-load what remained of their troops and cargoes began. Despite their dogged perseverance, Japanese efforts largely came to naught when the buzzard patrol went back to work. At 0555, Major Sailer rolled his SBD into a dive above the stationary targets below. Behind him were seven other aircraft from VMSBs -132 and -141, and the deadly work begun the previous day started all over again.

By early afternoon, Japan's largest and last major effort to regain Guadalcanal had reduced to bloody tatters. Adding to the destruction wrought by the aircraft of the buzzard patrol were newly arrived shore batteries of the Marine Defense Battalion that took two ships that lay within their range under accurate and effective fire, but perhaps the most spectacular work of the day was done by USS *Meade* (DD-602). Closing the beach until her hull almost scraped the bottom, her 5-inch guns and anti-aircraft batteries raked the beached ships and the few supplies that had been brought ashore. When she turned away to search for survivors of the previous night's naval engagement, there was precious little of value to the enemy left undamaged, but the buzzard patrol continued to scavenge the remains until early afternoon. The last air strike against the surviving Japanese came at 1350 that Sunday.

The end of the Naval Battle of Guadalcanal also marked the end of the campaign for VMSB-141. The flight echelon of the squadron was withdrawn from the Solomons on 19 November 1942 and transferred to Samoa, but the ground echelon remained on Guadalcanal until 19 January 1943, when it was withdrawn to the New Hebrides. It remained there until May and was then dispatched to Auckland, New Zealand for a well-earned period of R&R before finally returning to the United States in September 1943. After the mud, mosquitoes and sudden death of Gua-

dalcanal, New Zealand must have seemed like heaven on earth to the tired survivors of the squadron. While the ground echelon of VMSB-141 "toured" the South Pacific, its flight echelon returned to MCAS, El Toro. It remained there and was redesignated VMBF-141 on 14 October 1944. Upon its redesignation, it was re-equipped with the F4U Corsair, but the squadron's career as a fighter-bomber squadron was short-lived. In May, 1945, it was redesignated VMTB-141 and served as a replacement training squadron at El Toro for the Marine torpedo squadrons engaged in the Pacific Theater. After the Japanese surrender, VMTB-141 was deactivated on 10 September 1945.

The following officers commanded the squadron during its final weeks in combat and in the period following its service on Guadalcanal: Lieutenant Robert M. Patterson, 9 – 12 November 1942; Lieutenant Walter M. Bartosh, 13 – 18 November 1942; Major George M Sarles, the squadron's first commanding officer and winner of the Distinguished Flying Cross, 18 November through 16 December 1942; Captain Claude J. Carlson, Jr., 17 December 1942 through 8 March 1943; Lieutenant Oscar J. Camp, Jr., 8 March through 1 April 1943; Major Edward F. Bowker, Jr., 1 April through 14 May 1943; Captain Middleton P. Barrow, 15 May through 25 August 1943; Lieutenant John E. Lepke, 26 August through 23 October 1943; Captain John H. McEniry, Jr., 24 October 1943 through 21 January 1944; Major Wayne M. Cargill, 21 January through 15 December 1944; Captain Lee J. Crook, 16 December 1944 through 15 March 1945; Chief Warrant Officer William H. Sherman, 15 March through 11 May 1945; Major Richard E. Figley, 11 May through 25 June 1945; and Major Thaddeus Levandowski 26 June 1945 through 10 September 1945.

VMSB-141 was awarded the Presidential Unit Citation for its service in the Guadalcanal Campaign during the period 7 August through 9 December 1942, and the squadron was credited with the destruction of three Japanese aircraft in aerial combat.

The squadron was among those World War II squadrons that led a second life among the Reserves when it was reactivated in 1946, and it was redesignated a fighter squadron, VMF-141, and assigned to NAS, Oakland, California. In 1949, it had the distinction of being commanded by Colonel James E. Swett, who had been awarded the Medal of Honor for the destruction of seven Aichi D3A1 Val dive-bombers in a single combat of 7 April 1943 while a member of VMF-221.

In the early 1960s, the squadron was redesignated VMA-141 and reequipped with early models of the A-4 Skyhawk, the A-4B. It served until it was deactivated on 30 June 1965 at MCAS, El Toro.

The insignia of VMSB-141 depicted is a reproduction made from an original dating from the period between the squadron's return to the United States from the South Pacific and its redesignation as VMBF-141. The original design of the insignia of VMSB-141 is attributed to a member of the squadron, Technical Sergeant Rodney C. Anderson. Its symbolism of the traditional bulldog of the Marines with the remains of a Rising Sun battle flag in its teeth and the ribbons of the Presidential Unit Citation and Asia-Pacific campaign on its chest and posed on a bomb representative of the squadron's mission.

No record of the squadron's insignia used during its service in the Reserves has been found. It is likely that the squadron's earlier insignia was used during this period, minus the scout-bomber designation. However, this is speculation.

MARINE TORPEDO BOMBER SQUADRON 143

THE DEVILDOG AVENGERS

A.K.A., THE ROCKET RAIDERS

THE RAGIN' CAJUNS (POST-WWII RESERVE VMF)

via Holmberg

The squadron was activated on 7 September 1942 as a scout bomber squadron, VMSB-143, under the command of Major Graham H. Benson. After starting his dissimilar assembly of men on the road to becoming a cohesive combat unit, Major Benson turned command of the squadron over to Major John W. Sapp, Jr. on 27 November. As typical of many of the newly activated squadrons during this time, aircraft were slow to arrive. On 30 November, VMSB-143 had only seven of its normal complement of a dozen SBD-3 Dauntless scout bombers on hand. Aircraft losses of all types had been heavy in the four carrier battles contested from May through October of 1942, and the carrier squadrons were deemed to have a higher priority for new aircraft than their land-based counterparts. In addition, several Marine scout bomber squadrons had been committed to the heavy fighting in the Solomons, and aircraft wastage among them was high, requiring immediate replacements to be made available to them. There was also the small matter of the Allied invasion of North Africa, Operation *Torch*, which demanded a considerable number of the scarce carrier aircraft for the carriers operating in support of the assault.

Several additional factors further complicated this situation. One must bear in mind that the United States had been at war for less than a year, and the veritable avalanche of armaments

that would flow from America's factories that would occur later in the war had not yet reached anything near its eventual proportions. Much of the equipment with which the battles of 1942 were fought was on hand at the time of the Pearl Harbor strike. Also, the SBD was only the third type of monoplane scout bomber to be accepted for Navy and Marine service. Beginning in April 1936, the total production of the first two types, the Northrop BT-1 and the Vought SB2U-1, -2 and -3, was a mere 195 aircraft. Over the intervening years, some of these had been lost to operational mishaps, and the remainder was suitable only for advanced training. A few Atlantic Fleet squadrons flew the SB2U in the early months of the war but saw no combat while equipped with the aircraft. Only VMSB-241 flew the SB2U-3 in combat at Midway, and that squadron's experience with the type gave very ample proof of the Vindicator's ineffectiveness as a frontline combat aircraft in 1942.

Nonetheless, the squadron carried on with its training as best it could as additional aircraft slowly trickled in. However, before the squadron could be deployed to the South Pacific, it was redesignated VMTB-143 on 31 May 1943. Whether or not the earlier shortage of scout bombers had any effect on the decision to redesignate the squadron cannot be determined, but shortly after that, its full complement of Grumman TBF-1 Avengers was on hand. Its training completed, VMTB-143 was declared combat-ready and after a short period of leave for as many of the squadron's personnel as possible, it departed San Diego on 28 December 1942 and arrived on Efate in the New Hebrides on 16 January 1943. A month later, the flight and ground echelons of the squadron were separated, with the ground echelon remaining in the New Hebrides, while the flight echelon was dispatched northwestward to Guadalcanal. The squadron's aircrews and aircraft were in place on the recently secured island by 18 February. Their arrival coincided with the arrival of something new in the war of Japanese shipping in the Solomons. The Navy had developed a 1,600lb. aerial magnetic mine using a captured German model as a prototype. Due to the weight of this weapon, the TBF was the only single-engine Navy/Marine aircraft capable of carrying it.

On 20 March, Major Sapp led a total of forty-two Avengers from VMTB-143 and three Navy squadrons on a mission to sow this advanced type of mine in the waters off Kahili on Bougainville in the Central Solomons. While exact details of the effectiveness of these mines cannot be determined, it is known the Japanese reported the loss of two large merchantmen sunk and a destroyer damaged in this area during April. No other agency claimed these vessels, so it must be assumed they fell victim to the minefield. Despite the probable effectiveness of the mines, however, the mission was not repeated for more than two months. Charts of the waters off Bougainville were noted for their inaccuracy, and in order to prevent a friendly vessel accidentally blundering into the minefield at a later date, the position of the actual field itself and the placement of the mines within it had to be plotted with a high degree of accuracy. This called for considerable precision with regard to navigation and straight and level flight paths while the weapons were being sown. Also, the Kahili-Shortlands area was heavily defended, and despite the fact the mission was flown at night, the Avengers were easily detected by searchlights and came under heavy, accurate medium and large caliber anti-aircraft fire as they made their relatively

A Warrior at Rest
A well-worn example of the TBF Avenger aircraft is shown at rest on a hastily constructed airfield typical of the Solomons. [USMC photo]

low-speed runs at altitudes of from 800 to 1,300 feet, the altitude range required to place the mines accurately. This presented the Japanese gunners with a succession of relatively easy targets. As a result, losses among the four squadrons were heavy.

Despite their effectiveness, it is a fact the airmen of all nations heartily detested mine-laying missions. As related previously, the requirement to fly low and slow while dropping mines made the aircraft very vulnerable to any defenses in the area. Also, it could be anywhere from several days to weeks or months before the results of the missions became known, if at all. While a bomb drop or torpedo run might well entail greater risks to the airmen, the results, good or bad, were known immediately – the weapon was either a hit or a miss. It was one thing to risk one's life in the course of mission during which the aircraft were armed with bombs or torpedoes, but at least the crews knew whether the risk was worth the reward. A mine mission was something else altogether. It may be that this dislike of mine laying may have played a part in the decision not to carry on with more of these missions. After all, those commanding the Marine squadrons in the area were aviators themselves, and they understood this dislike quite well.

After the mine mission, the squadron flew a number of bombing and anti-shipping strikes against Kahili and the adjacent areas. On several occasions, night missions were flown against enemy shipping located by the prowling, radar-equipped PBY Catalina patrol bombers that probed the darkness with their all-seeing electronic eye. The Japanese realized the folly of sending supply ships into the area, except under heavy escort, due to the steady growth of American air power based on Guadalcanal, and the TBF was the first single-engine American strike aircraft

to carry radar. This, coupled with its range and ability to carry a ton of ordnance, made it ideal for hunting enemy shipping on the darkest of nights and during less than ideal weather conditions. The enemy was denied virtually all of nature's concealment. It was during this series of missions that Major Warren G. Mollenkamp assumed command of the squadron on 15 May.

A change of pace with regard to mission type came in early July when the squadron rendered valuable service in the close air support role to American ground forces during the battle for New Georgia. Marine close air support techniques began to fulfill the expected ability to deliver ordnance within yards of the friendly troops. New Georgia was, in many ways, a proving ground for the Marine air-ground teamwork that would play such a vital role in the battles to come. Support of the Marine on the ground has been one of the primary reasons for the existence of Marine aviation in the first place, but at times this was more a theory than fact. From mid-1943 onward, however, the theory was practiced and refined to a point hardly dreamed of when Lieutenant Christian F. Schilt was awarded the Medal of Honor for his pioneering efforts in Nicaragua in the 1920s.

Regardless of whether by day or night, ashore or afloat, VMTB-143 continued to hammer the enemy. On 22 July, the squadron took part in a major strike against enemy shipping off the eastern coast of Bougainville. All 18 of the squadron's Avengers concentrated their attacks against the largest of the Japanese vessels, tentatively identified as a cruiser. The aircrews claimed seven direct hits and eleven near misses within 90 feet of the target with 2,000-pound bombs. Her back broken, the "cruiser" sagged amidships and went under. Japanese records, however, credit the squadron with "only" six direct hits. The target was later identified not as a cruiser but as a large, valuable naval auxiliary, the 9,000-ton seaplane tender H.I.J.M.S. *Nisshin.* She was bound for Buin with a cargo of 22 medium tanks and some 667 troops aboard. None of the tanks and precious few of the embarked troops reached their destination thanks to VMTB-143.

In August and September, VMTB-143 was again practicing its close air support techniques against Japanese positions on Vella Lavella beginning with the assault on 15 August. The island was targeted because it was only 90 miles from the major complex of enemy bases around Kahili. Enemy air attacks against the invasion forces were frequent, and the Marine fighter squadrons destroyed large numbers of enemy aircraft. Occasionally, however, enemy fighters made life interesting for the TBFs engaged in supporting the ground troops. Several enemy aircraft fell to the gunners of the squadron as they defended their aircraft against the Japanese interceptors.

At the completion of the Vella Lavella operations, the squadron was withdrawn to Espiritu Santo for a short rest. Losses in men and aircraft were made good, and the ample supplies of nutritious food, the occasional adult beverage and regular rest away from the stress of combat soon brought the VMTB-143 back to its earlier strength and readiness. While in the rear area, orders were put into effect that reorganized the scout bomber and torpedo squadrons and considerably increased their strength. On 31 October 1943, the squadron reported its aircraft strength at 27 Avengers. As the squadron prepared to return to combat, its flight echelon was divided into three parts. One was to remain at Espiritu Santo. The second went to Guadalcanal, and the third was ordered to the newly captured airfield at Munda on New Georgia. This latter element of the squadron added its weight to the assault on Empress Augusta Bay on Bougainville on 1 November. Fighting in the area was prolonged and bitter as the Japanese strongly contested the landing both on land and in the air. Losses on both sides were heavy, and VMTB-143 suffered the loss of a TBF and its crew on 3 November.

During the fall of 1943, command of the squadron changed twice. Lieutenant William O. Cain, Jr. assumed command on 12 November and Captain Henry W. Hise succeeded Lieutenant Cain on 27 November.

As the assault forces continued to battle the omnipresent mud of Bougainville as well as the Japanese, VMTB-143 turned to the task of close air support with a vengeance once again. It was on Bougainville that the Marines' techniques of air support were graphically proven superior to that of the other services. On 9 November, the squadron's aircraft delivered their loads of 100-pound fragmentation bombs on enemy positions as planned just moments before the ground assault on the enemy positions. Smoke and dust from the bombs still hung in the heavy tropical air as the mud Marines moved to the attack. Stunned by the bombs, the enemy did not have a chance to recover his equilibrium before the assault reached the defenses, and the Japanese hastily withdrew, leaving behind much of his equipment and a considerable number of his dead.

Other strikes by Navy aircraft using Marine support techniques a few days later were equally successful. These and later attacks proved that air power, when properly applied, was capable of easing the task of infantry and reduced friendly casualties. Against the enemy entrenched on geographical feature known as Hellzapoppin' Ridge, Marine aircraft struck from altitudes as

In the author's collection is a G-1 flight jacket with the Rocket Raider/ Captain America insignia of VMTB-143. [Author's Collection]

low as 75 feet and made dummy runs after their ordnance had been expended to keep the enemy's heads down as the ground troops advanced. In one of their final strikes against targets on Bougainville on 26 December, the squadron's TBFs, again armed with 100-pound fragmentation bombs, blanketed an area scheduled to be attacked by the ground troops that afternoon. As infantry patrols carefully probed the area in the wake of the air strikes, they reported 100% of the bombs fell within the target area. So thorough had been the bomb coverage that few trees were left standing, and the remnants of the estimated 800 enemy troops that had held the area had hastily withdrawn.

In January, the squadron moved from Munda to the newly captured airfields on Bougainville. This movement to Bougainville signaled the opening of a direct air campaign against Rabaul, which was now within range of the single-engine strike aircraft. With its large complex of air bases and the excellent naval facilities centered on Simpson Harbor, Rabaul was the foundation upon which Japanese power in the Southwest Pacific rested. The conquest or neutralization of Rabaul would effectively bring a major portion of the Southwest Pacific campaign to a close. The Japanese were as aware of this as were the Allies and were determined to resist to their utmost. It was estimated that almost 100,000 enemy troops stood ready to defend New Britain and the bases at Rabaul. A direct assault would have been extremely costly in view of the enemy's readiness to defend a lost cause to the last bullet. This Japanese determination turned

Rabaul into a killing ground and the graveyard of enemy power in the area as repeated Allied attacks took an ever-mounting toll on the defenders. The decision was made to avoid a direct assault against New Britain and to neutralize the Japanese power on the island by a concentrated application of air power. Japanese ground installations were pounded day and night. Scores of enemy warships and merchantmen were sunk or disabled, and hundreds of their aircraft were shot down or bombed and strafed into wrecks on the many airfields surrounding Rabaul. In an effort to prop up their crumbling aerial defenses, the Japanese ordered some of their carrier air groups to New Britain in an effort to stem the allied tide. Losses among these air groups had been murderous in the carrier battles of the preceding year, and they were ground into dust once again in the constant air battles that raged almost daily in the skies above Rabaul. As a result, Japan's carriers were effectively put out of action for many critical months until their air groups could be again rebuilt. The Japanese Combined Fleet would not challenge the U.S. Pacific Fleet again until June 1944. When the carrier forces clashed west of the Marianas in the Battle of the Philippine Sea, the extent of the damage inflicted during the Solomons campaign upon Japan's elite carrier air arm was made abundantly clear to all concerned. The American victory in the Philippine Sea was so one-sided that it became somewhat derisively referred to as the "Great Marianas Turkey Shoot," and Japan's carriers became almost irrelevant for the remainder of the war.

The Avengers of VMTB-143 contributed their share to the pounding of the enemy at Rabaul. On 24 January, a strike against enemy shipping in Simpson Harbor by VMTB-143 and the Navy's VC-40 accounted for five ships while the fighter escort claimed 23 enemy aircraft shot down in aerial combat. The battering of the enemy continued until early spring when the enemy's power centered on Rabaul was effectively reduced to impotence. As the campaign against Rabaul began to wind down, Major Arthur W. Little, Jr. assumed command of the squadron on 1 April 1944. He was succeeded by Captain Myron Sulzberger on 8 May, and Captain George A. Smith replaced Sulzberger on 27 May.

In June, VMTB-143 was withdrawn from the Southwest Pacific and returned to the United States, arriving at MCAS, Santa Barbara, California before the end of the month. Within hours, the squadron was reduced to a shadow of its former numbers as virtually its entire personnel strength was granted leave en route to their next duty station. On 30 June, Major George B. Woodbury arrived to command the squadron as it began to absorb the mass of replacements. Shortly after VMTB-143 began training in preparation for its eventual return to combat, the decision was made to assign Marine squadrons to carrier duty. In addition to incorporating Marine fighter squadrons into the air groups of the ships of the Fast Carrier Force, all-Marine air groups were to be assigned to at least four escort carriers to supply air support for the assault troops during amphibious operations. Each of these air groups was composed of a fighter squadron and torpedo bomber squadron, along with a Carrier Aircraft Service Detachment, C.A.S.D., to maintain the embarked aircraft. VMTB-143 was assigned to Marine Carrier Air Group 2, MCVG-2, aboard USS *Gilbert Islands* (CVE-107), where it would be teamed with the Corsair-equipped VMF-512.

As soon as the reorganized squadron completed the normal training regimen for a torpedo squadron, it began carrier training.

First came what surely must have seemed to be endless hours of field carrier landing practice, officially known as FLCP, but generally referred to as "bounce practice," a nickname that was more accurate than many would care to admit. The dimensions of a carrier's deck were outlined on a runway, and the Avengers and Corsairs of MCVG-2 made approach after approach exactly as it would be flown to an actual carrier, complete with a Landing Signal Officer to "wave them aboard." When the aviators reached the point that they were considered no longer an overt danger to either themselves or to the carrier, they proceeded to sea for the real thing.

No doubt perhaps the first and most lasting impression left by one's first actual carrier approach after the bounce practice was the flight deck outlined on the runway was neither rolling and pitching nor running away from the oncoming aircraft at its best speed. Also, while it is likely that most of the Avenger pilots secretly may have dreamed of exchanging roles with the supposedly more glamorous fighter pilots, it is equally probable that these initial carrier landings increased their appreciation of their somewhat porcine aircraft. The Avenger was the largest, heaviest aircraft to routinely operate from a carrier during World War II, but the stable, forgiving "Turkey" was a carrier aviator's dream

via Holmberg

around the boat. While the Corsair was arguably the best fighter of the war, it could, and frequently did, turn on the unskilled or the unwary with fatal results. The low speed and high drag configuration of an aircraft preparing to land aboard leaves little margin for error on the part of the man at the stick and throttle.

However, it may come as somewhat of a surprise that after the fearful operational losses among the first Marine squadrons deployed aboard the CVs of the Fast Carrier Force early in 1945, the operational loss rate of the Marine air groups aboard the escort carriers was much lower. This was the case despite the CVEs' much more lively motion in virtually any sea state and a flight deck only slightly more than half as large as that of an *Essex*-class fleet carrier. No doubt, reports of the heavy operational losses experienced in the first deployments, mainly attributed to insufficient training in carrier operations and instrument flying, led to additional training for the squadrons of the MCVGs. As a result, non-combat losses were reduced to an acceptable level.

The New Year brought a new commanding officer when Captain John E. Worlund assumed command on 2 January 1945.

The early months of 1945 were devoted to the final polishing of the squadron's skills and to maintaining its proficiency in carrier operations. Finally, on 12 April, the air group boarded *Gilbert Islands* and departed for the western Pacific. The little carrier and her Marines were bound for Okinawa where the concept of carrier-based Marine air groups dedicated to the close air support mission would be put to the acid test of combat for the first time.

The carrier arrived off the tortured island in May and immediately added its aircraft to those supporting the troops ashore as they battled the Japanese defenders for every yard of Okinawa. Again, the ability of the Marines to place their bombs, rockets, and napalm within a few yards of friendly troops saved American lives as the advance continued, ridge by ridge and cave by cave. By mid-June, the defenders had been compressed into a relatively small area at the southern portion of the island, and there were so many American aircraft in the air space above the Japanese-held end of Okinawa, a real danger of midair collision existed.

Gilbert Islands and her sister carrier, *USS Block Island* (CVE-106), with MCVG-1, composed of VMF-511 and VMTB-233, aboard were ordered south to Leyte, arriving there on 19 June. There they were teamed with the Navy-manned *USS Suwannee* (CVE-27) to form Carrier Division 22. CarDiv 22 was to provide air support for the assault on Balikpapan, Borneo to be made by the Australian 7th Division planned for 1 July.

So thorough had been the pre-invasion bombardment, there was little opposition to the actual assault. The Aussies dispensed with close air support after a flight of Navy aircraft bombed a target already occupied by friendly troops, several of whom lost their lives in the attack. The Australians had neglected to notify the aircraft of their capture of the objective, and this unfortunate tragedy served to underscore one of the most critical requirements for successful close air support – immediate, direct radio contact between ground troops and aircraft.

The carriers' stay off Borneo was brief, and they were withdrawn on 4 July, returning to Leyte once again. Upon their arrival, CarDiv 22 was disbanded. *Block Island* was ordered to Guam, and *Gilbert Islands* continued south to Ulithi. On 4 August, *Gilbert Islands* joined the logistics support group of Task Force 58, the Fast Carrier Force, in the waters off the southern coast of Japan.

After the Japanese surrendered, the carrier was among the ships assigned to evacuate allied prisoners-of-war from Formosa, and there were some tense moments as the American forces approached the island. The Japanese ashore initially refused to acknowledge any radio messages from the ships, and no one knew if the Japanese had heard the Emperor's order to surrender or if they would obey even if they were aware of it. As a result, the carrier readied a strike should it be needed. The leading destroyer safely navigated the defensive minefield and was guided to the pier by the Japanese, who finally decided it would be in their best interests to obey the surrender order. The evacuation was successful, but the prisoners were in such poor condition that more than 10% of the 1,160 evacuees had to be hospitalized immediately and repatriated later.

The mission of mercy completed successfully, the carrier and MCVG-2 departed the western Pacific to return to the United States. After their arrival, MCVG-2 and *Gilbert Islands* parted company. VMTB-143 and VMF-512 were ordered to MCAS, El Toro, California. The air group was deactivated, but the squadrons remained at El Toro as a component of MAG-46, where most of the Marines' carrier-qualified squadrons were based with the exceptions of those squadrons currently at sea.

VMTB-143 remained on the active roster into 1946. However, shortly thereafter it was deactivated on 10 March 1946, the common fate of all Marine torpedo squadrons. It remained inactive until the United States began to rebuild its badly neglected military strength after the outbreak of the Korean War. The squadron was reactivated and redesignated a fighter squadron, VMF-143. Several members of the squadron were called to active duty for service in Korea, but the squadron itself remained a Reserve unit. It was assigned to NAS, New Orleans, and was deactivated again before the end of the decade of the 1950s and has remained inactive since.

During its service, VMTB-143 was credited with the destruction of 7½ enemy aircraft in aerial combat, and these were claimed during the squadron's service in the Solomons and the air campaign against Rabaul. In view of its service record, it is somewhat surprising that the squadron was not recognized with the award of a unit citation or commendation.

The first of the squadron's insignia depicted in the accompanying dates from the latter months of service during World War II. This "Captain America" design is credited to Lieutenant Alex Raymond and was an unofficial insignia. It was never submitted to Headquarters, Marine Corps for approval. It is machine embroidered on Navy blue wool, and this particular example resides on an M-442A flight jacket in the author's collection. It has suffered some minor moth damage around the edges over time, but it is in remarkably good condition for a wool item that is considerably more than half a century old. On the left breast of the jacket opposite the insignia is a nametag carrying Naval Aviator's wings and the name H.D. Dawson, Lieutenant, USMC. Unfortunately, the author has no additional information on Lt. Dawson.

The author has seen photographs of a variation of this design that presents somewhat of a mystery. This insignia is virtually identical to the first one pictured, but it bears the parent carrier and its hull number in white on the body of the torpedo. Obviously, it dates from the period of early 1945 through the latter months of that same year, when the squadron was a component of MCVG-2 aboard *Gilbert Islands*.

It is probable this insignia is actually an example of two or three variations of the insignia of MCVG-2 in which members of VMTB-143 adopted this variant, members of VMF-512 adopted a variant in which the torpedo and the legend "VMTB 143" was replaced with something emblematic of a fighter squadron and its legend and the members of the C.A.S.D. may have adopted a third variation. Again, this is speculation but a likely explanation.

The "Devildog Avenger" insignia was designed by a squadron member, Philip Miller, and received official approval in 1943. Originals of this design were embroidered on wool in the United States.

via Holmberg

The insignia depicting the cutlass-wielding pirate is an example of the design adopted by the squadron after its activation as a Reserve unit and its redesignation as a fighter squadron and recognized by the association of the city of New Orleans with Jean Lafitte's pirates of Baritaria.

There is a drawing of another version of the squadron's insignia in the files of the National Archives and Records Administration in Washington, D.C. It depicts a comic pelican, Louisiana's state bird, charging forward wearing boxing gloves and carrying a lighted grenade in it mouth. The drawing is in black and white, and it bears stamps that it was received for approval by the Headquarters, Marine Corps, on 3 August 1956. However, there is no indication whether or not any insignia were made to this design.

In the author's collection is a G-1 flight jacket in very good condition, especially for a garment that is more than sixty years old. It carries the Rocket Raider/Captain America insignia of VMTB-143 on the right breast and a name tag that reads "H.D. Dawson, Lieut., USMC" on the left breast.

MARINE ATTACK SQUADRON 144, THE HENSAGLISKA SQUADRON

Author's Collection

The squadron was activated as Marine Scout Bomber Squadron 144 at San Diego on 7 September 1942 under the command of Major John L.D. Gabbert. A component of Marine Aircraft Group 24 at MCAS, Santa Barbara, VMSB-144 was brought up to strength in terms of flight and ground personnel and commenced training. By the end of November, records indicate it had a total of ten aircraft on hand, seven SBD-3 Dauntless' and three SB2U-3 Vindicators, the latter suitable only for training. As the squadron neared combat readiness, Captain Roscoe M. Nelson assumed command on 23 November.

As the Christmas season of 1942 approached, the squadron received a warning order for movement to the South Pacific, and it departed the West Coast in mid-January 1943. It arrived on Guadalcanal on 5 February after staging through Noumea, New Caledonia, and Efate in the New Hebrides, where the ground echelon would remain as a part of the aircraft maintenance and service pool. The arrival of the flight echelon of VMSB-144 on Guadalcanal coincided with the final withdrawal of the last of the Japanese defenders after a bitter, bloody six-month struggle for the island and its strategic airfield. With the enemy ejected from Guadalcanal, the American command cast its eyes northwestward to the islands further up the Slot, as the waters separating the two parallel strings of islands that form the Solomons was known. The purely defensive phase of the campaign was over, and the Allied offensive was about to begin.

But, the Japanese were not about to sit idle as the Americans prepared their next moves. The enemy shifted forces from one location to another, evacuated some islands deemed not worth defending and reinforced others. Most all these movements and

preparations were made by ship and did not escape notice by the daily search missions sent out from the growing American installations on Guadalcanal. Strike missions were mounted against the Tokyo Express runs of Japanese destroyers and shipping concentrations in the areas of Vila in the Shortlands, the island of Kolombangara and around Munda on New Georgia. These missions marked the entry of VMSB-144 into combat, and some bitter aerial battles were fought as the Americans struck at the enemy shipping, and several Allied fighter squadrons ran up large numbers of victories protecting the strike aircraft. Despite their best efforts, however, Japanese fighters occasionally succeeded in eluding the Allied fighters and attacking the scout and torpedo bombers. Before long, some of the rear cockpits of the squadron's SBDs began to sprout miniature "Rising Sun" kill symbols to mark the successes of the radiomen-gunners.

After five weeks of operations from Guadalcanal, the squadron's flight echelon returned to Efate on 12 March 1943. From there, it went to Australia for a brief period of R&R as the ground echelon, still in the New Hebrides, continued its maintenance duties to aid in maintaining the flow of aircraft northward to the Solomons. As the squadron completed its period of R&R, Captain Frank E. Hollar assumed command of VMSB-144 on 21 April, and the squadron prepared to return to combat. On 8 May, the squadron's ground echelon was ordered forward to Guadalcanal where it was joined by the flight echelon on 13 June after the latter drew a new complement of SBDs from the aircraft pool in the New Hebrides and completed another period of refresher training. Shortly afterwards, the ground and flight echelons were separated once again when the flight echelon shifted its base of operations from Guadalcanal to the Russells on 26 June. It continued to operate from there for a month until it returned to Henderson Field on 26 July. From Guadalcanal, it was withdrawn once again to Efate for a rest period followed by additional refresher training before moving northward again. The ground echelon was reunited with the flight echelon while at Efate.

In October, the flight echelon again moved forward and was in operation from the newly captured airfield at Munda, New Georgia, by 15 October while the ground echelon again remained at Efate. VMSB-144's presence on New Georgia was as a part of the concentration of allied air power there for the next, and largest, move to date of the Solomons campaign, the invasion of Bougainville. This island was the largest of the Solomons chain, and its capture would place the land-based Navy and Marine squadrons within strike range of the enemy installations at Rabaul, the strategic objective of the entire South Pacific campaign. The Japanese realized that the fall of Bougainville would further imperil Rabaul, and they would resist the assault to the utmost of their declining ability to do so. In turn, the Allies expected fierce resistance and prepared accordingly. The landings were scheduled for 1 November 1943, and the squadron furnished eight SBDs as part of the strike planned to thoroughly bomb and strafe enemy positions on and near the beaches five minutes before the assault forces of the 3rd Marine Division and the 2nd Raider Regiment went ashore.

The squadron contributed its load of eight heavy "daisy cutters," 1,000-lb. general-purpose bombs with extensions fitted to nose fuses to detonate the bombs aboveground, to the strike. The daisy cutters would blast away a large area of underbrush to reveal any enemy strongpoints within it to further attack. As can be

via Holmberg

ary, when it embarked for its return to the United States, arriving there on 2 February. Upon arrival, it was reduced to cadre status under the leadership of its Non-Commissioned Officer-in-Charge, Master Technical Sergeant Robert Edens. The cadre moved what remained of the squadron's possessions ashore to its new base on the West Coast where it would begin again the process of transforming itself into a squadron from a loose collection of individuals. VMSB-144 was formed anew on 9 March 1944, when Captain Archibald M. Smith, Jr., assumed command for two days pending the arrival of Major Arthur M. Moran on 11 March.

In the midst of the squadron's rebirth as a scout-bomber squadron, it was redesignated VMTB-144 on 14 October 1944. It turned its Dauntlesses over to the fleet aircraft pool and drew its complement of TBM Avengers to begin its conversion into a torpedo squadron. [The TBM was the version of the Avenger built by the Eastern Aircraft Division of General Motors Corporation. Production of the Avenger was shifted from Grumman to Eastern Aircraft to allow Grumman to concentrate on production of the superlative and vitally needed F6F Hellcat fighter.] It was notified that it would become a part of the Marines' carrier force and was redesignated VMTB(CVS)-144 on 5 November. The (CVS) designation was applied to all the Marine squadrons that would form the air groups of the escort carriers to be composed of all-Marine squadrons, but this was a paper designation change only. These squadrons dropped the (CVS) portion of their designations after a short while, and VMTB(CVS)-144 was officially redesignated VMTB-144 in May 1945, when it moved to MCAS, Santa Barbara, to complete its carrier training.

The squadron remained at Santa Barbara throughout June and July and reported aboard its designated carrier USS *Salerno Bay* (CVE-110) on 12 August 1945. By that time, however, the

imagined, these weapons also had a fearsome effect on any exposed personnel unfortunate enough to be within the blast radius of the bomb. The assault forces characterized this strike as "excellently timed and executed" in reducing enemy resistance to the amphibious assault. The squadron continued to provide pinpoint close support for the Marines ashore on Bougainville until 21 November. The following day, VMSB-144 was withdrawn to Efate for the final time and reunited with its ground echelon. On 27 November, Captain Morris T. Nelson assumed command.

Captain Robert H. Giffen, Jr., relieved Captain Nelson on 10 January 1944, and the squadron remained at Efate until 12 Janu-

Another Blow Against the Japanese
This photo shows a number of the squadron's SBDs as they taxi toward the active runway to begin another strike mission against the enemy. The hastily cleared jungle growth and rough condition of the airfield at Munda provides ample evidence of the speed at which the Navy's Construction Battalions, the SeaBees, could convert virgin jungle into an operable airstrip. [USMC photo]

atomic weapons had been employed against the Japanese cities of Hiroshima and Nagasaki, and, after much bitter, acrimonious internal wrangling and several attempted assassinations against those involved in the surrender negotiations by die-hard Japanese militarists, the enemy signaled his willingness to meet the surrender terms of the Allies. The war ended on 15 August 1945, and the mass reductions of American power began immediately. For the Marines, squadron after squadron was deactivated in the months that followed, and VMTB-144 was among the first to meet this fate. The squadron was struck from the rolls of active squadrons on 9 December 1945.

VMSB-144 was credited with the destruction of eight enemy aircraft in aerial combat during its tours in the Solomons in 1943.

The squadron was among those to be born again as Reserve units, and it was reactivated, redesignated a fighter squadron, VMF-144, and assigned to NAS, Jacksonville, Florida. Shortly thereafter, VMF-144 was redesignated VMA-144. It converted to jet aircraft in the 1950s and continued to serve until deactivated again in a Reserve force reduction.

The first version of the squadron's various insignia designs dates from its service in the Reserves during the 1950s. It appears the same insignia was utilized for its entire period of post-World War II service, whether the squadron was an attack squadron or a fighter squadron. The illustration was copied from an insignia decal made for application to coffee mugs or any other semi-stationary item that would have its appearance enhanced by the application of the squadron's insignia – in other words, just about anything.

The second example of the squadron's insignia in the accompanying plates is of the second variation of insignia of VMSB/VMTB-144 and was made for a squadron reunion. "Hensagliska" is a Sioux word meaning "little warrior-brave warrior" and was suggested by a member of the squadron, Reyn-

Author's Collection

olds "Chief" Moody. Gordon Baldwin was the artist who drew the design. Original examples of this design consisted of a decal applied to a leather background.

The third illustration is of an original example of the first version of the insignia of VMSB-144. These were made in Australia during one of the squadron's R&R visits to "the land down under." These were machine embroidered on a wool background, and Headquarters, Marine Corps, approved the design in 1943. Note the deletion of the squadron number and the "daisy cutter" fuse extension on the bomb in the second version of the design. Both were deleted from the design for security reasons.

MARINE TORPEDO BOMBER SQUADRON 151,
THE ALI BABA SQUADRON

Author's Collection

The earliest use of military aircraft was that of the observation of the activities of one's enemies. The age-old need for commanders to know what lay "on the other side of the hill" could be fulfilled by aircraft more efficiently than by any other means. Virtually any aircraft capable of getting airborne could serve as an observation platform largely invulnerable to countermeasures, at least at first. As a result, the armed services of the industrial-ized nations sprouted units of these fragile, strange craft, and the United States Marine Corps was no exception. Several observation squadrons were counted among the ranks of Marine aviation units by the 1920s. However, during the several reorganizations of Fleet and Marine aviation units that took place in the decades between the world wars, the Marine observation squadrons were either deactivated or redesignated, with the last two being redesignated scouting squadrons on 1 July 1937. This state of affairs was, however, destined to be of short duration.

As the United States began to expand its military forces in response to a worsening world situation of the late-1930s, Marine Observation Squadron 1, VMO-1, was activated at MCAS, Quantico, Virginia. In the last of the major reorganizations of Navy and Marine aviation prior to the U.S. involvement in World War II, VMO-1 was redesignated VMO-151 at Marine Corps Air Station, Quantico, Virginia, on 1 July 1941, and Major Thomas C. Green assumed command. As was the case with several Marine squadrons during this period, despite its observation designation, the squadron was organized, trained and equipped as a scout-bomber unit.

7 December 1941 found the squadron, equipped at the time with a dozen Curtiss SBC-4 Helldiver biplane dive-bombers, on maneuvers at New Bern, North Carolina, along with two other squadrons from its parent organization, MAG-11. The squadron remained in North Carolina until 9 December, when it returned to Quantico. In the flurry of activities that followed in the wake of the Japanese attack on Pearl Harbor, VMO-151 and many other squadrons of Id MAW hurriedly quit the East Coast for various installations in California. In the near-panic atmosphere that prevailed for a short time after Pearl Harbor, conventional wisdom expected the Japanese to follow the carrier strike with an attempt to invade Hawaii at the very least or, perhaps, to attempt the conquest of the West Coast. After a short time, cooler heads prevailed, and VMO-151 was ordered back to Quantico on 10 January 1942.

In late March, the squadron was alerted for movement to the South Pacific. It was shifted from Quantico to Norfolk, Virginia, and sailed for Samoa on 9 April 1942, still equipped with its hopelessly obsolete SBC-4s. This move was a part of the American response to the perceived threat to the tenuous lifeline that stretched

Helldiver on the Rocks!
This SBC of VMO-151 came to grief on a rock pile bulldozed away from the runways and taxi strips of the airfield in Samoa. Note the prewar style squadron markings clearly visible on the fuselage side. [USMC photo]

from the West Coast of the United States, across the vast stretches of the Pacific to Australia. VMO-151 arrived at Tutuila, Samoa on 9 May, and the following day, Major Green was relieved of command and promoted to the position of Executive Officer of MAG-13. Major Raymond B. Hurst arrived to command the squadron on 12 May. In June, a detachment of the squadron was ordered to the island of Satapaula, in British Samoa, that lay 100 miles northwest of Tutuila. Upon its arrival, it was paired with the 7th Defense Battalion to form the island's garrison.

The squadron was destined to spend 13 relatively quiet months in Samoa far removed from any active combat arena. While the members of the squadron likely felt somewhat abandoned during the stay there, it may have, in fact, been a blessing in disguise. In the explosive expansion of the immediate post-Pearl Harbor period, dozens of new squadrons were activated and existing ones were quickly brought up to something approaching full strength. As a result, many of these squadrons either were equipped with obsolete equipment that would have been useless in combat, their aviators were woefully under-trained or a combination of these two circumstances, and VMO-151 suffered from both maladies. It was still equipped with its SBC-4s, and of its twenty aviators, only three were considered "experienced."

At the very least, the squadron's stay in Samoa cured the problem of lack of experience among its aviators in all categories, with the exception of actual combat experience. The only enemies encountered were wretched living conditions, mud and several exotic tropical diseases. Alerts were frequent, and thousands of hours were spent aloft searching for an enemy that never came within range of the probing Marine aircraft. Despite their antiquated state, the SBCs were good training platforms for the fledgling dive-bomber pilots of the squadron. A good many 500-pound bombs were expended against practice targets to hone the aviators' skills, and no doubt several unfortunate whales and other marine creatures were mistaken for Japanese submarines and "sunk" by the Marines. In fact, Samoa and several other island groups in Micronesia were on the Japanese target list, but events in the Coral Sea and at Midway effectively derailed any enemy plans for further expansion of their ill-gotten empire.

On 15 September 1942, the squadron was redesignated VMSB-151, a belated recognition of the fact that it was, regardless of its previous designation, a scout-bomber squadron. Major Hurst was transferred, and Captain John E. Bell commanded the squadron for six days until the arrival of Lieutenant Colonel George A. Sarles on 9 December 1942.

The squadron finally bade a no doubt less than fond farewell to its SBC-4 versions of the Helldiver when its biplanes began to be replaced with Douglas SBD-4 Dauntless dive-bombers. Finally, the squadron was released from duty in British Samoa and began to move from there to the island of Uea in the Wallis Archipelago, a French possession, on 27 January 1943. Conditions in the French-owned islands were hardly better than those the squadron left behind in Samoa. Some idea of duty there can be gained from a notation in the war diary of an unidentified squadron member who served there that, "Wallis has gained the reputation as about the best spot on God's earth to keep away from." Several tropical diseases were endemic to the archipelago, with filariasis chief among them. For a time, non-battle casualties from disease were at such a high incidence that those suffering from them were evacuated by the shipload. Clearly, the war diary comment was quite close to the mark concerning the "tropical paradise" that was the Wallis Islands!

During its stay in this "garden spot," the two squadrons of MAG-13 were split to form two additional squadrons. On 1 October 1942, VMSB-151 gave up nineteen officers, 109 enlisted men, ten of its old SBCs and a single Grumman J2F-5 Duck amphibian to form VMO-155 under the command of Captain John P. Haynes, Jr.

During the waning months of 1942, the situation on Guadalcanal moved from crisis to crisis, and reinforcements of all kinds were scraped together from every possible source to prop up the American hold on the strategic island. On 10 December, 18 pilots and 21 gunners of VMSB-151 were flown to the New Hebrides. A dozen of the pilots were immediately reassigned to fighter duty and joined VMO-251. They were transferred from Espiritu Santo to Guadalcanal within a few days. [Records from this hectic period are far from complete and do not record the eventual assignments of the remaining six pilots or the gunners, but no doubt they found useful employment during the pivotal struggle for Guadalcanal.]

As these events were taking place, American forces were moved into the Ellice Islands to deny their possible use to the enemy. These islands lay only 700 miles from the Japanese-held Gilberts and were of immediate need of an aerial garrison. The primary island in the group and the only one suitable for airfield construction was Funafuti, a tiny speck of sand measuring 100 yards-by-seven miles. Within a month, the Seabees had worked their accustomed miracles, and the island's airfield, such as it was, was declared ready for business. However, it was 31 January 1943 before the first American combat aircraft arrived when Lieutenant Colonel Sarles led a half-dozen of the squadron's SBDs to the field in company with nine Wildcats. The next day, three more dive-bombers of VMSB-151 arrived, but they were withdrawn after three weeks.

Lieutenant Colonel Sarles was ordered to other duty on 2 June, and Major Maurice W. Fletcher assumed command the following day. [Sarles went on to command VMB-611 until his loss in action on 30 May 1945.] On 6 June, the entire squadron left Tutuila behind and moved to the Wallis Group again and was in operation from its base on Uvea Island on 10 June as a part of the permanent garrison of the islands. VMSB-151 would remain there throughout the remainder of 1943.

In mid-February 1944, the squadron was alerted to prepare to move forward from the Wallis Group to the recently captured Marshalls. The move would be made under the leadership of a new commanding officer, Major Gordon H. Knott, who assumed command on 24 February 1944. On that same day, the squadron began its movement to the Marshalls. The squadron's SBDs arrived at Engebi Island, part of the huge Kwajalein Atoll, after a five-day, 2,000-mile flight, and part of the squadron was then shifted to nearby Roi. Its moves completed, VMSB-151 began to fly patrol missions and strikes in support of additional landings against other islets that formed Kwajalein. These strikes were the first true combat missions for the squadron as they bombed Wotho, Ujae, and Lae to cover the Marines of the assault units. Occasional strikes were also flown against Ponape, some 360 miles away from the squadron's base. The distance represented the extreme limit of the combat range of the SBD and required very careful navigation and attention to throttle and manifold settings in order to avoid the flight terminating in the water instead of the squadron's bases. At first, these strikes were met by fierce anti-aircraft fire, but it soon dwindled away as the enemy's ammunition supplies were depleted. Other than infrequent visits by small craft running between Japanese-held islands of the atoll or the occasional submarine that managed to slip through the American patrols, the garrisons of many of the enemy-held islands of the Central Pacific were totally isolated. Considering what Fate held in store for many of the islands actually targeted for assault, these soldiers could consider themselves to be quite lucky, although probably very few realized it at the time.

The squadron remained in the Marshalls flying patrols and strikes against the bypassed enemy garrisons on islands, the capture of which was not worth the blood that would be spilt. During this period, a number of officers commanded VMSB-151. Major Randolph C. Berkeley, Jr., assumed command on 31 October 1944. Major Bruce Prosser followed Major Berkeley on 5 December, and Major Robert J. Shelley, Jr., assumed command on 26 January 1945. Major John H. Stock followed Major Shelley on 27 March.

The squadron continued to serve as a part of the Marshalls garrison through 31 May 1945, when it was ordered to stand down from combat operations and prepared to return to the United States. VMSB-151 was reduced to a virtual cadre status as most of the officers and many of the enlisted were transferred immediately. Warrant Officer Robert L. Harmon assumed command of the rump of a squadron on 6 June 1945, and it departed for the West Coast on 9 June aboard S.S. *Silverpeck*.

The remnant of VMSB-151 reached San Diego in late June and was ordered to MCAS, Santa Barbara. After its arrival there, the squadron was redesignated a torpedo squadron, VMTB-151, on 30 June 1945, and Major Walter J. Carr, Jr., assumed command on 1 July. Concurrently with the change in designation, the squadron was ordered to undergo carrier training for service aboard one of the close air support-dedicated escort carriers during the anticipated invasion of the Japanese Home Islands.

However, before the carrier training could begin in earnest, the Japanese surrendered. VMTB-151 continued to serve at Santa Barbara until it was deactivated on 20 March 1946. It has remained inactive since that date.

The insignia in the plate is a reproduction produced for a squadron reunion and is an example of the only design attributed to VMO/VMSB/VMTB-151.

MARINE ATTACK TRAINING SQUADRON 20

Author's Collection

via Holmberg

During the latter months of World War II, the success of the big F4U Corsair in the fighter-bomber role in the Pacific had hastened the end of the dedicated scout bombers and torpedo aircraft in Navy and Marine Corps service. Its accuracy as a bombing platform was proven to be virtually equal to that of the dive-bomber without the need for a second crewman and fighter escorts. The demise of the Imperial Japanese Navy as an effective fighting force wrote *finis* to the torpedo bomber. The months immediately following the Japanese surrender saw the deactivation of all of the Marines' scout and torpedo bombing squadrons and the Navy's adoption of the all-purpose "attack" mission designation in November 1946 for their remaining carrier-based bombing and torpedo squadrons.

However, it required the impetus of the Korean War to bring the attack squadron into Marine aviation some five years after the Navy adopted the designation. On 1 March 1951, VMF-121, based at NAS, Glenview, Illinois, was called to active duty for service in Korea. Ten weeks later, VMF-121 was redesignated VMA-121, the first Marine squadron to bear the attack designation. The squadron was equipped with the Douglas AD Skyraider and dispatched to Korea, where it arrived on 19 October 1951. Based at airfield K-3 at Pohang, South Korea, it flew its first combat mission, the first by a Marine "attack" squadron, on 27 October.

Other Marine fighter squadrons were redesignated attack squadrons but retained the Corsair and continued to operate in the ground attack role. About the only visible change as far as

these squadrons were concerned was the application of the VMA designation on the lower aft fuselage of the F4Us in place of the VMF designation. Some squadrons, however, would receive the AD, and it was realized by the powers that be that the smooth transition of these squadrons to the Douglas product would be facilitated greatly by the activation of an attack training squadron dedicated to this aircraft.

As a result, VMAT-20 was activated on 1 December 1951. Based at MCAS, El Toro, the squadron was busy with the training of aviators in the Skyraider to ensure a steady stream of replacements for the AD squadrons engaged in Korea as well as those for the other squadrons converting to the new aircraft.

The end of the Korean conflict on 27 July 1953 slowed the pace of operations somewhat but the need for AD-qualified aviators continued until the Marine Corps began to replace the Skyraider with jet aircraft later in the decade. With the phase-out of the AD in Marine service, VMAT-20 was deactivated on 23 June 1958.

The first insignia shown of VMAT-20 depicted in the plate represents the only design ever to be officially approved for use by the squadron during its service. The second and third designs date from the squadron's service at MCAS, Cherry Point, NC in 1953 and 1954 respectively, and official approval of either of these two has not been confirmed.

MARINE ALL-WEATHER ATTACK TRAINING SQUADRON 202

THE DOUBLE EAGLES

Author's Collection

Author's Collection

The squadron was activated on 15 January 1968 to serve as the replacement and training squadron for those air and ground crews destined for service in the Marines' all-weather attack squadrons. The first Marine squadrons to be equipped with the A-6 Intruder had been trained by one of the Navy's A-6 FRS squadrons, VA-42, at NAS, Oceana, Virginia. However, the Navy A-6 program was in full swing, limiting the time that could be dedicated to the needs of the Marines. As more and more Marine light attack squadrons were redesignated and began to receive the Intruder, the need for a Marine FRS unit was met by the establishment of VMAT(AW)-202.

The squadron served in this capacity for almost two decades until the decision was made to begin the conversion of the Marines' A-6 squadrons to the two-seat, all-weather version of the F/A-18 Hornet, the F/A-18D. Once this process was begun, the requirement for additional crews for the remaining A-6 squadrons could be met by the transfer of A-6-qualified personnel from a squadron as it was re-equipped with the F/A-18D to those squadrons that continued to fly the Intruder. Thus, VMAT(AW)-202 was deactivated on 30 September 1986.

Few among even the most ardent supporters of the Hornet would claim it to be superior to the Intruder as an all-weather weapons delivery system, but the decision by the Marines to surrender their A-6s is based upon a certain logic. By the mid-1980s, the basic A-6 design was 30 years old, having grown out of a requirement for an aircraft with like capabilities that was first drafted during the Korean War. The A-6 airframe was no longer in production, and the surviving aircraft were beginning to show their age. Among the problems were fatigue-related cracks in the wings, and the program to re-wing A-6 airframes with a new composite wing, designated the A-6F, was canceled due to budget restraints. Also, the supply system would be simplified by decreasing the number of airframes and systems for which parts must be maintained. In addition to these purely Marine concerns related to the A-6, the Navy chose not to adopt the F/A-18D, opting instead to wait until the ill-fated A-12 Avenger II became available. The eventual cancellation of the A-12 program for reasons both political and technical would eventually deprive the Navy of a true carrier-based all-weather strike capability shortly after the end of the war in Southwest Asia.

Of the three versions of the squadron's insignia in the plates, the first is the official insignia of VMAT(AW)-202 and the second commemorates the squadron's final months of service, its so-called "Twilight Tour." The third insignia is an example of the first version of the squadron's official, approved insignia design. The reason or reasons behind the change of background color from a deep red to Navy blue is unknown.

MARINE ATTACK TRAINING SQUADRON 203
THE HAWKS

Author's Collection

The lineal predecessor of today's VMAT-203, VMT-1, was activated in 1947 as a component of MTG-20. Subsequently, it was absorbed into the Force Aviation Headquarters Group. In 1958, it was separated from the higher command and became VMT-1 again and became a component IId MAW. Equipped with the two-seat TF-9J Cougar and the TO-2 Shooting Star, it conducted swept-wing jet transition and refresher training, instrument procedures and instrument ground school. After a short time, the TO-2 was retired from service, but the TF-9J remained with the squadron until 1967. The transition to newer aircraft began on 2 July 1967 when the first TA-4F Skyhawk was received.

VMT-1 was deactivated on 5 December 1967, and VMT-203 was activated on the same date at MCAS, Cherry Point, North Carolina. Its mission was type training for the A-4 Skyhawk and was equipped with a mixture of TA-4F and -4H aircraft. It was assigned as a component squadron of Marine Combat Crew Readiness Training Group 20, and both enlisted ground crews and aviators passed through the squadron en route to a permanent squadron assignment. The enlisted personnel were taught to apply the theoretical knowledge they had received in their various technical schools to the actual aircraft type they would service and maintain. The same could be said of an aviator. When a student aviator successfully completed the squadron's training syllabus, he went on to the weapons training squadron for the A-4, VMAT-102, at MCAS, Yuma, prior to being ordered to an operational squadron.

As the older types of training aircraft in use in the advanced training phase of Navy flight training reached the end of their useful lives, more of the TA-4-type aircraft, primarily the unarmed TA-4Js, were utilized in the latter portions of flight training. This served to reduce the requirement for the mission performed by VMT-203. As a result, the squadron was redesignated VMAT-203 on 1 May 1972, and it was devoted to weapons training for the A-4 series aircraft and became the East Coast's counterpart to Yuma's VMAT-102.

As the decade of the 1970s approached its middle years, the Marine Corps began to acquire the revolutionary AV-8 Harrier vertical/short takeoff and landing attack aircraft. The Harrier's ability to operate from unprepared landing sites close to a potential battlefield while carrying a useful war load promised a quantum leap forward in the ability of Marine aviation to carry out its primary mission of support of the Marine on the ground. The AV-8 served as a "force multiplier" in that the ability of the aircraft to operate close to the battlefield allowed fewer aircraft to place the same amount of ordnance on target than a larger number of conventional aircraft operating from more distant bases. In addition, the ability of the aircraft to operate without the need of fixed, vulnerable airfields makes a squadron equipped with the Harrier a much less attractive target for enemy counter-air operations. Further, the vertical take-off capability of the AV-8 allowed it to go to sea on virtually any vessel with open deck space greater that the dimensions of the aircraft. Amphibious

Cat on the Ramp
Although this TF-9J was assigned to VMT-103, this 1965 photo clearly shows the details of those examples of this aircraft type that were assigned to VMT-1 at the time. [DoD Photo]

A Hawk on the Wing
This TAV-8B of VMAT-203 was photographed above a broken undercast with an instructor and a fledgling Harrier driver aboard. USMC Photo via the VMAT-203 Website

assault ships such the LPH and LPD that were designed for the support of helicopter operations could now embark a potent strike capability in addition to their usual vertical assault mission. In theory, at least, this would relieve the Navy's carriers from being tied to a beachhead for extended periods of time.

VMAT-203, then under the command of Lieutenant Colonel H.H. Clark, was selected to be the Marines' Harrier conversion training squadron, and the first of its new aircraft began to arrive in late 1975. When the last of the squadron's Harriers arrived, it was transferred to MAG-32, and shortly thereafter completed carrier qualifications aboard USS *Franklin D. Roosevelt* (CV-42) although carrier operations were not to be a part of the squadron's training syllabus.

When an aviator reported to the squadron for training, he was first introduced to the vertical flight ability of the Harrier, no doubt an eye-opening experience at first, utilizing one of the squadron's TAV-8A two-seat trainers under the watchful eyes of an instructor in the rear seat. Once the student has been deemed proficient in the trainer, he progressed to the single-seat AV-8A, the then-current operational variant of the aircraft. Assuming the successful completion of the squadron syllabus, the student

received a "combat-capable" rating and was transferred to an operational squadron. Upon arrival there, his training would continue, and when fully integrated into the squadron, he was rated "combat-ready."

After almost nine years of operation of the first-generation Harrier, the Marine Corps began to receive examples of the second-generation aircraft, the AV-8B. VMAT-203 received its first example of the new aircraft on 12 January 1984 and immediately began to upgrade its training syllabus to match the increased capabilities of the -8B aircraft. With a more powerful engine, upgraded avionics and a new wing, it was capable of higher performance with a greater ordnance load and increased weapons delivery accuracy via the advanced Angle Rate Bombing System (ARBS). An earlier version of this system had been introduced into service in the A-4 series during the Vietnam War and gave these aircraft a considerable boost in bombing accuracy.

As the squadron prepared and launched its new training syllabus, it was still required to provide qualified aviators for the older models of the aircraft that remained in service with the operational squadrons. Most of these surviving models had been upgraded to AV-8C standards. The two training syllabi were conducted in parallel for the remainder of 1984, 1985, and the early part of 1986. During this two-year period, the squadron produced 120 qualified aviators, 950 qualified maintenance personnel and flew 12,000 hours. In recognition of these accomplishments, VMAT-203 was awarded the Meritorious Unit Commendation for 1985/86.

The squadron continues to operate from Cherry Point to fulfill its training mission and has included the night-attack version of the AV-8B in its training.

Of the four versions of the squadron's insignia depicted in the plates, the first is its current insignia design, and the second is an earlier version of this same insignia. VMAT-203 contracted with its insignia vendor for this second insignia, and almost as soon as the initial batch of insignia were delivered, they informed the contractor that they were changing their design to

Author's Collection

the one on the left. This somewhat midstream change makes the second insignia, the one on the right somewhat of a rare "bird" for collectors. Also, in the author's opinion, the insignia on the right is a more attractive design than the one on the left.

The third and forth versions of the squadron's insignia depicted are the original VMAT-203 design in the smaller size normally worn on the aviator's flight suit, and the fourth, larger version is an example of that worn between the squadron's activation in 1967 and its redesignation as VMAT-203 in 1972. Also, it should be noted that while the squadron calls itself "The Hawks," the bird featured in these two latter insignia looks suspiciously like a Bald Eagle.

(It should be noted that the brief squadron history posted on the VMAT-203 website states that the lineal predecessor of the squadron is VMT-1 but that this squadron's colors were "cased" prior to the activation of the Hawks. This indicated that VMT-1 passed into history at that time, and VMAT-203 is a wholly different unit. One member of each squadron is assigned the duty as Public Affairs Officer, and while that individual is conscientious in the performance of that duty, they are rarely professional historians. Also, while contentious, it can be said with justification that the majority of these officers place the additional duty as P.A.O. several rungs down the ladder of their professional responsibilities.)

Author's Collection

MARINE ATTACK SQUADRON 211, THE WAKE AVENGERS

Author's Collection

Author's Collection

The squadron was activated on 1 January 1937 as VF-4M at NAS, San Diego, California, but this designation was short lived, and, the squadron was redesignated VMF-2 on 1 July 1937, in accordance with directives concerning the reorganization of all of the aviation assets of the Navy and Marine Corps which became effective on that date, and the designations of Marine aircraft squadrons were changed accordingly. On that same date, Major Charles L. Fike assumed command, and as the United States belatedly began to increase its long-neglected military strength in the face of a worsening world situation, the squadron was ordered to prepare for overseas movement. A short time after the end of the Christmas festivities of 1940 were over, VMF-2 boarded a ship for its voyage westward. Its new home was MCAS, Ewa, Territory of Hawaii, where it arrived in January 1941. On 1 July 1941, VMF-2 was redesignated VMF-211. This change in designations served to align squadron designations within their parent air groups and air wings. Major Paul A. Putnam relieved Major Fike on 7 November.

In late November 1941, almost before the "shine" had worn off the squadron's newly arrived Grumman F4F-3 Wildcats, VMF-211 was loaded aboard USS *Enterprise* (CV-6) to be transported to Wake Island in the Central Pacific. In addition to its very considerable value as a strategic outpost in the central Pacific, the American possession of Wake had served as a stop-over and refueling point for the trans-Pacific flights of Pan American Airways, and, as the clouds of war began to grow

ever darker on the western horizon, VMF-211 had been ordered there to form the island's defensive fighter force. The veteran members of *Enterprise's* Fighting Six, who were, relatively, far more experienced in the operation of the F4F, imparted what they could of their knowledge of the Wildcat to the pilots of VMF-211 during the brief voyage. The squadron had been able to amass very few flight hours and only a little knowledge of their new aircraft before they were ordered to the Central Pacific, and the words of wisdom from VF-6 would prove their value in the near future.

During the morning of 4 December, *Enterprise* turned into the prevailing tradewinds, and the Wildcats of VMF-211 began their short runs down the teakwood flight deck of the "Big E." Also launched from *Enterprise* was one of her SBD Dauntless dive-bombers to provide navigational assistance to the Marine fighters. After a flight of two hours, VMF-211 arrived over the island's airstrip, and their guardian angel SBD returned to the carrier, which had already begun her return voyage to Pearl Harbor. During her return, *Enterprise* was slowed by heavy weather, and it was this unexpected delay that prevented the invaluable carrier from being either in the harbor or near enough to it that it would surely have fallen victim to the Japanese attack of 7 December.

A few hours after the strike on Pearl Harbor, the first Japanese bombing raid from Kwajalein, some 600 miles to the southwest, struck Wake. Having received word of the Japanese raid against American installations in Hawaii, VMF-211 had a defensive patrol airborne when the raid began, but the outpost lacked radar. As a result, the fighters were out of position and missed the enemy bombers. The resulting damage was heavy, and several of the squadron's aircraft were destroyed on the ground. The Japanese then began a brief series of air raids against the American defenses on Wake in preparation for an amphibious assault against the island. The enemy bombers flew without fighter escort, and VMF-211 claimed several victims from these raids. At least two are known to have fallen to the guns of Captain Henry T. Elrod's Wildcat.

Despite their losses to the Marine fighters and anti-aircraft guns, the enemy believed the damage inflicted on the island's defenses was much heavier than was the case, and, strictly adhering to their timetable, the first Japanese invasion attempt against Wake was made on the morning of 11 December. It was

Pre-war Splendor
The Grumman F3F-2 assigned to the squadron commander basks in the bright sun of a quiet day at the airfield. Note the squadron insignia on the vertical fin below the aircraft Bureau number. [USMC photo]

contested between the vessels of the Japanese invasion force on one side by the Marine shore batteries on the island and the Wildcats of VMF-211 on the other. The defenders held their fire until the enemy closed to almost point-blank range. Believing their intended victims capable of only feeble resistance at best, the Japanese confidently approached the silent island. Then the Marine defense battalion's 5-inch guns roared to life, hurling salvo after salvo into the startled enemy. The guns definitely sank one Japanese destroyer and damaged several other ships of the invasion force. The bombing and strafing attacks of VMF-211 sank another destroyer and damaged several additional ships. Total Japanese losses were two destroyers sunk, several other vessels damaged, and 500 to 700 men killed. One of the Marines' victims was H.I.J.M.S. *Kisaragi*, but the identity of the second destroyer remains unclear even more than six decades after the event. American losses in this first engagement were practically nil. Still beleaguered but encouraged by their initial success, Wake's garrison prepared for the next round.

The defenders of Wake did not have long to savor their victory. Stung and shocked by their repulse, the Japanese return would be accompanied by overwhelming power, and any attempt at subtlety would be replaced by brute force. Two of the six Japanese carriers that had struck Pearl Harbor, H.I.J.M.S. *Soryu* and *Hiryu*, were detached from the strike force as it returned to home waters and ordered to destroy American air power on Wake before another landing attempt would be made, and a second and more powerful invasion force was ordered to capture the island, regardless of cost. Enemy air attacks, both from land bases and from the two carriers increased in frequency and intensity. VMF-211 continued to extract a price from the Japanese, but without reinforcements to make good their losses, it was only a matter of time, and the last of the defending F4Fs was destroyed on the morning of 22 December. Thereafter, the surviving members of the squadron joined the rest of the defenders to fight as infantry when the next enemy assault came, and they did not have long to wait. The final assault began at 0245, 23 December. It was over quickly. Only about ten members of VMF-211 survived, and among those who fell was the gallant Captain Elrod, who was later to receive a posthumous award of the Medal of Honor for his conduct at Wake. Major Putnam was among those who survived and was captured. It is from among his papers that much

of the information concerning the squadron's conduct in the final battle of Wake comes, and he was awarded the Navy Cross for his conduct during the defense of the doomed island.

A few members of VMF-211 had remained behind at Ewa when the bulk of the squadron had been sent to Wake. It was

The First of Many
Captain Henry T. Elrod of Marine Fighting Squadron 211 was the first Marine aviator to be awarded the Medal of Honor for his service during World War II, but many months would pass before the full details of Elrod's heroism would emerge from the smoke of the gallant, but futile, defense of Wake. [USMC photo]

Squadron Hack
A Curtiss SBC-3 Helldiver wearing the insignia of VMF-2 was captured in this pre-World War II photograph. Note the aircraft number, 19, on the fuselage. During this period, the usual aircraft complement of Navy and Marine combat squadrons was eighteen, but many squadrons acquired, by one method or another, an additional aircraft or two. These were used as transports for squadron personnel, instrument trainers and to provide sufficient flight hours for non-aircrew squadron members, such as flight surgeons, to qualify for their monthly allotment of flight pay. [USMC photo]

around this surviving nucleus that a "new" VMF-211 was built under the command of Major Luther S. Moore, who was listed officially as the squadron's commanding officer as of 24 December 1941. It was also during this period that the squadron adopted the nickname the "Wake Avengers," indicative both of their pride in the accomplishments of the squadron on the island and of their desire to avenge their fallen comrades. On 9 February Major Harold W. Bauer assumed temporary command of the squadron for three weeks before Major Moore assumed command again on 1 March.

Rebuilt and re-equipped with new F4Fs, the squadron once again found itself aboard a carrier. Loaded aboard USS *Lexington* (CV-2) on 14 April 1942, the squadron was transported to the island of Palmyra in the South Pacific, where it assumed base defense duties. Having been told the base at Palmyra was fully equipped and functional prior to its scheduled arrival, the squadron received an unpleasant surprise when it learned the runways

and taxiways of the base's were barely complete, and the living conditions there were primitive, to say the least. VMF-211 was destined to spend thirteen months in this tropical "paradise." While on Palmyra, the squadron was commanded by a number of different officers: Major Radford C. West relieved Major Moore on 8 August 1943; followed by Major Charles N. Endweiss on 25 October and Major Harold J. Mitchener on 7 April 1944.

In May 1943, VMF-211 returned to MCAS, Ewa, where it exchanged its F4Fs for the superlative F4U-1A Corsair. Major Robert A. Harvey relieved Major Mitchener on 16 July, and after three months of training with their new aircraft, the squadron departed Hawaii for the South Pacific once again. This time their destination was Espiritu Santo in the New Hebrides. After two months at Espiritu, VMF-211 moved forward to the Russells where it commenced combat operations for the first time since December 1941.

From its base in the Russells, the squadron was one of those that provided air cover and support for the assault of Bougainville. It was also here that, almost two years after the fall of Wake, the squadron began to extract the revenge that it wanted so badly. After some early painful lessons at the hands of the experienced and eager Japanese fighter pilots, the Corsair equipped squadrons of the Solomons Fighter Command began to mount some impressive scores. The Navy's initial opinion that the F4U was unsuitable for carrier operations came as a blessing to the often hard-pressed Marine fighter squadrons in the Solomons. Big, fast and rugged, the Corsair was the first American fighter committed to combat in the Pacific that was capable of besting the performance of the vaunted Japanese Zero. By mid-1943, the Marine fighting squadrons in the area had completed the transition to the Corsair, and their squadron scoreboards began to display an ever-increasing number of kill marks. Desperate to maintain their hold on the Solomons and the Bismarks, the Japanese committed more and more of their diminishing numbers of experienced fighter squadrons to the defense of the area. Counting on a short war, the enemy never planned to fight a battle of attrition like that being contested in the South Pacific, and as a result, the Japanese naval air arm was dealt a continuous series of heavy blows from which it would never fully recover. Rather than rotate their experienced aviators from combat to training commands in the home islands, where their hard won knowledge of the enemy could be passed along to those in training, these veterans remained in combat until most were killed, suffered debilitating wounds or were rendered combat ineffective by one of the host of tropical diseases endemic to the area. The result was a downward spiral. Each veteran lost in combat meant fewer were available as leaders and instructors for their green squadron mates, and the mantle of leadership fell on those whose level of experience was lower than those who had come before them. By the summer of 1944, the Japanese naval air arm was reduced to a mere shadow of its former prowess. While no Marine squadrons participated in the great Central Pacific campaign of 1944, their earlier efforts in the South Pacific did much to assure its success.

After a month in the Russells, the squadron moved to the newly captured airfields on Bougainville and began to take part in the aerial assault against Rabaul. While operating from Bougainville, Major Thomas V. Murto, Jr. assumed command of VMF-211 on 27 January 1944. In March 1944, part of the squadron moved to the Green Islands. From its two bases, it continued to take part in the pounding of Japan's "Fortress Rabaul." Rabaul, located on the island of New Britain in the Bismarks chain, was the cornerstone of Japanese power in the south and southwest Pacific areas, and it was in their stubborn defense of the fortifications there that much of the remaining elite of the Japanese naval air arm that had survived Guadalcanal and the Central Solomons was slowly but steadily reduced to near impotence. Defeated in the Solomons and in the defense of Rabaul, Japan's naval air arm was still able to, at times, inflict painful losses on the Allied forces, but it was never able to again mount any serious threat to the eventual Allied victory.

By the early spring of 1944, Rabaul's usefulness to the enemy had effectively come to an end. VMF-211, under the command of Major Thaddeus P. Wojcik since 6 May, remained in the Northern Solomons/Bismarks area, where it continued its participation in the strikes against the largely defenseless Japanese garrison there until December. Early that month, the squadron was on the move again to a more active area of operations, the

Philippines, under the leadership of Major Stanislaus J. Witomski, who had assumed command on 20 October.

General Macarthur's much heralded return to the Philippines had commenced in earnest with a massive amphibious assault against Leyte in the middle of the vast archipelago. As events turned out, the campaign in the islands lasted much longer than expected, and the decision was made to employ Marine squadrons to augment the efforts of the Army Air Forces. A destructive foray through the Philippines in September by the Fast Carrier Forces revealed the enemy defenses in the archipelago were much weaker than expected. As a result, the strategic decision was reached to advance the timetable for the assault on the islands. While the decision was the correct one at the strategic level, it brought about any number of tactical problems, not the least of which was the fact an October assault on Leyte would mean airfield construction would be severely hampered by the rainy season. This, in turn, meant a commitment of the fast carriers in the direct support of operations ashore for a far longer period than was anticipated or desirable. Also, enemy resistance was more prolonged than had been expected, and when sufficient airfield space was available to release the Fast Carrier Force from its support duties, the fighting ashore was still raging. As a result of a combination of these factors, the Army Air Forces found themselves in the rather embarrassing position of having an insufficient number of squadrons, particularly fighter squadrons, available to support the ongoing campaign. As a result, the decision was made to send in the Marines.

On 6 December, VMF-211 saw its first action of the Philippines campaign when it attacked an enemy convoy of seven ships that was attempting to reach Ormoc Bay on Leyte's west coast, the primary destination of Japanese reinforcement attempts. The Marines were to attack the convoy itself, and Army fighters were supposed to provide the Marines with cover from enemy fighters. As it turned out, the Army aircraft did not show up, but the Marines went ahead with their attack. Anti-aircraft fire and enemy fighters cost the squadron three Corsairs, among them the aircraft of Major. Witomski, who was able to successfully abandon his stricken fighter. One Marine was lost with his aircraft and two were rescued, one of whom later died from his injuries. Major Witomski was rescued and returned to the squadron a few days later. The squadron extracted a measure of revenge the following day when aircraft of VMF-211, -218 and -313 again attacked the convoy. Armed with 1,000-pound bombs, the Marines claimed

Just Another Day in Paradise
A number of the squadron's Wildcats are pictured in repose in a hastily bulldozed revetment at an airfield in the Russell Islands. Note the largely untouched coconut palms and jungle growth in the background. [USMC photo]

Practice Makes Perfect
An AD-4N Skyraider
of VMA-211 sweeps
over the heads of
Marines "charging"
up the beach during an
amphibious exercise at
Onslow Beach, Camp
Lejune, NC in 1955.
[USMC Photo]

five ships sunk. The enemy successfully ran a number of rein-forcement convoys into the "back door" of Leyte at Ormoc Bay, and these reinforcements provided the additional strength to the Japanese to prolong the campaign on the island for a surprising period of time. The air-sea battles that usually raged in the skies above the convoys were often extremely bitter with frequent heavy losses to both sides. The initial convoy attack also served to illustrate the all too common coordination problems that plagued joint Army Air Force/Marine operations during this period. [Some would assert that these problems continue to plague the U.S. armed services even during this period of "jointness."]

By mid-December 1944, the squadron was in operation from the newly captured bases on the island of Leyte in the central Philippines. From there, VMF-211 participated in cover-ing the assaults on Ormoc Bay and the island of Mindoro. On 9 January 1945, it took part in the attacks in the area of Lingayen Gulf on the main Philippines island of Luzon. Targets were plen-tiful in the area as Lingayen was the most suitable point on the long coastline of Luzon for amphibious assault, so the Japanese strove mightily to defend the area. Even during this period of in-tense operations, command changes continued for the squadron when, on 30 January, Major Philip B. May assumed command of the squadron until Major Angus F. Davis relieved him on 21 March. From Luzon, it moved southward where it continued to take part in the reminder of the Philippines campaign and was still in the islands at the end of hostilities against Japan. While many other squadrons looked forward eagerly to their return to the U.S., other duties lay ahead for VMF-211.

During its combat operations in World War II, VMF-211 was credited with the destruction of ninety-one Japanese aircraft in aerial combat and numerous enemy ships of various sizes sunk and damaged during the course of its service in the Philippines in addition to the losses inflicted on the Japanese during the squad-ron's defense of Wake, and it received two awards of the Presiden-tial Unit Citation in recognition of its contributions to the eventual allied victory. The first was in recognition of its actions in the defense of Wake during the period 8 through 22 December 1941. The second award was for its participation in the Philippines cam-paign from 3 December 1944 through 9 March 1945. In addition, it was awarded the Navy Unit Commendation for service in the Southern Philippines from 10 March through 30 June 1945.

Author's Collection

After the formal Japanese surrender on 2 September 1945, VMF-211 was one of the squadrons ordered to move north-ward from their bases in the Philippines to form the aerial com-ponent of the occupation forces in China. It remained there for almost four years in the midst of the civil war that raged between the Nationalist Chinese forces and the Communist Chinese forces. In 1949, with the defeat of the Nationalists im-minent, the remnants of the American occupation forces were withdrawn from China. Among the last to leave was VMF-211, which departed in January. Its method of departure was some-what unusual, however. It was directed to quickly complete carrier qualification, and after its qualification, it was ordered aboard USS *Rendova* (CVE-114). The squadron boarded the escort carrier on 22 January and returned to the United States and to NAS, Edenton, North Carolina, via a WestPac cruise that lasted until 4 May 1949. Few other Marine squadrons served overseas longer than VMF-211, having departed Ha-waii for Wake in April 1942 and remaining away from U.S. soil for slightly more than seven years.

After the outbreak of hostilities in Korea, VMF-211 re-mained on the East Coast. At the time the shooting started, the squadron was in the midst of another round of carrier qualifi-cations. Its qualification completed, operational control of the squadron was passed to the Navy's Air Group 7 on 10 July 1950 when it boarded USS *Midway* (CVB-41), for a Med cruise that lasted until 10 November 1950. Despite the fighting raging in Korea, other commitments claimed their share of deployments as well. Upon their return from the Mediterranean, the squadron took its F4U-4 Corsairs back to NAS, Edenton.

In early 1952, the squadron was ordered to carrier qualifications again in preparation for yet another Med cruise. On 19 April 1952, VMF-211 joined CVG-4 aboard USS *Coral Sea* (CV-43), and departed the United States for the Mediterranean. While deployed, the squadron was redesignated VMA-211, effective 30 June. *Coral Sea* returned from the Med on 12 October, and VMA-211 was returned to the control of its parent Marine Air Group. The "new" attack squadron surrendered its Corsairs in favor of the Douglas AD-4 Skyraider. After the completion of its stand down period at the end of the cruise and its work-up period with its new aircraft, it was underwent carrier qualification again. This time, instead of another deployment to the Med, the squadron would return to the western Pacific aboard USS *Wright* (CVL-49). The deployment lasted from 10 May until 31 October 1954. The squadron's return from its tour aboard *Wright* marked the end of its conventional carrier deployments.

In 1957, VMA-211 ended its association with the big AD and was re-equipped with its first jet aircraft, the Douglas A4D-1 (A-4A) Skyhawk. This was the beginning of a relationship that would endure for more than three decades, during which the squadron would operate no fewer than five of the six single-seat versions of the A-4 series that saw service with the Marine Corps.

The remainder of the 1950's and the first years of the 1960s saw VMA-211 and its A-4s deploy and return to their home station in a normal, peacetime unit deployment rotational schedule. During this period of the squadron's history, the A4D-1 was replaced with the A4D-2. The -2 gave way to the night-capable -2N. The -2N was replaced by the A-4E, which added a more powerful engine and two more underwing hard points, thereby significantly increasing the warload of the aircraft. (The Navy's aircraft designation scheme, which identified type [mission], manufacturer, model from that builder and sub-type, was changed in 1962 at the direction of President Kennedy's Secretary of Defense, Robert Strange McNamara. The Secretary claimed the old Navy system was hard for him to grasp and was confusing to him – a fine statement from a Secretary of Defense! However, when considered in the context of some of his later decisions and actions, it is likely that his statement was, unfortunately, quite close to the mark.)

Shortly after the squadron received the A-4E, the war drums began to sound again in Asia. The Marines landed at Da Nang in South Vietnam in the Spring of 1965, and the United States found itself at war again although the bitter, bloody conflict in Southeast Asia was never legitimized by a declaration of war, it would become the longest, most divisive conflict in the nation's history. [The Afghan War has since become our longest conflict.] Soon the base at Da Nang was so crowded with U.S. aircraft that it became necessary to build an additional facility to handle the number of squadrons committed to Vietnam. The site selected was Chu Lai, some distance north of Da Nang. The Navy's Construction Battalions [CBs] began construction in early May 1965, and the base was declared operational on 1 June. The first Marine attack squadrons arrived that day and flew their first combat missions from the new field later that same afternoon.

The turn of VMA-211 to deploy to Vietnam came in mid-October 1965 and it came under the operational control of MAG-12, the Air Group that controlled all the Skyhawk squadrons based at Chu Lai. It immediately began to add the weight of

The First of Her Class
A CH-53 D Super Sea Stallion and the AV-8B Harriers of a VMA Det. Rest on the flight deck of USS Tarawa (LHA-1) in this photo dated 11 November 2007. [U.S. Navy Photo]

via Holmberg

its bombs, rockets and cannon fire to the support of the Marines engaged on the ground against the enemy. In addition to the in-country war against the Viet Cong, strikes were mounted into the southern areas of North Vietnam. The air war in the North was a completely different war from that in the South. Any aircraft venturing into North Vietnamese air space found itself faced with the most sophisticated air defense system in the history of aerial warfare. Arrayed in depth were layers of light automatic anti-aircraft guns, heavy radar directed batteries, surface-to-air missiles and MiG interceptors. Although enemy aircraft rarely ventured into the southern reaches of their country, the other defenses were a deadly, ever-present menace. Should the attacking aircraft attempt to approach a target at low level to avoid the radar-controlled guns and missile batteries, they were exposed to a

Thirsty Bird
A Harrier of VMA-211 gets a drink from a tanker aircraft as it lugs a pair of laser-guided munitions above the desert terrain of Southwest Asia while en route to its target. The distances from the Arabian Sea to the battle area dictated the requirement to "tank," usually on both the inbound and outbound legs of a sortie. Note the laser designator on the nose of the Harrier housed in the hump on the upper nose of the aircraft just above the refueling hose. [U.S.MC. Photo via the VMA-211 website]

Fill 'Er Up!
This Harrier of the Wake Avengers in flight above the waters of the Persian Gulf was captured as it approached a tanker as indicated by the deployed refueling probe above the port intake. The area in the jet intake is painted white to make it easier to see any objects that may have collected there to prevent foreign object damage upon starting the engine. [U.S.M.C. Photo via the VMA-211 website]

hail of automatic weapons fire. Conversely, an approach from an altitude in excess of 10,000 feet avoided the lighter weapons but placed the attackers within the envelope of the heavy weapons and missiles. In addition to strikes into North Vietnam, VMA-211 took part in its fair share of missions into neighboring Laos and Cambodia as well.

The squadron remained at Chu Lai until February 1966, when it was rotated to MCAS, Iwakuni, Japan for a brief period of R&R. VMA-211 returned to Chu Lai in May 1966, and it would remain there until February 1970. Squadron personnel and aircraft would continue to rotate on an individual basis throughout this period, but it was decided that the close support effort would suffer less disruption from individual rotations as opposed to the wholesale rotation of entire squadrons.

Richard Nixon became President in 1969 and shortly thereafter announced a policy of "Vietnamization" of the war. U.S. forces would withdraw gradually and a greater share of the burden of combat operations would be shifted to the South Vietnamese as a result. Among the first American forces to be affected by this policy were the Marines, and VMA-211 was withdrawn from Chu Lai to MCAS, Iwakuni, Japan on 12 February 1970. While a great deal of hard combat lay ahead before the final withdrawal of American forces from Vietnam more than three years later, the war in Southeast Asia was over for VMA-211. From Iwakuni, the squadron was transferred to MCAS, El Toro. After a period of time at El Toro, the squadron was transferred to MCAS, Yuma, Arizona in the realignment of Marine fighter and attack assets between the two air stations. The squadron was re-equipped with the final version of the Skyhawk to see service with the Marine attack squadrons, the A-4M. (While the -M model designation was a logical progression of models, the -M was flown exclusively by the Marines, and many claimed that designator stood for "Marine.")

In June 1990, the squadron surrendered its last Skyhawk and was re-equipped with the revolutionary night attack version of the McDonnell-Douglas AV-8B Harrier V/STOL attack aircraft. Almost as soon as the squadron's aviators became acquainted with the night attack-capable Harrier, it became the first to receive the radar-equipped version of the aircraft as well. The Harrier was originally conceived as a clear air mass day attack aircraft to provide close air support to ground forces engaged in battle, and at the time of its introduction, this was sufficient capability. However, the passage of time and technological advances conferred virtually around the clock combat capability on the armed forces of the United States, which was demonstrated in all of its awesome power in the deserts of the Middle East. As a result, the capabilities of their supporting arms had to be extended to match, thus the coming of the two advanced versions of the Harrier.

VMA-211 did not see service as a unit in either Operations *Desert Shield* or *Desert Storm* but provided aviators and support personnel to augment the squadrons in combat. In the meantime, the remainder of the squadron participated in the unit deployment rotation while their brother Marines fought the desert war. These rotational deployments were the norm throughout the decade of the 1990s.

On 28 May 1992, Detachment A of the squadron boarded USS *Tarawa* (LHA-1), marking the initial overseas deployment of the AV-8B Night Attack version of the Harrier. The Det. was composed six aircraft, nine aviators and the enlisted support personnel. While deployed, some of the Harriers landed aboard USS *Ogden* (LPD-5).

The squadron deployed to WestPac in 1993 and 1994 operating from bases in Japan Okinawa and the Republic of Korea, and in February 1995, Det. A was attached to HMM-262 (Rein.) returning to Yuma in May 1966.

In the wake of the tragic events of September 11, 2001, VMA-211 found itself at war again when it boarded USS *Bon Homme Richard* (LHD-6) and deployed to the Arabian Sea. Shortly after their arrival on station, the ship and squadron began to take part in the air support portion of Operation *Enduring Freedom*, as the effort to destroy the Taliban in Afghanistan was dubbed. In light of the long, bloody and ultimately failed Soviet campaign in that nation, many predicted that American arms would suffer the same fate. But to the surprise of these predictors of doom, the United States prevailed, and the free nation of Afghanistan emerged from the chaos of battle. VMA-211 remained engaged in *Enduring Freedom* from January to March of 2002. The squadron then returned to its home station at M.C.A.S., Yuma.

After its post-deployment stand down period, the squadron again prepared to participate in the normal deployment schedule, but once again, events in the Middle East intervened in these plans. The continued intransigence of the Iraqi dictator and that nation's continued defiance of a host of U.N. resolutions led to the decision to topple Saddam Hussein from power once and for all. In January 2003, VMA-211 again found itself in the familiar surroundings of the "Bonnie Dick" en route to the Middle East again. This time the destination was the Persian Gulf for participation in Operation *Iraqi Freedom*. In a month of intense combat operations, the squadron flew in excess of 360 sorties and 640 combat hours in support of ground operations against the enemy. In the wake of the Iraqi surrender, the squadron remained in the Gulf for a short period until it returned to Yuma in May by way of a series of long westward flights that included a trans-Atlantic hop.

After six months at home, the squadron returned to full operational status and began the first of three back-to-back MEU detachments beginning in December. In July of the following year, Det. A deployed to M.C.A.S., Iwakuni, Japan.

In July 2005, the entire squadron deployed once again to Al Asad Airbase in Iraq in support of 13th MEU in conducting combat operations in support of Operation *Iraqi Freedom* 04-6.2. It returned to Yuma in February 2006.

After six months among family and friends, the squadron returned to its previous base in Iraq's Al Anbar Province in support of *Iraqi Freedom* 05-7.2 and 06-8.1. While deployed, VMA-211 conducted 206 days of sustained combat operations and flew more than 2,700 combat missions and amassed 5,200 flight hours in support of both I and II MEF's. The Avengers returned home in March 2007.

Today, it continues its deployment schedule to the locales dictated by U.S. policy in addition to support of coalition forces engaged in Iraq.

The first of the squadron's insignia depicted is its current official insignia design, and the second is a flight suit shoulder patch indicating the squadron is equipped with the all-weather night attack version of the AV-8B. The third version of the squadron insignia is a flight suit-sized version of its official design. Note the slightly more orange color of the lion and the outline of Wake Island than the colors in the first and fourth insignia. This slight difference in color is just one more example of slight variations that occur from time to time in authentic, official insignia.

The fourth version of the insignia of VMA-211 is an older example of its official insignia that dates from the immediate post-Vietnam period.

The fifth and sixth insignia are examples of the World War II insignia of the Wake Avengers. The one on the left is an original period insignia. Unfortunately, it has suffered some discoloration due to age and moth damage to the wool background during the more than half-century since it was made, but it is in above average condition for its age. The example on the right is a reproduction of the same design. If one takes a moment to compare the two, it is easy to see that this is one of the better reproductions available to collectors unable to pay the $350.00-plus price that the original would command in today's collector's market. The author also has seen so-called "PX" patch versions of this same insignia. "PX" patches were sold in base exchanges in the U.S. and were usually silk-screened on heavy canvas, and their edges were stitched to prevent unraveling. While these were not "official" insignia in that they did not pass through the hands of serving squadron members, they were quite popular among collectors during the period and were often purchased for family members and/or sweethearts of those serving in the various units.

It should be pointed out that many current versions of the squadron insignia have a red centered white star on a blue disk between "VMA" and "211" in the ribbon at the bottom. This is a replica of the insignia on the wings of the two biplanes of the squadron seen above and serve to connect the current squadron to the early years of its lineage and history. While somewhat hard to discern, this insignia is replicated on the noses of the two Harriers pictured.

The seventh example of the squadron's insignia is a hand-painted reproduction of the insignia of VMF-2. It was painted in this manner deliberately to "antique" it.

The last insignia was made in Japan after VMA-211 was withdrawn from combat operations in Southeast Asia in 1970 and commemorates the squadron's participation in Operation *Steel Tiger*, as the long-running aerial campaign against the Viet Cong sanctuaries in Laos and Cambodia was dubbed.

Author's Collection

MARINE ATTACK SQUADRON 214,
THE BLACK SHEEP
A.K.A., THE SWASHBUCKLER

Author's Collection

VMF-214 was activated on 1 July 1942 at MCAS, Ewa, Territory of Hawaii, under the command of Captain Charles W. Somers, who led the squadron until 21 July, when Captain George F. Britt relieved him. The nucleus of the squadron was composed of some of the survivors of VMF-221 that had suffered so heavily at Midway the previous month. While VMF-221 had inflicted a few losses on the enemy, the Zeros escorting the Japanese strike decimated the Marines in return. The squadron lost 15 of its 25 aircraft and pilots at the hands of the Japanese Zeros. After exactly one day of combat, only two of the surviving aircraft of VMF-221 were fit to fly again. It is no wonder that some of those assigned to VMF-214 were somewhat less than eager to face the Japanese again so soon. [By the war's end, VMF-221 would extract ample revenge from the Japanese for its defeat at Midway. It ended the war as the second highest scoring Marine fighter squadron with 185 confirmed kills.]

The new squadron drew its allotted number of Grumman F4F-4 Wildcats from the aircraft pool at Pearl Harbor and began the business of preparing for combat, and when word was received of the landing of the Marines on Guadalcanal on 7 August, these preparations took on an added sense of urgency. Soon squadron after squadron was hurriedly dispatched to the Solomons and the New Hebrides and the coming of the New Year brought with it orders for VMF-214 to prepare for movement to the South Pacific. The squadron would soon find itself en route to combat, and in early February 1943, the squadron's personnel, equipment, and Wildcats were loaded aboard the aircraft transports USS *Wright* (AV-1) and *Nassau* (AVT-16) at Pearl Harbor. They set sail for the South Pacific bound for Espiritu Santo in the New Hebrides, where they arrived later that month.

At Espiritu, the flight echelon was separated from the ground echelon and was moved forward to the Guadalcanal area, where it arrived on 10 March. By this date, the island was firmly in American hands, and preparations were under way to begin offensive operations against the remainder of Japanese-held positions in the Solomons. The next item on the agenda was the establishment of bases in the Russells Islands that lay 55 miles to the northwest of Guadalcanal. These islands had been occupied in unopposed landings on 21 February, and construction began immediately on a series of new airfields – the new home of VMF-214 and its sister squadrons of MAG-21. The group and its squadrons were all ashore at the field on Banika by 4 April.

The Japanese had not been idle while these American moves were being executed. Admiral Yamamoto burned with a fierce desire to extract revenge for the loss of Guadalcanal and made his plans accordingly. In early March, the admiral's plan was ready. Known as Operation *I*, it called for a series of massive air attacks against the American and allied forces, and nearly two hundred Japanese aircraft were massed at bases in the northern Solomons for this purpose. In parallel the admiral planned a similar aerial onslaught against the Allies in New Guinea. By launching Operation *I*, he hoped to be able to buy enough time for the Japanese to strengthen their defenses and build up forces throughout the area sufficiently to delay or, hopefully, defeat the Allied offensives that were sure to follow their success at Guadalcanal.

The preliminary round of Operation *I* began on 1 April when fifty-eight Zeros came down the Slot to cripple the American fighter defenses and to pave the way for the strike aircraft. The defending Americans traded six of their Wildcats for eighteen Zeros in this preliminary bout, but the main event was yet

Slow Boat to the South Pacific
This photo of USS Wright (AV-1) was snapped during the quiet days prior to World War II as she steamed through quiet southern waters. Note the awning spread above the fantail to provide some degree of escape from the hot sun.
[U.S. Navy Photo]

Author's Collection

to come. The centerpiece of Yamamoto's plan was launched on 7 April when sixty-seven dive-bombers, escorted by no fewer than 110 Zeros were sent against the Americans. As reports were received from the coast watchers and from the search radar operators of the size of the inbound enemy raid, the warning, "Condition very red!" was broadcast. All available Navy, Marine and Army fighters, a total of 76, were scrambled to meet the oncoming Japanese juggernaut. In the battle that followed, the attackers sank three ships; a tanker, a destroyer and a New Zealand corvette. Despite the losses, this amounted to a minor skirmish compared to the aerial action that took place. Outnumbered almost 3 to 1, the American fighters waded into the massed ranks of Japanese aircraft. Soon the skies above the island and Savo Sound were alive with the screams of aircraft maneuvering at full power and falling bombs interspersed with the staccato hammering of machine guns and the deeper booming of aircraft cannons. Within moments of the first passes by the American fighters, the funeral pyres of falling aircraft marked the sky. Here and there, a parachute blossomed white against the blue sky.

When the last of the surviving Japanese turned northward away from Guadalcanal, it was found that the parachutes had been American and most of the funeral pyres had been Japanese. For the loss of seven fighters, the defenders had accounted

for thirty-nine of the enemy, and all of the American pilots shot down survived and were rescued. VMF-214 received credit for the destruction of ten of the enemy in its first and only dogfight of its first combat tour. These victories by VMF-214, along with those of VMF-221, were the final victories scored by Marine fighter pilots in the Wildcat.

By the end of May, all the Marine fighter squadrons then engaged in the Solomons had been re-equipped with the Vought F4U-1 Corsair. VMF-214 completed its first combat tour and was withdrawn from Guadalcanal on 17 May. The squadron converted from Wildcats to Corsairs in June and July during its period of R&R at Efate in the New Hebrides, and Major Henry A. Ellis, Jr. assumed command of VMF-214 on 9 June. The squadron even managed to add a few Japanese scalps to its scoreboard while in the rear area. It seems that for three days, the seaplane tender USS *Chincoteague* (AVP-24) had suffered intermittent attacks by enemy aircraft. These repeated assaults had left her dead in the water near Vanikoro Island, and during the morning hours of 18 July, three torpedo-armed Type 97 land attack bombers [Nells] closed in for the kill. *Chincoteague* hurriedly broadcast an appeal for help from any friendly forces in the area. Four F4Us of VMF-214 on a routine training flight and patrol from Espiritu overheard the broadcast and answered the call for help. Led by the commanding officer, Major William H. Pace, who had relieved Major Ellis on 12 July, the "Swashbucklers" quickly dispatched the Nells and saved the gallant little tender.

The squadron returned to combat from bases in the Russells Islands with its new aircraft on 21 July. Its second stay in the Russells was short, and following the capture of Munda, on the island of New Georgia, the squadron was moved there. The primary objective during this phase of the Solomons Campaign was the capture or neutralization of the island of Bougainville, the northernmost and largest island of the Solomons chain. In order to accomplish this, the large force of Japanese aircraft on the island would have to be destroyed or neutralized. The major enemy base on Bougainville was located at Kahili, and it was during one of the strikes aimed at the reduction of Kahili that the former enlisted Naval Aviation Pilot [N.A.P.] Lieutenant Alvin J. Jensen accomplished one of the most amazing single-handed feats of the Second World War. During a fighter sweep of Kahili, Jensen became separated from the other members of his flight

Our New Toy
This example of the near-obligatory "class photo" captures the Swash-
bucklers of VMF-214 posed before one of their new Corsairs as the
squadron nears the end of the conversion to the new aircraft at Efate in
mid-1943. [USMC photo]

Good as New
The USS Chincoteague (AVP-24) was underway in San Francisco Bay
on 27 December 1943 after her repairs at Mare Island of the battle
damage she suffered before she was saved by the timely interventions of
the Corsairs of VMF-214. [U.S. Navy Photo]

in one of the frequent, violent tropical thunderstorms prevalent in the area at the time. The Marine struggled with the controls of his aircraft, and as fate would have it, when Jensen's Corsair emerged from the storm, it was inverted and directly over the Japanese airfield. Quickly righting his big fighter, Jensen commenced a lone strafing attack against the enemy aircraft on the field. Diving to within a few feet of the ground, the Lieutenant opened fire on the long line of enemy aircraft before him. His attack was completed in a single pass, and he set a course out of the area and for home leaving considerable damage and numerous surprised and angry Japanese in his wake. Reconnaissance photos taken the next day revealed the burnt wrecks of 24 enemy aircraft: 8 Zeros; 4 Val dive-bombers and 12 twin-engine Betty bombers. For this feat of superlative marksmanship and courage, Jensen was awarded the Navy Cross.

The squadron's second combat tour ended early in September, and VMF-214, now led by Major John R. Burnett, departed the Solomons for a well-deserved period of R&R in Australia. It was at this point that, thanks to some behind-the-scenes maneuvering on the part of Major Gregory R. (Pappy) Boyington, the legend of the "Black Sheep" of VMF-214 was born.

While the "Swashbucklers" of VMF-214 were nearing the end of their second combat tour, Boyington was prowling the rear areas attempting to form his own squadron. The legendary Boyington truly was one of the "characters" that have populated the rich history of the Marine Corps from time to time. A pre-war Regular officer and aviator, he was one of those allowed to resign his commission to join Chennault's American Volunteer Group, the Flying Tigers, to fight for China against the Japanese. Boyington claimed six victories while in China although several sources dispute that number. Ever one to chafe under the restrictions of the military's rules and regulations, he had acquired the nickname "Rats" during his earlier service. Growing tired of some of what he considered to be some of Chennault's more "chicken" restrictions, Boyington resigned from the A.V.G. and departed China forever. Never one of the group's favorites, Chennault gave Boyington a "dishonorable discharge" from the Flying Tigers. This discharge, of course, carried no official weight, and Boyington returned to the U.S., where he requested, and was eventually granted, reinstatement in the Marine Corps. Captain Boyington had not yet acquired the nickname "Pappy" but was soon living up to his earlier moniker of "Rats."

Shortly thereafter, Boyington found himself on his way to the South Pacific, where he served with several Marine squadrons in the earlier stages of the Solomons Campaign. Advanced to the rank of Major, Boyington had the seniority and service record that warranted command of a squadron. His problem was that, unless a squadron commander was killed or wounded in action, felled by a tropical disease or relieved of command for some reason, thereby opening a slot, there were none available at the time. New squadrons that arrived in the combat area were for the most part fully staffed, and without cause, it was correctly felt that it would disrupt the unit cohesiveness so vital to combat effectiveness if a squadron commander were to be relieved simply to give the squadron to Boyington.

Finally, he hit upon the idea to form a squadron from pilots in the various replacement pools in the area that existed to supply replacements for those aviators lost or disabled in action or ordered to other duty. Permission was granted, and Boyington formed his squadron. Only one small problem remained. What was his squadron to be designated? Obviously the Marine Corps did not keep "spare" designations in a file drawer for use in a situation such as this. Never one to let such a minor point stand in the way for long, Boyington simply adopted [some would later say "usurped"] the designation VMF-214 while the members of the "old" VMF-214 were "down under" on R&R. According to popular folklore, the "Black Sheep" were a collection of brigands and misfits gathered from all over the South Pacific to join a squadron that was led by the biggest misfit of them all. Without question, Boyington was certainly a "character," who at times, displayed a lack of respect for regulations considered by him to stand in the way of the accomplishment of the task at hand. Despite that, however, the "Black Sheep" were no more misfits than was any of the majority of the Marine and Navy aviators in the South Pacific at the time. The squadron's lineage may have been somewhat questionable, and perhaps this had something to do with the popular legend. But, when it came down to the primary task of destruction of the enemy, the "Black Sheep" of the "new" VMF-214 took a back seat to no one. [Apparently, history failed to record the reactions of the members of the "first" VMF-214 to Boyington's theft of their squadron designation, and that is probably just as well.]

Boyington and "his" VMF-214 entered combat from the base at Munda in September 1943. The squadron continued to operate from there through the month of October, when it was withdrawn to Espiritu Santo for a short rest. By 28 November, the squadron had returned to combat from the new base at Vella Lavella. By this point in time, the Allies were able to direct most of their efforts toward the reduction of the foundation upon

Author's Collection

which Japanese power in the South Pacific was built, the huge complex of airfields, supply dumps and the harbor facilities at Rabaul on New Britain, and it was to this end that most of the efforts of VMF-214 were applied. The Japanese defended the airspace around Rabaul with all the tenacity of their infantry defending a jungle island, and the enemy interceptors occasionally gave the strike forces a very difficult time. Closely tethered to the aircraft they were escorting, the Allied fighters often were unable to prevent enemy fighters from getting through to the strike aircraft. Some, including Boyington, began to press for a series of pure fighter sweeps against the enemy. It was hoped the enemy would not realize that the force bearing down on them was made up of nothing but fighters hoping for nothing more than to engage the defenders in fighter versus fighter combat while they were unencumbered with escort duty. The upper echelons of command saw the wisdom of this proposal and gave it their blessings. The first pure fighter sweep against Rabaul took place on 17 December 1943. Led by Boyington, it was composed of 76 Marine, Navy and Royal New Zealand Air Force fighters. Despite radioed pleas from Boyington to the Japanese to come up and fight, few of the enemy proved foolish enough to attempt to get airborne in the face of a certain ambush.

Later, Boyington argued that seventy-six fighters were too many to fight or to be controlled effectively. He wanted the number reduced to a more manageable 36 to 48. Yielding to Boyington's request, the next sweep was mounted on 23 December and numbered a total of forty-eight fighters. It was preceded into the target area by a heavy bomber strike and their escorting fighters. The "heavies" always drew a stiff reception from the enemy interceptors, and more than forty Japanese fighters were still airborne when the fighter sweep arrived over the target. Caught unaware and ambushed by the Americans, 30 Japanese fighters were claimed with an even dozen falling to VMF-214. Of these twelve, Boyington claimed four, which brought his personal score to 24, including his six claimed over China. Over the next few days, Boyington killed another enemy fighter to bring his total to twenty-five, one short of the American record shared by Captains Joe Foss and Eddie Rickenbacker.

There was a great deal of interest in the prospect of someone bettering Rickenbacker's World War I record, both in the

Left, Author's Collection; Right, via Holmberg

military and without. Hardly a day passed without someone, often a member of the press, asking Boyington when he was going to break the record. As a result, he felt a great deal of pressure, some of which was self-imposed. In turn, this may have led to the taking of unnecessary chances that otherwise would have been avoided. On 3 January, Boyington led a section of four Corsairs over St. George Channel near Rabaul. Engaged by a large number of enemy fighters, his wingman, Captain George M. Ashmun, was hit. Attempting to assist his wounded companion, Boyington shot down three Zeros, but not before the captain was shot down and killed. The other two members of the "Black Sheep" witnessed the destruction of the first of Boyington's victims, but, heavily engaged and fighting for their lives, they were unable to come to their leader's assistance. They were fighting their own battle for survival against a superior number of enemy fighters that were between them and Boyington. They had no choice but to retire or be shot down. Upon their return, the two reported that both Ashmun and Boyington had been shot down and killed. Ashmun was awarded a posthumous Distinguished Flying Cross, and Boyington the Navy Cross for their actions on that day. Boyington's award also was posthumous, at the time.

The Major, however, had succeeded in bailing out of his flaming Corsair at low altitude. After entering the water, the remaining Japanese fighters strafed him for more than 15 minutes without hitting him. Finally tired of the game or out of ammunition, the enemy fighters left the area. Boyington was safe for the moment, but just after dark, a Japanese submarine surfaced and took him aboard as a prisoner. The Japanese did not, however, report his capture to the International Red Cross as required by the Geneva Convention, and it was believed that he had, indeed, perished on 3 January 1944. He was awarded a posthumous Medal of Honor, only to have the award presented to him in person when he was "resurrected" and repatriated after the Japanese surrender. His record of twenty-eight enemy aircraft is still at the top of the Marines' list of aces. [As was the case with some of the kills he claimed in China, some questions pertain to Boyington's final pair of kills. According to regulations, a claim must be corroborated by eyewitnesses, gun camera footage or wreckage. For obvious reasons these were lacking in this case, but the kills were awarded anyway. The decision to award the

Medal of Honor already had been made, and no one wanted any controversy regarding a recipient of the award.]

Ironically, Boyington came closer to death at American hands than at those of the Japanese. After six weeks at Rabaul under the almost daily Allied air strikes, he was evacuated to the huge Japanese base at Truk in the Eastern Carolines. The transport plane carrying him stumbled into the midst of the massive carrier strike launched against Truk on 17 February 1944. The aircraft in which he was an unwilling passenger reached an airfield unscathed, and almost before it stopped its landing roll, Boyington, the other prisoners, and the Japanese crew dived into a nearby slit trench seconds before the transport was strafed and destroyed by one of the attacking Hellcats. During a break in the attack a Japanese pilot, who landed to refuel, ran past the trench in which Boyington and his companions were hiding, and when he saw the prisoners, he ran up and began to boast in English of his prowess as a fighter pilot. Boyington replied, "Well, ain't you just the cheerful son-of-a-bitch!" Soon the Hellcats returned to the attack, and Boyington's last sight of the enemy pilot was of him running for cover from the American guns.

Upon Boyington's presumed death, Major Lawrence H. Howe assumed command of the squadron, and near the end of January 1944, VMF-214 was relieved from combat duty and ordered to return to the United States. It arrived at MCAS, Santa Barbara, California on 28 January where it was deactivated the following day. It was reactivated on 8 February 1944 with entirely new personnel under the command of one of the first of its newly reported officers, First Lieutenant Ransom R. Tilton. The squadron was soon back to full strength, and shortly thereafter began carrier qualifications under the leadership of Major Warren H. McPherson, who had assumed command from Lieutenant Tilton on 2 March.

After completion of its training and its carrier qualifications, VMF-214 was again ordered into combat in early 1945. It boarded USS *Franklin* (CV-13) on 4 February as a component of CVG-5. In addition to her normal complement of Navy squadrons in the air group, there was a second Marine fighter squadron assigned, the "Sky Raiders" of VMF-452. If VBF-5 is included in the total, *Franklin* went into battle with no fewer than four full fighter squadrons embarked, which represented approximately 75% of the air group's strength. [A pre-war carrier air group had consisted of one fighter squadron, one scouting squadron, one dive-bomber squadron and one torpedo squadron with a nominal strength of 18 aircraft per squadron. This change in the composition of the carrier air groups by this stage of the war was due to two factors. The first was the demonstrated superiority of a fighter aircraft, such as the Corsair, over the pure dive-bomber. The second was the growing recognition of the threat posed to the carriers by the Kamikaze.] The squadron entered combat again on 18 March when the Fast Carrier Force launched the first of a series of strikes against the Tokyo area. The weather was miserable, and the hunting was poor as few enemy aircraft ventured into the sky to oppose the American strikes.

The routine began again the following morning. *Franklin* had begun to launch the first of the day's strikes when a single Japanese aircraft, which had escaped detection in the low clouds and fog in the area at the time, attacked. Struck by two 550-pound bombs, the carrier became a raging inferno within minutes of the first bomb hit. Fed by the fully fueled and armed aircraft, the fires quickly turned "Big Ben" into a funeral pyre for more than 900 of her crew and air group. The aircrews suffered particularly tragic losses. The smoke from the conflagrations trapped many of the flight crews in their ready rooms, and they suffocated while attempting to escape the flames. The struggle to contain the fires lasted throughout the remainder of the day, but they were finally brought under control and, at last, extinguished. *Franklin* survived, but she was out of the war. She and the survivors of her crew and air group returned to the United States, but she was deemed too badly damaged to be worthy of repair at that stage of the war. No fewer than 393 decorations for valor were awarded to her crew and air group for the efforts in their battle to save their ship.

When *Franklin* reached the West Coast on her return journey to the U.S., the surviving members of VMF-214 were detached from Air Group 5 and ordered to MCAS, El Centro. Major Stanley R. Bailey assumed command on 11 April and was succeeded by Major James W. Merritt on 10 July, but he was soon transferred to other duty, and Lieutenant Robert J. McDonnell assumed command on 1 July. McDonnell was in command for a month until the arrival of Major George C. Hollowell on 1 August. During this period, the squadron remained at El Centro and was still there when the atom bombs brought the war in the Pacific to a close. Thereafter, the squadron was transferred to MCAS, El Toro and assigned to MAG-46.

During its service in World War II, VMF-214 was credited with the destruction of 127 Japanese aircraft in aerial combat, and it was the only squadron to receive an unprecedented four awards of the Presidential Unit Citation. The first was for its actions on 7 April 1943 in the repulse of the massive Japanese attack on Guadalcanal; Operation I. The second was for the period 17 July through 30 August 1943 for its actions during the Munda Campaign. The third was for the period 16 September through 19 October 1943 for its participation in the Northern Solomons Campaign and the fourth was for the period 17 December 1943 through 6 January 1944 for its service during the Vella Lavella-Torikina Campaign and the reduction of Rabaul. No other unit has been so honored during the history of the Citation.

The squadron was deactivated shortly after the end of World War II, but it was not to be in limbo long. VMF-214 was reactivated in 1948. It spent a majority of the next two years oper-

Big Ben
Resplendent in her "dazzle" camouflage scheme, USS Franklin (CV-13) was photographed in May 1944 at the Norfolk Navy Yard. Contrary to what most believed, she was not named for Benjamin Franklin, but for the Civil War Battle of Franklin, Tennessee. [U.S. Navy Photo]

ating from various carriers off the West Coast training Marine pilots in carrier operations. At the outbreak of the Korean War on 25 June 1950, VMF-214 had gained more experience in carrier operations than virtually any other Marine squadron. When the decision was made to intervene in the conflict, the squadron was one of the first ordered to depart for Kobe, Japan, where it arrived on 31 July. Under the command of Lieutenant Colonel W.E. Lischeid, VMF-214 flew aboard USS *Sicily* (CVE-118) on 3 August while the carrier was off the coast of Korea.

By the time of the squadron's arrival aboard *Sicily*, the United Nations forces were pinned in the Pusan Pocket around the South Korean port city of the same name. They were desperately trying to hold on to the territory within the Pocket as the North Koreans attempted to break the defenses in order to drive the defenders into the sea and complete their victory. The order of the day for the squadrons embarked aboard the carriers was close air support and lots of it. VMF-214 arrived aboard the carrier in the morning of 3 August and flew their first combat mission of the Korean War that same afternoon. When the first of the squadron's Corsairs lifted off the flight deck of *Sicily* that afternoon, it had begun the first of the Marines' contributions to a total of more than 275,000 combat sorties that Naval aviation would fly during the three years of the Korean War.

Gradually, American air power and the superior weight of fire from the defenders on the ground began to weaken the force of the enemy's blows that fell on the Pusan Pocket. The North Koreans suffered horrendous casualties in their repeated attempts to break the defenses. The true extent of these losses will never be known, but an idea of how bad they were can be discerned from a report that, in the wake of a failed attempt to force a crossing of the Naktong River on the Pocket's western side, the waters of the river were discolored by the amount of enemy blood in it.

The interdiction strikes flown by the Navy, Marines, and Air Force destroyed much of the enemy's supplies before they could reach the front, and the close air support missions that were the Marines' specialty took an increasing toll on the troops

Launch the CAP
An F4U-1D of VMF-214 photographed from the island structure of USS Franklin (CV-13) as it prepares to get airborne from the carrier's deck. The presence of the fuel tank beneath the right wing and an absence of external ordnance indicates the beginning of a long and at times boring combat air patrol [CAP] flight. The white diamond on the vertical stabilizer of the Corsair is the geometric identification symbol assigned to CV-13. [USMC photo]

A Legendary Pair!
This photograph was taken shortly after Lieutenant Colonel Gregory Boyington's return to the United States after his release from a Japanese prisoner of war camp. On the left is Rex Beisel, the chief designer of the magnificent Corsair series. Although this photo was undated, it likely must have been taken on 5 October 1945, the day after his receipt of the Navy Cross, the ribbon of which is below his aviator's wings. This is the date of his receipt of the Medal of Honor from President Harry S. Truman. [USMC photo]

and supplies already there. The North Koreans could not move in substantial numbers during daylight hours without drawing the wrath of the sea blue aircraft that constantly circled overhead. While it would not be correct to state that American air power was solely responsible for the defeat of the North Koreans at Pusan, it is extremely doubtful that the perimeter could have been held without it.

The immediate threat to the Pusan Perimeter had been averted, and MacArthur was about to launch his counter-attack. Rather than a long, hard ground offensive up the length of the Korean peninsula, MacArthur decided on a strategy that had become his favorite during the protracted New Guinea campaign in the southwest Pacific in World War II, an amphibious "left hook" against the port of Inchon, near the South Korean capital of Seoul on the peninsula's West Coast. Due to one of the largest tidal variations found anywhere in the world and the long trip up a shallow, winding channel past the heavily defended island of Wolmi-do to reach the port of Inchon itself, the North Koreans did not believe an amphibious assault against the area was possible. And, for that matter, most of the highly experienced American naval officers who would be required to execute the assault advised against the selection of Inchon. One officer believed that if one were to compile a list of geographical and topographical features which mitigated against a successful amphibious assault, Inchon possessed virtually all of them. However, with a supreme confidence in the abilities of those under his command [and, some would say, a colossal ego], MacArthur stuck by his decision. In the long run, the General's decision proved to be correct, and the amphibious assault at Inchon is considered by many to be a strategic masterpiece and the crowning achievement of MacArthur's long and brilliant career.

Early in the morning of 15 September 1950, the first wave of assault troops of the First Marine Division went ashore on the tiny Island that guarded the entrance to the port. The first wave touched the beach at 0633, and as it did so, thirty-eight Corsairs of VMF-214 and -323 swept overhead to strike enemy positions as little as fifty yards in advance of the assault troops.

Wolmi-do fell shortly after 0800, but the actual assault on Inchon would have to wait until late afternoon and the return of the tides that would mean water deep enough for the assault ships to approach their assigned beaches. Meanwhile, even the most obtuse among the North Koreans could hardly have failed to grasp that the landing on Wolmi-do was a harbinger of a full-scale amphibious assault at Inchon. Whatever small numbers of potential enemy reinforcements in the area began to converge on the port, and the task of delaying their arrival or destroying them fell to the "Black Sheep" and the other squadrons embarked aboard the carriers of Task Force 77. Many of the reinforcements dispatched to the area suffered heavily under the weight of the air attacks to which they were subjected.

Shortly after the landing, Marine aircraft began to move ashore, closer to the scene of the action, as the U.N. forces expanded their lodgment on the coast. Along with this movement ashore, changes were made to the command structure of the Marine squadrons, and as a result, VMF-214 was transferred from MAG-33 to MAG-12. However, these changes to the command organization had little effect on the day-to-day operations of the squadrons involved as they continued to hammer the enemy. When word of the successful assault on Inchon was relayed to the U.N. troops within the Pusan Pocket, they responded with a full-scale offensive aimed at the complete and utter destruction of the North Korean People's Army. At first, the enemy resisted with a fury and determination reminiscent of the Japanese during the bitter campaigns in the South and Central Pacific only a few years earlier.

Gradually, however, the enemy began to break under the hammer blows that fell upon them and began to retreat northward. The retreat quickly became a rout as the largely disorganized enemy streamed away from the front. The fall of Seoul to the American advance from Inchon largely sealed the fate of the North Koreans.

Most of the country's road network converged on the capital, and its capture by the Marines formed an anvil upon which the enemy would be hammered to pieces by the advance of the Eighth Army from the south. Although the enemy was in full retreat, he was able to extract a price in blood from his attackers, and Lieutenant Colonel Lischeid was killed in action on a close air support mission on 25 August. He was succeeded in command of the squadron by Major R.P. Keller on 25 September. Keller would be awarded the Silver Star and the Distinguished Flying Cross during his tour in command of VMF-214.

By mid-October, the fighting had moved from South Korean territory into that of North Korea. Shortly after the success at Inchon and the fall of Seoul to the Marines, MacArthur ordered the First Marine Division withdrawn from combat in order to prepare for another amphibious assault against the North Korean port of Wonsan on the peninsula's East Coast. The speed of advance of the U.N. forces was such that when the Marines finally went ashore after having been delayed by extensive mine fields laid in the offshore waters, their objective had already fallen to South Korean troops advancing on the port from its landward side.

After their delayed arrival in Wonsan, the First Marine Division began to advance deep into North Korea, moving northwest from the port, and along with the Marines on the ground came their organic air support. The airfield at Wonsan was put back into operation as quickly as possible to support the advance of

the ground units of the division. The first elements of VMF-214 arrived on 13 October, and within days, the squadron's Corsairs were again in action. The "Black Sheep's" stay ashore was a brief one as they again returned to *Sicily* as the Marine squadrons rotated between shore bases and the carriers of the Seventh Fleet. *Sicily* and VMF-214 were so closely associated with one another that the carrier came to be called the "Sheep's Jeep."

As the U.N. forces advanced deeper into North Korea, ominous rumblings were heard from the Communist Chinese. It had been only slightly more than a year since they had driven the Nationalists off the mainland, and they were intent on consolidating their hold on the vast population of China. The Communists also

The Sheep's Jeep
This beautiful color shot of USS Sicily (CVE-118) was taken from a fleet oiler as the carrier made her approach to the oiler to refuel. Note the fuel hose rigged from the boom of the after end of Sicily's island. The aircraft on deck are Grumman AF Guardian anti-submarine aircraft, which dates the photo as having been taken in 1952 when she deployed to Korea in the anti-submarine role. [U.S. Navy Photo]

A Sheep's Banjo
One of the F2H-4 Banshee all-weather fighters of VMF-214 is pictured on the ramp at the squadron's home field, MCAS Kaneohe, on the island of Oahu. The F2H series of aircraft was nicknamed the "Banjo," and the additional size of the F2H-4 led to it being called the "Big Banjo." [USMC photo]

A Flying Blue Gas Station
An FJ-4B Fury snuggles up to the port refueling drogue of a KB-50
aerial tanker of the U.S. Air Force in this photo from the late-1950s.
[USAF Photo]

Author's Collection

were worried that the U.N. advance would not stop at the Yalu River but would continue northward to attempt to overthrow the fledgling communist regime. Even should the U.N. advance halt at the Yalu as stated, this would deprive the Chinese of a "buffer state" between them and the Free World, a complication they were not prepared to accept. As a result, the Communists let it be known through several neutral nations, primarily India, that they would intervene militarily on behalf of the North Koreans if the advance continued. The U.N. command, especially in the person of General MacArthur, dismissed these warnings as being of no concern whether true or not. The general is said to have stated that a Chinese attempt to save North Korea would "lead to the greatest slaughter" of the Chinese. Unimpressed with MacArthur's dire warning of their fate, the Communists began to send large numbers of troops, euphemistically referred to as "volunteers," south.

Shortly after the advance to the northwest began to enter areas considered to be too close for comfort, the first of these Chinese Communist "volunteers" were encountered. They struck the spearheads of the U.N. forces a series of hard blows and then seemed to disappear. At first, no one knew what to make of these initial contacts with the Chinese. Were they, in fact, the volunteers their nation claimed them to be, or were they the advance elements of a massive Communist Chinese intervention in the fighting? The Chinese had escaped detection despite scores of aerial reconnaissance sorties flown over the north, and the interrogation of several prisoners taken during these initial attacks and examination of the many enemy dead left behind when the attackers withdrew did nothing to increase any sense of urgency that may have been felt in MacArthur's headquarters. They viewed the evidence of the presence of Chinese forces as merely a handful of volunteers that would have no military impact. Perhaps these views were aided by the rose colored glasses worn by virtually all of the general's staff and the General himself.

Such questions had little immediate effect on the daily operations of those engaged in the fighting as the advance continued

Author's Collection

Fire Bomber
An A4-E SkyHawk of VMA-214 sits on the ramp at Chu Lai, RVN load-
ed with a centerline fuel tank and a pair of napalm bombs on the wing
stations. [USMC photo]

deeper into North Korea. VMF-214 again moved ashore on 13 November to the airfield at Yonpo, near the North Korean port of Hungnam, which had become the logistical base for the advance of the First Marine Division. True to their warnings, in late November, the Chinese struck the advancing U.N. forces on both sides of the Korean Peninsula with tremendous force. In the west, the Eighth Army reeled backwards under the force of the massive enemy attacks directed against it. Many units simply disappeared beneath the onrushing Chinese tide, and some began a fighting withdrawal southward under tremendous enemy pressure.

In the East, the First Marine Division weathered the initial blows and held its ground in the face of continuous heavy enemy attacks. Part of the success of the Marines to this point was due to the tactical acumen of the commanding general of the division, Major General O.P. Smith. While the commander of the Tenth Corps had urged Smith to advance with all possible speed, the cagey Marine had continued to advance in a careful manner after the initial contact with the Chinese. Instead of a headlong advance into the unknown, Smith advanced methodically, with each move planned and coordinated carefully. Units were kept intact, instead of becoming spread out and separated into smaller and smaller fragments by the rugged terrain. Smith's stubborn insistence on the maintenance of tactical integrity had much to do with the survival of his command in the days to come.

After blunting the initial enemy blows and inflicting heavy casualties on the attackers, it was obvious that the Marines' position amid the high plateaus near the Chosin Reservoir was untenable, and the division began its epic march to the sea. Despite periods of poor weather, every effort was made to provide the Marines with the air support that would prove pivotal in their eventual survival. Overhead were, among others, the "blue airplanes" of VMF-214. [During later interrogation, Chinese prisoners stated that were more frightened of the "blue airplanes" than any of the other weapons they faced.] The successful fight-

ing withdrawal of the First Marine Division has been covered elsewhere in this account, and it is sufficient to state that the Corsairs of VMF-214 played their part. The squadron remained in action in Korea throughout the hostilities.

After the armistice was signed, the squadron returned to the West Coast. VMF-214 was one of the few Corsair-equipped Marine fighter squadrons that was not redesignated an attack squadron during or shortly after the Korean War. Instead, the squadron surrendered its Corsairs in favor of the McDonnell F2H-4 Banshee. Known as the "Big Banjo," the F2H-4 was among the first of the Navy's jet-powered all-weather fighter/interceptor aircraft. The squadron was redesignated an all-weather squadron, VMF(AW)-214, on 31 December 1956. However, the "Black Sheep" were not destined to serve as an all-weather fighter squadron for but a short period, and on 9 July 1957, the squadron was redesignated VMA-214 and was re-equipped with the North American FJ-4B Fury fighter-bomber. After three years of operations in the North American product, the squadron transitioned to the Douglas A4D-2 Skyhawk. The last Fury left the squadron on 23 January 1962 – the last of their type active in a Marine squadron.

Shortly after their transition to the A-4, a portion of the squadron was ordered to carrier qualification. This sub-unit of the squadron was designated Detachment N (Det. N). After the completion of its carrier qualification, the detachment was assigned to Carrier Anti-Submarine Group 57 (CVSG-57) and deployed to the Western Pacific aboard USS *Hornet* (CVS-12). The growth of the Soviet submarine threat had led the Navy to establish dedicated anti-submarine carrier air groups composed of fixed-wing anti-submarine squadrons equipped with the Grumman S2F Trackers and helicopter anti-submarine squadrons equipped primarily with the Sikorsky HS-3 submarine-hunting helicopters. No other aircraft types were normally assigned to the CVSGs. In addition, the anti-submarine support carri-

A Pretty Bird
An A4-M of VMA-214 reposes on the ramp at MCAS, Yuma, Arizona. [USMC photo]

ers themselves were the earlier *Essex*-class carriers – vintage 1942/43. These vessels were little modified from their earlier form of a decade or so before. For example, a majority of them were still equipped with the Korean War-era hydraulic catapults that were incapable of launching any of the current generation of Navy fighter aircraft. To make the situation even worse, their anti-aircraft batteries had been reduced and were, in any case, composed of the same weapons the ships had carried in World War II. Clearly, in the face of virtually any type of hostile air threat, these ships would be almost literally helpless.

Enter the A-4 detachments from several of the Marine light attack squadrons. One of the guiding design principles behind the Skyhawk from the beginning had been to keep the design as light and simple as possible while maintaining the structural strength and ordnance delivery capability required. As has already been noted, the A-4 was a useful air-to-air combat aircraft when not burdened with a heavy load of external ordnance. It also carried a pair of 20mm cannon in the wing roots. To further enhance its capabilities as an air defense aircraft, its underwing pylons were wired to allow it to carry a pair of heat-seeking AIM-9 Sidewinder missiles. [Should anyone doubt the air-to-air combat capabilities of the A-4 series, they should give careful consideration to the fact the Skyhawk was utilized as the primary MiG-17 simulator in the adversary squadrons that proved indispensable in the Navy's Top Gun program and its Marine equivalents. When flown by a competent aviator well versed in air-to-air combat, these tough little aircraft were often capable of giving such advanced aircraft as the superb F-14 Tomcat all they could handle and more.] These Marine detachments were a stop-gap, and eventually, the Navy formed two specialized squadrons with the rather incongruous designation of Anti-Submarine Fighter Squadrons to supply these detachments, but in the interim, Marine squadrons fulfilled this need. One of the first to send a detachment to sea was VMA-214. Its Det. N deployed aboard

Hornet on 10 October 1963 and returned to the West Coast on 15 April 1964.

It was planned that the Marines would continue to supply the detachments in the near term, but, before 1964 ended, the United States found itself ever more deeply committed to the war in Southeast Asia. 1965 would find much of the combat air strength of the Fleet Marine Forces, Pacific, deployed to Vietnam. Also, when the anti-submarine carriers deployed to WestPac, they were in company with one or more attack carriers that were more than capable of supplying the needed fighter cover for the entire task force, including the CVSs, or the Navy VSFs furnished the fighter detachments needed by the anti-submarine carriers.

VMA-214 deployed to Chu Lai, Republic of Vietnam in June 1965, and it remained in combat there until February of the following year, when it was rotated to MCAS, Iwakuni, Japan, for a period of R&R and replacement of aircraft and personnel. During the squadron's nearly eight months in country on this first tour, VMA-214 flew 3,971 combat sorties totaling more than 5,200 combat hours. The squadron's respite from combat at Iwakuni was of short duration, lasting barely three months, before it returned to Chu Lai for another combat tour. It arrived back in Vietnam in May 1966 and remained in combat for the next 12 months. Upon completion of its second tour, VMA-214 left Vietnam behind for good. During their two tours there, they flew more than 13,200 sorties and expended more than 10,000 tons of ordnance in support of Free World Forces.

The years following the end of the war in Southeast Asia saw the "Black Sheep" taking part in the Unit Deployment Schedule in a normal unit rotation with deployments to Okinawa, Japan, and Korea, and in 1982, the squadron received the prestigious Lawson H.M. Sanderson Award in recognition of its selection as Marine Attack Squadron of the Year for fiscal year 1981 by the Marine Corps Aviation Association.

Another Great Marine Day!
Harriers of VMA-214 are pictured on the flight deck of Essex during an at sea period during its 1994 deployment. [USMC photo via the VMA-214 Website]

In 1989, VMA-214 surpassed 30,000 hours and more than six years of accident free flight operations, and in June of the same year, it became the first operational squadron to receive examples of the advanced AV-8B Night Attack version of the Harrier II in place of its long serving A-4M Skyhawks. The added night/all-weather capabilities of this version make the AV-8B even more remarkable and represent a significant increase in the usefulness of the Harrier to the Marine Corps. The squadron did not participate in either Operations *Desert Shield* or *Desert Storm* during the early months of 1991, but it became the first squadron to deploy with the night-capable Harrier when it took 20 of its aircraft to M.C.A.S., Iwakuni, Japan in October where it conducted operations for the next seven months.

In July 1993, the squadron took its aircraft to 29 Palms, California, where it spent three weeks "chasing the moon" during which its operations were designed to gather medical data on the effects of the operation of high speed jet aircraft while the pilot was equipped with night vision goggles. These had been in use for many years, but their users had been primarily ground troops and helicopter crews who had reported some difficulties with them due to the reduced field of vision, especially peripheral vision, of the goggles. If a helicopter pilot flying at 100 knots had a problem with the goggles, one can easily imagine the situation in the cockpit of a jet at three to five times that speed. However, these exercises were completed without mishap, and a great deal of data was gathered.

Initiating an intense period of operations, the squadron took its Harriers to sea for the first time when it deployed aboard USS *Peleliu* (LHA-5) in December of the same year, for operations both off the coast of Somalia in Operation *United Shield* and Operation *Southern Watch* over the southern regions of Iraq. Also, during this deployment, the squadron's Det. B took part in the evacuation of noncombatants during Operation *Distant Runner* in Burundi and Rwanda.

Upon its return from this deployment, VMA-214 hurried to become reacquainted with friends and family before preparations

began to go to sea again. In October 1994, the squadron deployed aboard USS *Essex* (LHD-2) in support of the 13th Marine Expeditionary Unit in Operations *Southern Watch* off Iraq and *United Shield* off the coast of Somalia. The next deployment came in April 1996, when again paired with 13th, VMA-214 boarded USS *Tarawa* (LHA-1) and departed the West Coast for the now-familiar waters of the Persian Gulf for another round of operations in support of Operation *Southern Watch*. These were interrupted briefly for the squadron's participation in combat during Operation *Desert Strike* in Northern Iraq.

The squadron spent the holiday period at home and operated within the U.S. during 1997 while a detachment went aboard *Peleliu* to conduct fleet testing of the Automatic Targeting Hands-Off System. The ATHS provided a significant advancement in the accuracy of ordnance delivery in close air support of ground operations. In October, VMA-214 received its third Lawson H.M. Sanderson Award as the Marine Attack Squadron of the Year in a formal ceremony at its home station.

Early in the New Year, the Black Sheep deployed again, and their floating home for the next few months was USS *Boxer* (LHD-4). In place of the usual round of port calls in Pearl Harbor and other stepping-stones across the vast Pacific, the ship deployed directly to the north Arabian Gulf. Primary among the reasons for the direct crossing was the continued Iraqi deception with regard to and lack of cooperation in the mandated weapons inspection program mandated by the United Nations in the wake of the Persian Gulf War of 1991. A condition of the cease-fire agreement that ended the conflict was that U.N. inspection teams were to receive unfettered access to all suspected sites and full disclosure on the part of Iraqi officials, both at the sites to be inspected as well as those higher in the government. Almost from the first visit, the Iraqis seemed to do all within their considerable power to thwart the inspection effort, despite repeated and unheeded warnings from the international body concerning failure to comply with the numerous resolutions concerning the nation's conduct. Finally, in early October 1998, the chief weapons inspector withdrew the inspection teams based on the belief that unless or until a greater degree of cooperation on the part of the Iraqis could be forced, these site visits were largely a waste of time and no small amount of trepidation with regard to the inspectors' physical safety.

Against a background of high level wrangling at the United Nations, the United States and Great Britain were determined to teach the Iraqis a stern lesson and force cooperation with the inspections. Unfortunately, the majority of the members of the U.N. lacked the will to enforce their own resolutions, preferring instead an unending series of largely meaningless words and threats. In response to this barrage of nothing more lethal than words, Saddam Hussein thumbed his nose at the world body and continued to pursue his chosen course as if he had been victorious in the 1991 war.

Dubbed Operation *Desert Fox*, the United States and Great Britain launched a series of cruise missile and air strikes on suspected Iraqi weapons of mass destruction sites. Secretary of State Madeleine Albright described the aim of these strikes as being to "degrade" suspected Iraqi ability to manufacture and employ WMD, as opposed to their elimination. The initial strikes were launched during the night of 16 December and were concluded on 19 December 1998, and VMA-214 shouldered its share of the

Ready for the Cat Shot
An aviator of VMF-214 braces himself for" the kick in the pants" by the hydraulic catapult of USS Sicily (CVE-118) off the coast of Korea in August 1950. The protruding warhead of the third rocket inboard on the starboard wing of this F4U-4 identifies it as an armor-piercing "RAM' rocket, which was especially useful against the T-34 tanks of the North Korean forces. [USMC photo]

load in these attacks. Regardless of whether the ultimate goal of *Desert Fox* was "elimination" or "degradation," many of the selected 100 targets throughout the country received a thorough pounding during the seventy hours of attacks. Estimates of the effectiveness of the strikes on Iraq's WMD capabilities vary widely, but it seems the primary victim of the attacks was that nation's ability to manufacture and employ ballistic missiles, which would have been the primary means to employ WMD against its neighbors. As far as the Iraqi ability to employ WMD on the battlefield was concerned, it was likely that they retained a considerable portion of whatever capability that existed prior to the attacks. And, while the material damage inflicted may have been considerable, its effect on Saddam Hussein's willingness to cooperate with the various U.N. resolutions seems to have been effectively zero. VMA-214 returned to its home station in 1999, where shortly thereafter, the entire Harrier fleet was grounded for a safety review in response to several recent accidents that were subsequently attributed to circumstances inherent in the operation of jet aircraft rather than any systemic problem with the Harrier or aircrew training.

After the grounding was rescinded, the squadron was split into two detachments that were deployed separately in support of two different MEU(SOC)s [Marine Expeditionary Unit, Special Operations Capable]. Half the squadron deployed to M.C.A.S., Iwakuni. Det. B deployed aboard *Tarawa* in support of 13th MEU. Among the missions that kept the Marines busy was their participation in humanitarian operations in East Timor, Indonesia and Operation *Determined Response*, the U.S. recovery of USS *Cole* (DDG-67) in the wake of the suicide bombing attack against her while she was taking on fuel in the port of Aden, Yemen. Seventeen of her crew lost their lives in the attack, and *Cole* suffered severe damage to her port side amidships. This damage was deemed severe enough to preclude her making the long voyage home under her own power, and *Tarawa* was among the ships dispatched to render aid to the stricken vessel. During the recovery operations, VMA-214 was tasked

A Sad Voyage
USS Cole (DDG-67) is pictured aboard the Norwegian salvage vessel MV Blue Marlin as she begins her voyage that eventually would return Cole to Pascagoula, Mississippi on Christmas Eve, 1990. Note the severe damage sustained on the ship's port side. [U.S. Navy Photo by PH2 Leland Comer]

with providing a highly visible fixed-wing aircraft presence that would serve to stabilize a potentially volatile situation. The answer to the question of how to return *Cole* to the U.S. was provided by the arrival of the Norwegian Navy's semi-submersible salvage vessel MV *Blue Marlin*. The battered DDG was loaded aboard and carried home. After *Cole*'s departure from Aden, *Tarawa* moved northward from the Horn of Africa and entered the Persian Gulf were she took part in Exercise *Iron Magic* from 15 through 26 November and then moved ashore for additional exercises conducted with Joint Task Force, Kuwait. The deployment lasted through the holiday period and then the Black Sheep and *Tarawa* returned to the United States.

The squadron spent its post-deployment stand-down enjoying the pleasures of its return and then re-entered its training cycle in preparation for its next deployment. Then came the shock of September 11, 2001, and the Black Sheep responded to the heightened alert status that came in the wake of the attack throughout the remainder of 2001 and the early months of 2002 until it answered the call for the global war on terrorism.

The continued intransigence of the Iraqi dictator Saddam Hussein regarding inspections under the auspices of the various U.N. resolutions in force finally pushed the coalition to the point of enforcing compliance with these U.N. actions by force of arms. As a part of this overall effort, VMA-214 deployed sixteen aircraft and more than 250 personnel to Ahmed Al Jaber Air Base, Kuwait. As the only land-based Harrier squadron, the Black Sheep flew in support of the assault of the I MEF northward into Iraq from the opening shot until after the fall of Baghdad and through the following summer. Its missions included close air support, aerial interdiction and armed reconnaissance. During operations, the squadron compiled more than 1,900 combat sorties and expended more than 236,000 pounds of ordnance. During this period, a detachment of the squadron flew in support of 31st MEU, and after a year in the Middle East, the Black Sheep returned unscathed to Yuma.

In May 2004, the squadron was ordered to the Middle East, this time in support of Operation *Iraqi Freedom*. The circumstances were realistic in that the squadron received less than a week's notice, and within that short timeframe, ten of the Sheep's Harriers were in operation from As Asad Air Base, Iraq. These aircraft were equipped with the new LITENING II targeting pod that provided a significant increase in weapons accuracy. Simultaneously, within this short notification period, a half-dozen of the squadron's Harriers were deployed aboard USS *Belleau Wood* (LHA-3) in support of the 11th MEU. Over the nine months of this split deployment, the Black Sheep completed a total of 1,978 combat sorties against targets in An Najaf, Al Fallujah, Baghdad, Ramadi, and other smaller objectives in the Al Anbar province in Western Iraq. The squadron's record during this deployment and the brief warning prior to its commencement provided ample proof of the ability of Marine air to go to war on short notice.

2005 saw the squadron called upon to conduct multiple simultaneous deployments again. A pair of six aircraft detachments departed Yuma in opposite directions, while the balance of VMA-214 remained at Yuma. Det. B deployed to Japan in support of the 31st MEU. Meanwhile, Det. A deployed to the North Arabian Gulf aboard USS *Peleliu* (LHA-5) in support of the 11th MEU. Like the British Empire of old, the sun did not set on the Black Sheep, at least in 2005!

The three parts of the squadron were reunited by August 2006 and immediately began to prepare for its next deployment which would come some five months later. In January 2007, VMA-214 deployed to Japan, again in support of the 31st MEU. Halfway through the anticipated 6-month deployment, the squadron learned that its time in Japan had been extended to a full year, due to the need to prepare units to support the surge of American forces into Iraq. As it turned out, the squadron was away from slightly less time than expected and was back at Yuma in time for Christmas.

The Black Sheep spent 2008 training and operating for its next deployment. In January 2009, Det. A boarded *Boxer* along

Now That's What I Call a Hole in the Ground!
This Harrier of VMA-214 was pictured in flight above the crater of Mt. Pinatubo on the Philippine island of Luzon during one of the squadron's deployment to the Western Pacific. [USMC Photo via the VMA-214 Website]

with 13th MEU and sailed for the waters off the Horn of Africa. In a new experience for the squadron, it conducted anti-piracy operations in the Gulf of Aden off the coast of Somalia and returned to the U.S. in August of that year.

While the Det. was busy chasing pirates, the remainder of VMA-214 was assigned to MAG-40 of 2nd MEB and deployed to Kandahar, Afghanistan, in May. Although at less than full strength, the squadron compiled 3,200 flight hours in 1,375 combat sorties. On 2 July, the Black Sheep provided close air support for the largest helicopter-borne troop insertion since the Vietnam War. The squadron returned to Yuma the night before Thanksgiving 2009, truly a reason to give thanks.

On 22 May 2010, VMA-214 received the Attack Squadron of the Year Award from the Marine Corps Aviation Association during that group's annual convention in Dallas, Texas.

Immediately after the receipt of that prestigious award, the squadron deployed to Alaska for Exercise *Red Flag 10-03*. This was the largest Red Flag ever conducted in Alaska, including forces from 8 nations, 120 aircraft and more than 2,500 troops.

Today, the Black Sheep of VMA-214 proudly carry on a proud record of service that began in 1942 and continues to the present day in the traditions firmly established by their predecessors who were proud to wear the squadron's black sheep. Of the versions of the squadron's insignia in the plates, the first eight are different examples of the squadron's current array of insignia. Four are different variants of the squadron's official insignia. The first three are virtually identical in color and detail and differ only in size, while the fourth carries a shade of blue somewhat lighter that that of the first three. This design has been worn virtually without change since the squadron's redesignation as an attack squadron in 1957.

The other four are representative of the "Black Sheep's" version of the popular shoulder rectangle adopted by virtually all the Harrier-equipped squadrons for wear on the flight suit.

A Sortie Begins
A Harrier of VMA-214 is pictured during its take-off run down the deck of Boxer. [USMC. Photo via the VMA-214 Website]

The ninth insignia is the squadron's cruise or "float" patch from its Det. N aboard *Hornet* in 1963-64.

The tenth is an example of its design that dates from the latter part of the Korean War-era. Note this one has a black ram in place of the ewe of the earlier insignia. This insignia is fully embroidered and appears to be Japanese-made.

The eleventh insignia is an example of one worn in 1951 that is unusual in that the aircraft has an unexplained red propeller boss, something unique among all the variants of this classic insignia design worn by members of VMF/VMA-214 for more than half a century.

Also, the two insignia described immediately above illustrate something of a mystery concerning this insignia. Note the late Korean War-period insignia depicts a black ram on it while the design from 1951 depicts a black ewe. The immediate post-Korean examples of the insignia reverted to the ewe, and the current design features the ram once again. Thus far, the author has been unsuccessful in attempting to determine the reasoning behind the changes in the sheep's gender from time to time. Even a former member of the squadron who served with VMF-214 throughout the Korean War was unable to shed any light on the reasoning.

The next example is that design worn during the Second World War after Boyington re-formed VMF-214. This insignia received official approval in 1944, and original examples of this design were embroidered on white wool, first in Australia and later in the United States. The example depicted is one of the latter. Pen Johnson originated this design.

Last is the "Swashbucklers" design worn between June and September, 1943. The Latin motto *Semper Vincere* translates as "Always to Conquer." This design never was submitted to Headquarters, Marine Corps for approval. These were made in Australia during one of the squadron's periods of R&R in 1943 and were embroidered on a wool background. The design of this first insignia of VMF-214 is attributed to Lieutenant Harry Hollmeyer.

Author's collection

MARINE ATTACK SQUADRON 223,
THE BULLDOGS
A.K.A., THE RAINBOW SQUADRON (WORLD WAR II)

Author's Collection

The lineage of today's VMA-223 begins at MCAS, Ewa, Territory of Hawaii on 1 May 1942 with the activation of VMF-223, under the command of Captain John Lucien Smith. A former artilleryman from Oklahoma, Captain Smith was a strict taskmaster from the old school of pre-war Marine regulars who began the difficult task of molding the raw material given him into an effective combat unit. Although an excellent aviator and tactician, many of those who served under him considered Smith to be cold and aloof, but in view of the trials that lay less than six months into the squadron's future, few would argue that he was among the best suited for the tasks that would come all too soon. At the time of VMF-223's activation, the United States and its Allies were reeling before an unbroken string of Japanese victories that had begun with the attack on Pearl Harbor five months previously. This series of successes were unprecedented in military history, but, a week after the squadron was activated, allied fortunes began to change for the better.

The Battle of the Coral Sea was contested on 7 and 8 May between the carrier forces of the United States and the Imperial Japanese Navies. The action was brought about by the American code breakers' ability to "read the enemy's mail," and when they warned Admiral Chester W. Nimitz, the commander of the Pacific Fleet, of a pending Japanese attempt to capture Port Moresby, New Guinea by sea-borne invasion, he dispatched the carriers USS *Lexington* (CV-2) and *Yorktown* (CV-5), along with the remainder of their respective task forces, to stop them. The result of Nimitz's action was history's first carrier-versus-carrier naval engagement in which the ships of the opposing fleets neither sighted nor fired a shot at their opponents. The Americans lost *Lexington*, a fleet oiler, and a destroyer, and *Yorktown* suffered moderate bomb damage. These losses were in exchange for a Japanese light carrier, H.I.J.M.S. *Shoho*, sunk. In addition, the air group of the fleet carrier H.I.J.M.S. *Zuikaku* was severely

mauled by the Americans and her sister ship, H.I.J.M.S. *Shokaku*, suffered heavy damage from multiple 1,000lb. bomb hits at the hands of the American dive-bombers, and, shorn of its air cover, the invasion force was turned back. As a result, the assault on Port Moresby was postponed indefinitely. Thus, in terms of ships and aircraft lost, Coral Sea was a tactical victory for the Japanese, but in strategic terms, it was a stinging defeat for them. The Japanese victory train had run off its rails, never to run again.

A month after the Battle of the Coral Sea, the turning point of the war in the Pacific occurred in the waters northwest of the tiny atoll of Midway in the central Pacific. The Battle of Midway was fought on 4 through 7 June 1942 and is considered by historians to be one of the most pivotal and decisive naval actions in history. In an attempt to capture the vital American outpost and to force the battered and heavily outnumbered Pacific Fleet into a decisive battle, the Japanese were ambushed by three American carriers and suffered a crushing defeat, their first in more than four centuries. The Americans lost the hastily repaired *Yorktown* and a destroyer, but in exchange for these ships, they tore the heart out of Admiral Nagumo's Japanese carrier forces, the *Kidō Butai*. The opening round of the battle went to the Japanese. Their strike against the island inflicted considerable damage, and the initial American attacks against the Japanese were beaten off with crippling losses to the attackers, but American fortunes changed with dramatic suddenness. Three squadrons of American dive-bombers arrived over the enemy carrier force undetected and commenced an attack of approximately six minutes' duration. Three enemy carriers received their deathblows in that incredibly short span of time and a fourth carrier was mortally damaged later that same day. Sunk were H.I.J.M.S. *Akagi, Kaga, Soryu* and *Hiryu*. Lost along with these four carriers were many of the irreplaceable veterans of their air groups and

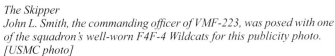

The Skipper
John L. Smith, the commanding officer of VMF-223, was posed with one of the squadron's well-worn F4F-4 Wildcats for this publicity photo. [USMC photo]

The Eyes of an Ace
What more can be said about this portrait of Major General Marion Carl, USMC? [USMC Photo]

a heavy cruiser. When the remaining elements of the Japanese fleet turned away from Midway on their sad journey back to the home islands, Japan had lost the initiative in the war in the Pacific and would never regain it.

Despite the distance from Hawaii to Midway, Smith and some of his pilots, along with their opposite numbers of their sister squadron, VMF-224, played a very minor supporting role in the drama that was played out around the atoll. They were dispatched to Barking Sands on the island of Kauai, Hawaii, as a precaution against another Japanese attack on the Hawaiian Islands. In case the efforts of the code-breakers were incorrect with regard to Japanese plans toward Midway, it was wise to be prepared for another lunge against the islands. When the first contact from the American patrol bombers revealed the advance of the enemy on Midway, an audible sigh of relief was heard among the members of the code-breaking unit at Pearl Harbor. While Captain Smith and the others spent some time amid the sand and palms of Kauai, the remainder of the squadron, under the Executive Officer, Captain Rivers J. Morrell, Jr., remained at Ewa to continue its training. When it was confirmed the Japanese fleet was steaming toward the home islands after the conclusion of the crucial battle, Smith and the rest of his detachment returned to their parent squadron at Ewa.

Shortly after the Battle of Midway, an Allied reconnaissance aircraft noted the Japanese had begun construction of an airfield on the island of Guadalcanal in the southern Solomons Islands from which the enemy had summarily ejected the meager Australian forces based there in April 1942. The Solomons lay across the Coral Sea northeast of Australia and north of New Zealand, and an enemy airfield in that location would be pointed like a dagger at the jugular of the supply lines that stretched across the vast Pacific to America's southernmost allies. A British protectorate before the war, the lower Solomons had fallen to the Japanese as part of their overall strategy that led to the Battle of the Coral Sea. Indeed, severing this supply line was precisely what the Japanese planned when they moved into the Solomons.

Immediately, the Americans began to plan the capture of Guadalcanal and its vital airfield. On 7 August 1942 the First Marine Division (Reinforced) landed on the island and its small neighbors of Tulagi and the twins of Gavutu and Tanimbogo that lay across Savo Sound from the airfield on Guadalcanal's north shore. The airfield fell to the Marines the first day of the assault, and the situation appeared favorable for the Americans early on. However, this was short-lived. Early the following morning in the first of a series of savage night naval engagements that would be fought in the area during the coming months, a

Japanese surface force of cruisers and destroyers surprised and severely mauled the Allied naval force supporting the landings. Totally unprepared for a surface action of any kind, especially a night battle of the type in which the Japanese excelled, the Allies lost the heavy cruisers H.M.A.S. *Canberra,* USS *Astoria* (CA-34), *Vincennes* (CA-44) and *Quincy* (CA-39) and a destroyer, USS *Jarvis* (DD-393). A torpedo hit blew the bow off USS *Chicago* (CA-29). Down with these ships went more than 1,000 American and Australian sailors. The Japanese suffered hardly a scratch in return, and the door was opened that would have allowed the Japanese to slaughter the nearly defenseless amphibious shipping that lay off the island. But, fearing that he would be at the mercy of the supporting American carriers if he remained off Guadalcanal any longer, the Japanese commander, Admiral Mikawa, turned his ships northward out of harm's way before he could attack the transports that carried the Marines' supplies.

Unknown to Admiral Mikawa, due to a signal failure on the part of the usually reliable Japanese long-range search aircraft, the commander of the American carriers, Rear Admiral Frank Jack Fletcher, had withdrawn out of range of the Japanese ships the previous day. With the coming of daylight, the American transports, now without air cover and within range of enemy aircraft attacking from bases located further up the Solomons chain, hastily unloaded what supplies they could and departed the area posthaste. This naval retreat left the Marines ashore to their own devices, at least temporarily. It would be some months before the Marines overcame their bitter feeling of having been abandoned by the Navy.

Utilizing mainly captured enemy equipment and supplies, the engineers of the First Marine Division immediately went to work on the airfield on Guadalcanal. In the meantime, five days before the Marines went ashore on the island, VMF-223 departed Pearl Harbor aboard the escort carrier USS *Long Island* (CVE-

Author's Collection

Taxi Service
USS Long Island (CVE-1) was tied up alongside a pier in Pearl Harbor when this photo was taken on 17 July 1942, shortly before she departed for Espiritu Santo with VMF-223 aboard. Most of the aircraft on her flight deck are SBDs, but at least one TBF is tied down forward. Long Island was a product of the Royal Navy's idea of an escort carrier, with a flush deck. Following classes of U.S.-designed CVE's were completed with a small island to starboard.
[U.S. Navy Photo]

1) bound for Espiritu Santo in the New Hebrides. VMF-223 was typical of the average American fighter squadron at this stage of the war. At its nucleus was a core of experience among the commanding officer and a few others, but the bulk of its ranks were filled with relatively inexperienced aviators who averaged far fewer flight hours in their assigned aircraft compared to their likely opponents in Japan's naval air arm. Destined to be the first fighter squadron ashore on Guadalcanal, Captain Smith arrived at Espiritu Santo determined to attempt some horse-trading with Major Harold W. Bauer, the commanding officer of VMF-212. The aviators of VMF-212 had left the U.S. prior to the departure of VMF-223, and while they had departed with approximately the same level of experience as the aviators of VMF-223, VMF-212 had enjoyed the benefits of additional training after their arrival in the South Pacific. Bauer had driven his troops hard during their time on Espiritu Santo prior to the arrival of VMF-223, and each hour they spent in the air would pay handsome dividends when they entered combat. With this in mind, Smith managed to exchange eight of his least experienced aviators for a like number of the more experienced members of VMF-212. Since -212 could expect to remain at Espiritu as the base's defensive fighter force for some weeks to come, the former members of -223 would have time to accumulate additional flying hours in their Wildcats prior to their being committed to combat.

Shortly after the deal between Smith and Bauer was consummated, VMF-223 and VMSB-232 were loaded aboard the hard-working *Long Island* once again and departed the New Hebrides for Guadalcanal. During the afternoon of 20 August, the carrier reached a point some 200 miles southeast of the island. She turned into the wind and began launching the 19 F4F-4 Wildcats of VMF-223 and the twelve SBD-3 Dauntless dive-bombers of VMSB-232. Marine air support was finally on its way to the beleaguered defenders of Guadalcanal, and at 1700 that afternoon, the thirty-one aircraft of MAG-23 entered the landing pattern above the airstrip carved out of the surrounding jungle. As yet unnamed, it soon would take its hallowed place among the icons of the Marine Corps as Henderson Field named in honor of Major Lofton R Henderson, the commanding officer of VMSB-241 who was killed at Midway.

In the early hours of the following morning, the 900 infantrymen of the Ichiki Detachment dispatched to Guadalcanal in the first Japanese attempt to recapture the island from the American invaders struck the Marine perimeter surrounding the vital airfield. The Marines' heavy defensive fire slaughtered the attackers, and shortly after dawn, the survivors had been driven into a coconut grove near the mouth of the Tenaru River. Marine infantry/armor teams, aided by the strafing aircraft of VMF-223 soon reduced these few survivors to a handful of scattered, fleeing individuals. Very few of the 900 Japanese who had attacked with such confidence the previous night survived to tell their tales to those who followed them to Guadalcanal, which was soon to become known to the Japanese as "The Island of Death." As soon as the Wildcats of VMF-223 landed from their attacks on the remnants of the Ichiki Detachment, their ground crews met them and hastily began to refuel and rearm the aircraft. Word had reached the island that an enemy air raid was headed for Guadalcanal. The squadron shortly would get its first taste of aerial combat.

The incoming enemy raid was intercepted at 1207. In the fights that followed, Captain Smith killed a Zero for the squad-

via Holmberg

ron's first confirmed victory, and one Wildcat crashed due to battle damage upon landing, but its pilot, Technical Sergeant J.D. Lindley, survived. [Editor's Note: Lindley was assigned to VMF-212 but was one of the early members of that squadron to see action at Guadalcanal.] The Marines had met their enemy in combat and had come out even in their first engagement. Within days, the men of VMF-223 would begin to add significant numbers of enemy scalps to their belts.

The Japanese continued to reinforce their troops on Guadalcanal in an ongoing effort to build sufficient strength ashore to drive the pesky Americans from the island for good. This effort on the part of the Japanese precipitated the first of four major naval engagements that would be contested during the next three months for control of the island. The Battle of the Eastern Solomons was fought on 24 August. The Japanese lost the light carrier H.I.J.M.S. *Ryujo*, and once again, the air groups of the other carriers suffered crippling losses. In return, USS *Enterprise* (CV-6) suffered moderate damage from three bomb hits. The damage to *Enterprise* resulted in Guadalcanal's Cactus Air Force receiving a welcome reinforcement to its striking power with the arrival of eleven of the SBDs of Bombing 6 of the veteran air group of *Enterprise*.

While the carriers were trading blows east of Guadalcanal, Japanese air attacks against the island's defenders continued unabated. At 1420 on 24 August, VMF-223 intercepted twenty-seven enemy aircraft that had been launched from *Ryujo* prior to her demise. None of the enemy reached the airfield, and sixteen of them joined their late carrier in its watery grave. Three fell to the Wildcat flown by Captain Marion E. Carl, and three other pilots, Lieutenants Zenneth A. Pond and Kenneth D. Frazier of VMF-223 and Marine Gunner Henry B. Hamilton, of VMF-212, accounted for two apiece. Four of the Wildcats were lost, along with three of their pilots.

Despite their losses, the Japanese were determined to eject the invaders and kept coming at the Marines. The squadron's next big fight came on the 29th when Marine fighters claimed eight more enemy aircraft. The next day, VMF-223 added fourteen more Japanese aircraft to their scoreboard. Four and three of these fell to Smith and to Carl, respectively. It appears that among Carl's victims in this fight was the redoubtable Japanese ace Lieutenant Commander Junichi Sasai, who was credited with twenty-seven victories at the time of his death. Assigned to VMF-223 as the squadron's engineering officer, Carl claimed his first enemy aircraft as a member of VMF-221 on 4 June during the Battle of Midway and was awarded the Navy Cross for his conduct during the battle. Captain Smith's equal in experience and skill, Carl was among the squadron's most steadfast members during its stay on Guadalcanal. He went on to a long and extremely distinguished career in the Marine Corps, retiring as a Lieutenant General. [Tragically, General Carl met his death at the hands of an intruder in his Oregon home while attempting to protect his wife of many years. The intruder was later captured, convicted of Carl's murder and sentenced to life in prison.]

Daily combats, as well as losses, continued to take place. While the Marines took a higher toll of the enemy than losses they suffered, the enemy could replace his losses more easily than could the Americans. Disease and fatigue were other constant drains on the air strength on the island. Clearly, a continuous stream of aerial reinforcements and replacements was needed if Guadalcanal was to be held. The first American aerial reinforcements reached the island on 30 August in the form of VMF-224 and VMSB-231, and the late afternoon of 11 September saw a major and welcome, though unplanned, reinforcement of the fighter strength of the Cactus Air Force when 24 F4F-4s of the Navy's Fighting 5 arrived on the island. Previously assigned to the air group of the USS *Saratoga* (CV-3), Fighting 5 had been ashore at Espiritu Santo since 31 August when *Saratoga* was damaged for the second time by a Japanese submarine's torpedo.

September dragged into October with almost daily fierce air combats above the island. VMF-223 and the other American squadrons continued to give better than they received, but finally and inevitably, VMF-223 was able to fight no more. Many of the original complement of pilots had been lost in battle, suffered incapacitating wounds or were wracked by malaria or any one of a half-dozen or more exotic tropical diseases that were endemic to the Solomons. The last of the squadron's survivors were withdrawn from Guadalcanal on 16 October. In less than two months on Guadalcanal, they had accounted for 111 1/2 enemy aircraft destroyed in aerial combat. (The fractional kill was the result of two pilots from two different squadrons sharing in the destruction of the same enemy aircraft.) For its services at Guadalcanal during the period 7 August through 9 December 1942, VMF-223 was awarded its first Presidential Unit Citation. (Unit citations are usually awarded for service during a particular campaign or battle. When awarded for a campaign, the dates of the award cover the entire campaign, regardless of the time of the unit's actual participation in it.) In addition, Smith received the Medal of Honor, the Navy Cross and the Distinguished Flying Cross for his service at Guadalcanal. Other members of the squadron received their share of decorations as well. Carl, Frazier, Morrell and Pond and Lieutenant Eugene A. Trowbridge received the Navy Cross, while Lieutenants Fred E. Gutt, Charles H. Kendrick, Willis S. Lees III received their awards posthumously. Lieutenants Hyde Phillips and Orvin H. Ramlo received the Distinguished Flying Cross. Seven members of the squadron's aviators attained the coveted but unofficial title of ace by achieving at least five kills: Smith, 19, Carl, 18½, including those at Midway, Trowbridge, 12; Gutt, 8 Pond, 6, Phillips, 5 and Ramlo, 5. These honors and achievements were not attained without cost, however. Of a complement of 21 aviators actually carried on the roster as members of VMF-223, six were killed in action, two were wounded severely enough to require evacuation and

via Holmberg

Author's Collection

one was injured in a crash and was evacuated. Hardly any of the others escaped the island without contracting at least one of the many tropical diseases so common throughout the Solomons.

The squadron arrived in San Francisco on 1 November 1942. After a short period of leave to enjoy more comfortable surroundings than those the squadron had endured over the past few months, it was transferred to MCAS, El Toro for R & R and retraining, and the squadron was among those to be re-equipped with the F4U Corsair. Major Smith was transferred to other duty, and Lieutenant Conrad G. Winter temporarily assumed command of the squadron on 1 January 1943 pending the assignment of a permanent commander. On 14 January, Captain Howard K. Marvin assumed command but was succeeded by an officer familiar to VMF-223, Major Marion Carl, on 26 January. On 4 February, Major Robert P. Keller relieved Major Carl who, along with Major Smith, was ordered to a war bond tour. During all these changes of command, the squadron enjoyed almost seven months of relative comfort and extensive training before it was sent into battle again. In July 1943, VMF-223 departed the West Coast for the Pacific once again.

The first destination of VMF-223 and its new Corsairs was the island of Midway. It remained at this mid-Pacific "paradise" for nearly five months undergoing further training and serving as a part of the outpost's defense force. When the squadron departed Midway in November, it was divided into two parts, with the ground echelon being sent to Efate in the New Hebrides and the flight echelon being sent to Vella Lavella, which lies at almost the mid-point of the Solomons. In February 1944, the squadron was reunited at Piva Yoke airfield on Bougainville. During this period the campaign against Rabaul was in full swing. In addition to the ongoing effort against Rabaul, the American airfields on Bougainville were under what, at times, seemed to be constant enemy fire from the portions of the island that remained in Japanese hands. It was during this period that the squadron's ground crews were among several that received commendations for their actions under enemy fire.

The arrival of VMF-223 on Bougainville coincided with the crescendo of the Allied aerial campaign against the Japanese fortress at Rabaul. The squadron was one of thirty-three Marine squadrons that would eventually take part in the pounding the enemy garrison received on a daily basis. By the time the "Rainbows" began to fly missions against Rabaul, however, it had been reduced to a point of relative ineffectiveness in the Japanese war effort. By mid-February, the Japanese tacitly admitted defeat and withdrew the battered remains of their naval air forces. Shorn of its protective aerial shield, the base would not be a threat to the continuing allied advances, provided the Japanese on New Britain remained in a defensive posture. Toward this end, American and Allied aircraft continued to rain tons of bombs on the enemy in an ongoing effort to ensure the base and its large complement of troops remained impotent. [The aerial stranglehold on Rabaul was so effective that the large Japanese garrison was forced to subsist on ever-shorter rations. The Japanese people of the World War II period were inveterate diarists, and many of the diaries faithfully kept by troops at Rabaul offer vivid descriptions of daily life beneath the rain of allied bombs and of the elaborate gardens many of the troops cultivated in order supplement their meager diets and to prevent starvation.] VMF-223 remained engaged in this duty for the remainder of 1944 under Majors David Drucker and Robert F. Flaherty, who assumed command of the squadron on 3 July and on 14 October, respectively.

While Rabaul continued to receive large amounts of high explosives, the tide of war continued to roll northwestward. The Americans had returned to the Philippines in late October 1944 and the assault against the island of Leyte had precipitated the largest naval engagement in history, the Battle of Leyte Gulf. Fought on 24 through 26 October, the battle was comprised of four separate actions and featured all the elements of a modern fleet, from Patrol Torpedo boats and submarines to Dreadnought battleships and carrier aircraft. American losses were comprised of the light carrier USS *Princeton* (CVL-27), three escort carriers, two destroyers and a destroyer escort. Japanese losses were four fleet carriers, three battleships and a large number of the Imperial Navy's remaining cruisers and destroyers. The once proud and all-conquering Imperial Japanese Navy was reduced to a handful of fleeing remnants scattered throughout the Empire and home waters. It was claimed by many that after Leyte Gulf, the Japanese Navy was, from that point forward, in possession of its rightful half of the Pacific, the bottom half! While the battle itself was an exclusively Navy action, it paved the way for the rapid commitment of most of the aviation assets of the Marine Corps that were in the South Pacific to the campaign to liberate the Philippines from the yoke of Japanese occupation.

Author's Collection

The crushing defeat of the Japanese Navy at Leyte Gulf had the effect of moving the time frame for all phases of the land campaign in the Islands forward. Instead of a slower, island-by-selected island advance through the Philippine Archipelago, the Americans were in a position to conduct several simultaneous assaults against separate objectives. In turn, this created the need for far more land-based air power than was initially planned for, and the Army Air Forces did not have the available resources in the Pacific to meet the unexpectedly expanded need. In turn, this led to the sudden call for all available Marine squadrons to be rushed forward to the Philippines and among these squadrons was VMF-223. MAG-14, the parent MAG of VMF-223, was alerted for movement from the Green Islands on 8 December 1944. The first units of MAG-14 moved forward to the island of Samar on 8 January, and the Rainbows arrived on 14 January. The squadron then took part in the liberation of the Philippines until June. While engaged in the Philippines, Major Robert W. Teller assumed command on 25 March 1945 and was followed by Major Howard E. King on 17 April.

In May, the squadron's ground echelon had been ordered to Okinawa, but the flight echelon remained in the Philippines for another month. During this period, the squadron was re-equipped with the -4 version of the Corsair. With a top speed in excess of 440 M.P.H., the F4U-4 was considered by many to be the zenith of the superlative Vought fighter.

Arriving at Kadena Airfield on Okinawa on 8 June, the squadron waited for nearly two weeks before they had the opportunity to test their new mounts against the Japanese in the air. VMF-223 engaged the enemy on two successive days, 21 and 22 June, and scored four kills each day. These engagements were each notable for different reasons. The combat of 21 June marked the squadron's first aerial engagement since March 1944, a period of 14 months. The combat of 22 June came as a result of the massed Kamikaze raid launched against the American naval forces that lay in the waters around the island. The four kills scored that day brought the squadron's total of kills to 132 1/2 during the Second World War, and one of those four was the 21st and last kill scored by Captain Kenneth A. Walsh, formerly of VMF-124.

Major Julius W. Ireland assumed command on 24 July, and VMF-223 remained in the area of Okinawa until the Japanese surrender and returned to the United States in company with the other units of MAG-14. It arrived at NAS, North Island in San Diego, on 28 February 1946.

For its service during World War II, VMF-223 received two awards of the Presidential Unit Citation. The first award was for service during the Guadalcanal Campaign and covered the period 7 August through 9 December

1942. The second award was for its service during the Okinawa Campaign and covered the period 11 June through 14 July 1945.

After its return to the United States, VMF-223 was detached from MAG-14 and assigned to Marine Air, West Coast as a component of MAG-33. The rigors of war behind them, the members of the squadron settled into the routine of the peacetime military and hoped their squadron would not be among the scores that were deactivated in the months following the end of hostilities against Japan. The end of man's most costly and bloody conflict brought a mass demobilization of the bulk of the wartime strength of the American military. By a considerable margin, those who wore the uniforms of the U.S. armed services were reservists who were released from active duty almost en masse. The result was nothing short of chaos among the units remaining on the active roster of the armed services.

[As indication of the speed with which the United States went about dismantling the greatest military force in history, the reader is asked to consider the following figures. On 31 August 1945, a total of 116,628 Marine Corps personnel were assigned to aviation duties and organized into 103 tactical squadrons. Ten months later, by 30 June 1946, that total had been reduced to 36,144 personnel and 27 tactical squadrons. As drastic as these reductions were, however, more cutbacks lay ahead. Four years later, on 30 June 1950, six days after the start of the Korean War, the numbers were 14,163 personnel and 16 tactical squadrons!]

On 9 June 1947, VMF-223 ceased operations as a combat squadron and assumed the duties of a transitional training squadron for the Corsair. In addition to the need to train newly minted aviators in the intricacies of the F4U, all of the Marines' scout bomber, horizontal bomber and torpedo squadrons had been deactivated, and many of the Regular Marine Corps pilots from these squadrons were ordered to the fighter squadrons to take the places of the mass of wartime reservists who had been released from the ranks. For an aviator accustomed to the docile flight characteristics of the SBD Dauntless dive-bomber or the big, stable Avenger torpedo bomber, the F4U presented quite a challenge. It would have been interesting indeed to take part in the first bull sessions among these former bomber and torpedo pilots after their initial experiences in the Corsair. Designed at the outset to be a carrier-based Navy fighter, the initial models of the F4U series were deemed to be unfit for carrier duty due primarily to its landing characteristics. This led to the decision to send it to the Marines as a land-based fighter, and while each successive model of the Corsair brought improvement in its speed, firepower, and handling characteristics in carrier operations, it remained a true thoroughbred throughout its long career.

After its period of service in MAG-33 as a transition training squadron, VMF-223 was shifted to MAG-11 and was redesignated Marine Fighter [as opposed to "Fighting"] Squadron 223 on 1 August 1948. Concurrently, it relinquished the training role and returned to the ranks of the Marines' operational squadrons. Shortly after joining its new air group, the squadron was ordered to carrier qualification in preparation for its first shipboard deployment. Upon completion of its carrier qualifica-

tions, the entire group came under the operational control of the Navy and deployed to the Med aboard USS Leyte (CV-32) on 6 September 1949. The cruise lasted until 17 January 1950.

Shortly after its return from its deployment, the squadron received word that it would be converted to jet aircraft in the near future. Initially, it was to be equipped with the McDonnell F2H Banshee, but these plans were changed in favor of the Grumman F9F-2 Panther. VMF-223 received its first jet in early July, and in two weeks, its full complement of a dozen aircraft were on hand.

Despite the heavy commitment of U.S. combat forces to the Korean War, VMF-223 was not destined to see service there. Instead, it was one of the units held in readiness should the fighting in Korea spread to other locations in the Far East or lead to the nightmare scenario of another war in Europe against Soviet Forces.

Fortunately, neither of these events occurred. Other than a sudden relaxation of the purse strings and an increased level of readiness, the Korean fighting had little effect on the squadron's activities.

Shortly after the end of the Korean War, VMF-223 began to surrender its F9F-2's in favor of the final model of the Panther, the F9F-5, and the squadron was redesignated VMA-223 on 1 December 1954. After once again being declared combat-ready with its new aircraft, the squadron was ordered to carrier qualification in preparation for its second carrier deployment. On 23 April 1956, the Navy's Carrier Air Group 15, CVG-15, assumed operational control of the squadron and it deployed aboard USS Wasp (CVA-18) for the western Pacific. VMA-223 returned to the U.S. on 11 October 1956 when it bade the Navy a fond farewell and returned to El Toro.

After five years in the Grumman products, the squadron began to receive the first examples of its first "true" attack aircraft, the North American FJ-4B Fury. Its first Fury arrived in mid-August 1957, and VMA-223 would operate this aircraft for slightly more than three years. In mid-January 1961, the squadron began to receive the first types of the aircraft that it would operate for a greater length of time than any other aircraft in the squadron's history, the Douglas A4D-2N Skyhawk. VMA-223 received its first Skyhawk in 1961 and was one of the last Marine squadrons to receive this remarkable product from the drafting board of the design genius Ed Heinemann. After receiving its "Scooters," the squadron began the process of attaining combat readiness in a new aircraft once again.

Before many years had passed, the rumble of guns could once again be heard across the vast Pacific from the squadron's home at El Toro. The civil war in Southeast Asia began to grow in violence on what seemed to be a daily basis. In response to the late President Kennedy's pledge to "pay any price," the U.S. began to commit more and more forces to aid its allies in the region. By April 1965, what had begun as increased material aid and a few advisors had grown into a full-scale war with the commitment of Marine ground combat forces to protect the enclave at Da Nang, and along with the Marine ground forces came their air support.

However, the first experience of VMA-223 in the growing war in Southeast Asia came in the form of another carrier deployment for a portion of the squadron. Det. T was formed and went aboard USS Yorktown (CVS-10) as a component of CVSG-55. Its mission was to provide the anti-submarine carrier with some measure of air defense, and to the surprise of some, although none of the Skyhawk operators, the Scooter was quite

A Hazy Day at Sea
USS Leyte (CV-32) pictured during operations in the North Atlantic in November 1948. [U.S. Navy Photo]

Car Quals
This F9F-2 Panther of VMF-223 sits on the deck-edge elevator of USS Franklin D. Roosevelt CVB-42) during the squadron's carrier qualifications in 1950. [U.S. Navy Photo]

effective in the air-to-air role. This was further enhanced when the outboard weapons stations were wired to accept the AIM-9 Sidewinder infrared missile. *Yorktown* deployed on 23 October 1964 and returned to the United States on 17 May 1965. While the Det. was aboard her, Lieutenant R.E. Ennis had the honor of making the 99,000th arrested landing of the carrier's long and distinguished career. Upon the return of the "Fighting Lady," as the venerable carrier was fondly nicknamed, VMA-223's Det. T was separated from CVSG-55 and returned to El Toro where it was reunited with the rest of the squadron.

While the squadron detachment had been at sea the remainder of VMA-223 had not been idle. As the war in Vietnam con-

tinued to build in intensity, the bulk of the squadron had been preparing for their eventual deployment to Southeast Asia. By the time of the detachment's return to its parent squadron, the first Marines had gone ashore at Da Nang, and Marine squadrons of all types were added to the growing roster of American air power in country. Even the massive base at Da Nang was soon swamped with the arrival of more squadrons than the facility could effectively support. In view of this, the decision was made to expand the number of bases available for U.S. use. Construction was begun on a new base at Chu Lai to the north of Da Nang in early May 1965. This base was to be used almost exclusively throughout their commitment to Vietnam by Marine attack squadrons equipped with the A-4. So rapid was the pace of construction that the first tenant squadrons began to arrive before the end of the month. First on the scene were VMA-224 and -311.

The squadron departed the West Coast for MCAS, Iwakuni, Japan on 1 September 1965 in preparation for its eventual deployment to the war zone in Southeast Asia. The turn of VMA-223 came on 15 December 1965 when they relieved the "Tomcats" of VMA-311. By the time the "Bulldogs" settled into the alien surroundings of Vietnam, American forces were engaged in heavy combat with the enemy on virtually a daily basis. The squadron was committed immediately to a heavy load of close air support missions for friendly ground forces in the northern operational area of South Vietnam, known as I Corps [pronounced "Eye Corps"], and missions into the southern portion of North Vietnam that lay across the nearby DMZ. Strikes were also flown into neighboring Laos and Cambodia. The squadron's first tour in Vietnam lasted one year, and VMA-223 was then withdrawn to Iwakuni for a short period of R&R. This move provided a three-month period for the squadron's personnel to catch their second wind before returning to combat in March 1967.

Immediately upon its return to Southeast Asia, the squadron found itself heavily committed to the support of Free World Forces in their almost daily battles against the Viet Cong and the regulars of the North Vietnamese army. This was the most intense period of combat operations for U.S. forces in Vietnam and the pace of the squadron's operations was extremely heavy.

Vietnam Years
This A4-E of VMF-223 was photographed in the midst of a JATO [Jet Assisted Take Off] run from the hastily constructed airstrip at Chu Lai, RVN. After the aircraft was airborne, the JATO bottles fell away. [USMC photo]

A Bulldog Fury
One of the FJ-B4s of VMA-223 that was photographed while parked on the crowded ramp of MCAS, El Toro, in late-1958. The aircraft color scheme was light gull gray upper services and insignia white undersurfaces. The squadron's traditional WP tailcode is in black, and the fuselage and tail stripes were white, outlined in insignia red, and carried red lightning bolts. [USMC photo]

In May 1967, the squadron amassed a total of 1,234 combat sorties, the highest monthly sortie total of any Marine squadron in Southeast Asia up to that time. VMA-223 was destined to remain in Vietnam for the majority of the Marines' commitment there, and a policy of rotation of squadron personnel on an individual basis rather than entire squadrons was put into place. It was felt that such a policy would result in less of a disruption of a unit's operational tempo as opposed to the wholesale rotation of squadrons. Although the faces changed as individuals completed their combat tours and were rotated to other duty, the "Bulldogs" remained at Chu Lai until the Marines' commitment to the war in Vietnam was drastically reduced in late 1969 and early 1970. During its service in the Vietnam War, VMA-223 flew a total of more than 32,000 combat hours, a record of which all hands could be justifiably proud.

VMA-223 was the first of the Marines' A-4-equipped light attack squadrons to be withdrawn from Southeast Asia. Their 20 A-4Es departed Chu Lai in company with the F-4B Phantoms of VMFA-542 on 28 January 1970. Their method and route of withdrawal was unusual in that they returned to the U.S. via a direct trans-Pacific ferry flight of 8,000 miles, with stops at NAS, Cubi Point in the Philippines, in Guam and in Hawaii. All the squadron's aircraft arrived safely at MCAS, El Toro on 8 February.

Their commitment to the Vietnam War behind them, the members of VMA-223 returned to a more peaceful existence as their fellow Skyhawk squadrons continued their involvement in an unpopular war that seemed to be without end. The remainder of the decade saw the squadron's A-4Es replaced with the upgraded A-4F model of the SkyHawk. In its turn, the -F was replaced with the ultimate version of the A-4 series, the A-4M. They continued to operate this outstanding aircraft throughout the 1970s and until the later years of the 1980s when they were re-equipped with one of the most revolutionary aircraft in the history of military aviation, the British Aerospace/McDonnell-Douglas AV-8B Harrier.

Declared combat ready by the AV-8B training squadron, VMAT-203, VMA-223 returned to the unit deployment schedule and prepared to take its new aircraft to sea for the first time. In May 1989, the bulk of the squadron deployed to the Med for the first time in almost four decades when it boarded USS *Nassau* (LHA-4) in support of the 26th Marine Expeditionary Unit. Concurrently, a detachment of the Bulldogs deployed to the Canadian Forces Base, Cold Lake, Alberta, for joint exercises with the military forces of our northern neighbor.

The V/STOL Harrier represented a quantum leap forward in the capability of a Marine squadron to support their fellow Marines on the ground. The ability of the Harrier to operate from unprepared areas only slightly larger than the dimensions of the aircraft itself provides the Harrier squadrons with tremendous capability to affect the course of an engagement or a campaign. Not the least of these is the ability to operate closer to the actual battle area than any other fixed-wing tactical aircraft. This acts as what is termed a "force multiplier" allowing fewer Harriers to deliver more ordnance in a shorter period of time than a larger force based at a location more distant from the battlefield. Also, the ability to vector the power plant's thrust nozzles in forward flight bestows maneuverability on this remarkable warplane that is second-to-none. While the Harrier lacks the supersonic speed of other strike aircraft and would appear to be "easy meat" for an enemy fighter, appearances can be deceiving. Should the enemy choose to close with the AV-8B and fight on the Harrier's terms, he likely will be in for a rude, if brief, awakening. [The AV-8B is scheduled for eventual replacement by the V/STOL version of the F-35 Joint Strike Fighter, but as this was written, the present administration has ordered a slow-down in the JSF program. Whether this decision was budgetary or political or a combination of the two is a matter of some contention, but it will, without doubt, drive up the unit cost and open the door for further cutbacks or delays. This is, by no means, the first example of such decisions, but without exception, they have had a deleterious effect on the program in question.]

In 1990, the squadron provided a detachment aboard USS *Saipan* (LHA-2) in support of the 22nd MEU. Deployed to the Med once again, the Marine amphibious force also was engaged in Operation *Sharp Edge*, the evacuation of foreign nationals from Liberia when that nation was torn apart in a bloody civil war.

Coming Home to Roost
This pair of the squadron's A-4s was photographed while on final approach to the active runway at MCAS, El Toro, CA. The pair of 300-gal. underwing fuel tanks carried by each aircraft indicate the flight was of considerable duration. [Photo from the Webshot Community web site]

Ready to Sortie
An AV-8B Harrier II + of VMF-223 carrying a load of six Mk.83 inert 1,000lb. bombs photographed as it prepares to begin a training sortie. [USMC photo]

In January 1991, a six-aircraft detachment of VMA-223 was dispatched to Rota, Spain, during Operation *Desert Shield/ Desert Storm*. It remained at Rota and saw no combat during operations against Iraq, but instead, it conducted a series of exercises with units of the Spanish Navy that also were equipped with export versions of the Harrier. The squadron returned to its base at Cherry Point in February.

In June 1991, a ten-aircraft detachment of the squadron boarded USS *Wasp* (LHD-1) for a Mediterranean /Persian Gulf cruise. The squadron maintained a high operational tempo in support of the Special Operations Capable MEUs in the post-Desert Storm period.

In 1994, VMA-223 converted to the latest Night Vision Goggle compatible night attack versions of the AV-8B and continued its operations from Cherry Point.

A pair of the squadron's aircraft was prominently on display in the climactic action sequences of the 1996 motion picture *True Lies*, starring Arnold Schwarzenegger, another in the lengthy list of movie and television credits amassed by Marine aviation over the years.

During the period 1999 through 2001, the squadron made a full unit deployment aboard USS *Bataan* (LHD-5) to Greece and another to the Caribbean as a part of the unit deployment rotation schedule during which the Harriers divided their time between operations ashore and shipboard.

In the wake of the events of 11 September 2011, the squadron soon found itself in combat for the first time since its return from Vietnam in 1970. It was deployed in support of 26th MEU(SOC), and after taking part in Exercise *Bright Star* in Egypt during which it honed its desert combat skills, it was repositioned to the Persian Gulf for Operation *Enduring Freedom*. The night systems of the Harrier proved to be particularly welcome in this environment.

VMA 223 deployed to Iraq in support of Operation *Iraqi Freedom* in the summer of 2005, and the deployment was a busy one as the Bulldogs have supported the objectives aimed at bringing stability to this troubled region. During a mission on 10 February 2006, the squadron surpassed the 60,000 accident free flying hours milestone made all the more remarkable when one considers the rigors of combat and the accident rate of the aircraft itself.

In January 2003, the squadron deployed to Southwest Asia again aboard USS *Kearsarge* (LHD-3) as a unit of 2nd Marine Expeditionary Brigade. After its arrival on station, VMA-223 was transferred to *Bataan*, where it joined VMF-542 to complete the "Harrier carrier" force attached to III MAW. It then took part in Operations *Southern Watch* and *Southern Force* from 5 through 18 March. With the outbreak of hostilities in Operation *Iraqi Freedom*, missions were flown in support of the offensive by 1st Marine Expeditionary Force. The squadron expended some 87,500 pounds of ordnance during *Iraqi Freedom*.

Flying Purple
In a demonstration of today's "purple" environment of joint military operations, a pair of Marine Harriers takes on fuel from an Air Force tanker aircraft while the AV-8Bs are en route to their targets in Iraq. [USAF Photo]

Morning Sortie, Iraq
An AV-8B of VMA 223 captured as it taxis into take-off position at Al Asad airbase in January, 2006. [USMC Photo]

VMA-223 continues to conduct operations in support of our national objectives in Iraq and Afghanistan and other missions as directed by National Command Authority.

An interesting tidbit of trivia concerning VMA-223 is that its "colors aircraft," which is assigned to the squadron commander and is usually the only one to wear full-color markings in these days of drab shades of gray carries the names of John L. Smith and Marion E. Carl on its canopy rails to honor the two most illustrious aviators in the long and proud history of the squadron.

Currently, the personnel assigned to the squadron continue to proudly carry forward the service of VMF/VMA-223 to this nation. It is actively engaged in the ongoing military operations in Southwest Asia, and there is no doubt that it will continue to carry out the missions assigned to it by our nation's leaders in such a manner that will swell the breasts of its former members with fond memories and pride in their old squadron.

Among the baker's dozen examples of insignia in the plates, the first is a current example of the squadron's officially approved insignia, and the second is a flight suit-size unofficial design. The third and fourth are examples of the flight suit shoulder rectangle of VMA-223. Both were obtained from the squadron at different times and represent another example of changes made to a unit's insignia from time to time with no specific explanation for the change or changes. A squadron-specific version of this rectangular insignia is common to all the Harrier-equipped light attack squadrons in the Marine Corps.

The next pair of insignia represents examples of Far East-made items. Note the absence of the traditional wings on the bulldog in the insignia with the gold background. Over the years, the wings have appeared and disappeared at random times. The insignia with the blue background is one made in the Philippines whose origin is identified by the relatively coarse quality of its embroidery.

Numbers seven and eight span the Korean War with regard to time. The insignia on the left, number seven, is embroidered

via Holmberg

on a gold twill background and dates from 1948, while the eighth dates from 1953. A slightly earlier version of number seven has been identified, which is identical with regard to the design and differs only in the embroidery style. The earlier version of this design is of American chenille embroidery.

The ninth insignia is a current reproduction available to collectors. When compared to the one to the right, which is an original, Australian-made example embroidered on a background of gold wool, the quality of the reproduction is obvious. In the decades since this last insignia was made, it has suffered some minor moth damage around its outer edge. Despite this, however, it is in surprisingly good condition.

The next insignia commemorates the squadron's return to the U.S. at the end of its participation in the war in Southeast Asia. In case that some readers may wonder what is special enough about that event to warrant the designing of an insignia should consider the following. The cockpit of the A-4 was a tight fit for virtually all who flew it, and the prospect of spending hours with one's backside on the hard seat cushion of an ejection seat for what seemed like hours on end between stops surely is an episode worth a patch!

The final design was designed and procured by and for those who made up the squadron's Det. T that deployed aboard CVS-18 in 1964/65.

The bulldog in boxing gloves, the presence or lack of wings notwithstanding, was designed for the squadron by the Walt Disney Studios and has served the VMA/VMF-223 for more than sixty years.

via Holmberg

Author's Collection

Coming Aboard
An AV-8B Harrier of VMA-223 is just moments from touching down aboard USS Nassau (LHA-4) on 26 October 2009 during the pre-deployment Composite Unit Training Exercise (COMPUTEX) conducted *by all units preparing to deploy. On the right is a CH-53E of the heavy-lift detachment of the composite unit. [U.S. Navy Photo by MC1 Brien Aho]*

MARINE ATTACK SQUADRON 231,
THE ACE OF SPADES

Author's Collection

Today's VMA-231 was activated on 1 January 1921 as the First Air Squadron, United States Marine Corps. There were three other squadrons activated on that date, and these four were the first permanent squadron organizations in the Marine Corps. Thus, no other squadron can claim a lineage pre-dating that of VMA-231. Effective 1 July 1922, the squadron was redesignated Marine Observation Squadron 1, VO-1. Also, photos dated as early as 1922 depict the squadron's Vought VE-7Fs wearing the squadron's Ace of Spades insignia on their vertical tail surfaces. So, it seems wholly appropriate that one of the Marines' original squadrons still wears what is perhaps the earliest example of a Marine squadron insignia as well.

On 29 May 1924, the Chief of Naval Operations directed via Letter SC 111-78:1 that the letter "M" be added as a suffix to the squadron number of Marine Corps squadrons in order to differentiate between those of the Navy and Marine Corps. [Prior to that date, there was a Marine VMO-1 and a Navy VMO-1 in service concurrently, and the CNO's directive was aimed at the elimination of any confusion that naturally could come about in the existing designation system.] Thus, the squadron became VO-1M. On 1 July 1927, the squadron was redesignated VO-8M as a part of the general reorganization of Naval Aviation that took place on that date. At this time, VO-8M was a component of the West Coast Expeditionary Force, San Diego.

The newly redesignated squadron's initial overseas station was at the city of Santo Domingo in the Dominican Republic. The decision to base the squadron in the Caribbean republic was due largely to the perpetual state of unrest that plagued the Caribbean Basin and Central America during the years following the end of the First World War. In addition to forces in the Dominican Republic and Haiti, Marines battled rebels on the ground in Nicaragua, and Marine aviation units were stationed in that strife-torn nation as well. The squadron remained in the Dominican Republic for the next six years and then shifted its operations westward across the Caribbean to Nicaragua, where it arrived

in February of 1927. For a time earlier that year, it had appeared that the civil war being waged there was nearing a peaceful solution. However, on 27 July 1927, the rebels under Augusto C. Sandino attacked the town of Ocotol in reaction to the American intervention that Sandino believed would prevent his eventual rise to power as the Nicaraguan strongman. (The rebels under Sandino took the name "Sandinistas" after their leader and would find their name appropriated by the latter-day Communists some six decades later in the troubled history of that nation.)

In response to the attack on Ocotol, VO-8M launched its first bombing strike, the first such operation conducted by the Marine Corps since the end of World War I. Five DeHavilland DH-4s and Boeing O2Bs under the squadron's commanding officer, Major Ross M. Rowell, struck the rebel positions surrounding the town. As the aircraft completed their bomb runs and began to pull up, the rear gunners opened fire on the Sandinistas. The squadron's bombing attack broke the back of the rebel efforts to occupy the town, and the battered Sandinista forces withdrew into the hills. Thereafter, the squadron continued its operations in Nicaragua until the Marines were withdrawn in 1933.

The next change in the squadron's designation took place as a result of the creation of the Fleet Marine Forces by the issue of General Order No. 241 dated 8 December 1933. This was soon followed by General Order No.67 of 20 December 1933, which reorganized the aviation assets of the Marine Corps by the assignment of all combat squadrons to Aircraft One [Fleet Marine Force, Atlantic] or Aircraft Two [Fleet Marine Force, Pacific], and the squadron became a component of Aircraft Two, Fleet Marine Force, San Diego.

The next major change in the squadron's lineage occurred as a result of the fleet reorganization that took place on 1 July 1937. On that date, the squadron was redesignated Marine Scouting Squadron 2 [VMS-2], and shortly afterward, the squadron was relocated from its base in San Diego to MCAS, Ewa, Territory of Hawaii. Despite its pleasant tropical surroundings, service in

Marines in Nicaragua
This two-seat Curtiss F8C-1 fighter was among the aircraft of VO-8M that served in Nicaragua. Shortly after this photo was taken, 20 March 1928, these aircraft were redesignated as OC-1s. [U.S. Navy photo]

VMS-2 or any other unit of the armed forces of the United States during that period was a hard life. America was only beginning to emerge in fits and starts from the depths of the Great Depression, and these years were lean ones in the extreme for all branches of the military. Pay was meager and promotions, both for commissioned officers and those in the ranks, were painfully slow in coming, even for those most deserving. Further, most of the Navy's small budget appropriations were spent on research and development, particularly with regard to Naval aviation. Building a carrier force of even minimum strength consumed a great deal of the available funding, and the ongoing rapid advances in all areas of aeronautics claimed their shares of the scarce dollars. As a result, there was little left over for anything else. But, even in the midst of this period of budgetary darkness, there was some benefit. For most of those who served, the military truly was their home, and the men who remained with the colors would form the hard core of professionalism around which the great American military machine of the Second World War would be built. However, that lay in the future. In the meantime, those in uniform were left with little to do but to carry on as best they could.

The coming of the Second World War to Europe on 1 September 1939 caused America to belatedly begin to strengthen its armed forces. Suddenly the purse strings that had been held so tightly during the previous two decades began to loosen ever so slowly. On 1 July 1941, VMS-2, still based at Ewa, was redesignated Marine Scout Bomber Squadron 231 [VMSB-231], and was under the command of Major Clarence J. Chappell, Jr. As such, it was the first squadron of MAG-23 of the IId Marine Aircraft Wing. (At the time, the scout bomber squadrons were concentrated in MAG-23.) Equipped with the Vought SB2U-3, the squadron continued to prepare for a war that nearly all were convinced was sure to come soon.

Just prior to the Japanese strike on Pearl Harbor, the squadron boarded USS *Lexington* (CV-2) for transfer to the island of Midway. Fortunately, *Lexington* was at sea when the Japanese struck. Hurriedly recalled, the carrier, with VMSB-231 still aboard, returned to Pearl Harbor on 10 December. No doubt all were shocked and saddened by the shambles they beheld as the carrier entered port. The Japanese raiders largely reduced the once neat, ordered base into acre upon acre of smoking ruins. Sunken and damaged ships still spread a thick carpet of fuel oil on the harbor waters; and fires still burned aboard the remains of the battleship

Depression-Era Operations
Three Vought SU-2s of VO-8M in flight over San Diego in 1933. The center aircraft is piloted by the squadron's commanding officer, Major F.H. Lamson-Scribner; aircraft #3 is flown by CWO Ross Jordan and aircraft #5 by Master Sergeant William Ward. [USN via Northrop Grumman]

USS *Arizona* (BB-39). Her broken hulk entombed the remains of more than 1,100 of her crewmen, and sputtering cutting torches could be seen as rescue efforts to reach those trapped aboard the capsized battleship USS *Oklahoma* (BB-37) and the former battleship-turned target ship USS *Utah* (BB-31) continued at a hectic pace. The once-mighty battle line of the Pacific Fleet lay sunken at its moorings along Battleship Row or trapped by other wrecks alongside. Only USS *Nevada* (BB-36) had succeeded in getting under way during the attack, but she had been beached at Hospital

Point to keep her from being sunk in the narrow channel and trapping seaworthy ships in the harbor. The island's air bases and air stations had received similar treatment from the Japanese aircraft that had struck so suddenly and without warning. No doubt that some members of the squadron were struck by the symbology of their squadron's insignia, the ace of spades, the traditional playing card symbol of death, and hoped that it would convey just that to the enemy. The squadron began its preparations for its eventual entry into combat.

On 17 December, 17 of the squadron's Vindicators completed their earlier mission when they were flown to Midway to form the striking arm of the garrison of that vital outpost. The men and aircraft of the squadron remained on Midway until 1 March 1942, when some of the squadron's personnel were returned to MCAS, Ewa. Those who remained behind on Midway were redesignated VMSB-241 on that date. (Three months later, under the command of Major Lofton R. Henderson, the former members of VMSB-231 took their newly arrived SBD Dauntlesses and their obsolescent Vindicators into battle against the cream of the Japanese fleet during the Battle of Midway.) On 30 June, most of those former members of VMSB-231 who had survived the battle returned to Ewa and rejoined the squadron.

Midway was to be the only combat action for the SB2U in the Pacific. It had been revolutionary when introduced into the fleet in 1937. It was the Navy's first monoplane dive-bomber, but later developments in the aeronautical world rapidly passed it by. It was considered to be obsolescent by the time of Midway, and it was quickly replaced in Navy and Marine Corps squadrons. VMSB-231 quickly surrendered their remaining SB2U-3s for the SBD-3 in early July and quickly began to get acquainted with its new aircraft. (Despite its age, the Vindicator had performed adequately at Midway and had surprisingly suffered a lower loss rate than the newer SBD-3s that had equipped the carriers' scouting and bombing squadrons and a portion of VMSB-241.) While this was going on, Major Raymond C. Scollin had assumed command of the squadron on 1 March 1942. However, he remained at the helm for less than two weeks before Major Charles J. Schlapkohl relieved him on 11 March, and Major Leo R. Smith assumed command on 21 June.

On 7 August, the First Marine Division (Reinforced) had landed on Guadalcanal and captured the island's vital airfield that same day. The field was the key to possession of the island, and utilizing primarily captured enemy equipment and supplies, it was rapidly prepared to receive aircraft. The first two Marine squadrons reached Henderson Field on 20 August and immediately joined the fray against the almost daily Japanese air raids and sea borne reinforcement attempts. As vital as the arrival of these first two squadrons was, more were needed as rapidly as they could be moved forward to the island. The second wave of Marine aircraft reached Guadalcanal on 30 August with the arrival to two more squadrons of MAG-23, VMF-224 and the dozen SBD-3 Dauntlesses of VMSB-231. The squadron's executive officer was Captain Elmer Glidden, who had flown with the contingent of VMSB-231 that had formed VMSB-241 at Midway. Captain Glidden had taken part in the attack launched by the latter against the advancing Japanese fleet on 4 June and survived to return to his parent squadron. He received the Navy Cross for his service during the battle.

Almost before the new arrivals of VMF-224 and VMSB-231 were afforded the time to unpack their meager belongings

Author's Collection

in their spartan new surroundings they began to fly missions against the Japanese. The daily routine for the fighter pilots was interception of the incoming enemy air raids. For the pilots and gunners of the scout bombers, it was alternating between support of the Marines on the ground as the latter sought to expand their perimeter around Henderson Field, and strikes against enemy supply dumps that were sometimes spotted amid the dense jungles. However, these activities quickly came to a halt in favor of strikes at the nearly continuous streams of enemy shipping that made up the infamous "Tokyo Express." The enemy convoys acquired that nickname for their regular attempts to build up and to sustain sufficient ground combat strength ashore to eject the Marines from their precarious foothold on the island. By early September, the Marine scout bombers began to launch their first offensive strikes against enemy bases to the northwest of Guadalcanal in an attempt to blunt the Japanese reinforcement attempts. Gizo Harbor, which lay 200 miles away at the limits of the offensive range of the bombed-up SBDs received early and frequent attention.

While the American attempts to halt the large organized Japanese convoys met with a fair amount of success, the near nightly runs by enemy destroyers hauling troops and supplies were far more difficult to counter effectively. The enemy would linger just beyond effective range of a potential strike by American aircraft until just before nightfall. They would then commence a high-speed run toward Guadalcanal. Upon reaching the island, the ships were able to unload their cargoes and run northward to be out of range before it was light enough for them to be attacked. The success of these destroyer supply runs led to the battles of mid-September. The squadron took part in the efforts to support to the embattled Marines of Colonel Merritt E. "Red Mike" Edson on 14 September as they struggled to hold their ridge-top positions against the attacks of the Kawaguchi Brigade in what became known as "The Battle of the Ridge." At times the American hold on the high ground was precarious in the extreme, but attack after Japanese attack was beaten back with heavy losses. With the coming of daylight, the heavy air support given by VMSB-231 and other units broke whatever remained of the Japanese effort against the Marine raiders' and parachutists' position as they blocked this latest enemy attempt to break through the Marines' positions and recapture the vital airfield. Forever after, this torn, blood-soaked patch of ground would be known to the Marines as "Bloody Ridge." The retreating enemy was harried along his journey by VMSB-231 aircraft.

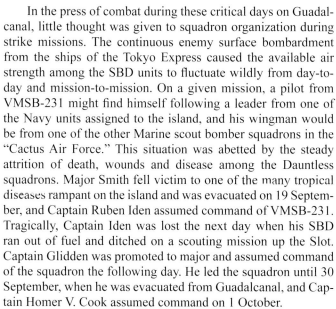

A Time of Transition
A Vought O3U-6 CORSAIR of VO-8M pictured just prior to the squadron's redesignation as VMS-2 on 1 July 1937. [Northrop Grumman]

Author's Collection

In the press of combat during these critical days on Guadalcanal, little thought was given to squadron organization during strike missions. The continuous enemy surface bombardment from the ships of the Tokyo Express caused the available air strength among the SBD units to fluctuate wildly from day-to-day and mission-to-mission. On a given mission, a pilot from VMSB-231 might find himself following a leader from one of the Navy units assigned to the island, and his wingman would be from one of the other Marine scout bomber squadrons in the "Cactus Air Force." This situation was abetted by the steady attrition of death, wounds and disease among the Dauntless squadrons. Major Smith fell victim to one of the many tropical diseases rampant on the island and was evacuated on 19 September, and Captain Ruben Iden assumed command of VMSB-231. Tragically, Captain Iden was lost the next day when his SBD ran out of fuel and ditched on a scouting mission up the Slot. Captain Glidden was promoted to major and assumed command of the squadron the following day. He led the squadron until 30 September, when he was evacuated from Guadalcanal, and Captain Homer V. Cook assumed command on 1 October.

The coming of October brought an increase in enemy reinforcement attempts. Several enemy ships were damaged, and others were sunk by the bombs of the SBDs. The bombers were especially active and effective in the aftermath of the naval Battle of Cape Esperance that was fought between the opposing navies on the night of 12-13 October. Several enemy destroyers felt the lash of the Dauntless's bombs, and those who did crawled northwest trailing fuel oil from rents in their hulls and fighting fires resulting from the hits. The following night brought the heaviest enemy naval bombardment of the long campaign. A few minutes before 0200 in the morning of 14 October, two Japanese battleships, H.I.J.M.S. *Haruna* and *Kongo*, fired 918 rounds of 14-inch projectiles into the area of Henderson Field. If there was any

blessing in all this, it was that almost two of every three of the big shells were armor piercing rounds. Because they penetrated so deeply into the earth before detonating, such projectiles are not nearly as effective in shore bombardments as instantaneous-fused high-explosive rounds. Also, their bursting charges were relatively smaller than the bombardment projectiles. Still, it was a terror-filled night for those on the receiving end, and the coming of first light revealed a sea of tangled, smoking debris around the airfield. Forty-one Americans had been killed, and only four of the 39 SBDs were flyable. This night would forever be known as the night of "The Bombardment" in the annals of the Marine Corps.

As soon as the damage had been surveyed, the hard-working ground crews turned to the task of trying to perform a miracle, patching the least damaged of the SBDs to provide the defenders with some measure of offensive punch. Others were pieced together from the numerous wrecks that littered the area. The need to do so was urgent in the extreme. One of the undamaged SBDs had struggled aloft from Henderson Field shortly after first light to scout the waters to the northwest for the enemy ships that all ashore knew were coming. The Dauntless reported eight enemy destroyers and six transports 140 miles away and closing. Another search in the afternoon found one battleship, three cruisers and four destroyers 180 miles away. Clearly, the enemy would attempt another bombardment to destroy whatever remained of American air power on the island.

By late afternoon, the ground crews had worked enough of a miracle to launch two separate flights of scout bombers, totaling thirteen aircraft, against the oncoming Japanese, who were only seventy miles away at the time. These two attacks were made up of aircraft from all the Dauntless-equipped squadrons on the island and their crews were an equal mix from all the Marine dive-bomber squadrons on the island. Here and there, a Navy-manned SBD joined in the strikes. Quickly reaching the enemy's position off the southeastern tip of Santa Isabel Island, the SBDs split their dive flaps and rolled into their precise, near-vertical 70-degree dives. Unhindered by Japanese fighters, the pilots' hands and feet played lightly on the controls as they kept their sights aligned with their selected aiming points among the rapidly maneuvering ships below. In the rear cockpits of the SBDs, the radiomen-gunners manned their twin 30-caliber machine guns and scanned the skies above and behind for any sign of the deadly Zeros, which never came. Occasionally, the diving aircraft would be rattled slightly by a near miss from the curtain of anti-aircraft fire loosed by the enemy ships as they twisted and turned below in their violent maneuvers to escape the attacking dive bombers.

As the dive-bombers reached their release points, each of the pilots' right thumbs pressed the bomb release switches on the top of their sticks. At the same time their left hand tugged the manual release handle to ensure a good drop. The long, black, ship killing 1,000-pounders and the lighter but still deadly 500-pounders began to fall away from the undersides of the American aircraft. As soon as a pilot felt his bomb release, he began to ease out of his dive, closing his dive breaks as he did so to increase his aircraft's speed as they began to jink and weave away from the enemy's fire. And then the bombs began to hit. Several direct hits and damaging near misses were claimed, and one of the ever-present Allied coast watchers reported seeing a large transport sunk. However, the Japanese were just as courageous and determined as the American adversaries, and they kept coming.

After this strike, American air power at Henderson Field was spent for the time being. There was not enough time remaining to get another strike into the air before the coming of darkness, and the Japanese were able to reach their landing areas at Tassafaronga, only ten miles from the Marines' perimeter. To add insult to injury, later that night, two Japanese heavy cruisers added 752 8-inch projectiles to those fired by their battleships the previous night, and once again Henderson Field and the surrounding area took a beating. So confident were the Japanese that they had finally succeeded in eliminating the American air power on Guadalcanal that the Japanese transports were still unloading their cargoes of troops and supplies when daylight

Sightseeing, Marshalls Style
This relatively pristine radar-equipped SBD-5 of VMSB-231 was photographed in flight over the lagoon of Majuro with a backdrop of naval vessels and the small islets surrounding the sheltered waters of the lagoon. The peaceful nature of the flight is indicated by the lack of armament aboard the aircraft and the stowed position of the radioman-gunner's twin 30-caiber guns. [U.S. Navy photo]

came. The miracle-making ground crews had been hard at it almost as soon as the last of the cruisers' shells had fallen during the night, and, slowly, one-by-one, the aircraft damaged by successive nights of naval bombardment were patched up and readied for combat once again. As soon as an aircraft was deemed to be airworthy, it was fuelled, armed, and checked once again before its assigned flight arrived to take it aloft.

Providing that the major structural members of the airframe of a given aircraft remained intact, it was possible to repair it, given enough time, but time was short, and more than one fighter or dive-bomber that otherwise would have been restored to flight was dragged to the "bone yard" near the runway. As soon as the discarded aircraft stopped moving, ground crews swarmed over the new arrival to scavenge whatever was useable and needed by another less-damaged aircraft. Occasionally, a shout of joy akin to those heard at a children's Easter egg hunt were heard as a begrimed Marine ground crewman found the object of his search. The hastily repaired results of these scavenger hunts often resembled a martial patchwork quilt as a particular aircraft sported an engine cowling from one wreck, a flap from a second and a rudder or wing panel from yet a third. But, despite their perhaps odd appearance, they could fly and fight, and that was all that was required.

Of the first three SBDs that attempted to get airborne, two were wrecked due to the damage sustained by the airfield, but four sorties were able to survive the problems of the conditions of Henderson Field and get airborne by 0700. They quickly reached the enemy's landing area off Tassafaronga and scored two hits. However, the subsequent single-plane attacks were too costly to the attackers. It was too easy for the ships' anti-aircraft gunners to concentrate their fire against a single attacker, and the Zeros that had not put in an appearance the previous afternoon off Santa Isabel were active over their ships. Four SBDs were lost along with their crews before Brigadier General Roy S. Geiger, commander of the Cactus Air Force, made the decision to halt the costly single-plane attacks. He correctly reasoned that to continue in this mode, no matter how desperate the need, would quickly reduce his strength to the point of ineffectiveness. He ordered all efforts to be made to husband their strength until the defenders could launch a coordinated attack.

By 1000 that morning, the Americans were able to get a dozen SBDs from all the squadrons present on the island into the air. Every undamaged fighter, as well as those that could be patched up to the point that they represented a greater danger to the enemy than to their pilots, covered the dive-bombers. Once again, the ritual of the dive-bombers began above the Japanese ships off Tassafaronga. Down came the SBDs, and their bombs began to strike home. The raging fires the SBDs' bomb hits left behind them consumed the Japanese ships, and a high percentage of the troops and supplies that had been brought ashore, but the merciless aerial pounding continued as the Americans threw every flyable aircraft into their repeated attacks, including the PBY-5A Catalina named the "Blue Goose," which was the personal aircraft of General Geiger. All the torpedo aircraft had been destroyed by the enemy's naval bombardments of the previous two nights, but while the torpedo aircraft had ceased to exist, their torpedoes had not. Geiger's pilot and aide, Major Jack Cram, loaded one of the 1-ton weapons under each wing of the PBY and managed to coax the straining aircraft into the air.

That was the easy part of the mission. The PBY was an excellent long-range patrol aircraft, but it was never expected to do the job of a TBF Avenger torpedo bomber, especially in broad daylight against alert and angry defenders. It was lightly armed, slow and vulnerable to fighter attack, and there were 30 Zeros prowling the area. In spite of this, Cram and his crew pressed on to the target. [While Major Cram's attack is not directly a part of the history of VMSB-231, it shall forever remain one of the most heroic actions in the annals of Marine aviation. For this reason, and to further illustrate the conditions under which VMSB-231 fought at the time, it is included here.]

Their attention drawn to the attacking SBDs, the Japanese either did not see the big patrol bomber approach the area or did not believe it would take part in the attack. As soon as Cram saw the first SBD roll into its dive, he pushed the nose of the PBY over and dived to the attack. With an additional two tons slung beneath its wings the "Blue Goose" built up speed at an alarmingly rapid rate. When it reached 240 knots, far above the safe speed specified in the design of the aircraft, its big parasol wing flapped violently in protest against the abuse it was receiving. More alarmed by the prospect of the wing separating from the fuselage than by the enemy before him, Major Cram immediately cut back the throttles and began to ease the "Goose" out of its headlong dive. As the aircraft settled on to its attack heading and drop altitude for the torpedoes, Cram selected the nearest enemy transport and released his two weapons.

As soon as the second torpedo fell away, Cram hauled the big PBY around in a turn that strained every rivet and ran for the somewhat dubious safety of Henderson Field. Initially, the Zeros had either ignored the patrol bomber or believed it presented no danger to the Japanese shipping. However, as soon as the first torpedo dropped, the Japanese fighters came howling after the "Blue Goose" in full cry. The swift enemy fighters quickly overhauled the lumbering PBY and began their gunnery passes as Cram's gunners fought back with courage born of desperation. While enemy fire riddled the fleeing American, the defenders' return fire and the wild maneuvers of the of the man at the controls saved the aircraft until it began its straight-in approach to the fighter strip on Guadalcanal, Fighter 1. Still, one of the Zeros persisted in its attacks. It would surely have made a kill had it not been for the timely intervention of Lieutenant Roger Haberman of VMF-121. Haberman was also returning to Fighter 1. His aircraft was smoking from damage received in the swirling dogfights that raged above the Japanese ships. As Cram approached the end of the runway, the Zero continued to fire at the fat, easy target ahead. Haberman simply turned into the landing pattern behind the unsuspecting Japanese fighter and shot it down, its blazing remains coming to rest just off the end of the runway of Fighter 1. When General Geiger surveyed the damage to his PBY, he launched a tirade of tongue-in-cheek threats to court-marshall Cram for destruction of government property. The general then wrote a commendation for Major Cram and awarded him the Navy Cross for his heroism. Not only was this attack among the most courageous in a day filled with heroism, but at least one of Cram's pair of torpedoes scored a hit on one of the enemy transports.

The actions just described proved to be the final major combats for VMSB-231 in the fighting at Guadalcanal. Major Glidden returned from the hospital after a bout with malaria and as-sumed command on 1 November. The squadron was relieved on 2 November and returned to the United States for badly needed rest and retraining. It arrived at NAS, San Diego on 19 November, where it stayed throughout the remaining days of 1942. For its service during the Guadalcanal-Tulagi Campaign of 7 August through 9 December 1942, VMSB-231 was awarded the Presidential Unit Citation. Major Glidden received his second Navy Cross for his actions during the campaign.

In early January 1943, after a period of welcome leave for the squadron's surviving personnel, it was transferred from San Diego to MCAS, El Toro located in Orange County, a short distance inland from NAS, Los Alamitos. Upon its arrival there, the squadron's preparations for its return to combat began in earnest. VMSB-231 remained at El Toro for six months regaining its strength, training replacements and preparing to enter combat again. This return to the Pacific Theater came on 18 July 1943, when VMSB-231 departed the West Coast bound for Midway, where it arrived on 15 August. In the fifteen months since the decisive battle for control of the island, Midway had become a backwater staging area for the coming American Central Pacific campaign against the Japanese. Many miles to the west and south, the campaign to drive the enemy from the Solomons still raged as the squadron settled into its new surroundings and continued its preparations for active combat. However, the squadron would not see the Solomons again, and there is little doubt the surviving first-tour veterans shed few tears over that fact.

The squadron remained on Midway throughout the remainder of 1943 and the first few days of the New Year, but it quit the mid-Pacific outpost in late January of 1944 for the island of Majuro in the Marshall Islands. The capture of the Marshalls was the opening move of the vast 1944 Central Pacific Campaign, and the first aviation units began to move ashore on Majuro almost before the guns fired in the fighting had cooled. The advance echelon of VMSB-231 arrived on Majuro on 3 February. The squadron's SBDs arrived there on 21 February from the escort carrier USS *Gambier Bay* (CVE-73). Composed of literally hundreds of atolls large and small, the Japanese had garrisoned virtually every inhabitable speck of land in the Marshalls, but the Americans captured only a few of the larger atolls and bypassed the rest. The task of VMSB-231, now a component of MAG-13, was to pound the bypassed enemy garrisons into impotence and to see they remained that way. They were engaged in this duty for virtually the remainder of 1944.

At first, enemy opposition to these strikes was fierce and in the first six months following the islands' capture, thirty-six American aircraft were lost to the defenders' anti-aircraft fire. For a time, it appeared as if the enemy had an inexhaustible supply of ammunition, but, gradually, cut off from any source of re-supply or reinforcement, the enemy garrisons' ammunition stores were expended, and they were pounded into virtual impotence by the continuous American attacks. [By this period of the war, the Japanese had begun using a large percentage of their remaining submarine force to run small shipments of supplies to their bypassed garrisons in the Pacific, but many perished in the attempt as they had to run the gauntlet of destroyers, destroyer escorts, and hunter-killer groups that combed the waters between these islands and the nearest Japanese base.] During the service of VMSB-231 in the Marshalls, Major Glidden compiled a remarkable record. By the time the squadron had been relieved

Author's Collection

The Iron Man
Major Elmer C. Glidden, USMC, looks on as his radioman-gunner applies more mission marks to the fuselage of the Major's SBD. These provide ample proof that Glidden more than earned his "Iron Man" nickname. Just visible on the far left of the photograph is a portion of the insignia of VMSB-231. [USMC photo]

on Guadalcanal, Glidden had made a total of twenty-seven combat dives against the enemy, including those at Midway. While serving in the Marshalls, he and his radioman-gunner, Master Sergeant James Boyle, made seventy-seven more. Glidden's record of 104 combat dives was the most for any American pilot in World War II. He truly lived up to his nickname of the "Iron Man." He continued to lead the squadron until he was relieved of command of VMSB-231 by Major William E. Abblitt on 5 September 1944 and returned to the U.S., his combat finished. He received the Distinguished Flying Cross for his performance and leadership in the Marshalls.

In October 1944, the squadron was redesignated VMBF-231 when it was re-equipped with the F4U-1A Corsair. However, this designation was short-lived, and the squadron was again designated VMSB-231 on 30 December. Major Abblitt was transferred to other duty on 3 February 1945, and Major Joseph W. White, Jr. assumed command the following day. On 9 August, Captain John G. McAllister succeeded Major White.

The squadron remained in the area of the Marshalls until August 1945, when it was redesignated VMTB-231 and ordered back to the United States to undergo carrier training. However, it was destined never to go into action in its new role as a torpedo squadron. The war was over, and the aerial torpedo had largely fallen out of favor among naval aviation tacticians, and as a result, VMTB-231 was deactivated on 20 March 1946. All the other Marine scout-bomber and torpedo squadrons fell victim to the deactivation axe shortly after World War II.

The squadron remained on the inactive list for nearly three decades until it was reactivated on 15 May 1973 and designated VMA-231, under the command of Lieutenant Colonel "Rocky" Nelson. The occasion for the squadron's reactivation was to form one of the first Marine squadrons to be equipped with the remarkable British Aerospace/McDonnell-Douglas AV-8A Harrier V/STOL (Vertical/Short Take-Off and Landing) attack aircraft. By January 1975, the newly reactivated squadron had completed its transition to the Harrier under the guidance of the staff of VMAT-203 and was declared combat ready. Five of the squadron's aircraft were loaded aboard USS *Inchon* (LPH-12) for carrier qualifications.

The following September, an additional five aircraft were deployed to NAS, Roosevelt Roads, Puerto Rico, marking the first deployment of the AV-8A to the American commonwealth in the Caribbean.

Mid-summer of 1976 saw the entire squadron ordered to carrier qualifications once again in preparation for a carrier deployment. Its carquals completed, VMA-231 was detached from the operational control of MAG-32 and transferred to the Navy's CVW-19. On 4 October 1976, CVW-19 deployed to the Med aboard USS *Franklin D. Roosevelt* (CV-42). This marked the first full-strength deployment of a Harrier-equipped squadron as a component of a Navy air wing. One of the high points of the deployment came when a dozen of the squadron's aircraft boarded USS *Guam*, (LPH-9) for a transit of the Suez Canal and the Red Sea into the Indian Ocean. The destination of *Guam* was Kenya on Africa's east coast, where the ship and its aircraft were on display as a part of that nation's Independence Day celebrations. After the sojourn into the Indian Ocean, the squadron was reunited and *Roosevelt* returned to the United States on 20 April 1977. Upon arrival, VMA-231 was detached from the control of CVW-19 and returned to its parent MAG at Cherry Point. Largely as a result of its outstanding performance during the deployment, VMA-231 was selected as the V/STOL Squadron of the Year, the first time this award was presented.

In February of the following year, the squadron operated from Fort Bragg, North Carolina, operating in conjunction with the U.S. Army during Exercise *Devil Strike VII*. After visiting the Army, the squadron returned to Cherry Point.

On 28 June 1978, a half-dozen of the squadron's Harriers deployed aboard USS *Saipan* (LHA-2) for operations in Northern Europe. This marked the first operations of the AV-8A aboard an LHA-class vessel, and while deployed, the squadron took part in Exercise *Bold Guard*. This marked the first northern

European operations for a Marine Harrier unit and the first occasion in which U.S. Harriers operated with their counterparts of 899 Squadron of the Royal Navy.

In 1980, VMA-231 was divided into two parts for operations. Det. A deployed to Kadena, Okinawa while the remainder of the squadron deployed to Northern Europe again aboard *Saipan* in August. While in Europe, the squadron took part in Exercise *Teamwork 80* in August. For the squadron's return to Cherry Point, it cross-decked to USS *Iwo Jima* (LPH-2). During its return voyage, the squadron had occasion to visit their Royal Navy counterparts at Yeovilton, England. The squadron returned to Cherry Point on 3 November.

On 8 April 1981, the squadron boarded USS *Nassau* (LHA-4) for operations in the Med. The "Tigers" of VMA-542 also were aboard *Nassau* for this short deployment, which lasted until 29 June.

In September 1982, the squadron again boarded *Nassau* for yet another deployment to Northern European waters to take part in Exercise *Bold Guard/Northern Wedding*. The squadron remained aboard *Nassau* until near the end of the year.

By the time of the squadron's next deployment in April 1983, U.S. troops were ashore in Lebanon. VMA-231 spent the next seven months aboard USS *Tarawa* (LHA-1) in support of their fellow Marines in their ill-fated peace keeping efforts.

In September 1984, the squadron deployed to Northern Europe again aboard *Inchon*. In addition to the usual round of exercises and at-sea periods, the ship and the embarked squadron visited the United Kingdom, Norway and the Netherlands. Upon its return to Cherry Point, VMA-231 stood down to be re-equipped with the newer and far more capable AV-8B version of the Harrier. Its last flight in the AB-8A version of the Harrier took place on 2 August 1985, and receipt of the AV-8B began on 19 September.

The squadron was again declared combat-ready with its new aircraft in July 1986. In early 1987, VMA-231 took its Harrier IIs aboard USS *Coral Sea* (CV-43) for carrier qualifications. Its qualification completed, the squadron returned to Cherry Point to complete its preparations to deploy to Europe again. This deployment began with a trans-Atlantic flight to take part

in several NATO exercises, and in November a half-dozen of the squadron's aircraft boarded *Saipan* for Exercise *African Eagle* during which these six aircraft completed a total of 332 sorties without a single abort. Several other exercises and operations in locales as diverse as Honduras and the Med kept the squadron busy throughout the remainder of 1987 and early 1988. On 27 March of that year, all the squadron's aircraft and personnel were reunited at MCAS, Cherry Point.

The decade of the 1980s was a noteworthy one for VMA-231 in many respects, and the squadron's excellence was recognized three times by the receipt of the Marine Corps Aviation Association's Attack Squadron of the Year Award for 1981, 1982 and 1984.

VMA-231 deployed to MCAS, Iwakuni, Japan in June 1990, marking the squadron's first operations in the Pacific since the end of the squadron's service in World War II. While deployed to Japan, the squadron took part in a number of exercises and spent a considerable amount of time dodging the half-dozen typhoons that marched in succession across the western Pacific areas of the squadron's operations. But before VMA-231 could return to the United States, it found itself at war again. Iraqi forces invaded the Kingdom of Kuwait in August, and President Bush initiated Operation *Desert Shield*. The squadron deployed directly from Iwakuni to Sheik Isa, Bahrain, where it arrived on 22 December. The route of the flight was eastward and required crossing the Pacific, the Atlantic, and the Mediterranean. The squadron was initially informed that it would see action only when the ground phase of operations began, and it would operate in the close air support role.

However, when the Coalition launched Operation *Desert Storm*, VMA-231 was in action from the initial air strikes. Its first strikes were against Iraqi artillery positions in the area of Khafji that were firing on Marine positions across the border on the first day of *Desert Storm*. VMA-231 silenced the Iraqi artillery, for which the Marines on the receiving end of the hostile fire were extremely grateful. Throughout the remainder of January, the squadron accumulated a total of 966.2 flight hours in combat, tops for the deployed Marine Harrier squadrons. This

Close Air Support, Harrier-Style
An AV-8B of VMA-231 delivers a load of 500lb. bombs on targets on a practice range near MCAS, Yuma, AZ.
[Photo via the Webshots web site]

total of flight hours bested the record set by VMA-231 the previous month, when it flew a total of 904 hours. The "Aces" were extremely active throughout the period of operations in Southwest Asia, and it flew a total of 987 combat sorties comprising a total of 1,195.8 combat hours. In the course of the missions, it delivered 1660 Mk.82 500lb. bombs, 62 Mk. 83 1,000lb. bombs, 969 Mk.20 Rockeye cluster munitions, 78 Mk.77 firebombs and 22,709 rounds of 25mm ammunition, for a grand total of 1,692,000 pounds of ordnance. Had those on the receiving end of this ordnance been aware of its significance, they certainly would have agreed that the Ace of Spades is a symbol of death. The squadron suffered its only loss of the conflict on 9 February, when a SAM brought down the Harrier flown by Captain Russell A.C. "Bart" Sanborn. He ejected from his mortally wounded aircraft and was taken prisoner by the Iraqis. After the cease-fire was signed, the captain was released.

VMA-231 returned to MCAS, Cherry Point in March 1991, and after a stand-down period, it began a normal deployment cycle. It was during a deployment aboard USS *Kearsarge* (LHD-3) in support of the 24th MEU (SOC) in the recovery of Air Force pilot, Captain Scott O'Grady whose aircraft was brought down over Bosnia on 2 June 1995.

The squadron received the CNO's Safety Award for 1991, 1992, 1995, and 1996 and was selected as the Attack Squadron of the Year again for the year 1992.

In April 2003, the squadron entered the war in Iraq in support of the Coalition forces in bringing down the brutal regime of Saddam Hussein. After the end of the campaign, the squadron returned to the U.S., and after a welcome period of R&R, it entered the unit rotation schedule again.

It returned to the Middle East in the spring of 2007 in support of Operation *Iraqi Freedom* 06-08.1, operating from Al Asad Airbase. During this deployment, VMA-231 completed 1,738 combat sorties and amassed 5,158 flight hours in combat.

On 8 February 2009, the squadron entered its 90th year of service to the nation and its Corps.

At the present time, the classic ace of spades continues to take wing on the squadron's aircraft. As this was being written, the squadron continues to support our nation's operations in the war against global terror.

The first of the squadron's insignia depicted in the plates is its current insignia, but as noted earlier, the basic design of the Ace of Spades on a simple black disc has been worn by all squadron members since the squadron was first activated in 1919. The "A" and "S" recall Air Squadron 1, the first Marine squadron.

The second example is a patch commemorating the squadron's selection as the Marine Attack Squadron of the Year for 1992. This would only be presented to squadron members who served with VMA-231 during the period for which the award was given.

The third and fourth insignia are flight suit patches denoting the wearer's status as a qualified VSTOL aviator and his or her completion of a minimum of 500 flight hours in type.

The fifth insignia is a cruise patch from the 1981/82 deployment of the squadron's Det. B.

The final example is a World War II period original. It is American made and embroidered on black wool. Unfortunately, it has suffered the attention of some moths over the years, but it is in quite good condition for a wool insignia that is six decades old.

Home Away from Home
U.S.S. Kearsage (LHD-3) is under way on a calm day. (USN Photo)

MARINE ATTACK SQUADRON 233
THE FLYING DEATH HEADS (AS WORLD WAR II VMTB)
BULLDOGS & RAINBOW (AS WORLD WAR II VMSB)

Author's Collection

The squadron was activated at MCAS, Ewa, Territory of Hawaii, on 1 May 1942. Upon activation, the squadron was designated a scout bomber squadron, VMSB-233, under the command of Major Benjamin W. Norris who remained in command for only three weeks and was then replaced by Major Clyde T. Mattison. [Major Norris was transferred to VMSB-241 at Midway as that squadron's executive officer and was killed in action at the head of his section of the squadron on 4 June 1942, the first day of the Battle of Midway, where he earned a posthumous Navy Cross.]

After slightly more than six months of training, VMSB-233 departed Hawaii bound for Espiritu Santo in the New Hebrides, where it arrived on 12 December. On Christmas Eve, the squadron's flight echelon moved forward to Guadalcanal, and the ground echelon joined it on the island on 18 January 1943. Captain Elmer L. Gilbert, Jr. assumed command of the squadron on that date. By the time of the squadron's arrival on Guadalcanal, the battle for control of the vital island had been decided in favor of the Americans. The final Japanese reinforcement attempt had come the previous November and had precipitated the bloody, three-day engagement that came to be known as the Naval Battle of Guadalcanal. The battle ended in a costly Japanese defeat, and the enemy reluctantly came to the conclusion that they would be unable to drive the Americans from the island. As a result, there was little action to be found other than support of the troops involved in the final push to drive the diseased and starving remnants of the Japanese forces from the island.

Despite American efforts to the contrary, however, the Japanese succeeded in evacuating their surviving forces under the cover of darkness in late January and early February. Conducted by multiple destroyer runs carefully timed to arrive within strike range of aircraft operating from Guadalcanal under the cover of darkness, load troops at locations around the island's northern extremity at Cape Esperance and steam away in time to be out of strike range by dawn, the withdrawal of the remains of the Japanese garrison was a tactical masterpiece and ranks among the most successful operations of the Imperial Japanese Navy after the first six months of the war. So successful were the Japanese that when some of their ships were sighted steaming southward, it was assumed they were attempting to reinforce the garrison on the island. It was only when the Americans launched what they believed would be their final push against a heavily entrenched enemy did the truth come to light. Only a handful of starving, diseased enemy troops who had failed to reach the evacuation points were encountered, and these were disposed of quickly.

As the fighting around Guadalcanal and the adjacent islands to the north across the infamous "Ironbottom Sound" entered something of a lull, the squadron's flight echelon departed Guadalcanal on 22 April and returned to Espiritu Santo where it was joined three weeks later by the ground echelon. Shortly after the squadron arrived at Espiritu, Captain Gilbert was ordered to other duty, and Major Claude J. Carlson, Jr. assumed command on 1 May but was replaced by Major Howard F. Bowker, Jr. on 25 May. The command changes continued when Major Robert H. Richard assumed command on 9 June, only to be followed by Major William J. O'Neill on 1 July.

On 22 May, while still at Espiritu, the squadron was reorganized as a torpedo squadron and exchanged its SBDs for Grumman TBF Avengers. However, it retained its scout bomber designation despite the change of aircraft and tactical mission. After six weeks of training and patrolling the waters around Espiritu, the squadron again moved forward to Guadalcanal, where it arrived in early August. Unfortunately, Major O'Neill was killed in an aircraft accident on 3 September, and Major Royce W. Coln assumed command the following day.

Author's Collection

By the time VMSB-233 returned to the once bitterly contested island, the war had begun to move northwestward, up the ladder of the Solomons toward the campaign's ultimate objective, Rabaul. The first steps toward the northwest were taken when the Russells and the islands of the New Georgia group were captured in a bloodless, unopposed assault. The move from Guadalcanal to the Russells placed Allied aviation units some sixty to ninety miles closer to their next objectives. This advance, however slight it may have been, allowed a vital few additional minutes of flight time for the F4F Wildcat to escort strike aircraft. The F4F was notorious for its "short legs," and the big, long-ranged F4U Corsair was just coming into widespread service with the front line squadrons in the South Pacific. This increase in escort range literally could prove to be the difference between life and death to the sometimes hard-pressed strike aircraft.

The next move north was to the large island of New Georgia in the central Solomons, and Marine squadrons, among them VMSB-233, quickly moved into the area around Munda and commenced operations against the remaining enemy forces within striking range. During its operations in the New Georgia area, the squadron flew from bases at Munda, Piva and Cape Torokina.

Shortly after the turn of the New Year, the great Japanese base at Rabaul was finally pounded into impotence by the weight of continuous Allied air strikes, and the decision had been made to avoid a costly invasion by bypassing it and allowing it to "wither on the vine." After the reduction of Rabaul, the long, bloody Solomons campaign slowly ground to a halt. The Allies had run out of objectives in the South Pacific, and a large number of Marine squadrons that had taken part in the campaign were returned to the United States for rest and retraining before they were committed to further action. The turn of VMSB-233 to go home came in March 1944 when it returned to MCAS, Santa Barbara. Major Coln was detached from the squadron temporarily on 20 March, and Captain Russell R. Riley assumed command pending Major Coln's return on 17 May. However, Coln was permanently detached on 4 July, and Captain Edward J. Montague, Jr. assumed command for a month until the arrival of Major Robert W. Vaupell on 4 August. Major Coln was awarded the Distinguished Flying Cross for his leadership of the squadron.

In October, the squadron's designation finally recognized its mission as a torpedo squadron when it was redesignated VMTB-233. Shortly after its redesignation, the "new" torpedo bomber squadron was ordered to carrier training. While undergoing this training, the squadron lost its commanding officer when Major Vaupell was killed in an accident on 14 February, and Captain Edmund W. Berry assumed command the following day. Major Vaupell was the second commanding officer of the squadron to die in a flying accident during the war. VMTB-233 was the only Marine squadron to claim this dubious distinction.

Upon completion of its carrier training, the squadron was ordered to Marine Carrier Air Group 1 (MCVG-1) aboard USS *Block Island* (CVE-106) where it was teamed with VMF-511. *Block Island* departed the West Coast bound for the western Pacific on 20 March 1945. By early May, VMTB-233 was again in combat as a part of the escort carrier forces committed to the support of the bitter fighting that still raged on Okinawa. The squadron's initiation into the Okinawa campaign came on 5 May 1945 when they conducted close air support missions against Japanese strongpoints in the Naha area, and it alternated be-

All Dressed Up and no Place to Go
A fully armed SBD-4 of VNSB-233 is receiving a great deal of tender loving care from its ground crew as it rests in the sun at Guadalcanal's Henderson Field in the early winter of 1943. The aircraft just visible behind the tail of the Dauntless is a PBY-5A Catalina patrol bomber. [USMC Photo]

tween support of the Marines and strikes against the complex of airfields at Sakashima Gunto on Miyako Island some 175 miles southwest of Okinawa. These bases were a staging area for kamikaze attacks against the fleet off the bloody island. *Block Island* remained in the Okinawa area until early June when it was relieved and ordered to Leyte in the Central Philippines.

When the carrier arrived at Leyte, she was teamed with USS *Gilbert Islands* (CVE-107) that had embarked MCVG-2, composed of VMF-512 and VMTB-143, and USS *Suwannee* (CVE-27) with CVEAG-40 (VF-40 and VT-40) aboard. The three escort carriers formed Carrier Division 22 [CarDiv 22] whose mission was to provide air support for the assault of the Australian Seventh Division against Balikpapan on the Japanese-held island of Borneo in the Netherlands East Indies.

VMTB-233 flew air support missions for the Australian forces in the Netherlands East Indies until 4 July 1945 when *Block Island* was ordered to return to Leyte. With its departure, its days in combat were at an end, but still had a role to play in the aftermath of the horrific drama that was World War II when it took part in the surrender of the Japanese forces on Formosa Should any of the former enemy forces considered resisting the surrender, no doubt the sight of armed American aircraft circling above them likely had a quieting effect on their potential hostile actions Its duties there completed, the carrier and her embarked Marines set course to return to the United States.

VMTB-233 returned to the United States in November and subsequently was assigned to MAG-46 at MCAS, El Toro. Shortly thereafter it suffered the same fate as the other Navy and Marine bombing and torpedo squadrons and was deactivated on 10 March 1946. The squadron was credited with eight kills of Japanese aircraft in aerial combat during its service.

However, it was among the squadrons to be reactivated and assigned to the Reserves in 1946. Upon beginning its Reserve service, it was redesignated VMF-233 and was based at NAS, Norfolk, Virginia. It was initially equipped with the F4U-4

Some Quiet Moments
USS Block Island (CVE-106) was captured in silhouette as she rides at anchor with the aircraft of MCVG-1 arrayed on her flight deck. Although the original photo states the picture was taken "somewhere in the Pacific," its date of 30 April 1945 makes it very likely it was taken during a quiet interlude in the anchorage of Kerama Rhetto of the western coast of Okinawa. [U.S. Navy Photo]

Corsair, but these quickly gave way to the FH-1 Phantom. The FH-1, in turn, was replaced with the F9F Panther and the F2H Banshee shortly after the squadron was reactivated during the Korean War in October 1951. VMF-233 remained at Norfolk and served as a conversion and refresher squadron for individual reserve aviators recalled to the colors.

The squadron was released from active duty shortly after the armistice that ended the conflict went into effect in July 1953, and it was redesignated an attack squadron, VMA-233, a few months later. The attack squadron gave up its jets in favor of the big AD-5 Skyraider, the "wide-body" model. These gave way to the A-4 Skyhawk as the VMA-233 returned to jet operations as a light attack squadron. It continued to function in this capacity until its second deactivation in 1969, when the Reserves were restructured and reduced.

Regarding the two insignia depicted in the plates, the first shown is a reproduction of the insignia utilized in the latter months of the squadron's service, the period after October 1944 when it was redesignated as a torpedo squadron. The insignia's design is attributed to Ronald Crowell, and original examples were embroidered in the U.S. on a wool background. Although it was not confirmed by photographic evidence, it is very likely that this design was adopted again when the squadron was redesignated an attack squadron in the wake of its active service during the Korean War. It would have represented a return to its early history.

The second insignia is an original example of the squadron's service in the post-war Reserves. It is rather badly soiled and may be handmade, but aside from the soiling, it is in very good condition. It is embroidered on what was likely a white wool felt background and is backed with cotton gauze.

Regarding the symbolism of the insignia, it represents the relaxed, flying club-like attitude prevalent in the Reserves in the months following V-J Day. This attitude did much to lend credence to the rather disparaging epithet of "Weekend Warriors" applied to these squadrons. The aviator, astride his Corsair, is dressed in one of the more offbeat styles of the time, the zoot suit. The "bomb load" carried by the F4U is made up of school books to represent one of the better benefits made available to former members of the armed services, the G.I. Bill, which made sure that many of these men were able to obtain or to complete their college degrees.

If an insignia design was produced for the squadron during its relatively brief service as a scout-bomber squadron, no record of it survives.

Author's Note: The author must admit to an "Oops" as far as this squadron is concerned. It was included in his earlier work on Marine fighter squadron insignia and lineage. He was unaware of its post-Korean War redesignation as an attack squadron at the time the earlier work was published. The additional history was included in its proper place as an attack squadron.

MARINE SCOUT BOMBING SQUADRON 236
THE BLACK PANTHERS
A.K.A., THE HELLRAIDERS

Author's Collection

Marine Scout Bombing Squadron 236 was activated on 1 January 1943 at MCAS, Mojave, California, under the command of Captain William A. Cloman, Jr. As additional personnel reported, and more SBD Dauntless dive-bombers were assigned to the squadron, it began to take shape as a tactical unit, and portions of the California desert heaved and shook from the concussion of the many tons of bombs the squadron expended during practice sorties against the numerous targets that populated the many practice ranges in the area while the denizens of the desert scurried for cover.

Captain Robert L. Knight assumed command on 11 March, and shortly thereafter, VMSB-236 was alerted to prepare for overseas movement. This precipitated a flurry of activity as last minute details were taken care of, and "midnight requisitioning" details from the squadron fanned out across the air station to procure any useful items that had yet to make their way through the supply systems to VMSB-236. Others armed themselves with a selection of the items on hand in an overabundance to trade the excess inventory for things in short supply. Often these men served a dual purpose. Not only were they busy trading items with other organizations on the air station, they also served as scouts to locate caches of supplies that would be of interest to the night raiders after the coming of darkness. While no specific details of these activities exist, anyone who has ever lived a part of their lives at the tender mercies of a military supply system can attest to the fact such practices are part and parcel of the life of any unit as it prepares for deployment. In fact, this exists on a lesser scale all the time. After all, one must stay in training and be ready for any similar situations in the future.

In April, the squadron was transferred from Mojave to MCAS, Ewa, Territory of Hawaii. There, the squadron had little time to enjoy its lush surroundings that stood in stark contrast to its previous station as it worked to polish its skills before it was committed to combat. On 16 April, Major Floyd E. Beard, Jr. assumed command of VMSB-236, and as summer drew to a close, the squadron was notified of its pending deployment to the South Pacific. As preparations were underway for its entry into combat, a portion of the flight echelon was detached from the squadron and ordered to Guadalcanal. It arrived on the island on 4 September 1943 and relieved VMSB-234, which was withdrawn for a short period of rest. The remainder of the squadron was en route to Guadalcanal as its detachment moved forward to airfields in the central Solomons and flew missions against the enemy on the islands to the northwest.

On 23 September, the squadron's SBDs participated in the first strike by dive-bombers against the Japanese troops entrenched on Bougainville. This mission signaled the opening round of the pre-invasion attacks aimed at the destruction of the enemy's defenses in preparation for the amphibious assault against the island, which was planned for 1 November 1943. Located midway up the West Coast of Bougainville, the actual targets of the assault were Cape Torokina and Empress Augusta Bay. The Marines repeatedly struck targets all over the island with a dual aim in mind. The first objective was to reduce the enemy's overall strength on Bougainville and several smaller islands in the area that were also targeted for capture. The second, and perhaps more important, reason was to avoid tipping the Japanese to the actual target of the assault until it was too late to shift his forces and concentrate his strength around Cape Torokina.

As the squadron's detachment participated in pre-invasion attacks against Bougainville, the remainder of VMSB-236 arrived in the Solomons. Its ground echelon and the rest of the squadron's aircraft moved ashore at Munda on New Georgia on 22 October, and the detached element was reunited with the larger portion of the squadron there on 25 November. From Munda, the full strength of VMSB-236 was added to the forces pounding the enemy on Bougainville. The assault was executed as scheduled on 1 November, and VMSB-236 added the weight of its bombs on targets throughout the area, and in the midst of these operations, a familiar face returned to the squadron. On 11 November, the recently promoted Major William A. Cloman, Jr., the squadron's first commanding officer, again assumed command and led the squadron for the next seven months.

On 25 January 1944, the squadron's forward echelon moved further northward to the newly captured airfield at Torokina. From there, it took part in the strikes against Rabaul. As Allied air power turned its full attention to the reduction of Rabaul, the Japanese initially resisted these strikes with all the considerable power at their command. Frequently, defending fighters swarmed after the strike aircraft, and the Allied fighters escorting the strikes destroyed large numbers of enemy aircraft. Hundreds of miniature Japanese flags were added to the scoreboards of the fighter squadrons as increasing numbers of the enemy interceptors fell to the wide-ranging escorts. Despite the best efforts of the fighters, however, the Japanese fighters were sometimes able to get among the strike aircraft. When this happened, the strike aircraft tightened their formations until their wing tips almost overlapped, and the radiomen-gunners in the

Nothing but Water
Three Marine SBDs are shown as they were being ferried from one island location to another. The presence of the under-wing fuel tanks on the wing bomb racks indicate this mission was devoted to getting the aircraft to their new location rather than hitting the enemy. As the Marine scout-bombing squadrons moved to various far-flung bases, this was the fastest and most efficient way to get them there. [U.S. Navy photo]

via Holmberg

rear cockpits cleared their twin .30-caliber guns for action. In these air battles above Rabaul, the gunners of the squadron were credited with four kills.

Early in February, the squadron was divided when the ground echelon was moved from Munda southeastward to Efate in the New Hebrides, and after almost three months of routine operations and boring patrols from New Georgia, the flight echelon of the squadron was moved in the opposite direction, to Ocean Field on Green Island. The movement into Green and several other islands to the north of New Britain completed the so-called "ring around Rabaul." The once-mighty enemy base was doomed. It now lay surrounded by a solid ring of Allied airfields, and barring a decision on the part of the Japanese high command to risk a major naval engagement to relieve the fortress, it would be pounded into ever smaller fragments of rubble. Even if the enemy decided upon an attempt to relieve Rabaul and if it were to succeed, the relief would be temporary at best, and as a result, Rabaul was left to its fate. VMSB-236 continued its operations from there from 24 April until 20 May when it returned to Torokina. By now, Rabaul had been reduced to impotence in the face of the overwhelming Allied air power. Its usefulness to the Japanese as a base of operations was at an end, and the only thing left for the defenders to do was to kill as many Americans as possible if and when New Britain became the target of the amphibious forces. In view of the Japanese ability to resist amphibious assault and inflict sometimes heavy casualties on the attackers, the decision was wisely made to bypass most of

New Britain and continue to subject the defenders to air attacks which would continue intermittently until the end of the war.

VMSB-236 was reunited at Munda in June and moved to Torokina again in August. It continued to take part in the ongoing strikes against Rabaul and the Japanese positions on nearby New Ireland throughout the remainder of 1944. It must have been a strange contrast for the members of the squadron who had flown in the earlier attacks against Rabaul when it was at the height of its powers to now make their dives unopposed except for occasional weak and ineffective anti-aircraft fire. As these attacks continued, Major Edward R. Polgrean assumed command of the squadron on 14 June.

From the late spring of 1944 until the end of the year, Marine aviation had little to do in the way of real contributions to the overall effort to defeat the Japanese. Certainly, it was necessary to continue the attacks against Rabaul and the other bypassed enemy garrisons scattered throughout the upper Solomons, New Britain and New Ireland, but one can legitimately question whether this represented the most effective use of the units involved. The combat effectiveness of the majority of the squadrons involved in these missions had been honed to razor sharpness by many weeks of strikes when the enemy was capable of strong and often effective resistance, but now many of the Japanese garrisons were more heavily involved fighting starvation than in fighting the Allies. To be sure, the enemy would occasionally claim an unlucky or unwary victim, but most of the strikes mounted against the bypassed Japanese were routine and boring. Without doubt, more than a few of the flight crews were satisfied to spend their time pounding a near comatose enemy rather than to risk their lives against an enemy more able to resist. And, such an attitude among those whose necks are on the line certainly is understandable, but it was short sighted on the part of those in the higher command echelons to not find more useful employment for these veteran squadrons and leave the strikes on bypassed enemy territory to be used as a "finishing school" for new units. For example, the decision to form escort carrier air groups to specialize in the demanding mission of close air support of amphibious assaults should have been made much sooner than it was. During this relatively quiet period of the squadron's history, Major Glen H. Schluckebier assumed command on 15 October but led the squadron for only two weeks. Major James A. Feeley, Jr., replaced him on 1 November, and Major Fred J. Frazer took command on 9 December.

MacArthur's long awaited and much publicized return to the Philippines served to rescue Marine aviation from their routine existence in the latter half of 1944. The first Marine fighter squadrons moved to the Philippines in late 1944, and by shortly after the New Year, much of the available Marine aviation combat power formerly in the southwest Pacific had moved to the islands. Marine fighter squadrons had moved ashore on Leyte shortly after the October 1944 assault and were ordered to counter the enemy's reinforcement convoys that landed additional troops and supplies through the island's "back door" at Ormoc Bay on the island's western shore, but the impetus for the movement of the dive-bomber squadrons to the Philippines was the assault on the main island of Luzon on 9 January 1945. The target of the amphibious forces was the Lingayen Gulf area on the west coast of Luzon and only some fifty miles northwest of Manila.

Among the initial targets of the assault forces was the area near Mangaldan that lay just inland from the southeastern shore of Lingayen Gulf. An airfield was to be constructed in the surrounding rice fields, and Mangaldan would serve as the center of the activities of the Marine scout bomber squadrons on Luzon. By the end of January, no less than seven Marine scout bomber squadrons, including VMSB-236, were based there and comprised some 168 Dauntless's. This assembly of air power came to be known as "The Diving Devil Dogs of Luzon" in the stories filed by the combat correspondents and the infantry units to which their efforts were largely devoted. The first strike in which VMSB-236 participated came on 30 January when the squadron's SBDs, combined with those of VMSB-341, sent thirty-six aircraft against Tuguegarao. The enemy used an airfield near the town extensively as a staging base for aerial reinforcements and re-supply, and numerous supply dumps were located close to the airfield. The strike proved to be an outstanding example of the bombing accuracy of which the SBDs were capa-

Hard Work in the Hot Sun
Although this photo is not of the highest quality, it shows ground crewmen of VMSB-236 hard at work repairing battle damage to the tail section of one of the squadron's SBDs. [USMC Photo]

ble. The airfield was left cratered and unusable, and eight enemy fighters dispersed around it were left in flames as well. Supply dumps were thoroughly blanketed with bombs, and ten barracks were destroyed. Also, three direct hits destroyed a former school building used by the enemy as a headquarters. If anyone doubted the ability of the Marine dive-bombers beforehand, this strike erased any reservations they may have had.

Equally impressive was the fact that the Marines came ashore ready to fly their assigned missions almost from the moment their boondockers were on dry land. Proof of this is offered by the statistics regarding their operations in the last week of January. The first squadron did not arrive at Mangaldan until 26 January, and by the end of operations on the 31st, the squadrons based there had dropped more than 207,000 pounds of bombs and expended 25,895 rounds of machine gun ammunition. Initially though, some of the Army commanders, not to mention their troops, were somewhat leery of the Marine version of close air support. Whereas the Army Air Forces rarely, if ever, willingly bombed within 1,000 yards of friendly forces, the Marines' definition of "close" was literal, often placing quarter- and half-ton bombs a hundred yards or less from American troops. Target after target was reduced to smoldering ruin by the pinpoint strikes, and it did not take many days before the praise lavished on the Marines by the Army became almost embarrassing. In a roundabout fashion, the Japanese complimented their opponents when captured anti-aircraft gunners admitted they were reluctant to open fire on "the little planes that dive" for fear of revealing their gun positions to other dive-bombers. As successful as these operations were, however, the enemy occasionally claimed one of the SBDs. For example, on 3 February, Major Schluckebier was forced to jettison his bomb and crash-land his aircraft after it apparently was struck by enemy ground fire. Fortunately, units of the 1st Cavalry Division were close at hand and reached the

Major and his gunner, Sergeant Donald M. Morris, almost before they were able to extract themselves from the wreckage of their aircraft. The two Marines were returned to Mangaldan the following day.

Operations on Luzon continued until late March, and VMSB-236 flew its last mission on the island on 23 March when seventeen of the squadron's SBDs struck targets in the area of Balete Pass, a route frequently used by Japanese reinforcements and supply columns. Over the next two days, the Marine dive-bomber squadrons were withdrawn from Luzon and sent to the southern island of Mindanao. As the Marines left Luzon, their record there was nothing short of phenomenal. Attached to the Fifth Army Air Force, the seven Marine squadrons flew 36% of the average daily number of that far larger organization's total of sorties. During the campaign, the SBD squadrons flew a total of 8,842 sorties and expended over 1,500,000 rounds of machine gun ammunition and 19,167 bombs, ranging in weight from 100-pounds to 1,000-pounds. From the first mission in late January through 14 April, the Marines averaged 116 sorties per day, or more than sixteen sorties per squadron each day.

On 10 March 1945, the Americans landed at Zamboanga on the western tip of the large southern island of Mindanao, and the SBD squadrons of MAG-32, including VMSB-236, were redeployed from Luzon to Mindanao beginning on 24 March. The first two squadrons of the group to head south were VMSB-142 and VMSB-236. The 650-mile flight was made safely by 42 of the squadrons' aircraft, and the five that were delayed on Luzon by mechanical difficulties made the trip the next day. The squadrons' destination was Moret Field, named for Lieutenant Colonel Paul Moret, who had been killed in the crash of a transport aircraft on New Caledonia two years earlier.

Although the level of combat operations on Mindanao was lower than the squadron had experienced during the Luzon campaign, the close air support expertise the Marines demonstrated there was carried over to the fighting on Mindanao. No enemy strong points were capable of withstanding the pinpoint attacks of the SBDs. In addition to operations against the enemy on Mindanao, Moret Field was ideally located to allow aircraft operating from there to support amphibious operations against the Japanese in the Sulu Archipelago, which lies between the western tip of Mindanao and the east coast of Borneo. The primary locations of enemy strength in the Sulus were on the islands of Jolo and Sanga Sanga. Those two islands actually lay

closer to Zamboanga than many of the squadrons' targets on Mindanao itself.

The fighting on Mindanao was officially declared to be at an end on 30 June, and combat operations came to end shortly thereafter. On 24 July, Major Frazer turned command of the VMSB-236 over to Chief Warrant Officer Herman E. Rasmussen and departed for other duty. Rasmussen's tenure of command marked one of the very few occasions in Marine aviation that a squadron was not commanded by a commissioned officer. However, warrant officers occupy a unique niche in the Marine Corps, and there is little doubt that VMSB-236 was well served while in Rasmussen's charge.

MAG-32 officially ceased all tactical operations on 1 August, and the group's four squadrons were notified they would be returned to the United States, beginning on 15 August. However, not all the squadrons were destined to make the journey. During the afternoon of 1 August, Warrant Officer Rasmussen posted the orders deactivating VMSB-236.

For its service in the Philippines, VMSB-236 received two awards of the Navy Unit Commendation. The first award was for the period 23 January through 15 March 1945 in recognition of its service during the Luzon campaign. The second award was for the period 16 March through 30 June 1945 for its service in the operations in the southern Philippines and Sulu Archipelago.

VMSB-236 was one of the squadrons that served in World War II that received a second lease on life in the post-war reserves. The squadron was reactivated in 1946, redesignated VMF-236, and assigned to the Naval Air Reserve air station at Denver. It continued to serve in this role until deactivated for a second and final time on 30 June 1959. It remains among the inactive until the present day.

The first insignia depicted in the accompanying plate is an example of the second variant of the same basic insignia design worn by VMSB-236 while the second pictured is the first variant of the squadron insignia. As can be seen, Captain Walter Jordin's initial design carried forward from one version to the other. The first insignia were made in Australia during one of the squadron's R&R visits there, and the examples of the second version were made in the U.S. No doubt the squadron designation was deleted for security reasons.

Research to the point of this writing have been unsuccessful in whether or not the squadron changed its insignia during its years of service in the Reserves.

MARINE SCOUT BOMBING SQUADRON 241
THE SONS OF SATAN

via Holmberg

Marine Scout Bombing Squadron 241 was sired by VMSB-231, which was transferred to Midway on 17 December 1941, bringing its seventeen SB2U-3 Vindicators from MCAS, Ewa, Territory of Hawaii, to the tiny, strategic outpost. Despite the critical shortages of all types of equipment and supplies, and aircraft in particular, in the Pacific Theater in the chaotic weeks following the Japanese strike against Pearl Harbor, VMSB-231 was ordered to the mid-ocean atoll to form the strike component of its aerial garrison. When it was realized the Japanese had not planned to immediately follow their attack on the Pacific fleet with amphibious operations against either Midway or Hawaii, it was decided to return a cadre of VMSB-231 to Ewa, where it would be brought up to full strength again, and the portion of VMSB-231 remaining on Midway was activated as VMSB-241 on 1 March 1942. A component squadron of the Hawaii-based Marine Aircraft Group 22, its first commanding officer was Captain Lewis H. Delano, Jr., who led the squadron until 10 April and was succeeded by Captain Leo R. Smith the following day. Major Lofton R. "Joe" Henderson took command of VMSB-241 on 17 April 1942.

After the invasion scares that characterized the opening weeks of the war in the Pacific passed, the Japanese left Midway largely unmolested until the early summer of 1942, with the exception of occasional brief shelling delivered by one of the submarines that periodically prowled the surrounding waters in hopes of picking off an American vessel as it approached the atoll. However, the chain of events that would bring Midway's period of relative peace to a resounding end began in mid-April. The Commander-in-Chief of the Japanese Combined Fleet, Admiral Isoroku Yamamoto, did not concur with the Empire's decision

to go to war with the United States and had counseled against this course of action so vigorously that his life was in jeopardy at the hands of the more hotheaded among Japan's ample supply of militarists who were bent on a war of conquest. He had served a tour of duty in America as the naval attaché at the Japanese embassy and was far more familiar with the United States and its people than was the typical ranking Japanese officer. He knew that Japan's only chance for victory lay in a quick defeat of the United States Pacific Fleet, which, hopefully, would result in an American willingness to accept a negotiated peace on terms favorable to Japan. Also, he realized this had to be accomplished before the full industrial might of America was brought up to war production levels. Nor was he among those who believed Americans to be a weak, inferior people unwilling to fight. As a result, Yamamoto searched for an objective that was of great enough importance to bring the battered and heavily outnumbered Pacific Fleet into a decisive engagement that would lead to its destruction. This was particularly true with regard to its carriers, which had not been present in Pearl Harbor on 7 December 1941, and in the wake of the attack had carried out a series of hit and run attacks against Japanese installations which served to anger and embarrass the Imperial Japanese Navy.

The majority of the Japanese High Command disagreed with the admiral and wanted to concentrate on continued expansion of the Empire to the south and west, believing it would be months, if not years, before the Americans were ready to meet

Bomber Leader
Just a hint of a somewhat whimsical smile can been seen in this official portrait of Major Lofton R. "Joe" Henderson, the commanding officer of VMSB-241. Although it is undated, it appears to have been taken on the occasion of Henderson's promotion to Major. [USMC Photo]

the Combined Fleet in battle. These myopic beliefs came to a crashing end with Doolittle's raid on Japan on 17 April 1942. Despite President Roosevelt's flippant response to a reporter's query that the raiders had flown from "Shangri-La," the fictional paradise of James Hilton's novel *Lost Horizons*, Yamamoto knew the strike had come from the American carriers. Although the raid had caused little material damage, the psychological effect was the equivalent of a major earthquake, and, like an earthquake, the raid shook Japan to its very foundations. This was particularly true of the Imperial Navy, and it soon burned with the desire to avenge the stinging insult inflicted by Doolittle and sixteen Army Air Force B-25s.

Yamamoto wanted to strike eastward against the remaining American outposts in the central Pacific. He believed that only by mounting threats against strategic locations such as Midway could the Pacific Fleet be brought to battle. However, operations were already in motion that would be difficult to stop. Thus, the decision was made to proceed with an attempt to capture Port Morseby on the eastern tip of New Guinea, which resulted in the Battle of the Coral Sea in early May. The Japanese were turned back and lost a light fleet carrier sunk, a large fleet carrier damaged and the air group of another decimated. It would require some months to bring these two vessels back to an acceptable operational level. The absence of these two carriers, H.I.J.M.S. *Shokaku* and *Zuikaku*, well may have made the difference at Midway a month later.

[The inability on the part of the Japanese to have these two powerful fleet carriers ready for Midway starkly illuminated two critical weaknesses in the enemy war machine. Damage to *Shokaku* was by no means minor but it was not sufficiently severe to have kept her in port during the crucial battle had Japan possessed a reasonably acceptable industrial base upon which to build its war plans. The second weakness lay in the fact that the air group of a Japanese carrier was part of the ship's company and far more tightly integrated into the fabric of the ship than was the case in the U.S. Navy. The semi-independent status of a U.S. carrier air group made it comparatively easy to shift a particular air group from carrier to carrier. So should an air group suffer heavily in action, it could be replaced quickly and the parent carrier returned to action. Conversely, the Japanese were without the services of *Zuikaku* at Midway because, while she had escaped physical damage at the Coral Sea, her air group was decimated in that action, and the time required to make good the losses among the aviators rendered this powerful carrier impotent for a considerable time.]

Meanwhile, before the opening of hostilities, the Americans had succeeded in breaking the Japanese naval code used to transmit many of the orders to its fleet, as well as other message traffic. The Americans were able to read an average of approximately a quarter of each intercepted message and, with a lot of inspired guesses to fill in the gaps, they were able to shift their forces in response to the enemy's movements, an ability that did much to redress Japan's superiority in numbers. The Americans thus became aware of pending Japanese plans regarding an objective referred to as "AF" in the coded orders, but no message identified "AF." The Commander-in-Chief of the Pacific, Admiral Chester W. Nimitz, believed AF referred to Midway, but others, including the Chief of Naval Operations, Admiral Ernest J. King, believed AF could refer to any of several other

Before the Battle
In the days prior to the battle, the aircraft based on Midway flew mission after mission devoted to search and training. Pictured here is a pair of SB2U-3s of VMSB-241 departing on one such mission. The aircraft in the foreground, Number 6, failed to return from an attack against the Japanese fleet on 4 June. [USMC Photo]

locations, even the West Coast. And King was not a man whose opinions could be taken lightly so, in order to prove his thesis, Nimitz conceived an inspired bit of deception and, using a secure undersea cable, ordered Midway to transmit a false report that its water distillation plant had broken down. Within hours, a Japanese message was intercepted and decoded referring to a shortage of water at AF. With the primary Japanese objective identified beyond a reasonable doubt, Nimitz began to plan his countermoves accordingly.

Midway, its name derived from its location almost exactly "midway" between San Francisco and Tokyo, lay at the northwestern extremity of a submerged mountain range at whose opposite end lay the islands of Hawaii. Composed of a pair of tiny islets and a reef surrounding a beautiful lagoon, the vital airstrip was on Eastern Island, and the other facilities were on Sand Island. It was Nimitz's intent to turn Midway into an unsinkable aircraft carrier, and he ordered every available aircraft to the island prior to the coming battle. These reinforcements continued to arrive until it became virtually impossible to find sufficient parking space to accommodate them. Midway became a beehive of activity, and no doubt the primary species indigenous to the island, the ubiquitous "gooney bird," a variety of giant albatross, stared in wonder at the bustle that threatened the peace of its heretofore-quiet atoll home.

As the battle eventually unfolded, it represented the largest assemblage to date of the Japanese Combined Fleet. As was the enemy's custom, the operational plan called for a number of widely dispersed task forces converging on the objective from different directions in perfect timing. The remains of the Pacific Fleet, surprised and reacting to the tempo of the Japanese dance master Yamamoto, would be crushed in detail by the overwhelming power of the Imperial Japanese Navy, if, that is, everything went according to plan, that is, the Japanese plan. The centerpiece of Yamamoto's carefully choreographed naval ballet was surprise, and everything depended on achieving it. Critically, the notion that the Pacific Fleet would act in some fashion other than that called for in the Japanese battle plan simply was not considered. To the end of his days less than a year in the future, the Japanese admiral did not know that the chance of catching the Americans unawares were compromised long before the first ship of the Combined Fleet sailed from the Inland Sea into battle.

The Battle of Midway opened on the morning of 4 June 1942. The probing American PBY Catalina patrol bombers located various elements of the approaching enemy, including the carrier striking force, and reported the enemy's present position, course and speed. Another radioed the electrifying message, "Many planes heading Midway. Bearing 320, distance 150." With the enemy's forces definitely located and a large strike inbound, the Americans on Midway hurled a series of attacks against the Japanese. Every flyable aircraft took to the air to hit the enemy and to prevent their being caught on the ground and destroyed by the Japanese strike. VMSB-241 sent 27 aircraft after the Japanese carriers. Major Henderson led sixteen SBDs flown by the squadron's relatively more experienced aviators and eleven of the antiquated SB2U-3 Vindicators followed, led by Major Benjamin W. Norris, the Executive Officer of the squadron.

The portion of the squadron led by Major Henderson found the enemy at 0755 and attacked immediately. Due to the general inexperience of his squadron, Henderson elected to mount a more simple to execute glide-bombing attack in place of the usual but more difficult to master dive-bombing tactics. A glide-bombing attack is executed from a far shallower angle of approach, approximately 45-degrees, as opposed to a 70-degree dive. It has the advantage of allowing more time to locate the intended target and to correct errors before bomb release. Its disadvantage was that it exposed the relatively slow aircraft to enemy fire for a far longer period.

Had the Marines succeeded in surprising the enemy, the glide-bombing attack might have been effective, but that was not to be. VMSB-241 was beset simultaneously by enemy fighters and heavy, accurate anti-aircraft fire. Major Henderson's Dauntless was hit, set afire and crashed. Captain Elmer E. Glidden assumed the lead and continued the gallant but ultimately futile attack. Some of the Japanese Zeros appeared to wait until they detected the gunner in their intended victim in the act of reloading his guns and then attacked. In the rear seat of the SBD flown by Lieutenant Rollow, Private, First Class Reed T. Ramsey tossed a beer can overboard. Believing the can was an empty ammunition box, a Zero immediately swept into a firing run. Holding his fire until the enemy closed to point-blank range, Ramsey shot the surprised Japanese down in flames. History has failed to record whether the beer can was full or empty or what it was doing in the rear cockpit of an SBD that historic morning northwest of Midway, but regardless of the lack of exact details regarding the beer can, Ramsey's ingenuity and marksmanship were recognized with an award of the Distinguished Flying Cross.

The Marines pressed their attacks to extremely low altitude. Most released their bombs at no more than 500 feet, but not a single hit could be confirmed. Glidden later reported seeing two direct hits and a damaging near miss on one carrier, but all available evidence indicates that, despite their valor, the portion of the

squadron led by Major Henderson failed to score a hit. Henderson received the Navy Cross posthumously for his attack, and Glidden survived to receive his Navy Cross, the first of two he would receive. Their bombs expended, the first contingent of VMSB-241 turned for home, still beset by enemy fighters, who pursued the SBDs some forty miles. Of the sixteen Dauntlesses, half failed to return to Midway, and several of those that made it back were too badly damaged to take part in the remainder of the battle.

As the surviving SBDs turned away from the Japanese fleet, the second element of the squadron found the enemy and attacked. The enemy ships had been executing radical maneuvers to ward off the attacking Americans. As a result, Major Norris's Vindicators found themselves on the opposite side of the Japanese formation from the carriers. Realizing it would be suicidal to attempt to attain a position from which he could strike at the carriers, he led his charges in a glide-bombing attack against an enemy battleship, H.I.J.M.S. *Haruna*. Again, despite their best efforts, VMSB-241 failed to score any hits, but minor damage was inflicted by some near misses. Two of the lumbering SB2Us were shot down in the vicinity of the Japanese fleet and two more ditched short of Midway due to battle damage.

Despite their failure to secure any hits against the enemy, the valiant efforts of VMSB-241 and others played a major part in the resounding American victory that would follow shortly. The Japanese were forced to maneuver radically to escape the succession of attacks launched from Midway and the torpedo attacks from the American carriers. This enabled three squadrons of carrier-based dive-bombers to reach the enemy undetected later that morning. The first SBD rolled into its dive at 1024 that fateful morning and the last pulled out at 1030. Those six minutes are among the most decisive in history. Three of the four Japanese carriers were mortally damaged, and another strike later that day found and killed the fourth carrier of the Japanese Carrier Striking Force. The Battle of Midway ended for all practical purposes with the coming of darkness on 4 June. H.I.J.M.S. *Akagi, Kaga, Soryu* and *Hiryu* had been reduced to drifting, blazing wrecks by the Navy dive-bombers, and without their carriers, the Japanese faced a hopeless task. However, the final act of the battle would not be played out until the morning of 7 June.

Major Benjamin Norris assumed command of what remained of the squadron, and prepared for whatever lay ahead. Later that same day, despite their earlier efforts and losses, VMSB-241 was ordered to find and attack a damaged enemy carrier reported to be some 200 miles from Midway. Taking off at 1900, the strike failed to find the enemy due to poor weather in the target area, and the Vindicator flown by Major Norris was lost due to unknown causes. Captain Marshall A. Tyler had the somewhat grim distinction to become the third officer to command VMSB-241 on 4 June 1942. Both Tyler and Norris were awarded the Navy Cross for their actions at Midway, but, unfortunately, that to Norris was made posthumously.

With characteristic dogged determination, Yamamoto ordered the Japanese onward despite their crippling losses. Four heavy cruisers, H.I.J.M.S. *Kumano, Suzuya, Mogami* and *Mikuma*, were ordered to bombard Midway during the night of 4/5 June to wreck the airfield and reduce the island's other defenses preparatory to the amphibious assault. At the time the four cruisers received these orders, the invasion of Midway was to proceed despite the losses earlier in the morning. However, later

Coming Home
USS Tambor (SS-198) returns to Pearl Harbor after a war patrol. She is about to turn toward the submarine base in the harbor. Fiord Island is in the background. [U.S. Navy Photo]

that day, Yamamoto realized the battle was lost and ordered a general retirement. Only eighty miles from Midway when the order calling for the retirement reached them, the cruisers began to turn away from the island when, at 0215, they sighted the submarine USS *Tambor* (SS-198) on the surface nearby recharging her batteries after spending virtually the entire day submerged. In the midst of their turn away from Midway, another emergency turn was ordered to avoid *Tambor*. In the resulting confusion, *Mogami* plowed headlong into the starboard quarter of *Mikuma*, opening a fuel tank to the sea and a resulting long, iridescent ribbon of oil that would lead like a signpost to the cruiser with the coming of dawn. *Mogami* was in dire straits. Forty feet of her bow was ripped away, and, of the remainder, everything back to the forward 8-inch turret was bent at right angles to port. Her speed was reduced to 12 knots. *Mikuma* was ordered to escort her crippled sister while the other two cruisers retired at high speed. Two destroyers accompanied the limping cruisers.

Tambor was unable to gain a firing position, but she continued to trail the damaged enemy ships, and with the coming of dawn, reported their position, course and speed to Midway. At 0700, Captain Tyler led the dozen aircraft of VMSB-241 after the enemy. Tyler led six SBDs, and Captain Richard E. Fleming led a like number of SB2Us. They found the enemy at 0800 and attacked. First to go in were the Dauntlesses. Again, no hits were scored, but several bombs were near misses that caused some damage. After Tyler came the Vindicators under Fleming. Again, the old "Wind Indicators" made a glide-bombing attack. Fleming's aircraft was hit and burst into flames, but he kept the lead and dropped his bomb. It was a near-miss, and his flaming aircraft continued onward to strike the after turret of *Mikuma*, starting fires that suffocated most of her engine room crews and

reduced her speed to less than that of her crippled sister. It will never be known if Fleming's act was unavoidable or intentional. Lost with the Captain was his gunner, Private, First Class George A. Toms. A witness to Marine's act, *Mogami's* captain uttered Fleming's epitaph, "He was very brave." Others agreed with this assessment. Fleming was awarded a posthumous Medal of Honor, and Toms received the Distinguished Flying Cross, likewise posthumously.

[Some recently published works, such as *Shattered Sword*, by Jonathan Parshall and Anthony Tully, which made extensive use of Japanese sources, state that Fleming's aircraft crashed close aboard *Mikuma* in the way of her after turret, and the wreckage around and atop the turret were debris from her mangled after superstructure. But regardless of whether or not Fleming crashed aboard the cruiser, his selfless act of heroism fully deserved the award of the Medal of Honor.]

Again, the Marines' attacks failed to score any bomb hits, but their actions had dire results for the Japanese. During the morning of 6 June, the final full day of the Battle of Midway, Navy dive-bombers caught the cripples. A succession of 1,000-pound bomb hits almost literally tore *Mikuma* apart. Through a combination of excellent damage control and more than a little luck *Mogami* survived the beating she took, but it would be almost a year before she was ready for sea again. During the night, many of *Mikuma's* crew had been transferred to the escorting destroyers, and one of the Navy aircraft planted its bomb on the fantail of one of the destroyers, which slaughtered hundreds of those who had so recently quit *Mikuma*. As the attack ended, a crewman of one of the SBDs snapped one of the most dramatic combat photographs of World War II in which the final moments of *Mikuma* were captured. She is shown dead in the water, wallowing in the

Medal of Honor Recipient
A graduate of the University of Minnesota, it is believed that this por-
trait photograph of Captain Richard E. Fleming, USMCR, was taken on
the occasion of his graduation from flight school at NAS, Pensacola in
1940. [U.S. Navy Photo]

Close Air Support, Marine Style
Armed with a 500lb. bomb on the centerline rack and a 100lb. weapon
under each wing, a Marine SBD prepares for takeoff on another sup-
port mission among the thousands flown by Marine squadrons in the
Philippines. [USMC photo]

gentle seas. Her superstructure, from just aft of amidships to her after gun turrets, has been reduced to a tangled mass of smoking wreckage to the level of her main deck, and one of her complement of Type 93 torpedoes is shown partially ejected from its launcher. Standing in stark contrast to the light background formed by the smoke are what appear to be the remains of Fleming's Vindicator, locked in a mortal embrace with the aftermost 8-inch turret aboard *Mikuma*. Shortly after the photograph was snapped, the mangled cruiser lost her battle with the encroaching sea, and she slipped from the sight of mortal man.

In the days following the battle, Admiral Nimitz paid tribute to the Marines of VMSB-241 and VMF-221 with the following words, "Please accept my sympathy for the losses sustained by your gallant aviation personnel at Midway. Their sacrifice was not in vain. When the great emergency came, they were ready. They met, unflinchingly, the attack of vastly superior numbers and made the attack ineffective. They struck the first blow at the enemy carriers. They were the spearhead of our great victory. They have written a new and shining page in the annals of the Marine Corps."

In the aftermath of Midway, VMSB-241 remained on the atoll where it absorbed replacements and licked its wounds from the battle. No one could know with certainty that the Japanese

would not make another lunge at the island, and the squadron was quickly brought back up to full strength in terms of personnel and aircraft. The surviving Vindicators were flown back to Hawaii, and new SBD-3s were received to replace the last of these obsolete warplanes. Throughout the remainder of the year, the squadron spent many hours aloft searching for an enemy that would never return. During the remaining months of 1942 and into 1943, a succession of officers commanded the squadron. Captain William E. Clasen assumed command from Captain Tyler on 4 September, and Major Joseph P. Fuchs succeeded Clasen on 15 October 1942.

In March 1943, VMSB-241 departed Midway and returned to MCAS, Ewa. It remained there for less than a month and then was ordered to American Samoa. It arrived on Tutuila on 24 April, led by Major Wayne M. Cargill, who had assumed command from Major Fuchs on 15 April. Assigned to MAG-13 under the 4th Base Defense Air Wing, the squadron would operate from Samoa for the next eight months. At the time, the conditions on Tutuila were primitive in the extreme. The spartan living conditions, coupled with the equatorial climate, served to make each day a challenge, and after a short time, many of the squadron members probably longed for the "pleasures" to be found among the gooney birds and sand of Midway. While in Samoa, Major Cargill was transferred to other duty, and Captain William W. Wood assumed command on 12 October. Major James A. Feeley followed Wood on 16 November. The squadron continued its operations from Tutuila for eight months and then was ordered to Efate in the New Hebrides, where it arrived on 16 December 1943. After six weeks at Efate, VMSB-241 was ordered northwestward into the Solomons and was in operation from Piva airfield on Bougainville by 7 February 1944. From here it entered combat for the first time since 5 June 1942. The squadron took part in the continuing series of hammer blows against Japanese positions around Rabaul and other locations on New Britain and New Ireland. After five weeks of this duty, VMSB-241 was ordered to Efate once again on 18 March.

After a period of R&R in Australia, the flight echelon returned briefly to the New Hebrides but was immediately ordered forward to the newly captured island of Emirau, which lay to the north of New Britain and New Ireland. The capture of Emirau and the nearby Green Islands forged the last links in the "ring around Rabaul." The usefulness of the installations there ended earlier in 1944 when the Japanese fleet was driven from Simpson Harbor, one of the finest deepwater anchorages in the South Pacific. With their fleet gone, the defenses were reduced to near-impotence in two months of the most intense, concentrated aerial combat of the war in the Pacific. Now, with the occupation of the Greens and Emirau, Rabaul was completely surrounded by Allied air bases from which it would be bombed periodically for the remainder of the war. The thousands of Japanese troops who manned the fortress's defenses were of no further use to the Imperial war effort than they would have been had they held an outpost on the moon's Sea of Tranquility.

The ground echelon of VMSB-241 moved from Efate to Munda on New Georgia on 18 June 1944, where it would remain throughout the squadron's days in the South Pacific. The flight echelon joined it there on 8 July. The reunited squadron remained on New Georgia through the end of 1944, condemned to life in this now quiet backwater by the movement of active combat operations to the north and northwest. On 11 August 1944, Major James C. Lindsay assumed command of the squadron and led it until he handed command to Major Jack L. Brushert on 1 November.

General MacArthur made good on his promise to return to the Philippines on 20 October 1944, with the amphibious assault on Leyte in the middle of the Archipelago. From Leyte, the Americans attacked both north and south to complete the liberation of the islands. With the return of American forces to the Philippines, much of the ensuing combat would entail operations on relatively large land masses compared to the coral atolls of the central Pacific, allowing the Army troops to maneuver in a fashion which they were accustomed by the combat in the European Theater. Armored spearheads were able to conduct sweeping movements in the grand style of the old cavalry units that they had supplanted. In short, much of the fighting in the Philippines, especially that on the main island of Luzon would resemble European-style warfare conducted in a tropical setting. A key ingredient in this style of warfare was close air support in large quantities, and despite its preponderance of numbers and obvious power, the Army Air Forces, represented in this example by the Far Eastern Air Forces, were singularly ill prepared to meet this need. It seemed to have an intense institutional dislike for this type of mission in which relatively small numbers of aircraft were dispatched to place a few large bombs on a small target with great accuracy. Instead, the Army Air Forces appeared to prefer to dispatch large numbers of aircraft, ranging from twin-engine light bombers to large, four-engine heavies to saturate an area with several tons of high explosives. Such attacks were delivered in traditional, or if you prefer, classic level bombing attacks. Experience in the European Theater had proven that such saturation attacks usually either missed the targets completely or placed a percentage of the bombs dropped on friendly troops in the vicinity. This was due to the inability of the multi-engine aircraft to employ dive-bombing, as opposed to horizontal bombing, tactics.

In contrast to the Army Air Forces, Marine aviation had existed almost from its very beginnings to provide support for troops on the ground. As soon as the first Marine scout bomber squadron arrived on Guadalcanal, it flew a number of sorties in support of the periodic forays of the Marines outside their defensive perimeter. This close air support capability, with the addition of specially trained radio-equipped ground control parties, had been raised to a state of near-perfection with the shift of American operations in the Solomons from the defensive to the offensive. The lives of many a rifleman had been saved by the SBDs of the Marine scout bomber squadrons' ability to place a 1,000lb. bomb directly on an enemy strongpoint within fifty to 100 yards of the attacking Marines on the ground.

Clearly, this was an institutional problem. The Army Air Forces procured a number of both the SBD Dauntless and SB2C Helldiver dive-bombers, designated the A-24 and A-25, respectively, but for reasons unknown, these aircraft were never employed in combat. Also, the German Luftwaffe often employed its excellent Junkers Ju-88 twin-engine bomber frequently as a dive-bomber, proving that multi-engine aircraft were capable of executing a diving attack. In short, the Army Air Forces never accepted the fact that a single heavy bomb released at low level in a 70-degree dive was more effective in the support of ground troops locked in battle with the enemy than a large number of bombs released at medium to high altitudes that fell somewhere in the general vicinity of the intended target. Perhaps, it was merely a matter of style. But, strangely enough, in Europe, the Army Air Forces had developed a mirror image of the Marines' ground support capabilities, complete with fighter pilots on the ground in company with the attacking infantry and armor, but this ability was seldom, if ever, employed in the Pacific Theater. The situation in the Philippines becomes even more difficult to understand when one remembers that the Army Air Forces sent several squadrons of the dive-bomber variant of the P-51A Mustang, designated the A-36A Apache, into action in North Africa, Sicily and Italy with excellent results. Equipped with wing-mounted dive brakes, the A-36 was capable of great accuracy when flown by a pilot experienced in dive-bombing. Also, the early versions of the Mustang were excellent low-level fighters. Furthermore, the A-36 squadrons had been in action in the European Theater for several months before the Marines began to hang bombs on their Corsairs in the Pacific theater, but the procurement of this excellent aircraft was ended after the delivery of a relative handful of airframes. By the time of the cross-channel assault in Normandy, the A-36 had almost completely disappeared from the inventory.

As a result, the call went out for the Marine scout bomber squadrons to move to the Philippines. They would be first employed on the largest of the archipelago's islands, Luzon. The landings there were delayed by the heavier than expected enemy resistance in the Central Philippines and did not go ashore until 9 January 1945. Despite the delay, the first movements of the scout bomber squadrons that would participate in the campaign began six weeks earlier when VMSB-241 was ordered from New Georgia to Bougainville on 22 November 1944. On 16 December, the squadron boarded the ships that would carry them to Luzon and departed the Solomons for the last time. It sailed under its twelfth commanding officer, Major Benjamin B. Manchester III, who assumed command of VMSB-241 on 10 December.

The squadron was to be based at Mangaldan airfield on Luzon, where it arrived on 25 January 1945. Under the operational control of the Army Air Forces' 308th Bombardment Group, the Marines initiated combat operations on 27 January, when eighteen of the squadron's SBDs lifted off the airstrip for a strike against Japanese positions in San Fernando Province. The mission was successful, with a total of thirty-six 100-pound and eighteen 500-pound bombs placed on a series of targets composed of gun positions, bivouac areas, supply dumps and various structures. As they recovered from their dives, the aircraft thoroughly strafed the area. The SBD flown by Lieutenant Edward M. Fleming made a direct hit on a large oil storage area, which erupted into a sea of flames. Smoke from the burning dump could be seen from the SBDs as they prepared to land at Mangaldan, 35 miles away from the target. Fleming's accuracy was rewarded with the Distinguished Flying Cross.

On 30 January, the Marine squadrons were ordered to provide an aerial flank guard to the Army's First Cavalry Division as it made a dash for the Philippine capital of Manila. Nine aircraft were to be in the air on call for support from dawn to dusk. The necessary arrangements were made with the cavalrymen, and the troopers jumped off at dawn of 1 February. The primary mission of the division was to free the thousands of civilian internees and prisoners of war held in the Manila area. Therefore, speed, not combat, was to be the essence of the operation. As a result, the Marines were employed as aerial scouts as well as flying artillery. When alternative routes around strong enemy positions were located, instructions were radioed to the ground. When the enemy could not otherwise be avoided, they were subjected to the precision attacks of the aircraft, greatly reducing friendly casualties and maintaining the speed of the advance. The flexibility and quick reactions of the supporting Marine aircraft were demonstrated time and again during the advance. Diverted to a more important target while en route to a pre-briefed target, the SBDs thoroughly blasted the town of San Isidro just ahead of the advancing cavalrymen. All of the Marines' bombs fell within the target area, and later reports stated that, "the target was left in shambles." This was indicative of the support rendered by the Marines that contributed significantly to the Army's success. The troopers reached Manila sixty-six hours after they began their advance, having traversed more than 130 miles of hostile territory, and among others, the infamous Santo Thomas prison camp and its hundreds of Allied internees were liberated as a result. It is doubtful if this feat could have been accomplished without the superb support of the flying Marines, and the Army commanders were lavish in their praise of the support rendered by the scout bomber squadrons.

Perhaps somewhat struck by the novelty of observing Marine aircraft operating under Army control, the war correspondents in the area quickly dubbed the Marines the "Diving Devil Dogs of Luzon." And, the reputation was well earned. Japanese prisoners later related that some among them were reluctant to fire on American troops for fear of the quick retaliation from the SBDs. The army troops quickly came to appreciate the Marines' contributions and went to great lengths to protect their guardian angels when the need arose. Technical Sergeant Andy Bridgewater went single-handed to the aid of Lieutenant Kerwin W. Jacobs of VMSB-241 and his gunner, Corporal Samuel Scheinfeld, when their SBD was brought down by ground fire and crash-landed in no man's land. Bridgewater successfully brought the pair into friendly lines unhurt despite heavy enemy fire.

The accuracy of which the Marines were capable was demonstrated to all on behalf of the cavalrymen on 8 February. The troopers were taking heavy enemy fire in their attempts to dislodge the enemy from a ridgetop. The dive-bombers were instructed to hit the crest of the ridge and its reverse slope while the cavalry clung to the forward slope. The first bomb landed just below the ridge crest on the Japanese side, and the remainder landed further down the reverse slope. The cavalrymen quickly overran the enemy and found that eight machine gun positions and fifteen mortar emplacements had been destroyed in the pinpoint attack. Three hundred dead Japanese troops manned these weapons.

In addition to its daily routine of strike and support missions, the squadron found some time for some experimentation and innovation. It was the first to use an airborne strike controller in the rear seat of a Dauntless. In contact with liaison parties with the ground troops, the experienced controller in the air was able to more quickly convert target descriptions given from a "worm's eye level" to what would be observed from the air. The controller's aircraft then would lead the strike. This led to an even more rapid response to the fluid situations in which the ground forces often found themselves. As the Luzon operations continued, Major Jack L. Brushert assumed command of VMSB-241 once again on 20 February 1945.

As February became March, the pace of operations on Luzon began to slow. The Marines were beginning to run out of targets as the campaign on the island entered its final stages. As a result, the Marine scout bombing squadrons began to shift southward to the island of Mindanao. By 24 March, the four squadrons of MAG-32 had departed Luzon, but the three squadrons of MAG-24, VMSBs-133, -241 and -244 remained on the northern island for another two weeks.

While the overall pace of operations had slowed, the southward move of MAG-32 made for a busy two weeks for MAG-24. During the two weeks following the departure of MAG-32, the three squadrons of MAG-24 flew a total of 122 separate missions against the remaining enemy-held portions of Luzon. The Japanese were squeezed into smaller and smaller pockets, and, finally, on 2 April, MAG-24 was ordered to cease combat operations and to prepare to follow MAG-32 to Mindanao. During its stay on Luzon, VMSB-241 recorded a total of 180 missions and 1,518 sorties. On 10 April, the squadron's ground echelon boarded the ships that were to carry them south and sailed at 1500 that same day. The flight echelon followed on 20 April. The initial landings on Mindanao had been made on 10 March, near Zamboanga on the southern side of the island's westernmost tip, and the squadrons of MAG-32 went ashore a short time later. The turn of MAG-24 and VMSB-241 came on 17 April when American forces landed near Malabang south of Lake Lanao. VMSB-241 commenced operations from the airfield at Malabang on 22 April. The pattern of operations was virtually identical to that on Luzon, a steady diet of close air support sorties that hammered the Japanese to ease the always-bloody tasks of the ground troops. While in operation on Mindanao, VMSB-241 flew 250 missions, totaling 1,336 sorties, but by now the end was in sight.

Operations continued throughout the days of mid-summer, but at this point, it was clear to all that the next operations would come against the Japanese home islands. At least initially, the flying Marines' part of these operations would be primarily pro-

Author's Collection

new to the Corsair that were destined for active duty. The squadron was released from active duty after the war ended in July 1953 and returned to its more peaceful existence in the Reserves.

Shortly after its release from active duty, the squadron entered the jet age when it began its conversion to the Grumman F9F-5 Panther. After something on the order of three years in the Panther, these were exchanged for the swept-wing F9F-6 Cougar, which, in turn, gave way to the fighter-bomber version of the Cougar series, the F9F-8. As was the case with several squadrons equipped with the F9F-8, both active and Reserve, VMF-241 was redesignated VMA-241. In 1962, the squadron began to receive a true attack aircraft, the A4D-2 or A-4B as it became after the mandated change in the Navy's aircraft designation system that had served it well for half a century.

The squadron was deactivated at Los Alamitos in 1963 and has remained inactive since that time. Unfortunately, often virtually the only records reside in the minds of those who served in these units and for many years, there was no requirement for Reserve units to submit history reports like those required of Regular units. After several years service, VMF-241 was deactivated in the late-1950s and has remained inactive since that date.

During its service, VMSB-241 was credited with the destruction of six enemy aircraft in aerial combat. It was awarded the Presidential Unit Citation for its service at Midway and received two awards of the Navy Unit Commendation for its service in the Philippines, the first for its service on Luzon during the period 23 January through 10 April 1945. The second was for its service in the southern Philippines during the period 11 April through 30 June 1945.

VMSB-241 had the melancholy distinctions of having suffered the highest single day loss rate of any Marine scout bombing squadron throughout World War II and of having been commanded by three officers during the single day of 4 June 1942. But, in addition, Major Lofton R. Henderson lent his name to one of the most enduring symbols of the long, distinguished history of Marine aviation when Henderson Field on Guadalcanal was named in his honor.

The insignia of VMSB 241 is an original example and represents the only design attributed to the squadron during its World War II service. The Latin motto, "*ALERE FLAMMAN*," translates as "Flaming Downward," quite appropriate for a dive-bomber squadron.

The insignia shown for VMF-241 is an example of that worn during the squadron's service in the Reserves at N.A.S., Los Alamitos. No details regarding size, materials, etc. are known beyond what can be discerned from the illustration.

vided by the carrier air groups assigned to the escort carriers to provide close air support. The strike elements of these air groups were the carrier-qualified TBF/TBM squadrons. Also, the days of the SBD in Marine Corps service were drawing rapidly to a close, and only a handful of the scout bombing squadrons were re-equipped with the SB2C. VMSB-241 ceased combat operations on 16 July 1945 and turned its SBDs over to the Navy for disposition, and the "Sons of Satan" were deactivated. It fell to the squadron's final commanding officer, Captain Armon Christopherson, in command since 23 July, to read the orders for the squadron's deactivation on 1 August 1945.

The squadron was reactivated as a component of the Marine Corps Reserves at N.A.S. Los Alamitos, California in 1946 and designated VMF-241 although the exact date of its reactivation has thus far eluded the author. Upon its reactivation, it was equipped with the F4U-4 Corsair and carried on a rather routine existence as a member of the "Weekend Warriors," but that came to an abrupt end on 23 July 1950 when VMF-241 was called to active service in response to the start of the Korean War. Although called to active duty, it was one of the squadrons that was not deployed in response to the war. Instead, it served as a conversion and training squadron for individual Reserve aviators

MARINE SCOUT BOMBING SQUADRON 243
THE FLYING GOLDBRICKS

Author's collection

VMSB-243 was activated on the day prior to the opening of the Battle of Midway, 3 June 1942, at MCAS, Santa Barbara, California, under the command of Captain James A. Booth, Jr. The squadron spent the next seven months in Southern California training and preparing for its transfer to the South Pacific. On 23 November, Major William M. Hudson relieved Captain Booth as the squadron's commanding officer.

On 18 January 1943, the "Goldbricks" departed San Diego, bound for MCAS, Ewa, Territory of Hawaii. After six weeks there, the squadron was divided into two echelons and dispatched to quiet areas of the South Pacific. Half of the squadron was sent to Johnston Island, and the other half was sent to Palmyra, and the departure date for both echelons was 12 March. The divided squadron spent six months in the South Pacific conducting more training and many long, boring over-water patrols until both echelons were ordered back to Ewa, where the squadron was reunited in late September. While it is likely that many members of the squadron suffered from near terminal boredom during their stay on the two tiny islands, -243's war had not been too bad to this point, all things considered. Major Hudson had been detached and ordered to other duties on 22 July, and Captain James L. Fritsche commanded the squadron for four days pending the arrival of Major Thomas J. Ahern on 28 July.

On 26 October, the squadron left Ewa en route to the northern Solomons, where the final assaults to secure bases for the reduction of Rabaul was about to move into high gear. The squadron's flight echelon arrived at Munda on 20 November 1943, and the ground echelon was ordered to Efate in the New Hebrides. Immediately upon its arrival at Munda, VMSB-243 began

to fly strikes in support of the ongoing assault operations against Bougainville, which had begun with the landing on 1 November. The squadron's Dauntlesses took part in missions against Japanese installations at Ballale, Kahili and Kara in support of the Marines' assault on the island. After several weeks of action in the area, the squadron was withdrawn from operations and ordered to Efate, where it arrived in late December.

In March 1944, the squadron's flight echelon was ordered to Green Island, which lay to the east of New Britain, and with the occupation of this island, the fate of Rabaul was sealed. Surrounded by a continuous chain of Allied air bases and cut off from outside aid, the Japanese installations at Rabaul, which had been battered to the point that they posed little, if any, offensive threat were left to spend the remainder of the war under the bombs and rockets of Allied aircraft. Strikes were flown against the area to keep the enemy from rebuilding his strength, but the once-mighty and feared Japanese base was of no further use to Japan's war effort. This battering continued with varying levels of intensity until the Japanese surrendered. Gradually, the garrison was reduced to near starvation, particularly after the enemy's carefully tended vegetable gardens were added to the Allied target lists, a cruel but necessary move to keep down enemy strength.

In April, the flight echelon of VMSB-243 was withdrawn to Efate, and the squadron's ground echelon was on Emirau. With the end of the campaign against Rabaul, a lull descended over the Marine squadrons in the South Pacific. The aerial portion of General MacArthur's southwest Pacific campaign was almost totally an Army/Army Air Forces affair, and while the Marines would supply the vast majority of the assault forces for the coming central Pacific offensive, the air support for the great trans-Pacific amphibious campaign was to be provided by the Navy's carrier forces. A few Marine squadrons had been shifted to the Marshalls to hammer the remaining enemy garrisons that had been bypassed in the area, but VMSB-243 was not among them. As far as the South Pacific was concerned, the Marines had run out of worthwhile objectives, and in June, the squadron was united on Emirau when the flight echelon was ordered there from Efate. While at Efate, Major Joseph W. Kean, Jr. assumed command of the squadron from Major Ahern on 13 October 1944. Major Ahern was awarded the Distinguished Flying Cross for his service while in command of the squadron. While the Marine combat squadrons were no doubt enjoying their respite from the rigors of combat, MacArthur returned to the Philippines in October 1944.

The combat operations in the vast archipelago differed from those that had characterized the campaign in New Guinea. That earlier campaign had featured the strategy of bypassing strongly defended locations on the large island in favor of assaults against more lightly defended locales. The rugged geography of New Guinea aided the United States and its Allies in that it was very difficult to rapidly shift forces from one position to another via most of the overland routes. However, a political consideration outweighed all military considerations. Not one square yard of New Guinea or any of the smaller islands in the vicinity had been U.S. territory prior to 7 December 1941.

The Philippines, on the other hand had been a U.S. possession since the end of the war with Spain in 1898, and while several high ranking naval officers, most notably Admiral Ernest

Marines at Work
This grainy photo depicts an SBD of one of the several Marine scout-bombing squadrons as it prepares to attack enemy positions on the island of Luzon. [USMC photo]

J. King, argued the islands should be bypassed completely in favor of an assault against the island of Formosa and a landing on the coast of China, the decision was made to proceed with the liberation of the Philippines. The strategic benefits of either the Formosa/China option or the Philippines were approximately equal, but the decision in favor of the Philippines was influenced in no small measure by the eloquence of General MacArthur's impassioned appeal to make good his promise to return to the islands. This meant that, while certain of the smaller islands in the archipelago would be bypassed temporarily in favor of the larger or more strategic islands, once a given island was assaulted, none of the enemy garrison would be bypassed. The entire landmass would be liberated. Also, many of the islands in the archipelago were quite large by Pacific standards, with total land areas of many hundreds of square miles. However, virtually all the populated islands, regardless of size, would be liberated, not bypassed. In many ways, the fighting in the islands would more closely resemble the campaigns being waged in Europe than those in previous Pacific assaults that were characteristic of the advance through Micronesia.

The upshot of this was that there was a requirement for the type of precision close air support that the Marines had made their specialty and the Army Air Forces were not capable of providing. While the Army had received almost 900 SBDs, which were designated the A-24, the decision was made for whatever reason, not to commit them to combat. Most were relegated to training duties in the United States or used for inshore anti-submarine patrol along the Eastern seaboard and the Gulf Coast. In addition, there were many institutional differences between the Army Air Forces and the Navy/Marine Corps regarding the proper employment of air power. The former displayed a distinct preference for strategic bombing on a grand scale and was somewhat grudging in its use of tactical air power when it came to close air support of ground troops. However, during the decade of the 1930s, the army activated several "attack" groups and squadrons and spent a fairly large amount of its scarce funding on the development of attack aircraft. Despite this considerable investment, virtually none of the dedicated army attack groups saw combat as such, and virtually the only attack aircraft to see service in large numbers in the Pacific was the A-20

Havoc series. These excellent aircraft, however, were employed almost exclusively in the low-level light bombing role against airfields and shipping targets. Another factor that can leave one scratching their head regarding the Army Air Force's apparently negative attitude toward the employment of a dive-bomber is the considerable success enjoyed by the A-36 variant of the P-51A Mustang. Dubbed the Apache, the A-36 was fitted with slotted dive breaks above and below the wings and proved to be a more than satisfactory weapon in the close air support role. Powered by the Allison V-1710 engine, the P-51A/A-36 was limited in performance at higher altitudes, which was of little consequence in its operating environment. Used in North Africa, Sicily, Italy and to a lesser extent in the China-Burma-India theater, it is surprising that its production was ended at 500 examples, and it was not used in the southwest Pacific.

On the other hand, the Navy and Marines were almost totally devoted to tactical air power. As a result, the decision by the Army Air Forces to relegate its dive-bombers to non-combat roles is somewhat surprising. A decision that would satisfy the air support requirements was reached after much arguing and gnashing of teeth on both sides. It was decided that the Marine fighter and scout bombing squadrons that had been relatively idle in the South Pacific for more than six months would be moved forward to provide additional fighter strength and air support for the Army ground forces in the Philippines campaign.

The first portion of VMSB-243 to move to the Philippines was its much-traveled ground echelon, which departed Emirau on 25 December 1944. The flight echelon followed on 27 January 1945. By the end of the month, there were no fewer than seven scout bombing squadrons at the newly completed airfield at Lingayen Gulf on the northernmost, and largest, island of the Philippines, Luzon. After a day for aircraft maintenance, each of the squadrons turned to their newly assigned task of supporting the army armor/infantry teams as they fought to destroy the Japanese forces on the island. It did not take long for those troops to come to appreciate the Marines' ability. The same skills that had made the Navy and Marine dive-bombers so effective against Japanese shipping in the Solomons made them deadly close support weapons. American ground units often advanced under the shadow of the blue SBDs in the skies above them, and many

Japanese strongpoints were destroyed or neutralized as the Marines placed their bombs within yards of friendly troops.

Operations on Luzon continued until late March, when VMSB-243 and the other squadrons of MAG-32 were ordered to prepare for movement to the second largest of the Philippines Islands, Mindanao, at the southern extreme of the Archipelago. So effective had been the Marines' support during the fifty-six day campaign on Luzon that the commander of the Sixth Army, General Walter Krueger said, in part, "This support was of such high order that I personally take great pleasure in expressing to every officer and enlisted man in that group my appreciation and official commendation for their splendid work." General Krueger closed his remarks by stating, "As we approach the last ramparts of Japan, I and every soldier under my command would be pleased to have the 32nd Marine Air Group of the 1st Marine Air Wing serve with us again." High praise indeed from an army that was, at first, somewhat reluctant regarding the Marines! Even the Japanese expressed a certain admiration for the Marine dive-bombers, albeit in a roundabout fashion, when captured diaries and statements by the few prisoners taken among the anti-aircraft gun crews when they spoke of their reluctance to open fire on the aircraft at times because of the retribution that was sure to come as a consequence.

It was the same all over again on Mindanao. The support afforded the ground troops by the SBDs was nothing short of superb and without a doubt saved many American lives. Tactical operations were continued until 1 August 1945. Major Kean was detached from the squadron on 14 August, and Captain Donald E. Coyle assumed command the following day. Within two weeks the squadrons of MAG-32 were en route to the United States, and VMSB-243 arrived at San Diego in September.

For its service in the Philippines, VMSB-243 received two awards of the Navy Unit Commendation. The first was for its operations on Luzon and covered the period 23 January through 15 March 1945. The second award was for its participation in operations on Mindanao and covered the period 16 March through 30 June.

Shortly after its return to the United States, VMSB-243 was deactivated on 21 September 1945, but it was one of the squadrons to receive a second lease on life in the Reserves. It was redesignated VMA-243 and equipped with the Douglas AD Skyraider. Based at NAS, Atlanta, Georgia, it continued to serve in this capacity until the big AD was phased out of service with the Marines, and it was again deactivated during one of the reductions of the Reserves in the late-1950s. It has remained inactive since.

The squadron insignia shown is an example of those made for a recent reunion and is identical to that utilized by VMSB-243 during its active service, with the exception of the materials used in the insignia. Originals are embroidered on wool background, while the reproductions are made of modern, man-made materials. The original design is attributed to Lieutenant Robert Floeck.

It seems that only the enlisted personnel of the squadron wore the insignia. The proverbial "powers that be" did not look favorably on either the nickname or the insignia and it was never submitted for official approval.

The author has been unable to uncover any example of the insignia worn by VMA-243. It is likely the same design was used with "VMA" substituted for the former "VMSB."

MARINE SCOUT BOMBING SQUADRON 244,
THE BOMBING BANSHEES

Author's collection

Marine Scout Bombing Squadron 244 was activated as VMSB-242 on 1 March 1942 on Midway under the command of Captain Clyde T. Mattison, who led the squadron for less than six weeks before Captain Lewis H. Delano, Jr. succeeded him on 10 April. On the day after Captain Delano assumed command, the squadron was ordered to MCAS, Ewa, Territory of Hawaii, and after a short stay, it was ordered to MCAS, Santa Barbara, California, on 20 May. In the midst of preparations for its transfer to Santa Barbara, Major Edward E. Authier assumed command on 1 May. While at Santa Barbara, VMSB-242 was redesignated VMSB-244 on 14 September 1942. This represents one of the rare instances of a Marine squadron changing its numeric designation. Normally, after a number has been assigned, a unit will carry that same number throughout its history.

The squadron remained in the Southern California area until shortly after the New Year when it departed San Diego to return to Midway on 7 January 1943 after a short, intermediate stop at Ewa, where Major Robert J. Johnson assumed command on 18 January 1943. The squadron reached Midway for the second time on 20 March and was destined to spend the next five months as part of the island's garrison, but in the wake of their stunning defeat in the Battle of Midway in June 1942, Japanese forces never threatened the tiny island again. Only an occasional submarine ventured into the waters near the atoll, and the aviators of all the squadrons assigned to the island's garrison spent many hours aloft on routine patrols searching the empty sea and sky.

The squadron was divided into two echelons on 18 August and left Midway to return to Hawaii. From there, the squadron was alerted for further movement to the South Pacific. Both echelons reached Espiritu Santo in the New Hebrides in early October. The flight echelon moved forward to Guadalcanal on 16 October and then to Munda on New Georgia. From there, the many Japanese installations on Bougainville were within relatively easy striking distance. The first strikes from Munda against the Japanese on Bougainville were flown on 16 October, and during the next fifteen days, the three SBD-equipped squadrons based there flew no fewer than 413 sorties against the enemy. VMSB-

244 certainly contributed its share. The Marine dive-bombers pounded enemy installations at Kahili, Kara, Kakasa, and Buka on numerous occasions, and despite heavy anti-aircraft fire and several attempted interceptions by defending Zeros, losses, fortunately, were exceedingly light.

The squadron's flight echelon remained at Munda until 30 November 1943 when it was withdrawn to Efate where it was reunited with its ground echelon, and Major Harry W. Reed assumed command on 25 January 1944. After spending slightly more than two months in the rear area, VMSB-244 moved forward again. Again it was divided with the flight echelon being ordered to Piva, and the ground echelon was directed to Torokina. Operating from Piva, the squadron's flight echelon took part in the final stages of pounding Rabaul into passivity and was then withdrawn again to Efate by 25 March. Meanwhile, the ground echelon remained on Bougainville.

Major Reed was transferred on 30 April, and Captain Richard Belyea assumed command the following day. After two months at Efate, the flight echelon moved to Green Island under the command of Major Frank R. Porter, Jr. since 2 July. It was there for less than two weeks before it was ordered to Emirau Island, which lay to the northwest of New Britain, the island upon which Rabaul was located. With the occupation of Emirau to the northwest of Rabaul and of Green Island to the east coupled with assaults on Cape Gloucester on New Britain's western end, the fate of Rabaul was sealed. The once-mighty base with its large garrison and strong system of defenses against direct assault was cut off and surrounded. It was ringed by Allied air bases from which it could be pounded to rubble without the need for a direct and costly amphibious assault. With the neutralization of Rabaul, the long, bloody Solomons campaign was successfully concluded in favor of the United States and its Allies. Conversely, the campaign had proved to be nothing short of an unmitigated disaster for the Japanese. While none of the series of individual defeats suffered in the Solomons were as sweeping or as dramatic as the cataclysm of Midway, their cumulative effect was even worse, if possible. The campaign

The Beast
This fine aerial shot captures many details of the SB2C-3. Initially plagued by a host of problems, the aircraft was subjected to scores of changes that eventually made it a serviceable, not altogether popular, weapon, but virtually none of the squadrons that had the opportunity to operate both the SBD and the SB2C preferred the latter aircraft. [USMC photo]

had consumed ships, men and aircraft at an alarming rate. Further, due to limited Japanese industrial capacity, each loss was successively more difficult to replace than the one that preceded it. Air group after air group was withdrawn from their parent carriers and sent to bases in the islands. There, they were ground to bits by the increasing weight of the allied offensives, each of which was spearheaded by increasing numbers of higher quality aircraft manned by better trained crews. Admiral King's strategy to turn the Solomons into a vast sinkhole for Japanese naval and air power had worked to the fullest extent possible. In particular, the enemy's naval air arm would never recover from its losses suffered in the Solomons. When the Japanese finally realized the futility of further resistance in the Solomons, it was too late.

The aircraft of VMSB-244 departed Emirau on 24 June and returned to Munda. After three months there, the squadron was on the move again, moving forward to Green Island where it operated until December. While there, Major Porter was transferred to another assignment, and Major John L. Dexter assumed command on 17 December 1944. During the squadron's stay on Green Island, the long-awaited American return to the Philippines commenced. As events unfolded, the Army Air Forces proved unable to furnish air support in the quantities needed by the ground troops. As a result, the decision was made to augment the available support with many of the large number of relatively underemployed Marine squadrons in the South Pacific. Among these units was VMSB-244. The squadron was one of the component units of MAG-32 that moved to the Philippines to provide close air support for the army units engaged in the campaign to liberate the Islands from the yoke of Japanese oppression. As a component of MAG-32, the squadron's operations paralleled those of its sister squadron, VMSB-243.

Under the command of Major Vance H. Hudgins since 20 December, the "Banshees" were the last of the scout bomber squadrons of MAG-32 to arrive in the Philippines, but it was

soon heavily involved in its full share of missions. In addition to supporting army units, many sorties were flown on behalf of the native guerrilla army that had grown into a formidable force in the wake of the Japanese occupation. The guerrillas had inflicted a steady stream of casualties and damage on the Japanese, but, like all irregular forces, the Filipinos were not equipped with the heavy, crew-served weapons required to conduct more than hit-and-run raids and ambushes. When the Filipino forces began to conduct open combat operations after the American assault, air support became their substitute for conventional artillery and mortars. The squadron's efforts to support the guerrillas on 12 February 1945 drew particular praise from the leaders of the irregular forces when eighteen aircraft of VMSB-244 provided an extremely destructive attack for the aid of the guerrillas in the area of Bokod-Ambulac in northern Luzon.

During the latter part of the squadron's stay on Luzon, it was transferred from MAG-32 to MAG-24. As a component of MAG-24, VMSB-244 was among the last of the Marine scout bomber squadrons to leave Luzon for Mindanao in the southern reaches of the Archipelago. The "Banshees" did not depart for operations there until 22 April 1945. Soon after its arrival on Mindanao, VMSB-244 found itself again heavily engaged in the support of Army tank/infantry units. There was a short break in the tempo of operations for the squadron that began on 19 May when its SBDs were replaced with the Curtiss SB2C-4 Helldiver. On that date, the squadron received thirteen of the controversial aircraft. The SB2C had been dubbed "the Beast" by the Navy scout bomber squadrons that had been equipped with it. Upon its initial acceptance by the navy, the new aircraft had been beset by a host of problems ranging from structural weakness of the design itself to poor manufacturing quality. At one point, serious consideration was given by the Navy to the cancellation of the entire production of the aircraft, but by this time, the Helldiver program has acquired a life of its own. Three factories, includ-

Banshees at Work
This pair of SB2C-4s of VMSB-244 is in flight above the Philippines island of Mindanao on 12 June 1945. [USMC photo]

ing Canadian Car and Foundry in Montreal, had geared up to produce the Beast, and it was believed that it would be virtually impossible to cancel the SB2C. Perhaps the two major factors driving the requirement to phase out the Dauntless was that production of the SBD ended on 21 July 1944, and many of those remaining in service were growing more war weary with each sortie. Gradually a sufficient number of the bugs in the SB2C were corrected for the program to proceed. The "Beast" never received the affection of its crews that was afforded the SBD, but it was capable of carrying a heavier offensive weapons load and was faster than the Dauntless and was, theoretically at least, the superior weapon.

After a short period to become familiar with their new mount, the "Banshees" were back in action. The Mindanao campaign was officially concluded on 30 June, but scattered fighting and air support missions continued for some time after that date. But, by mid-July, the Marines had run out of worthwhile targets, and a realignment of Marine aviation assets was underway for the anticipated amphibious assault on the Japanese home islands. On 16 July, two of the three squadrons of MAG-24, VMSB-133 and VMSB-241, were deactivated, leaving VMSB-244 as the only tactical unit of MAG-24.

The squadron remained in the Philippines until after the Japanese surrender. It then returned to the United States where it was deactivated on 10 June 1946 and has remained inactive since that date.

For its service in the Philippines, VMSB-244 was twice awarded the Navy Unit Commendation. The first award was for service on Luzon and covered the period 23 January through 10 April 1945. The second award was for service in the southern Philippines and covered the period 11 April through 30 June 1945. In addition, the squadron was credited with three victories in aerial combat with Japanese aircraft during its service in the Solomons.

The insignia on the left above is a reproduction of its insignia that is available from a number of militaria dealers. This second example matches exactly to an illustration of the squadron's insignia that appeared in the publication "NAVAL AVIATION NEWS." Apparently, VMSB-244 made some changes to the basic design at some point during its service, but the exact date and reasons for the change remain a mystery.

The insignia on the right above is of the first design of the "Bombing Banshees," the stark, black and white hooded skull clutching a bomb in its teeth is an original example. The white portions on the insignia are embroidered on a black wool background. The design is attributed to Lieutenant Charles G. Fink, and original examples were embroidered on a black wool background during a period of R&R in Australia.

MARINE SCOUT BOMBING SQUADRON 245, THE RED MOUSIE SQUADRON

Author's Collection

A Sea-going Taxi Service
U.S.S. Copahee (CVE-12) pictured in her most frequent role as an aircraft ferry for the delivery of aircraft to the forward areas of the Pacific in this mid-1944 photograph. Her flight deck is crammed with at least four different aircraft types: from bow to stern; F6F Hellcats, SB2C Helldivers, F4U Corsairs and TBM Avengers. [U.S. Navy Photo]

VMSB-245 was activated at MCAS, El Toro, California on 1 July 1943 under the command of Major Richard L. Blain, who led the squadron until Major Julian F. Acers superseded him on 25 August. The squadron spent most of the remainder of 1943 in training at El Toro, but it was alerted for movement just before Christmas, and on 31 December, it departed the West Coast for MCAS, Ewa, Territory of Hawaii. Before the squadron could begin to unpack, it was ordered to Midway, where it arrived on 5 January 1944, and upon its arrival there, VMSB-245 was assigned to the island's garrison. During its stay on the tiny atoll, the squadron continued its training and flew many no doubt boring hours of patrol missions searching for an enemy that would never return to the waters around the island. After almost three months amid the sand and gooney birds of the "paradise" that is Midway, the squadron was ordered back to Ewa in 1 April.

After a month in Hawaii, the squadron boarded USS *Copahee* (CVE-12) on 5 May for transport to the Central Pacific. After slightly more than a week aboard the cramped little escort carrier, the squadron arrived at Majuro in the Marshalls on 13 May 1944. Its stay at Majuro was short, and the squadron was transferred to Makin in the Gilberts before the end of the month. After setting up shop on Makin, VMSB-245 began to take part in strikes against bypassed Japanese garrisons in the Marshalls. During the squadron's stay on Makin, Major Robert F. Halladay assumed command on 24 September, and the following month, the squadron returned to Majuro in order to place additional enemy garrisons in the islands within range of its aircraft. The enemy continued to feel the sting of the squadron's SBDs throughout the remainder of 1944 and the early months of 1945 until

its base of operations was shifted to Ulithi in the Palaus on 15 March 1945. On 15 July, Major John E. Bell assumed command of VMSB-245 on 15 July 1945, and the squadron continued to operate from Ulithi against the many bypassed enemy garrisons in the area until the end of hostilities against Japan. Shortly after the war's end, the squadron returned to the United States and was deactivated on 17 November 1945, and it has remained inactive since that date.

Regarding, the squadron insignia in the plate, the one pictured above is an original example of the Red Mousie insignia. It is silk-screened on heavy canvas and is much larger than most insignia of this period, measuring almost 6 ½ inches in diameter. Perhaps this example was made to be worn on the back of a flight jacket rather than the usual location on the right breast. The smaller is a reproduction that was made for a recent squadron reunion. These represent the second design worn by VMSB-245. Originally, the squadron insignia consisted of a bulldog wearing a red jersey, carrying a twin-barreled machine gun and riding a falling bomb. Both designs were drawn by the Disney Studios, but the second design was adopted at the insistence of the commanding officer in honor of his wife, whom he called his "little red mouse." Apparently, the squadron members were not happy with the second design and chose not to wear it outside the squadron area.

Author's Collection   *via Holmberg*

MARINE ATTACK SQUADRON 311,

THE TOMCATS

A.K.A., THE WILLIE LOVERS; THE PANTHER PACK (KOREA);

HELL'S BELLES (WORLD WAR II)

Author's Collection

VMF-311 was activated at MCAS, Cherry Point, North Carolina on 1 December 1942, under the command of Major Ralph K. Rottet, and after receiving its initial complement of Grumman F4F-4 Wildcats, it commenced training. Not long after that, the squadron was relocated to MCAS, Parris Island, South Carolina, on 18 April 1943 to help to relieve the crowding at Cherry Point, which, at the time, was the largest Marine aviation facility on the East Coast, if not in the entire Marine Corps. In the interim, however, VMF-311, like so many others during this hectic period, underwent a rapid turnover in command. Major Rottet was transferred, and Lieutenant Harry B. Woodman became the temporary commanding officer on 1 February 1943. Lieutenant Roy A. Neuendorf commanded the squadron from 5-15 February and was followed by Lieutenant Michael J. Curran, Jr. on 16 February. After ten days, Captain Jack D. Kane assumed command on 27 February and set a new record for tenure by remaining in command through 31 May 1943. He was succeeded by Major Harry B. Hooper, Jr. on 1 June and was followed by now Major Jack Kane from 6 July through 31 August. During the period 1 through 13 September, Major Robert L. Anderson commanded the squadron and was succeeded by Major Hooper again on 13 September 1943. While frequent command changes during wartime is nothing unusual, eight commanding officers in 7 ½ months may approach a record.

Shortly after its arrival at its new station, VMF-311 exchanged its F4Fs for the Vought F4U-1 Corsair and continued training with its new mount. After slightly less than five months at Parris Island, the squadron was ordered to prepare for overseas movement, and it departed the East Coast for MCAS, Miramar on 31 August. Almost immediately after its arrival on the West Coast, the squadron its personnel and aircraft were loaded aboard ship in San Diego and sailed for the Central Pacific in early September. Its destination was Pago Pago in Samoa.

After a brief stay on Pago Pago, VMF-311 moved to Wallis Island. Its flight echelon arrived there on 8 October, and the ground echelon arrived by ship on 19 October. The buildup of Marine aviation assets in the area was in anticipation of the coming amphibious assaults against the Gilberts, scheduled for November, and the Marshalls soon after the New Year. These moves were to mark the beginning of the great American Central Pacific offensive that, in the space of little more than a year, would drive the Japanese westward across vast distances to the very gates of the Empire itself. The squadrons waiting in the Samoa area were to form part of the garrisons of the newly captured atolls and suppress Japanese forces on bypassed islands by bombing and strafing the enemy until these cutoff locales were reduced to impotence.

The Gilberts fell to the Americans in November after a brief but very bloody assault, and in late January 1944, it was the turn of the Marshalls. The Americans learned a great deal from the bitter, costly Tarawa operation in the Gilberts, and these hard-won lessons were absorbed quickly and applied to the offensive in the Marshalls. The targeted atolls in these islands fell quickly and at a considerably lower cost to the attackers. VMF-311 moved from Wallis to Roi, one of the principal islands of Kwajalein Atoll and immediately began operations against other islands in the group still held by the Japanese. Located at the northern extremity of the atoll, Roi was home to the squadron

Okinawa Bound
Some of the cannon-armed F4U-1Cs of VMF-311 are pictured lashed down on the flight deck of USS Sitkoh Bay (CVE-86) en route to Okinawa. Note the wooden clamps used to prevent damage to the ailerons in case of high winds. [USMC Photo]

for two weeks before it moved to Kwajalein Island at the atoll's southern tip. After approximately a month there, VMF-311 returned once again to Roi.

On 30 July, the squadron suffered its first loss attributed to enemy action when the Corsair flown by Captain Michael J. Curran, Jr. was hit by enemy anti-aircraft fire while engaged in a strike against Wotje. Curran's aircraft was seen trailing smoke as it crashed into the sea approximately 500 yards off the beach, and despite repeated radio calls, Curran made no visible attempt to abandon his stricken fighter, and it is likely he was killed or disabled by the first enemy rounds to find their target.

The squadron spent the remainder of 1944 in the Marshalls pounding the bypassed Japanese garrisons on Wotje, Maloelap, Mille and Jaluit. At first, each strike was greeted by fierce resistance as the enemy gunners below filled the sky with the black puffs of heavy anti-aircraft rounds and shifting webs of tracers from the lighter weapons. Gradually however, enemy resistance weakened as ammunition supplies began to run short and, guns were destroyed, or their crews were felled by the bombs and strafing attacks. After a few weeks, the attacks became little more than "milk runs", as the enemy's ability to resist grew weaker with each passing day. Despite the lessening resistance offered by the Japanese, however, the Marines learned, sometimes to their cost, that the enemy below was still a dangerous foe ready to claim the unwary or the careless. During the squadron's stay in the Marshalls, Major Charles M. Kunz assumed command on 24 October 1944.

While VMF-311 was in the Marshalls, it was one of several Corsair-equipped Marine squadrons visited by Charles A. Lindbergh, and he flew several missions with them. He demonstrated the tremendous potential of the big gull-winged fighter as a fighter-bomber when he hauled 1,000lb. and then 2,000lb. bombs aloft and then deposited them on the nearest Japanese positions. Following Lindbergh's lead, VMF-311 and the other Marine fighter squadrons in the Marshalls increasingly began to use the Corsair in the strike role. VMF-311 also was one of the squadrons involved in the tests of the Corsair's accuracy as a dive-bombing platform when compared to the standard Marine scout bomber of the day, the SBD. These tests showed little practical differences in the bombing accuracy of which each aircraft was capable when flown by well-trained aviators, and the F4U had much to recommend it as a dual-purpose aircraft.

By the end of 1944, the Marine squadrons had reduced the remaining Japanese installations in the Marshalls area to little more than collections of rubble. The expenditure of more bombs against would serve little more than to reduce the rubble to dust,

and in view of this, the squadrons began to reduce and then to cease operations against what remained of the enemy installations within the atoll. Some units were withdrawn to Hawaii or to the West Coast while others remained in the area marking time and flying boring patrol missions and the occasional strike while waiting for orders to move forward to more active operational areas. VMF-311, commanded by Major Perry Shuman since 11 February 1945, was among the latter and remained in the Marshalls until the squadron and the others of MAG-31 were ordered to Okinawa. The Group's aircraft and personnel were loaded aboard the CVEs USS *Sitkoh Bay* (CVE-86) and USS *Breton* (CVE-23) for movement by sea to Okinawa, where they were to operate from Yontan airfield on the island. The little carriers arrived off the island on 6 April 1945.

As fate or luck would have it, on that morning, the new, cannon-armed F4U-1Cs of VMF-311 were among the first to be catapulted from the escort carriers and took station above the ships to act as their combat air patrol, or CAP. As this was taking

Before...
USS Laffey (DD-724) pictured as she appeared before her ordeal off Okinawa on 16 April 1945. It appears she had just backed her engines full because of the prop wash amidships. [U.S. Navy Photo]

place, the first and largest of the large, coordinated Kamikaze attacks of the Okinawa campaign struck the masses of shipping off the island. Suddenly, ten miles from the two CVEs, a twin-engine Kawasaki Ki-48 Japanese Army bomber, code-named "Lilly," was sighted low on the water on a course straight for *Sitkoh Bay* and *Breton*. The ships immediately began to maneuver radically and took the attacker under heavy fire. Overhead, the Corsairs of VMF-311 dived after the kamikaze. The ships' anti-aircraft fire seemed to have little or no effect on the enemy aircraft, and the Corsairs of VMF-311 plunged through the flak and closed on the enemy. They immediately began to rake the "Lilly" with 20-mm. rounds, and it caught fire from hits in both its engines, the fuselage and nose, but despite the heavy damage inflicted on his aircraft, the Japanese pilot never wavered from his attack as he singled out *Sitkoh Bay* as his intended victim. Suddenly, the right wing, weakened by the Corsairs' fire, tore away, and the "Lilly" cart wheeled into the sea in a blinding splash of fire and spray a mere fifty yards from the CVE. Captain Ralph G. McCormick and Lieutenant John J. Doherty shared credit for the destruction of the Kamikaze, and their victim was the first of the 71 kills credited to VMF-311 while operating in the Okinawa area. Both aviators were awarded the Distinguished Flying Cross and credited with saving the CVE from heavy damage, if not destruction.

On 16 April, the third massed suicide attack struck the ships off the island. VMF-311 shared credit with VMF-441 for saving the destroyer USS *Laffey* (DD-724) from certain destruction at the hands of the Kamikazes, but each lost a Corsair and its pilot as the result of a mid-air collision as they maneuvered to take the same enemy aircraft under fire. *Laffey* was reduced to little more than a battered wreck by multiple hits from the suicide aircraft, but, with the aid of the Marines, she claimed several of her attackers. She survived the heavy damage inflicted upon her, was repaired and continued to serve after the end of the war against Japan. Later she was modernized in the FRAM program of the 1960s and served well into the '70s. [*Laffey* operated in company with the author's ship in the Mediterranean in 1969.]

The next good day of shooting for the squadron was 27 April when it was credited with thirteen kills. A week later, VMF-311 had its best single day when it was credited with the destruction of seventeen enemy aircraft. Six of these fell to the

via Holmberg

squadron's Corsairs during a morning CAP mission. Eleven more were claimed during the dusk CAP when the Marines ran into a flock of Kamikazes. In the wild fight that followed, eight Japanese fighters and three reconnaissance aircraft-turned-Kamikazes were shot down. Four of the enemy fell to the guns of the Corsair of Lieutenant William F. Brown, and Lieutenant Roland T. Hamner destroyed three more. Both aviators received the Distinguished Flying Cross for the day's action. The heavy punch packed by the four 20mm cannons of the -1C model of the Corsair were proving to be especially effective in dismantling the lightly constructed Japanese aircraft because, even if the kamikaze was turned into a fireball, it was unlikely to be deflected from its trajectory unless its airframe was destroyed.

While the half-dozen or so massed suicide attacks the Japanese sent against the fleet gathered in the waters off Okinawa drew the most public attention, rarely a day passed without a nearly continuous stream of small raids lunging at the ships in

Author's Collection   *Author's Collection*   *via Holmberg*

the area. Often a series of single plane raids sniffed around the periphery of the massed amphibious shipping and radar picket destroyers like rabid wolves looking for the opportunity to pounce upon the unwary or the weak. A damaged or burning vessel attracted more Japanese aircraft in the same manner that a magnet attracts iron filings. In many ways these small attacks proved to be more costly and difficult to counter than the massed raids. Low cloud, mist, and fog are prevalent in the waters surrounding the Ryukus during the spring, and the weather provided ample cover for these small numbers of enemy aircraft. The radar technology of the day lacked the precision of more current sets, and the ranges and bearings provided were no more than relatively accurate approximations of the target's location and was not capable of accurately determining a target's altitude. As a result, the intercepting American fighters, which also lacked airborne radar of their own, were left to grope blindly in the murky conditions for the enemy. Added to the frustration felt by the aviators at this game of cloud shielded hide-and-seek was the knowledge that many of the gunners on the ships under attack were most likely to shoot first and then attempt to identify the target's remains if and when they could be located.

As the Okinawa fighting dragged on toward its bloody conclusion in early June, VMF-311 and most of the other Marine squadrons in the area began to fly missions against the southernmost of the Japanese home islands, Kyushu. The squadron continued these strikes until the Japanese surrender, and Major Michael R. Yunck assumed command on 15 June, the first of Yunck's eventual three tours in command of the squadron. Major Shuman received two awards of the Distinguished Flying Cross during his tour of command of the squadron.

VMF-311 was credited with seventy-one kills, which ranked second only to the "Death Rattlers" of VMF-323 in the number of victories scored in the Okinawa area. In addition, the squadron was awarded the Presidential Unit Citation for its service during the Okinawa-Ryukyus campaign for the period 7 April through 14 July 1945.

After the surrender of Japan, VMF-311 was ordered there as part of the American occupation forces. It remained in the Far East for nearly a year until it was ordered to San Diego, where it arrived on 4 July 1946. From San Diego, the squadron moved to

Miramar the following day. After less than two weeks, VMF-311 was reduced to cadre status of one officer, Lieutenant Rupert C. Wesley, Jr. With perfect military logic, Lieutenant Wesley was designated the commanding officer of VMF-311, in command of himself. After a short stay at Miramar, VMF-311 was ordered to MCAS, El Toro. After Wesley's arrival there, new personnel began to report to rebuild the squadron's ranks. It must be remembered that the vast majority of those who served in the armed forces of the United States during World War II were reserves whose term of service was "for the duration." To replace the departed reservists, a significant number of those ordered to VMF-311 were Regular aviators whose previous service had been in one of the deactivated scout bomber or torpedo squadrons or one of the multi-engine transport or bombing squadrons. No doubt these aviators found their first flight in the Corsair was quite an experience compared to the far more docile aircraft they had flown previously.

The squadron's assignment to the occupation forces undoubtedly played a part in its remaining in an active status when so many of its sister squadrons from the war years were deactivated with great haste almost as soon as the shooting stopped. For the first time since its activation, VMF-311 was granted the opportunity to enjoy the routine of a peacetime squadron, and in July 1948, its designation was changed from "Marine Fighting Squadron"-311 to the new, more fashionable one of "Marine Fighter Squadron"-311.

After its return to the U.S. from Japan in mid-1946, VMF-311, then under the command of Lieutenant Colonel John P. Condon, was selected to become the second Marine Corps squadron, and the first on the West Coast, to be equipped with jet aircraft. The squadron surrendered its Corsairs and began familiarization and training in the new world of jet aircraft operations. The first two jets to be assigned to the squadron arrived in mid-June of the following year when the squadron received a pair of Lockheed TO-1s, the Navy's version of the F-80 Shooting Star then being acquired by the Air Force. By August, a full complement of twelve of the new aircraft was on hand, and the squadron began preparations in earnest to become proficient in their new aircraft.

From the time of its selection as a jet squadron and 30 September 1949, VMF-311 served as the Marines' first training squadron located on the West Coast, despite its fighter squadron designation. The squadron's days as an independent unit came to an end on the following day when it was reassigned to MAG-12 as an operational squadron.

The Lockheed aircraft with which the squadron was equipped was never intended to serve with Navy and Marine squadrons on a long-term basis. Its adoption was strictly an interim measure until the first jet designed for naval and carrier service became available. That aircraft was the Grumman F9F-2 Panther. First flown in November 1947, the typically Grumman, i.e., stubby and strong, aircraft was first flown operationally by the "Black Aces" of the Navy's VF-41. VMF-311 was the first Marine squadron to receive the aircraft, followed in short order by VMF-115 and VMF-451. The squadron received its first F9F-2 in February 1950. It was during this period that the squadron adopted the nickname "The Panther Pack" in honor of their new aircraft. VMF-311 was in the process of working up to a combat-ready status in their new aircraft when the storm clouds of war broke over the tiny, divided nation of Korea on 25 June 1950. As bitter and often bloody combat raged up and down the Korean peninsula, few in the squadron could hardly fail to realize that VMF-311 soon would be committed to action there.

In November 1950, the squadron received a warning order to prepare for movement to Korea and shortly thereafter, VMF-311 was on its way to war again. In late November, the massive Chinese Communist counter-offensive against the United Nations forces had trapped the First Marine Division in the rugged terrain of eastern North Korea near the Chosin Reservoir. At first it was feared (except by the Marines themselves) that the division would be wiped out. But the division held its ground in the face of the initial massed Chinese assaults and extracted a fearful toll from among the ranks of the attackers. Then the division began what will forever stand as one of the most outstanding feats in the long history of American arms, their epic march to the sea and the port of Hungnam on North Korea's east coast. (When questioned by the press about his division conducting one of the few large-scale retreats in Marine history, the division commander is said to have responded with a brusque, "Retreat hell! We're just attacking in the other direction!") [Although this supposed quote made for good news copy, it is unlikely that the scholarly, somewhat reserved Major General O.P. Smith ever uttered these words.] While few could dispute the truly magnificent accomplishment of the officers and men of the First Marine Division, it is equally true that few could dispute that, without the near-continuous air support received from aircraft of the Navy and the Marine Corps, it likely would have been impossible.

VMF-311 arrived at the airfield at Yonpo, North Korea on the morning of 7 December 1950, and two of their F9F-2Bs, the fighter-bomber version of the Panther, flew the squadron's first combat sorties of the Korean War in support of their fellow Marines on the ground. The Panthers of VMF-311 were the first Marine jet aircraft to be committed to combat, and they added the shrill whine of their F9F-2Bs was added to the basso chorus of the Corsairs and Skyraiders. The blanket of friendly aircraft bombed, napalmed, rocketed and strafed the Chinese forces that struggled to halt the Marines' advance toward the sea and safety. Through a frozen hell of sub-zero temperatures, nearly impassable terrain and tens of thousands of Chinese, the First Marine Division fought their way to the sea beneath a curtain of air support. [Captured Chinese later stated they feared the "blue airplanes" more than any other weapon at the Marines' disposal.] When they reached the port of Hungnam, the tired, ragged, but unbeaten men of the Division formed ranks and marched into the perimeter. With them they brought their heavy equipment, their wounded, many stragglers from broken army units that had disintegrated under the Chinese attacks and, true to the Marine tradition of never leaving their dead on the field of battle, the bodies of their comrades who had made the supreme sacrifice. In their wake, they left untold thousands of Chinese dead and wounded. The magnitude of the losses inflicted in the Chinese forces by the Marines, both air and ground, will never be known with any degree of accuracy, but they must have been nothing short of horrific. Since this was the first time the masses of the Peoples' Liberation Army had met the firepower of a modern western military force. Many of the enemy formations that had been engaged in the fighting had been rendered unfit for further combat for many weeks, and in some cases, many months. On Christmas Eve, the last of the nearly 100,000 troops and 90,000 North Korean civilians who chose to flee the North were loaded aboard the waiting ships and evacuated the port. Overhead were the Navy and Marine aircraft that had contributed so much to the success of the operation.

However, the Panthers of VMF-311 were not among those aircraft. After four days of combat, they had been ordered south to the K-9 airfield near Pusan in South Korea. Immediately upon their arrival there, they were once again in combat, lending their

Into the Jet Age
One of the Lockheed TO-1 Shooting Stars of VMF-311 is secured on the ramp at MCAS, El Toro, shortly after the squadron began to receive the aircraft. Note the squadron's traditional WL tailcode. During this period, the underline was used to identify Marine squadrons. [USMC Photo]

A Fighting Cat
One of the Grumman F9F-2B Panther jet fighter-bombers assigned to VMF-311 is pictured at a bleak Korean airfield. Note the tremendous number of mission marks on the fuselage, an indicator of the pace of operations for many Marine squadrons in Korea. [USMC Photo]

support wherever it was needed. In December 1950 alone, the squadron logged more than 400 hours of combat. On 21 December, one of the more unusual incidents of the squadron's service occurred when Lieutenant Weldon R. Mitchell rolled into a strafing attack against an enemy supply column. During this period of intense cold that often brought what little motorized transport the enemy possessed to a halt, Mitchell expected to see one of the shaggy Mongolian ponies pressed into service by the Chinese appear in his gunsight. Instead, he was treated to the rather strange sight of a camel among the enemy. This unfortunate beast must have been loaded with all the ammunition it was able to stagger forward carrying because it, as well as several other pack animals, was literally vaporized in the detonation as the first of his rounds found their mark. Mitchell later would be awarded the Distinguished Flying Cross for his service in Korea. Strangely, any mention of the destruction of one armed enemy camel was absent from the citation that accompanied the Lieutenant's award.

On 26 December, the squadron suffered its first combat loss in Korea. The F9F flown by Captain Jerry E.A. Miller struck a ridgeline and exploded as it attempted to pull out after a bombing run on a bridge. It was never determined whether the Cap-

The Distinguished Senator from Ohio
In addition to his more-well known roles as a United States senator and astronaut, John Glenn was a combat aviator as well. During his service with VMF-311 in Korea, he acquired the habit of attracting enemy anti-aircraft fire, as evidenced by the damage inflicted by a direct hit from a 37mm round. [USMC Photo]

tain's aircraft was struck by enemy fire or that, perhaps suffering from target fixation, Miller committed the almost universally fatal error of pressing his attack to too low an altitude. Earlier, Miller had been awarded the Distinguished Flying Cross for his services with the squadron.

The New Year found the squadron still in combat, but the engines of their aircraft had begun to experience malfunctions. So acute were these problems that all the squadron's F9F-2Bs were grounded by 16 January. As a result, VMF-311 was withdrawn from combat and ordered to Japan until the engine defects could be resolved. The problems were promptly rectified, and the squadron returned to combat on 19 February. Just prior to its return to the K-3 airfield near Pohang, VMF-311 was detached from MAG-12 and reassigned to MAG-33 as a part of a general realignment of Marine aviation assets in Korea that took place at that time. The change, however, had little effect on the squadron's steady pace of close air support and armed reconnaissance missions.

VMF-311 remained the only jet-equipped Marine squadron in Korea until the arrival of VMF-115 in February 1952. However, this event meant little to the men of the squadron as its brisk operational tempo continued with only brief and infrequent respites until the Armistice that ended the fighting in Korea was signed on 27 July 1953. On that same day, Captain W.I. Armagost flew the final Marine jet mission of the Korean War. That mission, however, did not end the commitment of VMF-311 in the Far East. It was one of the squadrons selected to remain there until the repatriation of prisoners was completed. Even the return of the prisoners did not bring about the end of the squadron's service in Korea, remaining there until it boarded USS *Princeton* (CVA-37) on 27 April 1955 for passage to the United States. During its many months in Korea, the squadron had flown a total of 18,851 combat sorties, and for its service

Author's Collection

there, VMF-311 was awarded its second Presidential Unit Citation and the Navy Unit Commendation.

The next major milestone in the squadron's history occurred on 1 June 1957. Effective this date, it was redesignated VMA-311. At the same time, it was re-equipped with the swept-wing Grumman F9F-8 Cougar. This version of Grumman's long line of Cats served the squadron for only a year before it was replaced by the Douglas A4D-2 [later A-4B] Skyhawk. Like all the other Navy and Marine squadrons that flew the quick, nimble little A-4 at one time or another, the pilots of VMA-311 quickly came to appreciate the sterling qualities of the "Scooter." The A4D-2 gave way to the A4D-2N [A-4C], which possessed a fair night/bad weather attack capability to the squadron's arsenal. In turn, the A-4D-2N was replaced by the A4D-5 [A-4E], which added two more underwing stores stations, bringing the Skyhawk's total to five and a significant increase in its ordnance load.

While these events were taking place, America was moving closer to combat in the festering war in Southeast Asia. Marine rotary wing squadrons had been more or less involved in combat operations in support of the armed forces of South Vietnam since April 1962 with the initiation of Operation *Shufly*. Gradually, the number of Marine helicopter squadrons increased, but it was not until after the Tonkin Gulf Incident of 2 August 1964 that many gave serious thought to what might lie ahead. It was during this notorious episode that warships of the United States Navy were attacked on the high seas by North Vietnamese torpedo boats and the retaliatory Navy air strikes of 5 August, Operation *Pierce Arrow*, were conducted. For a short time, it appeared that the crisis would abate, but in early 1965, the Communists stepped up their attacks on installations throughout South Vietnam, and in response, the United States launched a significant number of air strikes on North Vietnamese targets from the carriers in the Tonkin Gulf. These strikes were known as Operations *Flaming Dart I* and *Flaming Dart II*. In early March, President Johnson ordered the commencement of sustained bombing of North Vietnam in Operation *Rolling Thunder*, and the first Marine ground combat units stormed ashore at Da Nang in an unopposed amphibious assault on 8 March to provide security for the large air base there. Marine aviation units soon followed, and America and its armed forces were soon deeply involved in another shooting war in Asia.

It quickly became apparent that mere static defense of important installations, such as the air base at Da Nang would do little more than provide the enemy with a large, stationary target for his rockets and mortars. Soon, the "grunts" launched offensive sweeps into the surrounding countryside to wrest the initiative from the enemy by disrupting his attacks before they could be launched. As the tempo of operations increased, the number of Marine squadrons ordered to Da Nang quickly outstripped the ability of the base to support them, and construction was begun in May 1965 on a new facility at Chu Lai, some fifty miles south of Da Nang. The new base was declared ready to commence operations by dawn on 1 June. The A-4Es of VMA-311 in company with the A-4Cs of VMA-225 arrived before noon that same day, and in a quick turnaround, VMA-311 flew its initial combat mission of its long war in Southeast Asia that same afternoon. The squadron remained at Chu Lai until it was withdrawn to MCAS, Iwakuni, Japan for a short period of R&R, but its respite was brief, and VMA-311 returned to Chu Lai in February 1966.

The Splendid Splinter, Marine Corps Style
Trained as a Marine aviator during World War II, baseball great Ted Williams was recalled to the colors for service in Korea. Although he was none too pleased at the interruption of his post-World War II baseball career, he, like so many other Reservists, served their country with distinction in yet another conflict. Williams is shown being awarded the Distinguished Flying Cross during his service with VMF-311. [USMC Photo]

The Last Bomb
The commanding officer of VMA-311, Lieutenant Colonel John Caldas, preflights his A-4 prior to take-off on what will prove to be the squadron's final combat mission of the Vietnam War on 27 January 1973. The weapons release sequence was set so that the scarlet and gold bomb upon which the colonel's left hand rests would be the last weapon to be dropped. [USMC Photo via www.Sykhawk.org]

It was destined to remain in combat in Vietnam longer and to fly more combat missions there than any other Marine squadron. The primary mission of all the Marine attack squadrons committed to Vietnam was the close air support of friendly ground forces. This primary mission, however, did not prevent VMA-311 from striking targets in the southern portion of North Vietnam as well as taking part in the "Steel Tiger" strikes into neighboring

Laos and Cambodia. The contrast between the relatively permissive operating environment of South Vietnam and the concentrated enemy air defenses of North Vietnam must have been quite startling when encountered for the first time. For reasons beyond the scope of this work, the decision was made to place a host of viable North Vietnamese military targets off-limits to air strikes for purely political reasons, and the strikes were halted at various times in the vain hope the enemy would realize the "error" of his ways, giving up his desire to overrun the South. These decisions were among those which allowed the enemy to construct one of the densest air defense networks in the history of aerial warfare. Aviators who had experience upon which to make the comparison stated the North Vietnamese air defenses were more formidable than those in many areas of the Third Reich during World War II.

During the battle for the Marine combat base at Khe Sanh, VMA-311 devoted many of its strikes to support of their fellow Marines on the ground, and during one of these strikes, the A-4 flown by Captain Bobby G. Downing was struck by enemy ground fire 21 January 1968. Downing ejected safely and was rescued by helicopter only ten minutes after abandoning his crippled aircraft. Two days later, Major William E. Loftus's aircraft was heavily damaged by enemy fire during a sortie near the besieged base. With his situation rapidly going from bad to worse, Loftus realized he would not be able to reach the safety of the Gulf of Tonkin before his aircraft quit flying, and he turned back toward Khe Sanh. Ejecting directly over the base, the Major's parachute descent ended with his shroud lines fouled in the barbed wire entanglements of the outer perimeter of the Marines' positions. As he struggled to free himself before any enemy troops could reach him, Loftus doubtless heaved a large sigh of relief when a Marine patrol arrived on the scene and retrieved him from the wire. Grinning at the young officer in command of the patrol, Major Loftus greeted him with the comment, "Lieutenant, if you weren't so damn ugly, I'd kiss you!" Uninjured, Loftus returned to Chu Lai later that same day, none the worse for his experiences. Within days, he was again flying sorties in support of his new found friends among the mud Marines at Khe Sanh.

Assigned to MAG-12, VMA-311, along with its sister squadrons in the group, VMA-121, VMA-211 and VMA-223, continued to fight the long, weary and unpopular war until American presence in Southeast Asia was reduced in January 1970. One by one, the squadrons of MAG-12 were withdrawn from combat and returned to the United States or were ordered to Japan. By 12 February, VMA-311 was the only Marine A-4 squadron in Southeast Asia. In late summer, the squadron shifted from Chu Lai to Da Nang, where it came under the control of MAG-11. It operated from there for the next nine months and flew what was believed would be its 47,663rd and last combat sortie of the conflict on 7 May 1971. On 12 May, VMA-311 withdrew its twenty-one A-4Es to MCAS, Iwakuni. The squadron expressed some, albeit small and less than heartfelt, regret that it was not able to reach the 50,000-sortie milestone during its more than six years of combat in Southeast Asia.

In response to the massive North Vietnamese Easter Offensive of March 1972, VMA-311 was one of the Marine squadrons committed to the renewal of heavy combat in Vietnam. Alerted for movement to combat again on 12 May, the squadron's Skyhawks departed Iwakuni for Bien Hoa, South Vietnam, five

Last of the Breed
One of the A-4M Sky Hawks with which VMA-311 was equipped in the late 1980s is depicted during its landing roll at the squadron's home station, MCAS, Yuma, AZ. The photo captures excellent detail of the A-4 in a landing configuration, and the presence of a pair of 300-gallon underwing fuel tanks indicates a flight of considerable duration. Also note the presence of a multiple ejector rack (MER) in the centerline station. [USMC Photo via Webshots]

days later. It flew combat sortie number 47,664 on 19 May and passed the 50,000 mark on 29 August. It remained in combat in Southeast Asia until the cease-fire on 23 January 1973. By this date, VMA-311 had flown a total of 54,625 combat sorties in four countries in Southeast Asia: Laos, Cambodia, North and South Vietnam. It was withdrawn from Bien Hoa and returned to Iwakuni on 29 January 1973.

To put these rather dry statistics into proper perspective, one should consider the following facts. During the eight months between the squadron's return to combat in May 1972 and the cease-fire, it flew nearly 7,000 sorties. It never had more than 21 aircraft on strength. This averages to more than 40 missions per aircraft per month for eight months – a lasting tribute to both the A-4 and to the pilots, ground crews and other personnel of VMA-311! In addition to being an outstanding tribute of the men of the squadron, it has much to do with the robust and reliable systems in the A-4. As great an aircraft as the A-6 Intruder proved to be in Vietnam and later, its relative complexity and high maintenance requirements would have weighed heavily against it in this environment.

The squadron remained at MCAS, Iwakuni where it continued its long and successful association with the various models of the A-4 series until some months after it returned to the U.S. After its arrival there, the squadron was reequipped with the final model to see service with the Marines, the A-4M, which features a still more powerful engine, a revised canopy and tail fin and the Hughes Angle Rate Bombing System [ARBS]. In addition to affording improved accuracy of the delivery of conventional munitions, the ARBS enabled A-4s equipped with it to employ precision laser-guided munitions, which are among those weapons generally referred to as "Smart Bombs."

VMA-311 was transferred to MCAS, Yuma, Arizona, in June 1988, where it continued to operate the A-4M until early-1989, when it began the process of conversion from the by now obsolescent Skyhawk to the AV-8B Harrier II. The arrival of the first AV-8B introduced the squadron into the new world of vertical/short take-off and landing, and it immediately began the process of working up to combat readiness in the new and revolutionary aircraft. It was during this period that the squadron received the Lawson H. M. Sanderson Award as the Marine Attack Squadron of the Year from the Marine Corps Aviation Association.

Shortly after the squadron was declared combat ready in the Harrier, VMA-311 was deployed for combat once again when it departed Yuma on 11 August 1990 to take part in Operation *Desert Shield/Desert Storm*. Operating first from Sheikh Isa, the Harriers were redeployed to Al Jubail, Saudi Arabia, closer to the eventual scene of combat operations in Kuwait. VMA-311 flew its first combat mission on the commencement of *Desert Storm* on 17 January 1991. During the war in the Persian Gulf, VMA-311 lost one aircraft in combat on 28 January, when the Harrier flown by Captain Michael C. Berryman was shot down by ground fire. The Captain successfully ejected from his doomed aircraft and was taken prisoner by the Iraqis. He was released from captivity upon the cessation of hostilities the following month. During its participation in the Gulf War, VMA-311 flew 1,017 combat sorties and expended 840 tons of ordnance on all varieties of Iraqi targets. The squadron returned to U.S. soil from Southwest Asia in April 1991 and to a normal deployment cycle once again. Shortly after its return, the squadron again received the Sanderson Award as the Marine Attack Squadron of the Year for 1991.

In April 1992, VMA-311 began to receive the night attack version of the AV-8B and was certified as a night attack squadron shortly thereafter.

The shock of the attacks of 11 September 2001 had barely begun to subside when the squadron deployed aboard USS *Peleliu* (LHA-5) and departed for the north Arabian Sea. Upon their arrival the squadron's Harriers became the first of their type to conduct combat operations in Operation *Enduring Freedom*, the destruction of the Taliban regime in Afghanistan. As the heaviest period of combat there came to an end, the squadron completed the remainder of its deployment and returned to its home station, where it enjoyed a brief period of R & R before preparations for the next deployment began.

In January 2003, the squadron departed U.S. soil bound for the Arabian Gulf in preparation for its next round of combat. On 21 March 2003, almost fifty-nine years to the day after the lineal predecessor of VMA-311 flew its initial combat sortie in World War II, the squadron flew its initial sorties in Operation *Iraqi Freedom*. By the time the cease-fire was signed, VMA 311 had expended 77 tons of various types of precision guided munitions against 132 different targets, as well as much more weight in conventional munitions.

As this was written, the squadron continues to participate in the ongoing combat operations of America's global war on terrorism.

Of the insignia of VMA-311 depicted, the first pair is representative of the squadron's current design, which it has worn with minor variations since the mid-1960s. As can be readily seen, they are virtually identical in design and vary only in size and shades of color. The third is a Det. B "float" patch. Number four is a variant dating from the early 1970s featuring the cartoon character "Bill, the Cat," that was in vogue at various times for inclusion in unofficial insignia designs. The fifth is a design adopted in 1961 and, according to the squadron history, worn until the current design came into use.

Modern Marine Light Attack Aviation
This fine shot of an AV-8B Night Attack Harrier II of VMA-311 is "what it's all about" in Marine light attack until the advent of the V/STOL version of the much-heralded Joint Strike Fighter, if that aircraft ever enters service. [Photo via Webshots]

Coming Aboard
This AV-8B Night Attack Harrier of VMA-311 is just moments away from touchdown aboard USS Bon Homme Richard (LHD-5). Note the vertical positioning of the exhaust nozzle of the Pegasus engine and the extended Lift Improvement Devices under the belly of the aircraft. These LIDs capture air as it rebounds from the surface of the landing aircraft, in this case the Bonnie Dick's flight deck, and provide additional aid in landing. [USMC Photo]

The sixth and seventh insignia are original examples of the squadron's insignia adopted when the squadron was redesignated an attack squadron.

Number eight is the last officially approved insignia design of VMF-311 and dates from the squadron's post Korean War service while based at MCAS, El Toro. Headquarters, Marine Corps, approved this design in 1957. The eighth insignia is an example of one of many variations on this theme. All date from the period between 1951 and 1954 and, while the central figures of Sylvester the Cat on the jet engine represented by a flaming stovepipe are the same, the materials differ. Some are bullion on a wool felt background, and some are on a twill background, etc.

The final pair of insignia pictured are examples of the World War II insignia of VMF-311. The example on the left is a fully embroidered original from the years immediately after the war, and the one on the right is a hand-made reproduction of the

Coming Aboard the Boat
This AV-8B of VMA-311 is just moments away from touchdown aboard USS Peleliu (LHA-5) on this beautiful day in the South China Sea in the waning days of its 2008 deployment, which lasted from 4 May until 4 November. Operations were conducted in the South China Sea, the Persian Gulf, and the Red Sea, and the squadron's detachment was under the operational control of HMM165 (REIN). Judging by Peleliu's paintwork, not much time was spent in port. [USMC Photo]

squadron's earliest insignia. The lack of the squadron's nickname and designation on the reproduction conform to wartime security regulations, which were regularly violated by many squadrons. Unfortunately, the identity of the artist who designed this insignia has been lost over the years.

The December 1944 supplement of the "National Geographic" devoted to the insignia of the U.S. armed forces depicts the insignia of VMF-311 to be very similar in detail to the reproduction but on a rectangular background.

Regarding the changes in the squadron's insignia since the tomcat was adopted, it is likely that the interest on the part of the "powers that be" regarding insignia design and content following World War II led to the demise of the nude "belle." And, while the reasons for the selection of the tomcat have been lost in the nearly half-century since its adoption, it is appropriate in that these animals have a well-deserved reputation as fierce combatants and of being ready to fight at a moment's notice when their territory is threatened.

The heart came into use in the various insignia in the immediate post-World War II period. The issuance of Aviation Circular Letter No. 156-46 on 7 November 1946 called for, among other things, the assignment of two-letter tail codes to all Marine squadrons. VMF-311 was assigned the code WL. [The underscore was used to denote Marine units.] In the phonetic alphabet in use at the time, WL was pronounced "William Love," leading to an unofficial reference to the squadron as the "Willie Lovers." When the original "Hell's Belles" design fell into disuse, the heart was incorporated into all subsequent insignia used by the squadron.

via Holmberg

Author's Collection

MARINE ATTACK SQUADRON 322,
THE FIGHTING COCKS
A.K.A., THE GAMECOCKS,
THE CANNONBALL SQUADRON (WORLD WAR II)

Author's Collection

The lineal predecessor of VMA-322, Marine Fighting Squadron 322, was activated on 1 July 1943 at MCAS, Cherry Point, North Carolina, under the command of Major Frederick M. Rauschenbach. Shortly after its activation, the squadron was transferred from Cherry Point to MCAS, Parris Island, South Carolina, for training. After approximately six months at Parris Island, the squadron was declared combat-ready and was alerted for movement westward. It departed Parris Island for the West Coast in January 1944, but its stay there was destined to be a short one, and from California, the squadron was ordered to MCAS, Ewa, Territory of Hawaii. Operations from Ewa, in the form of additional training, continued until the late summer, when the squadron was alerted for further movement to the South Pacific.

VMF-322 arrived at Emirau on 18 September 1944. By this time, however, all active combat in the Solomons and the Bismarks area had ground to a virtual halt. The great Japanese base at Rabaul had been reduced to the point of ineffectiveness the previous February, and the entire area was now a quiet backwater far removed from the active combat arenas. However, strikes continued to be mounted against Rabaul and the other bypassed enemy installations in the south and southwest Pacific, and the purpose for these was twofold. First, it was necessary to ensure that these now passive bypassed garrisons were kept in their present state of impotence, and they provided a useful means to "blood" a new unit by providing relative benign targets for them to engage in their initial combat sorties.

Elsewhere, however, the war continued unabated. Three days prior to the squadron's arrival on Emirau, the First Marine Division assaulted the island of Peleliu in the Palaus where,

to quote an official recount of the ensuing battle, "some of the fiercest and most confused fighting of the Pacific war" would rage for the next several weeks. But the scene of this fierce struggle was far removed from the peaceful haven that was now the backwater of Emirau.

After nearly a month at Emirau, the squadron was ordered southeastward to Espiritu Santo in the New Hebrides, which was even farther from any active theater than Emirau. The flight echelon arrived there in October, and the ground echelon joined it there the following month. VMF-322 remained in the New Hebrides until early March of 1945 when it was ordered forward for the forthcoming assault on Okinawa, Japan's last bastion standing between the advancing Americans and the sacred soil of the Home Islands. This island was destined to be the scene of the bloodiest combat in the entire Pacific war, and although none knew it at the time, the last battle of this long and fiercely contested struggle against the Japanese Empire.

Japan had annexed Okinawa in 1879, and over the ensuing sixty-six years, it had come to be regarded by most Japanese as virtually a part of Japan proper, at least as far as the island itself was concerned. The native Okinawans, on the other hand, were looked upon as an inferior race suitable only for laborers and servants As a result, there was little love lost between the Japanese who lived on the island and the natives. The island lay only 325 miles to the southwest of Kyushu, the southernmost of the home islands and within easy reach of aircraft from virtually anywhere in the homeland. The great naval engagements of 1944 had reduced the seemingly once-omnipotent Imperial Japanese Navy to scattered remnants furtively seeking shelter

Author's Collection

from the rampaging carrier task forces and the ever-present submarines of the United States Pacific Fleet, but despite the series of crushing defeats inflicted upon the enemy fleet, few among the Allies harbored any doubts that the struggle for control of the island would reach epic proportions in the air and on land. Unfortunately, these beliefs were to prove right on the money.

The long and bloody battle that lay ahead would witness the largest concentration of Marine air strength of the entire Pacific war. VMF-322 was a component of MAG-33, which was, in turn, one of four groups that composed the Air Defense Command of the Tactical Air Force that was organized to support and to protect the assault forces. Among them the four MAGs of the Tactical Air Force controlled a total of fifteen Marine fighter squadrons – an even dozen day fighter squadrons and three night fighter squadrons. Before Okinawa was finally declared secure, all were destined to see their full share of combat.

After the preliminary capture of some of the small islands that lay close to Okinawa off its western shore, the main assault went ashore on Easter Sunday, 1 April 1945. The vital airfields of Yontan and Kadena fell to the unchallenged American advance just after noon on the first day. Work commenced to restore these fields to operation as soon as they fell into American hands in order to ready them to receive the waiting squadrons of the Air Defense Command. By the coming of darkness on that Sunday, more than 50,000 American troops, both Army and Marines, were ashore, and the vital airfields at Yontan and Kadena were in American hands. What little resistance that had been encountered had been scattered and fleeting, and, happily,

casualties had been almost nil, but this period of light resistance proved to be the calm before the proverbial storm, a storm of blood and suffering.

The actual assault had been far easier than expected in terms of enemy resistance and casualties among the assault forces. At sea, however, this first day proved to be a different story. In an instance laden with bitter irony, the heaviest casualties of the day were suffered by the Second Marine Division, which had made a feint against beaches in a different sector of the island in an attempt to draw the Japanese defenders away from the actual assault beaches. A transport and two LSTs carrying troops of the division fell victim to Japanese suicide aircraft. The Kamikaze, which had made its first appearance of the Pacific war late the previous October in the Philippines, had claimed its first victims at Okinawa. VMF-322 suffered its first casualties of the campaign on 3 April when *LST-599*, with 30 officers and 169 enlisted men of the squadron aboard, was struck by a Kamikaze. Seven men were wounded, and all the squadron's vehicles and cargo that she had been carrying were lost.

From Guadalcanal to Okinawa, the Japanese had never defeated an American amphibious assault – a fact of that the Japanese were painfully aware. Often, the enemy had thrown away much of his strength in screaming, suicidal Banzai charges that were doomed to destruction before they were launched. Before the first American set foot on Okinawa, the defenders had given up all hope of victory or even survival for that matter. Their objective was to hold each in a series of heavily fortified defensive lines that lay across the southern portion of the island for as long as possible and then withdraw into the next line. In this, the Japanese unknowly adopted much the same strategy as that employed by the Germans in Italy in 1944. By such a strategy, the Japanese hoped to inflict the maximum number of casualties on their attackers and to prolong the land battle for as long as was possible. This represented a major strategic change in the manner in which the Japanese conducted the vast majority of the battles in the Pacific to date. Should their plan to come to fruition, the American fleet would be tied to the support of their troops ashore to allow maximum time for the Kamikazes to do their deadly work. By depriving the Navy, particularly the carriers, of its prime asset of strategic mobility, it would be exposed to land based air attack from the string of bases that stretched, ultimately, from the islands just to the north of Okinawa to Hok-

Damage Control
LST-599 with LCT-876 stowed on her main deck is shown ablaze after being hit by a kamikaze in the anchorage of Kerama Retto on 3 April 1945. LSM-79 is coming alongside to render aid and assist in firefighting. Fortunately, there were no fatalities among the personnel of VMF-324 who were aboard the LST. [U.S. Navy Photo]

kaido. If enough damage could be inflicted on the Pacific Fleet, any assault against the home islands could be postponed for a considerable time, or possibly indefinitely. Should this come to pass, perhaps the Allied Powers would accept a negotiated settlement to the war. In the end, it proved to be a forlorn hope, but it was virtually all the Japanese had left to them. In this strategy of keeping the American fleet near Okinawa, the Japanese were painfully successful. The first of several mass suicide attacks struck the assembled ships of the invasion fleet on 6 April, and while the soldiers and Marines ashore were still searching for their elusive enemy, few now harbored any illusions that the campaign would be easy or short.

It was critical to get the airfields ashore operational as soon as possible to ease some of the burden of the carrier based fighter squadrons, and Kadena airfield was declared ready for operations on 9 April. As soon as this welcome news was re-

via Holmberg

Author's Collection

ceived, the squadrons of MAG-33, including VMF-322, moved ashore and began operations immediately, but the squadron's ground echelon did not arrive at Kadena on 1 May. In addition to VMF-322, MAG-33 had two other day fighter squadrons, VMF-312 and VMF-323. -312 and -323 began to run up large strings of victories almost immediately, but this was not the case for VMF-322. It was a matter of being in the wrong place at the wrong time and of being tasked with a larger number of close air support sorties for the squadron, but when opportunities for aerial combat presented themselves, VMF-322 made the most of them.

The squadron's first opportunity came late in the afternoon of 13 May, when Lieutenants Richard S. Wilcox and Forrest B. Warren were assigned a combat air patrol mission covering Kerama Retto, a small island fifteen miles west of Okinawa. One of the islands captured prior to the main assault, the sheltered anchorage of Kerama Retto was used as a repair facility for ships struck by Kamikazes. The two pilots of VMF-322 intercepted a pair of Aichi D3A1 Val dive-bombers attempting to strike the already wounded ships in the harbor. The enemy singled out the destroyer USS *Bache* (DD-470) as their intended victim. Another of the destroyers present splashed one of the attackers, and Lieutenant Warren went after the other. He chased the stubborn Val through "friendly" anti-aircraft fire for 2,000 yards, closed on the enemy and set the Japanese aircraft afire. The enemy aircraft spun and struck *Bache* a glancing blow. A hit from one of the ships' 40mm guns knocked part of a wingtip from Warren's aircraft, forcing him to bail out, but he survived his unintentional saltwater bath. Five minutes later, Lieutenant Wilcox intercepted and destroyed a Zero attempting to attack the anchored *Bache*. Again chasing the enemy through the withering barrage of the ships' anti-aircraft fire, the Zero was shot down in flames before it could close the anchorage. After the Marines broke up these attacks, *Bache's* captain sent the following message to VMF-322, "Admirable and courageous work....please convey to these pilots the gratitude of the officers and men of *Bache*." Both Warren and Wilcox were each awarded the Navy Cross for their actions of 13 May.

The squadron continued its steady diet of close air support missions when not assigned to combat air patrol. As vital as the protection of the ships that lay off Okinawa was, it was realized that the Kamikaze attacks would continue until the island was secured, and the fleet was no longer tied to the relatively constricted area around the southern Ryukus. But, the fleet could not depart until the land campaign was successfully concluded, so the sooner the enemy ashore was defeated, the sooner the fleet would be able to seek the protection of the vast ocean to help to defeat the suicide attacks. The slow, bloody advance of the troops ashore was carried out under a continuous blanket of air support as the airmen labored to ease the task of the ground troops. The Corsair was the most numerous of the aircraft engaged in the support effort, and the accuracy of their strikes and the heavy ordnance loads carried by the aircraft earned the F4U the sobriquet "the sweetheart of Okinawa" during the campaign. VMF-322 certainly contributed its share to the luster of the Corsair's reputation in the skies above the tortured island.

Despite the heavy load of close air support missions, VMF-322 also continued to share the task of "capping" the ships offshore. As the second month of battle edged toward an end, the Kamikazes continued their assaults.

The morning of 25 May began with 165 Japanese suicide aircraft swarming after the radar picket ships stationed at intervals around the island. These destroyers, along with their accompanying retinue of smaller ships called the "pallbearers," bore the brunt of these attacks. The smaller ships were positioned near the destroyers on the picket stations to provide additional weight to the anti-aircraft fire and, should the worst occur, to rescue survivors, hence their grim nickname. The picket ships had already suffered horrendous losses from suicide attacks, but their mission of providing early warning of incoming raids was vital and continued throughout the campaign.

By 0830 that morning, air battles were raging near virtually every picket station that surrounded the island. American fighters claimed seventy-five Japanese aircraft, and of these, Marine fighter squadrons accounted for more than half the total with thirty-nine kills. VMF-322 was credited with eight kills in a series of savage, no-quarter fights. Lieutenant James E. Webster was the squadron's high scorer for the day with three kills, earning a Distinguished Flying Cross. However, despite the desperate, valiant work of the fighters of all services, eleven more ships were added to the doleful tally of sunken and maimed vessels.

The Kamikazes returned in force only two days later, but rather than a single massive assault, small raids of two to four aircraft hurled themselves at the ships continuously for more than nine hours. It was the longest continuous alert of the campaign, and during Okinawa's "longest day," it is estimated that 56 separate raids took place composed of approximately 150 enemy aircraft. Again, the Marines scored heavily and claimed 32 of the enemy with VMF-322 again contributing to the total. After the big raids of late May, there were no more large enemy attacks, but hardly a day passed without at least a few Kamikazes lunging at the fleet. These attacks continued to contribute to the alarming total of battered and blackened ships and the tremendous number of enemy aircraft destroyed in aerial combat.

As May drew to a close, Major Rauschenbach was ordered to other duty. He departed on 30 May, and Major Walter E. Lischeid assumed command the following day, and in June, VMF-322 was heavily committed to the assault by the Second Marine Division against Iheya Shima, a small island that lay to the northwest of the northern tip of Okinawa. Thanks to the support offered by VMF-322 and other squadrons, the American casualties were mercifully light, and the small island quickly fell to the assault troops. On 12 June, VMF-322 carried out the first Marine attack mission from Okinawa against the Japanese mainland. Their target was the airfield at Kanoye on the island of Kyushu, which received a thorough bombing and strafing attack by the squadron's Corsairs.

The battle for Okinawa ground to its inevitable conclusion on 21 June after 82 days of fierce combat. VMF-322 had been engaged for 73 days and had recorded 29 kills. This was in addition to the squadron's contribution to the astounding total of 14,244 close air support sorties flown during the campaign. For its service during the period 9 April through 14 July 1945, the squadron was awarded the Presidential Unit Citation.

On 15 July, VMF-322 moved its base of operations from Kadena to Awase, where it was based until the Japanese surrender. The squadron remained there until February 1946 when it, along with the other squadrons of MAG-33 returned to the United States, and its officers and men, both regular and reserve, prepared for the future in a world at peace, at least as far as America was concerned.

VMF-322 survived the wave of post-war deactivations that swept many of the most celebrated squadrons of the Marine Corps into limbo. In 1946, it was assigned to the reorganized MAG-15, which was the only air group assigned to Aircraft, Fleet Marine Force, Pacific. The squadron spent the immediate post-war years at Midway and at MCAS, Ewa. It returned to the U.S. aboard USS *Princeton* (CV-37) in April 1949 and was assigned to MCAS, Edenton, North Carolina. During this period, the Truman administration was slashing defense expenditures to the bone, and along with many other squadrons, VMF-322 was deactivated on 30 November 1949.

VMF-322 was among the many deactivated squadrons that later were reactivated as components of the Marine Reserves. The Korean War was a major force behind many of these squadrons receiving a reprieve. VMF-322 was reactivated on 6 July 1951 and was assigned to NAS, Squantum, Massachusetts. In December 1953, the squadron was moved to NAS, South Weymouth, twelve miles from Squantum.

VMF-322 finally retired its last Corsair in March 1955, and re-equipped with its first jet aircraft, the swept-wing Grumman F9F-6 Cougar. It was redesignated VMA-322 in May 1958. VMA-322 flew the Grumman product for eighteen months before it was re-equipped with the North American FJ-3 Fury, which served in the squadron's colors for almost three years.

In September 1962, VMA-322 was re-equipped with the Douglas A4D-2 [A4-C] Skyhawk. In turn, these were succeeded by the A4-E and the A4-M models of the superlative little product of Douglas that were to continue to serve with the squadron until VMA-322 was deactivated on 30 June 1992 in the wave of force reductions in the wake of the Cold War. [Several sources give the date of the squadron's deactivation as 1 July 1992.] The squadron's 27th commanding officer, Lieutenant Colonel Daniel Ventre, presided over the ceremony that saw the colors of VMA-322 retired. In addition to the Presidential Unit Citation streamer, its colors carried the Asiatic-Pacific Campaign streamer with Bronze Star and the World War II Victory streamer. The squadron was awarded a Unit Citation upon deactivation.

Author's Collection

Home to Roost
An A4-M Skyhawk of VMA-322 rolls out after touchdown at its home station. Notice what appears to be a dummy missile of the type used ACM exercises on a store station on the starboard wing. [USMC Photo]

When VMA-322 was deactivated, seven members of the squadron whose service totaled 145 years also retired, and the squadron that had been ranked as the most combat ready squadron in the Marine Corps Reserve for ten consecutive years passed into history.

Regarding the insignia of the squadron, the first two pictured are, on the left, an example of the last version of the squadron's officially approved insignia and the flight suit shoulder "bullet" specific to the aircraft type with which the squadron was equipped. The next two are a slightly older version of the official design and a flight suit insignia. These represent the insignia worn by the squadron from the date of its designation as an attack squadron until its deactivation. They differ only in detail and slightly in color.

The last three pictured are examples of variants of the insignia of VMF-322. These were worn by the squadron during its service as a fighter squadron from the time of its activation in 1943 until its deactivation in 1949. They differ in size, detail and materials. The first is American-embroidered on twill, and the second is silk-screened on aircraft fabric. The "Fighting Cocks" insignia was a product of the Disney Studios.

Note the first of the squadron's insignia from the latter days of World War II. In the closing days of the war, the Marine fighter squadrons took on more and more of a fighter-bomber role. As a result, the squadron's insignia was modified, with the cock clutching three HVARs in its right foot.

MARINE ATTACK SQUADRON 324

THE DEVIL DOGS

A.K.A., THE VAGABONDS

THE DEVIL PACK (WORLD WAR II)

Author's Collection

Marine Fighting Squadron 324 was activated on 1 October 1943 at MCAS, Cherry Point, North Carolina, under the command of Major Philip R. White, and almost immediately after its activation, the squadron moved from Cherry Point to the nearby auxiliary airfield at Oak Grove due to the crowded conditions at the former location. After setting up shop at its new base, the squadron commenced its training, but a month after arriving at Oak Grove, VMF-324 was on the move again. Its new home was the primitive Simmons-Knott Field at nearby New Bern, North Carolina. During this period, Cherry Point was a literal beehive of activity. It was the largest Marine Corps Air Station on the East Coast, if not the largest in the entire Corps. Scarcely a week passed without the activation of one or more new squadrons there, and the construction of new facilities was losing the race with the growth in the numbers of new units and personnel. As a result, many new units, such as VMF-324, were ordered to one of the many outlying airfields that made up the massive Cherry Point complex. Although the nickname "Vagabonds" was not adopted until much later in the squadron's service, it would have been appropriate from the very beginning. During this series of moves, the squadron's command changed hands several times. Major White was detached on 9 November, and Captain Robert W. Van Horn assumed command until Captain George W.

Wilcox succeeded him on 12 November. Major Carl M. Longley relieved Captain Wilcox on 15 November. Even during the most arduous of conditions, pomp and ceremony remain near and dear to the hearts of many Marines everywhere, but three change-of-command ceremonies in less than a week surely were enough to tax the most ardent of parade ground Marines. After Major Longley's arrival, the squadron returned to the more pressing business of its preparations for combat.

Its command arrangements settled for the time being, and with a full complement of aviators and aircraft on hand, the squadron began to conduct training exercises beginning with the formation of sections composed of a leader and his wingman. The two aircraft section was the basic tactical formation, and these were combined into four plane divisions of two sections. Regardless of the eventual size of any formation of single-engine tactical aircraft, the section and division are its building blocks and the integrity of the two aircraft section is a vital key to survival in aerial combat. After the squadron's aviators attained a sufficient level of proficiency in section and division formations and tactics, training in formations up to squadron strength were undertaken. These were interspersed with instrument and gunnery training and cross-country navigation exercises as the squadron approached combat readiness.

VMF-324 remained on the East Coast until 15 July 1944 when it departed New Bern bound for MCAS, Miramar, near San Diego, and shortly after arriving on the West Coast, a portion of the squadron was detached and ordered to MCAS, Mojave, in the California desert for training in the delivery of the massive 11.75-inch "Tiny Tim" rocket and heavy bombs with its Corsairs. The detachment spent three weeks at Mojave blowing large holes in the vast and sparsely populated desert while the remainder of the squadron prepared for movement to the South Pacific. The warning order for movement was received shortly after the return of the detachment, and all hands immediately turned to the completion of the myriad of last minute tasks that always accompany the preparation for such a move.

Its preparations more or less complete, the squadron sailed from San Diego on 30 August, and after staging through MCAS, Ewa, on the island of Oahu, VMF-324 arrived on Midway on 16 September. By this date, Midway had been left far behind the battlefront, and while all hands expected to be ordered to the Western Pacific at any time, Midway was to be as close to the Japanese as VMF-324 would get during World War II. During its sojourn in this now-quiet backwater of the war, Major Longley was transferred to other duties on 28 July 1945, and Major Robert C. Hammond, Jr. assumed command on 29 July. Less than a week later, he was succeeded by Major James W. Merritt on 4 August. All the while, the aviators of VMF-324 spent many hours aloft preparing to meet an enemy that had given up all hope of conquering Midway many months before, and after eleven months there, the squadron was ordered to return to Ewa, where it arrived in late August 1945. It remained in Hawaii until after the formal Japanese surrender, and the squadron returned to the United States shortly after the enemy's formal surrender on 2 September. It was one of the many squadrons to be deactivated in the months that followed the end of hostilities in the Pacific. Major Merritt read the formal orders deactivating VMF-324 on 15 October 1945.

The outbreak of hostilities in far-off Korea on 29 June 1950 found the armed forces of the United States hardly better prepared for war then they had been on 7 December 1941. The seemingly endless rounds of reductions in force levels and military expenditures in the years immediately after V-J Day had long since trimmed away any fat and cut deeply into the bone and muscle of America's military establishment. In one vital area, however, the United States was far better prepared than perhaps at any other time in our history. World War II had ended less than five years earlier, leaving the United States with a vast pool of superbly trained manpower that was still of military age, and tens of thousands of these veterans were recalled to the colors. In the case of Marine aviation, dozens of squadrons that had been deactivated or transferred to the Reserves were reactivated and recalled to active duty. The fighting in Korea would drag on for thirty-seven frustrating and often bloody months, and VMF-324 was reactivated on 17 March 1952 and redesignated VMA-324 upon its activation. Despite the heavy commitment of Marine aviation assets to the fighting in Korea, VMA-324 would not meet the enemy in combat. Instead, it was assigned to MCAS, Opa Locka, Florida, near Miami. The majority of those assigned to the squadron were recently returned veterans of the fighting in Korea, and no doubt most of them found their new surroundings in South Florida to be a pleasant change from the alternately freezing and sweltering climate of the small, distant Asian peninsula. However, VMA-324 was afforded little time to enjoy the change of pace.

As the war in Korea entered its third summer, the Navy found itself with somewhat of an embarrassment of riches in certain respects. So many carriers had been taken out of mothballs and reconditioned for service in the Far East and to meet the host of other military commitments of the United States that the Navy did not have a sufficient number of squadrons to man them adequately. As had been the case in early 1945 and as is the case today, the solution was to assign Marine squadrons to car-

USS Saipan (CVL-48)
Saipan at sea in the early-1950s with FH-1 Phantoms and a HOS-3 helicopter on her flight deck.
(Naval History Center Photo)

rier duty until the Navy had sufficient squadrons to cover its carrier commitments. As a result, the decision was made to assign VMA-324 to USS *Saipan* (CVL-48) for the carrier's scheduled deployment to the western Pacific.

The negotiations to end the fighting in Korea had been alternately stumbling forward, halting, and then restarting once again for nearly two years, and while it appeared certain that the fighting eventually would be brought to an end at the conference table rather than on the battlefield, no one knew with any certainty when the shooting would stop or whether the enemy would honor the terms of any ceasefire agreement. As the squadron pressed ahead with its deployment preparations, it was not known whether the ship would be sailing into peace or into war. It was during this period prior to its deployment that VMA-324 acquired its nickname "Vagabonds." It seems that one of the squadron's favorite watering holes in the greater Miami area was known as the Club Vagabond, and the squadron adopted the name of its favorite haunt as its nickname. This was no doubt due to the many "arduous" hours spent there taking on fuel in preparation for the remainder of the evening.

The Korean ceasefire was signed in late July, and the shooting officially stopped on the 27th of that month. However, due to the uncertainty of what might follow, the decision was made to continue the deployment as scheduled and to consider it to be a combat deployment. VMA-324 completed its carrier qualifications aboard *Saipan* in August, and the final shakedown cruise was conducted in the waters off Mayport, Florida, from 30 September through 8 October. After a brief stay in port to take on supplies, make last minute repairs, and tie up any remaining loose ends, *Saipan* and VMA-324 sailed from Florida for the western Pacific on 13 October. At the time of their departure, none of those aboard were aware of the near-epic proportions of the months to follow. Instead of a relatively routine deployment followed by a return across the Pacific to the U.S., the ship and

squadron had sailed on what would become the first and, to date, one of a relative handful of round the world cruises by a Marine squadron. In many ways, the honor of the world cruise was in recognition of the many outstanding achievements of the ship and her embarked squadrons during their deployment. One of the more noteworthy events to occur during the voyage was the squadron's delivery of twenty-four AU-1 Corsairs to the hard-pressed French forces in Indochina. The ill-fated action at Dien Bien Phu had begun, and the French forces were in dire need of additional ground attack aircraft to support their embattled, and ultimately doomed, garrison of paratroopers and legionnaires. [Editor's Note: The AU-1 version of the long-lived Corsair was an outgrowth of the Korean War. It was a specialized ground attack version of this redoubtable fighter, with an engine rated for maximum power and speed at low altitudes. It also included considerable additional armor in the lower fuselage and around the oil coolant radiators located in the wing roots.]

On Easter Sunday morning, 18 April 1954, *Saipan* turned into the wind and began to launch the Corsairs to be transferred to the French into the muggy morning sky. Although they carried no air-to-ground ordnance, each of the AU-1s carried a full ammunition load for its four 20mm cannon. No one knew whether or not the incoming aircraft would draw fire from the Communist forces in the area of their destination, the airfield at Tourane, which would become known to a later generation of Americans as Da Nang. The Corsairs were launched without incident and arrived at their destination without being fired upon. There they broke into the landing pattern above the airfield and touched down in this strange land. Upon landing there were several brief but heartfelt reunions between some of the waiting French aviators and the Marines who had been classmates during flight training at Pensacola or Corpus Christi. The reunions completed, the Marines boarded a helicopter for the flight back to their carrier. This operation completed successfully, *Saipan* and her embarked

At the Break
A half-dozen AD-4B Skyraiders of VMA-324 prepare to break into the landing pattern above USS Lake Champlain (CVS-39) as she steams across a glassy Mediterranean seascape during their 1955/56 deployment. (USN Photo)

squadrons continued operations in the western Pacific until mid-May when word was received that the ship would return to Mayport by steaming around the world. King Neptune and his Royal Court boarded the ship when she "crossed the line" on 1 June, and after the appropriate ceremony [and punishment], the carrier was manned completely by trusty shellbacks.

After brief port calls at Colombo, Ceylon [now Sri Lanka] and Aden on the Red Sea, *Saipan* transited the Suez Canal on 19 June, becoming an operational component of the Sixth Fleet in the process. Additional port calls were made at Naples, Italy; Ville Franche, Nice and Cannes, France; Barcelona, Spain, and Lisbon, Portugal during operations with Sixth Fleet before the carrier set a course westward for Mayport. The squadron flew its Skyraiders off *Saipan* for the last time on 18 July and made a brief stop at NAS, Jacksonville, before heading southward for the familiar surroundings of the greater Miami area. This departure marked the end of the first round the world cruise by a Marine squadron and the longest continuous association between a Marine squadron and a carrier up to that time. However, the end of the cruise aboard *Saipan* marked the beginning of a long association of VMA-324 and the Navy's flight decks that would see the squadron deploy aboard a carrier on five more occasions during the remainder of its active service.

The summer of 1955 found VMA-324 preparing to go to sea once again. It completed its preparatory carrier qualifications and was detached from its parent MAG and assigned to CVG-6 for a Med cruise aboard USS *Lake Champlain* (CVA-39). The carrier departed Mayport on 9 September and set a course eastward. For the next seven months, VMA-324 and its sister squadrons were engaged in the usual rounds of exercises, war games and "showing the flag" operations, interspersed with port calls, that make up the routine of a Med cruise. The ship completed its deployment without incident and returned to the U.S. on 31 March 1956, and on that date, to the operational control of the Marine Corps again.

Shortly after its return from its latest Med cruise, the squadron began to exchange its AD-4B versions of the versatile Skyraider for the latest version of the aircraft, the AD-6, and when the normal work-up period following the receipt of a new aircraft was completed, VMA-324 was once again ordered to carrier qualifications pending its return to the Med. The squadron would deploy aboard *Lake Champlain* for a second time. In the year since its last deployment, the carrier had undergone conversion from an attack carrier, a CVA, into an anti-submarine warfare carrier, a CVS. This resulted in a higher complement of helicopters aboard and a de-emphasis of strike operations in favor of submarine hunting. For this cruise, the air group of the carrier was entirely composed of the squadrons of MAG-26, which marked just the second and final occasion that the entire aircraft complement of an *Essex*-class fleet carrier was filled by Marine squadrons. *Lake Champlain* and MAG-26 sailed for the Med on 5 September 1957 and returned to the U.S. on 30 October after a short two-month deployment.

After the squadron's return from this deployment, it was clear that the days of the Skyraider were numbered as far as the Marine Corps was concerned, although it would be almost another decade before the venerable AD disappeared from the strike role in the Navy. Many of VMA-324's sister attack squadrons had begun to move into the new arena of jet aircraft opera-

tions, and the members of VMA-324 looked forward to the new challenges of high-speed aircraft performance. Still, the big, stable Skyraider was a superlative attack aircraft, and, as anxious as the squadron was to move forward aeronautically, most would miss the 'flying dump truck," as the AD series had become known. In early 1959, the squadron was notified to begin preparations to transition to another Douglas attack aircraft, the A4D-2 Skyhawk. Shortly thereafter, the first A4Ds began to arrive, and the squadron set about learning its new mount, and the nimble little "Scooter" quickly claimed the respect of all hands. Upon completion of the transition and work-up, the squadron was ordered to carrier qualifications in preparation for another carrier deployment.

On 19 September 1960, operational control of VMA-324 was transferred from MAG-24 to CVG-15 aboard USS *Coral Sea* (CVA-43), but instead of another deployment to the Med, *Coral Sea* was bound for WestPac. Three weeks after their departure, VMA-324 welcomed VMA-121 aboard the carrier where the two Marine squadrons would form the light attack component of her air group for the next six months. While at sea, VMA-324 was redesignated VMF(AW)-324 on 1 February 1961. No doubt this marked the only occasion when a Marine All-Weather Fighter squadron was equipped with a light attack aircraft, the Skyhawk possessed a respectable air-to-air combat capability, although it was, by no stretch of the description, an all-weather fighter. On the return leg of the deployment, VMA-121 was detached from the air group on 10 April, leaving VMF(AW)-324 as the sole Marine aviation contingent aboard the carrier. The ship returned to the U.S. on 27 May, and the squadron was detached from CVG-15 upon arrival to return to a normal operational status with its parent MAG.

Four months after the squadron's return from the western Pacific, it was again redesignated, becoming VMF-324 on 8 October. In an instance more reminiscent of the Navy's methodology with regard to changing squadron designations rapidly, VMF-324 was redesignated VMA-324 later the same day. [While the author is very familiar with the terms "the needs of the service," he has yet to encounter anyone that can satisfactorily explain happenings such as that. Why not, in this case, just redesignate the squadron VMA-324 in the first place and be done with it?]

After two years away from the deck of a carrier, the squadron was again ordered to carrier qualifications in the summer of 1963. Their qualification completed, VMA-324 was transferred to the control of CVG-7 aboard USS *Independence* (CVA-62). Bound for the Med once again, the ship departed the U.S. on 6 August 1963 and returned to the U.S. on 4 March 1964.

After its return from its latest deployment, the squadron was re-equipped with the much-improved A-4E version of the Skyhawk. With two additional store stations and a more powerful engine, the –E boasted a considerable increase in useful war load over its predecessors and was the most numerous version of the series. Their transition to the new version of the Skyhawk was followed by the now-somewhat routine preparations for VMA-324's sixth carrier deployment. Again teamed with the Navy squadron of Air Wing 7 [formerly Air Group 7] aboard *Independence* for another Med cruise that began on 13 June 1966 and lasted until 1 February 1967. This cruise was the first deployment for the carrier since her return from the Tonkin Gulf the previous year. During her 100 days on the line off Vietnam,

Replenishment at Sea
The ability of the U.S. Navy to replenishment its ships at sea did much to enhance its global reach. This view shows USS
Coral Sea (CVA-43) and USS Duncan (DD-874) alongside USS Bellatrix (AF-62) during the squadron's deployment.
(U.S. Navy Photo)

the air wing had suffered the loss of thirteen aircraft in combat. In addition, four others were lost to operational causes. No doubt all concerned were, at the same time, somewhat relieved by the thought of their not having to return to the deadly skies of North Vietnam in the near future and somewhat angered by the knowledge they would not have the opportunity to avenge their previous losses. At the same time, as far as the Marines were concerned, while none were aware of the fact at the time, the completion of this deployment marked the end of the long association of VMA-324 with the carriers of the United States Navy.

After its return from its 1966/67 cruise, VMA-324 continued to operate from various air stations up and down the East Coast, those in the Caribbean, and other locales as a part of the normal unit rotational schedule and was not among the Marine

light attack squadrons deployed to southeast Asia. VMA-324 continued to operate the –E version of the Skyhawk for the remainder of the decade of the 1960s until it was superseded in 1971 when the first –Ms began to roll off the production line. The A4-M represented the culmination of the development of the A-4 series and would see service only in the Marine Corps. With its more powerful power plant, improved avionics and the Hughes Angle Rate Bombing System [ARBS], this aircraft would remain at the forefront of Marine light attack aviation until it was replaced by the remarkable AV-8 Harrier series. However, VMA-324 would not operate the Harrier and continued to be equipped with the –M Skyhawk until it was deactivated on 29 August 1974. The squadron was among those of all aviation branches of the U.S. military that was fated to be deactivated in

The CO's Scooter
Aircraft Number 1, traditionally assigned to the squadron's command-ing officer, waits on the ramp for its next sortie. [via www.Skyhawk.org]

the wake of the war in Southeast Asia. The war there had been long, bitter and extremely frustrating for all concerned, both military and civilian, and when it finally crawled to its less than satisfactory end, most civilians wanted nothing more than to put the entire experience behind our society, but the military entered a long period that was, in many ways, even more frustrating than the war had been. It was more than a decade before the armed forces of the United States were able to rid themselves of the malaise of the post-Vietnam era.

Of the four insignia pictured, the first was adopted in the late-1950s and was worn by the squadron from the date of its adoption until the deactivation of VMA-324. The red dog's or wolf's head is the source of the squadron's "Devil Dog" nick-name and is in keeping with the devil's face in the insignia of VMF-324 of World War II. The crossed swords are Mamaluke sabers of the full-dress uniform of Marine officers and com-memorate the presentation of such a saber to Lieutenant Pres-ley N. O'Bannon, who led his Marines in the actions along the North African littoral celebrated in the line from the Marine Hymn, "…to the shores of Tripoli."

The second and third insignia are examples of the design worn by VMA-324 in the period following its reactivation in 1953. The one on the left is the more accurate of the two, and

Author's Collection

that on the right is an example of a reproduction most commonly seen for sale today.

The last is an example of the World War II insignia of VMF-324. It was designed by Lieutenant Russell N. Moubleau and is one of no fewer than nineteen Marine squadron insignia from the World War II period that included a representation of the F4U Corsair in one form or another despite the official prohibition against the inclusion of a specific aircraft type in an insignia.

What, if any, changes were made to the squadron's insig-nia during the ten months in 1961 when it was designated an all-weather fighter squadron is unknown. If any changes were, indeed, made, it is likely that they were limited to changing the squadron designation in the scroll at the bottom of the insignia.

MARINE ATTACK SQUADRON 331

THE BUMBLEBEES, THE KILLER BEES

THE DOODLEBUG SQUADRON (WORLD WAR II)

Author's Collection

Marine Scout Bombing Squadron 331 was activated at MCAS, Cherry Point, North Carolina on 1 January 1943, under the command of Captain Robert B. Cox who would be the first of several officers to command the squadron during its early months of service. He was succeeded by Major James L. Beam on 26 January, and Beam was followed by Captain James A. Feeley on 1 February, who commanded the squadron until 15 April 1943, and Major Paul R. Byrum, Jr. assumed command the next day. The fact that the squadron was commanded by four officers in 3 ½ months speaks volumes to the state of flux of Marine aviation at the time due to its almost exponential expansion.

While its command arrangements were being determined by higher authorities, VMSB-331 received its initial complement of SBDs so it could begin its training. It moved from Cherry Point to one of that station's outlying fields at nearby Bogue in June 1943, where the squadron began the process of becoming proficient with the aircraft it would later take to war in the Pacific. The long, bloody struggle for control of Guadalcanal had begun to wane by the date of the squadron's activation, and preparations were under way to begin the planned march up the Solomons to Rabaul. The elimination of the Japanese fortress on the island of New Britain was the ultimate strategic objective of the entire Solomons campaign.

In September, the squadron was ordered to San Diego as the first step of its journey into combat in the Pacific. By this date, American forces had driven the Japanese back to the upper Solomons and were preparing to assault Bougainville to establish bases from which the reduction of Rabaul could begin in earnest. Only a year earlier, the "Slot," as the New Georgia Sound, the body of water dividing the two parallel strings of islands that compose the Solomons was nicknamed by the Americans, had

been the favored route of the Japanese forces steaming southeastward to contest the American possession of Guadalcanal. Now, it was an American highway running northwestward that terminated at Rabaul. No doubt all hands in VMSB-331 expected to be dispatched to the Solomons in short order. However, other destinations lay ahead for the squadron. In late September, the squadron sailed from San Diego, but it was not bound for the Solomons, the expected destination. It was ordered instead to the Central Pacific for support of the coming assault against the Gilbert Islands that was scheduled for late November. VMSB-331 arrived at Tutulia in October and staged forward to Wallis Island. Wallis was only an intermediate stop as the squadron soon moved to Nukufetau, a small atoll seventy-five miles northwest of Funafuti. Upon its arrival, it was assigned to the Ellice Defense and Utility Group, designated Task Group 57.4, on 15 November 1943.

The Second Marine Division went ashore on Tarawa, the main objective of the Gilberts campaign, on 20 November. The action that followed was brief but extremely bloody. The division suffered almost 1,000 men killed in the seventy-six-hour fight for the tiny atoll that was the most intense of the entire Pacific war. Air support for the assault and capture of the atoll was mostly a Navy affair provided by the squadrons aboard the escort carriers that saw their first action at Majuro other than serving as aircraft ferries in the Gilberts. The Marine squadrons, among them VMSB-331, were to provide local patrols and air defense in the area of their bases until the airfields on Tarawa and Makin, the other major assault objective in the Gilberts, that were won at such a high cost could receive them. The squadron moved to Tarawa on 30 November, where it again engaged in local patrol duty and the aerial escort of friendly shipping in the

Another Mission Underway
Armed with a 500lb. bomb on the centerline and a 100lb. bomb on each wing rack, a lineup of SBDs of VMSB-331 taxsi toward the runway at the field on Majuro. [USMC Photo]

area. VMSB-331's stay on the blood-soaked speck of coral was short, and it returned to Nukufetau on 26 December, but perhaps the most vivid memory many of the members of VMSB-331 took with them was the pervading stench of death that hung over the tiny atoll for many weeks after the battle there ended. It would remain there until after the next major assault in the Central Pacific, the capture of the Marshalls Islands, scheduled for shortly after the New Year. There can be no doubt that the scene that greeted the members of the squadron upon their arrival came as a shock to many among them. The shattered desolation and the stench of death served as grim reminders of the reality of the ground troops' war.

In late February 1944, MAG-31, including VMSB-331, began to move forward to new bases in the Marshalls. The squadron's flight echelon arrived on Majuro on 25 February and was joined there by the remainder of the squadron on 2 March. Majuro was in the heart of the Marshalls, and many of the heavily fortified Japanese-held islands in the group had been bypassed rather than to incur the unnecessary casualties that would result from assaulting these islands. VMSB-331's base was within easy reach of four major enemy garrisons. The closest, Mille Atoll, was only sixty-five miles from Majuro, and the most distant, Wotje Atoll, lay 160 miles away. These atolls were easily within range of a fully loaded SBD, and as a result, they received an almost daily pounding from the Marine squadrons based on Majuro and Kwajalein. At first, Japanese reaction to the American raids was fierce, but the enemy's ability, if not his will, to resist was reduced by each successive attack. The war in the central Pacific moved westward rapidly, and the Japanese garrisons left behind were reduced to simply attempting to survive as their supplies were consumed by the troops on the islands or were destroyed by the Marines' attacks. Soon, the strikes became "milk runs" that were seldom opposed by more than a few scattered bursts of anti-aircraft fire. Despite their severely reduced circumstances, the enemy below was still the enemy and would occasionally smite the unwary or the unlucky.

On 4 March, VMSB-331 carried out the first raid by the Marshalls-based Marine squadrons against Jaluit Atoll, which, at a distance of 243 miles, lay near the limit of the SBD's range as a bomber. Despite the 498 tons of bombs deposited on Jaluit by Army and Navy aircraft since the previous November, Japa-

nese anti-aircraft fire was intense and accurate, and 40% of the Dauntlesses participating in the strike were damaged by enemy fire. The following day, SBDs, this time from VMSB-231, struck Jaluit again. Their targets were the anti-aircraft batteries that had raked VMSB-331 so accurately the previous day. These two squadrons then began to alternate missions against the heavily defended atoll. Gradually, the weight of the bombs dropped by VMSB-231 and -331 wore down the enemy opposition until strikes against Jaluit took on the character of the milk runs being flown against the other Japanese installations in the Marshalls.

During the Bee's tour in the Marshalls, Major James C. Otis assumed command of the squadron after Major Byrum was transferred on 9 May 1944. In October 1944, VMSB-331 was redesignated VMBF-331 in expectation of exchanging its SBDs for F4U-1A Corsair fighter-bombers. This change of aircraft took place, but the squadron was redesignated VMSB-331 again on 30 December and exchanged its newly arrived Corsairs for SBDs once again shortly thereafter. The squadron continued to operate these aircraft against targets in the Marshalls until the Japanese surrender. On 18 December, Major John H. McEniry assumed command of the squadron and was followed by Major Winston E. Jewson on 3 February 1945.

Wide Body
A "wide-body" AD-5 Skyraider of VMA-331 flies over the calm waters of the Atlantic near NAS, Miami in the days following the end of the Korean conflict. The stores stations under the starboard are carrying a full load of practice ordnance. [USMC Photo]

Even before the end of the Second World War, it was obvious the sun was setting on the pure scout bomber in Navy and Marine service. The mighty Corsair had proven its ability to double in spades as a strike aircraft, and within months after the Japanese surrender, all of the Marines' scout bomber squadrons, including VMSB-331, were deactivated. The squadron's colors were retired on 21 November 1945. The squadron remained inactive for the better part of a decade until it was reactivated and redesignated an attack squadron in the wake of the Korean War. America, it seemed, again had learned to its cost the folly of its chronic lack of peacetime military preparedness in an unstable and dangerous world. Upon its reactivation on 23 April 1952, VMA-331 was equipped with the successor to the Dauntless, the Douglas Skyraider. The squadron received the "wide-body" AD-5 two-place version of the aircraft initially, and the drone of the squadron's aircraft was added to that of the others operating from MCAS, Miami.

The "wide-body" AD-5 quickly gave way to the single-seat AD-6 model in 1956, and VMA-331 continued to operate the big Skyraider in a normal squadron rotational deployment schedule for the next three years, but in early 1959, the squadron received word that it would soon convert to its first jet aircraft, the Skyhawk. The switch from props to jets came later that same year when the squadron began to receive the A4D-2 version of the "Scooter." Concurrent with the receipt of its new aircraft, VMA-331 moved its base of operations from Miami to MCAS, Cherry Point. After again being rated as a combat ready squadron with the Skyhawk, the squadron again began to deploy in support of America's commitments at home and abroad.

The A4D-2, which later became the A-4B, was replaced by the improved A-4E model, and the squadron began preparations for its first deployment aboard a carrier. Shortly after the completion of carrier qualification, the squadron was ordered aboard USS *Forrestal* (CVA-59) as a component of Air Wing 8 and deployed to the Med on 10 July 1964. It returned to Cherry Point on 13 March 1965.

By the time of the squadron's return to its home station, the United States was fully committed to the war in Vietnam, but VMA-331 did not deploy there. It remained based at Cherry Point and carried out its share of the Marines' deployments up and down the East Coast and in the Caribbean. After another round of carrier qualifications, VMA-331 went to sea again in 1970. It joined CVW-8 aboard USS *Independence* (CVA-62) and deployed to the Med on 23 June 1970. It returned to the U.S. on 1 February 1971.

While many Marine attack squadrons were reequipped with the -F model of Skyhawk, VMA-331 continued to fly the -E for most of the next eight years until it began to equip with the A-4M, the final single-seat model of the Skyhawk to see service with the Marine Corps. With its uprated engine and avionics, the -M represented the ultimate in the Skyhawk series.

It may be interesting to note that among the A-4Ms operated by VMA-311 was the 158th and last A-4M to be built. Coincidentally, this aircraft was also the final example of the entire A-4 series built, #2960. It rolled off the end of the production line at the Douglas plant in El Segundo, California on 27 February 1979. For the occasion of the completion of the last Skyhawk, the aircraft was resplendent in a special color scheme with the flags of the seven nations that had operated the A-4 painted on the fuselage side aft of the air intake. (Since that date, several other nations have received reconditioned models of the aircraft.) After the completion of the requisite speeches and ceremonies, the aircraft was presented to representatives of VMA-311. Soon after its arrival at Cherry Point, the aircraft was re-painted in the standard color scheme. In 1983, the squadron's Skyhawks were replaced by the AV-8B Harrier, ending VMA-

Man, What a View!
This section of AD-6 Skyraiders of VMA-331 was captured in flight above some spectacular scenery in this photo dated 1959 shortly before the squadron began its transition to the Skyhawk. The significance of the diagonal stripe on the fuselage side below the cockpit on aircraft #9 is unknown. [U.S. Navy Photo]

331's nearly twenty-five years with this remarkable little Douglas aircraft. While the Harrier offered a quantum leap forward in capability in the close air support mission, the "Scooter" was to be remembered fondly by all of those who flew it.

After their working up period with their new aircraft, the squadron returned to a normal schedule of deployments. This routine continued until the massive deployment of U.S. forces to Southwest Asia for Operations *Desert Shield* and *Desert Storm*. The deployment of VMA-331 was unique in that it was the only Marine fixed-wing squadron to deploy aboard a naval vessel for the Persian Gulf War. Control of the squadron was shifted from its parent MAG-32 to MAG-40, a provisional air group that was activated for the duration of the crisis in the Persian Gulf, for deployment there in October 1990. The squadron boarded the amphibious assault ship USS *Nassau* (LHA-4) and arrived in the Gulf the following month.

Initially, it was planned that the coming ground attack against the Iraqis occupying Kuwait would include an amphibious assault near Kuwait City, but the Iraqis laid extensive mine fields in the waters from which the assault would be launched. This, coupled with the strength of the enemy's defenses, the fear of high casualties among the attacking Marines, and with what would necessarily be heavy destruction in the actual area of the proposed landings rendered the amphibious assault a feint. Another factor that weighed heavily against the cost of the planned amphibious assault was the unprecedented speed with which the coalition forces overran their Iraqi opponents and advanced into Kuwait. However, the mere threat tied down large numbers of Iraqi troops defending beaches against an attack that would never come.

The eventual diversionary nature of their original mission did not prevent the squadron from taking part in air strikes in the Kuwaiti Theater of Operations. Most of the sorties involved "shaping the battlefield," in the terminology in vogue at the time. This "shaping" cost the squadron one aircraft on 27 February 1991 when the Harrier flown by Captain Reginald C. Under-

wood was shot down. Unfortunately, Captain Underwood was lost with his aircraft. After the successful completion of *Operation Desert Storm, Nassau* and VMA-331 returned to the U.S. After its post-war stand down period, the squadron returned to a normal deployment rotation.

After enjoying its post-deployment stand down period, the squadron began preparations for its next scheduled deployment, which came in February, 1992. Aboard *Nassau* again, the squadron departed the United States for a new destination for most of its members, the North Atlantic. There VMA-331 took part in Exercise *Teamwork 92*, along with the 4th Marine Expeditionary Brigade.

The deployment completed, the squadron returned to the United States, and as has been the case in the wake of every war, long or short, in our history, a series of cuts were being imposed on the military budget and force structure. Among the victims of this round of reductions was VMA-331, which was deactivated in September, 1992, and the squadron has remained among the inactive over the ensuing two decades.

Author's Collection

via Holmberg

A Hazy Day in the Med
USS Forrestal (CVA-59) conducting flight ops during operations with the U.S. Sixth Fleet in the Mediterranean. [U.S. Navy Photo]

The first insignia pictured is the current insignia of VMA-331. It is fully embroidered on a twill backing. The second example is one of the current aircraft type insignia popular among Navy and Marine aviators. It indicates the aircraft with which the squadron is equipped and is worn on the shoulder of the flight suit. The "VL" is the tail code of VMA-331, and "Killer Bees" is the more popular current squadron nickname.

The third is a larger example of the same basic design, but it dates from 1972. Note the differences in detail of the body of the bee and that the insect is wearing goggles on this insignia that are not shown on the first picture.

The fourth insignia is an example of the squadron's insignia that dates from the early 1960s and is Japanese-made.

The fifth and sixth insignia date from the 1950s during the period after the squadron was reactivated and designated an attack squadron.

The last one is an example of the insignia of VMSB-331 that is embroidered on a wool felt background, which has suffered some moth damage around its lower edge over the many decades since it was made. Note that the details of the bee are virtually identical in each version of the insignia.

The squadron's insignia design is attributed to a squadron member, Captain John J. Tooley.

Not pictured is that worn by the squadron upon its reactivation in 1955. It differed from the current design in background color and the angle at which the bomb is falling.

via Holmberg   *Author's Collection*   *Author's Collection*

A Colorful Bee
An early example of the A4-M version of the Skyhawk in the colors of VMA-331 sits on the ramp on an overcast day.
[USMC Photo]

MARINE TORPEDO BOMBER SQUADRON 341,
THE TORRID TURTLES

via Holmberg

Marine Scout Bombing Squadron 341 was activated on 1 February 1943 at MCAS, Cherry Point, North Carolina, under the command of Captain William E. Clasen. Additional personnel reported during the next few weeks to round out the squadron's roster, and training commenced as soon as a sufficient number of SBD Dauntless dive-bombers and crews were on hand. During this period, the physical facilities at Cherry Point were outstripped by the rapid rate at which new squadrons were activated, and, as a result, VMSB-341 moved from the main facility to nearby MCAAF, Atlantic Field, a satellite installation to Cherry Point, to continue its training. The move was completed by 31 May 1943, and the squadron remained at the auxiliary field for sixty days, and it returned to Cherry Point on 1 August. Shortly thereafter, the squadron's flight echelon was alerted to prepare for movement to the Pacific theater.

The ground echelon departed from New Bern by train and arrived at what was then the Marine Corps Air Depot, Miramar on 9 September. The flight echelon began a cross country flight on 1 September and arrived at NAS, North Island on 5 September, and after the arrival of the ground echelon, a group of mechanics and technicians was sent to the naval air station to prepare the squadron's SBDs for shipment by sea. On 25 September, the squadrons aircraft and the flight echelon were loaded aboard USS *Nassau* (CVE-16) and sailed for the South Pacific that same afternoon. The ground echelon beat the aviators to sea when it sailed aboard the army transport U.S.A.T. *Pueblo* on 20 September. Major Clasen was detached temporarily on 30 September while the squadron was en route to the South Pacific, and Major George J. Waldie, Jr., served as the squadron's interim commander until VMSB-341 reached its destination, Pago

Pago, American Samoa, where it arrived on 6 October. Clasen returned and assumed command once again on 8 October.

The Japanese had planned to move against allied positions in Samoa and other islands in the area during the summer of 1942. Their plans, however, had been derailed, first by the crushing defeat at Midway in June, and then by the American assault against Guadalcanal and the Lower Solomons, which sucked Japanese resources into the ever growing sinkhole that was the Solomons at an alarming rate from their point of view but much to the allied plan. After a struggle lasting six months, the Japanese had withdrawn the pitiful remnants of their forces from Guadalcanal in February 1943, and the Americans had gone over to the offensive in the Solomons immediately thereafter. These reversals of American and Japanese fortunes ended any Japanese plans for expansion toward Samoa or any place else, for that matter. As a result, the American forces in Samoa formed garrisons for outposts in this now quiet backwater of the war. By the latter part of October, the squadron was ashore and had begun flight operations where combination of mechanical failure and bad luck claimed the squadron's first casualties when one of its SBDs crashed on the Samoan island of Savaii. Second Lieutenant Louis F. Zimmerman and his gunner, PFC James P. Madden were killed in the crash. [This peaceful island is reputed to have been the inspiration for Robert Louis Stevenson's novel *Treasure Island.* The author resided in the islands when he wrote the classic story.

Commanded again by Major Waldie since 31 October, the flight echelon moved from Efate to the airfield at Munda, New Georgia, just after the New Year and joined the Solomons Strike Command in hammering the Japanese at Rabaul. It participated in its first strike against the fortress when it contributed sixteen SBDs to the attack of 17 January 1944. Targeted against shipping in Simpson Harbor, the 117 aircraft of the American strike were met by seventy-nine enemy fighters that rose from the complex of airfields that guarded Rabaul. Marine fighters claimed eleven Japanese fighters, and the strike aircraft were credited with sinking five ships and inflicting varying degrees of damage on others. More than 18,000 tons of vital shipping was subtracted from the roster of the Japanese merchant marine that was beginning to shrink precipitously steadily from the losses inflicted by American aircraft and submarines.

Rabaul had fallen to the Japanese in January 1942. Located on the eastern end of the island of New Britain, it, along with New Ireland, are the principal islands of the Bismarck Archipelago. The Japanese had rapidly built up their defenses at Rabaul until it became the cornerstone of their positions in the southwest Pacific. Rabaul's Simpson Harbor was the finest deep-water port in the entire area, and, guarded by thousands of troops and a complex of five airfields and with nearly impenetrable jungle on its western flank, it was thought by the Japanese to be impregnable. However, the reduction of Rabaul had been the primary strategic objective of the entire Solomons Campaign. The long and often bloody march up the island chain had been conducted with the plan in mind of placing sufficient Allied air power within range of Rabaul to pound it into impotence. This aerial might was in position by mid-December 1943, and the campaign against Rabaul commenced in earnest on 17 December. Each day the weather permitted, the Japanese were attacked without mercy, and their defenses were beaten down over the next two months. Finally, on 19 February 1944, the Japanese admitted, at least to themselves, that they were incapable of halting the allied aerial onslaught and withdrew the bulk of what remained of their defending aircraft from the Bismarks. When the inevitable, as far as the Japanese were concerned, ground assault against the fortress came, the Emperor's troops would be expected to defend their positions to the last bullet and man and considerably slow the Allied juggernaut while inflicting maximum casualties on the assault forces. However, by this time, the Allied strategy of "island hopping" had been fully developed. It had been proven unnecessary to assault and reduce each island held by the enemy, and where suitable alternatives could be found, strongly held islands would be bypassed in favor of assaults against those that were left relatively unguarded. Bases were to be established on these islands and would serve as springboards from which continuous air assaults would be mounted against enemy garrisons left behind to "wither on the vine." This strategy saved a great deal of time and uncounted Allied lives, and it would seal the fate of Rabaul. Attacked from the air for the remainder of the war, the Japanese defenders were gradually reduced to near-starvation existence. Eventually, the vegetable gardens the Japanese planted to supplement their meager diets were added to the target lists of the attacking aircraft. The number of enemy troops who perished as a result of the disease and starvation brought about by these tactics are unknown but must have numbered in the thousands.

VMSB-341 played its part in the campaign against the fortress. It participated in many of the strikes against the enemy there from the 17 January attack until the Japanese withdrew their air and naval forces a month later. From Munda, the squadron moved forward to the complex of airfields in the Piva area of Bougainville to shorten the range for missions mounted against Rabaul. During this period of intense operations, Major James T. McDaniel assumed command on 24 January 1944.

From Bougainville, the squadron continued to participate in the strikes against Rabaul until March, when it was withdrawn from combat for a short period of R&R, and after its tour of the wonders of Australia ended, VMSB-341 was reunited at Efate in the New Hebrides for a few weeks. On 6 March 1944, the Green Islands, a short distance due east of Rabaul, had fallen to the continuing American advance, and VMSB-341 was among the first squadrons to be ordered to the newly captured airfields there. The "Torrid Turtles" spent their second combat tour taking part in the continued pounding of Rabaul.

At the end of its second period in combat, the flight echelon departed for Australia once again. The ground echelon moved also, but instead of Australia, it moved to Emirau on 29 April. When the squadron's aviators returned from Australia, they went first to Efate and then were reunited with the ground echelon on Emirau on 24 June. VMSB-341 continued to participate in the strikes against the Japanese at Rabaul throughout this period and was ordered to the Green Islands in July. These islands were the final links in the chain of Allied airfields that continued to strangle Rabaul into a state of near-impotence, and the squadron continued to take part in missions against the area for the rest of 1944.

By mid-1944, the Solomons-Bismarks area had been transformed from a scene of bitter daily combat into one of a relatively quiet rear area. Strikes continued to be flown against Japanese positions on New Britain and New Ireland, and there was no shortage of routine search and patrol missions to be flown. But, the Marine aviators in the South Pacific had driven the enemy from the skies and seas of the area. There was little in the way of useful strategic goals that remained to be accomplished in

the theater. As a result, this considerable assemblage of aerial striking power languished in the doldrums for some months. It was during this quiet period of the squadron's service that Major Walter D. Parsons assumed command on 20 May. He was followed by Major Christopher F Irwin, Jr., on 15 August.

The American return to the Philippines in the latter part of October 1944 was the catalyst that served to awaken the slumbering power of Marine aviation in the south and southwest Pacific. For reasons already discussed, the Army Air Forces proved incapable of providing the precision close air support called for in the Philippines campaign, and the combat in the Archipelago was too protracted for the fleet carriers to provide this type of support on a continuous basis. These factors generated a call for the Marine scout bombing squadrons that sat virtually unemployed in the South Pacific. With regard to the "Turtles" of VMSB-341, its flight echelon was ordered from the Green Islands back to Emirau on 22 December 1944 in preparation for its deployment to the Philippines. The squadron's ground echelon remained on Emirau until January 1945, when it boarded the ships of the convoy that would carry it to Luzon, the northernmost and largest island of the Philippines. The flight echelon flew north to the island on 26 January 1945, and by day's end on 28 January, seven Marine scout-bombing squadrons were in place at Mangaldan Airdrome on Luzon. These squadrons had at their disposal a total of 168 SBDs, along with more than 3,500 officers and men. This represented the largest single concentration of Marine scout bombing squadrons during World War II.

VMSB-341 began operations in the Philippines on 30 January when the squadron, along with VMSB-236, sent a total of thirty-six SBDs against targets located near the town of Tuguegarao in Cagayan Province. Among the list of targets there was an airfield used by Japanese aircraft that were flown from bases on Formosa as reinforcements for their forces on Luzon. The results of the strike were devastating. Seven large craters were gouged in the runway by 1,000lb. bombs, and eight well-camouflaged enemy aircraft located nearby were destroyed. Several supply dumps were thoroughly bombed, strafed, and left engulfed in flames. Ten barracks buildings were destroyed, and a large structure, formerly a school building, identified by friendly guerrillas as a headquarters facility, was leveled by three direct hits. It would be a considerable period of time before the facilities in the area were of use to the Japanese again.

The Marines had been in operation from Mangaldan for only two weeks when word came that they would take part in operations in the southern Philippines also. Among the first squadrons to participate in operations on Mindanao would be VMSB-341, and the ground echelons of the three squadrons identified to move south began to pack in preparation for the shift of forces. In yet another example of the way things often happen in the military, some of these forces had been ashore on Luzon for only one day when they began to make ready for another move. The members of the headquarters squadron of MAG-32 began to refer to themselves as "Stevedores Union, Local 32" in reference to their many hours spent in preparing and loading cargo for movement by sea. The ground echelons of the squadrons of MAG-32, which now included VMSB-341, boarded the ships of the convoy that would carry them south to Mindanao and sailed on 23 February. The flight echelon of VMSB-341 remained on Luzon for another two weeks, taking part in a continuing series of strikes there before they moved

The Weapons of War
These SBD-5s are nearing completion on the assembly line at Douglass Aircraft El Segundo, California plant in 1943. [U.S. Navy Photo]

south. Targets at Nichols Field near Manila and the island of Corregidor were among the unfortunate recipients of the squadron's bombs during this period.

The 24 SBDs of VMSB-341 departed for points south on 22 March and arrived at Moret Field at Zamboanga, Mindanao shortly thereafter. The squadron's ground echelon had moved ashore from its convoy on 15 March and was ready to receive the squadron's Dauntless's when they arrived. MAG-32 would be based at Zamboanga on the western tip of Mindanao, and the squadron's SBDs arrived there on 23 March 1945. Marine aircraft from the other groups on Mindanao supported landings north of the island, which allowed more than the usual amount of time for the aviators of MAG-32 to settle into their new surroundings before they were committed to operations. VMSB-341 flew its first sorties from its southern base on 9 April, when it was among the squadrons that provided support for the Army's 41st Infantry Division on Jolo Island in the Sulu Archipelago which lay to the southwest of the Philippines. Forty-four SBDs of the squadrons of MAG-32 were among the aircraft that supported the initial assault.

These islands were populated by the Moros, the fierce Moslem warriors who made the lives of the Japanese invaders miserable and often quite short. Clannish and wary of outsiders they considered to be "infidels," the Moros did not welcome even American airmen who found themselves on the ground in Moro territory. Among the main target of the sorties flown after the landings were against Japanese positions centered around Mount Daho, a 2,247-foot peak that dominated much of the surrounding terrain. It was estimated that some 400 men of Japanese Special Naval Landing Force, the nearest Japanese equivalent of U.S. Marines, held the area and were heavily supplied with automatic weapons ranging from light machine guns to twin 20mm cannon.

Despite five days of heavy air attacks, the initial assault by the 41st Infantry Division met a bloody repulse, and the Marine aircraft were called in again. A total of 33 SBDs, including fifteen

from VMSB-341, struck an area measuring approximately 600 by 200 yards in which the enemy's defenses were concentrated. The infantry's renewed attack followed closely on the heels of the air strike and quickly captured its objectives. The scene in the area subjected to the air strike must have evoked visions of Dante's Inferno. Later descriptions spoke of "...not a whole tree in the area. Concussion in there [from the detonations of multiple 1,000-pound general-purpose bombs] must have been unbearable. Dead were everywhere – parts of bodies splattered about..." More than 230 enemy dead were attributed to the strike.

Major Robert J. Bear assumed command of the squadron on 4 May 1945, and operations on Mindanao continued after the official end of the campaign there on 30 June. Additional missions were flown against the Japanese in the Sulu Archipelago, the last major effort in the area coming on 12 July. On 1 August 1945, VMSB-341 and the other squadrons of MAG-32 were ordered to cease tactical operations and to turn in its aircraft in preparation for their return to the United States. Major Bear was detached and Lieutenant Robert J. Morrissey assumed command on 15 August 1945. The "Torrid Turtles" of VMSB-341 returned to the United States and were deactivated on 13 September 1945.

VMSB-341 was credited with the destruction of two enemy aircraft in aerial combat during its service in the northern Solomons. Both were credited to Corporal Martin A. Houlroyd, one the squadron's gunners. In addition to these aerial victories, the squadron also received two awards of the Navy Unit Commendation. The first was for its service on Luzon during the period 23 January through 15 March 1945, and the second was for service in the Southern Philippines during the period 16 March through 30 June 1945.

The example of the insignia of VMSB-341 in the accompanying plate was made for a squadron reunion and is accurate in detail and color. Originals of the insignia were embroidered on wool during one of the squadron's R&R periods in Australia. The design is attributed to a squadron member, Dwayne Ustler.

MARINE SCOUT BOMBING SQUADRON 342
THE BATS FROM HELL

via Holmberg

VMSB-342 was activated on 1 July 1943 at MCAS, Cherry Point, North Carolina, and the first officer to command the squadron was Major Joseph W. Kean, Jr. A component squadron of Marine Aircraft Group 34, it received its personnel complement and a handful of aircraft and commenced its training immediately following its activation. According to aircraft return reports, on 1 August, VMSB-342 had a total of fifteen aircraft on hand. This total was composed of four SBD-4 Dauntlesses; nine of the newer SBD-5s; one Grumman J2F-1 Duck amphibian and a single example of the Vultee SNV-1, the Navy version of the Army Air Force's BT-13 "Vibrator" advanced trainer to serve as its hack and instrument trainer. The squadron continued its training at Cherry Point throughout the remainder of 1943 and into the early spring of 1944. In April, it was transferred from the main air station to nearby MCAAS, Atlantic Field, to ease the crowding at Cherry Point. After completion of the move, some of the squadron's aircrews were detached and temporarily as-

signed to NAS, Boca Chica, near Miami, for additional training. VMSB-342 remained at Atlantic Field until mid-summer, when it was transferred to the field at Newport, Arkansas, in early August. Major Kean was detached on 12 August, and Lieutenant Richard B. Fielder assumed to duties of interim commanding officer the following day.

The latter half of 1944 was the low point of World War II for Marine aviation in terms of useful employment in any active campaigns. The Solomons Campaign had reached its successful culmination earlier in the year. The Japanese fortress of Rabaul had been beaten into submission in a furious aerial campaign that saw the enemy tacitly admit defeat and withdraw the remnants of his aircraft in February, leaving the garrison there to extract whatever it could in blood to slow the Allied advance. The decision had been made to exclude the Marines from participation in the European Campaign, and the war in the Pacific was progressing so well with far lower than anticipated losses in aviation personnel that the Navy had made the decision to reduce the numbers of students undergoing aviation training.

The upshot of all this was that a significant number of well trained and combat experienced Marine squadrons were languishing in quiet rear areas throughout the Pacific Theater. The only active combat operations for the Marines during this period were in the Palaus, where the bloody fighting for the miserable, hellish sun-baked ridges of Peleliu raged, but only a small number of aviators were engaged there. As a result of the lack of gainful employment for the squadrons already deployed to the Pacific, many of those in the United States that previously had been engaged in hurried preparations for deployment experienced a rapid slowing of their own operations. For many, this time in the doldrums would spell their doom.

As far as VMSB-342 was concerned, many of its personnel were transferred to other duties, and Captain James R. LePhew assumed command from Lieutenant Fielder on 23 August. His term at the reins of the squadron would last for only two days, pending the arrival of Major Paul L. Andre, Jr., on 25 August 1944. The squadron remained at Newport until it was deactivated on 10 October 1944. In light of the massive commitment of Marine aviation to the war in the Pacific, it is somewhat ironic that Newport, Arkansas was the westernmost point of deployment of VMSB-342 during its history.

To date, research has failed to locate an example of the insignia of VMSB-342. The design depicted is an illustration, and it represents the only design attributed to the squadron during its short months of service.

MARINE ATTACK SQUADRON 343
GREGORY'S GORILLAS (WORLD WAR II)

Author's Collection

VMSB-343 was activated on 1 August 1943 at MCAAF, Atlantic Field, North Carolina, under the command of Major Walter E. Gregory. In December, the squadron was transferred to Greenville, South Carolina, to continue its training. It remained at Greenville until 15 July 1944, when it was alerted to prepare for movement to the Pacific, and shortly thereafter, VMSB-343 began its journey westward. The squadron's next stop was MCAS, Miramar, where it remained for only a few days before it sailed from San Diego, on 31 August, bound for MCAS, Ewa. After its arrival at Ewa, the squadron was issued new aircraft and began to get acquainted with its new mount, a somewhat rare "Beast" among Marine scout bomber squadrons, the SB2C. The Battle of the Philippine Sea in June 1944 had been the last hurrah for the SBD Dauntless among the Navy's carrier-based dive-bomber squadrons. Even then, the SBD had been largely replaced aboard the carriers by the Curtiss SB2C Helldiver, and only Bombing 16 of USS *Lexington* (CV-16) had flown the SBD in this, the last of the great carrier-vs.-carrier battles. Although VMSB-343 had been trained and initially equipped with the Dauntless, the squadron received the Helldiver while at Ewa. After almost two months in which to become familiar with their new aircraft, the squadron departed Ewa on a 1,100 mile overwater flight to its next station at Midway on 27 August.

All the squadron's aircraft arrived safely at Midway, and it was assigned to the airstrip on Eastern Island where it was under the control of the Hawaiian Sea Frontier. By this date, the war had moved far across the vast central Pacific, and Midway was a quiet backwater and a stop over point for ships and units coming and going to the scene of active combat operations. VMSB-343 was

destined to spend thousands of long, boring hours aloft under the mid-Pacific sun searching for an enemy that was no longer present. The routine of these patrol flights was broken only by anti-submarine escort flights for friendly ships while they were operating within the squadron's areas of responsibility, but these patrols seldom bore any fruit in the form of submarine sightings, let alone any attacks. While the Imperial Japanese Navy was able to boast of a considerable submarine force during the first half of the war, by mid-1944 its strength had been reduced to a large extent, and those that remained were seldom employed against allied supply lines. Instead, they were employed almost exclusively in hunting warships and the unprofitable stand in role as supply vessels to the bypassed Imperial garrisons spread out across the Pacific.

On 1 April 1945, VMSB-343 shifted its base across the atoll's lagoon to Sand Island, the other principal landmass of the flyspeck that was Midway. After settling into its "new" surroundings, the squadron went back to its routine of patrol and anti-submarine missions that were to continue until the Japanese surrendered. As World War II entered its final month, the squadron under went several changes of command with Major Harold G. Schlendering assuming command on 3 August 1945. He was followed by Major Perry H. Aliff on 18 August and Major Jack Cosley on 31 August.

Almost before the last shot was fired against the Japanese, the civil war between Nationalist and Communist Chinese forces flared again in mainland China. The Japanese invasion of China had brought about a temporary, uneasy truce of sorts between the Nationalists and Communists as they both turned their energies and mutual hatred against the Japanese. Now, however, Japan lay prostrate before the victorious Allies, and both sides in the Chinese Civil War returned to their old ways, clawing at each other with a renewed fury and armed with both those weapons seized from the Japanese, as well as those supplied to both sides by the Allies during the war. In an attempt to bring some measure of stability to a land torn by war for nearly two decades, several Marine aviation units were moved into China from the bases they had occupied at the time of the Japanese surrender. VMSB-343 was one of the squadrons ordered to China, where it arrived in late October 1945. Upon its arrival, it was assigned to MAG-32 at Tsingtao, and for the first time in its history, the squadron was about to engage in something other than countless hours of boring sea patrol missions. The first "show-of-force" patrols over both Nationalist and Communist territory were flown on 1 November. Neither side had any interest in stopping the fighting, and Nationalist and Communist alike frequently fired upon these patrols. It is somewhat ironic that VMSB-343, a squadron that been activated at the height of World War II, saw the first shots fired at its aircraft in anger after the war's end by forces who were ostensibly friendly to the United States.

Despite the frequent ground fire, the patrols continued without loss until 8 December when six of the squadron's SB2C-5s of a flight of twelve were lost in a blinding snowstorm over Communist-controlled territory near Laichow. The Helldivers crashed with the loss of all twelve men aboard. Unfortunately, the remains of only eight were recovered, and in a somewhat strange turn of events, the villagers in the area wrote touching notes about the loss of "our friends, the Americans." They even returned the reward they had received for finding the bodies of the Marines. Suffice to say China in those days was a maze of emotional and political twists and turns as bizarre as any in that nation's long and often contradictory history.

By the spring of 1946, the United States began to appreciate the likely hopelessness of these peacekeeping efforts and that there was little the U.S. could do to influence events there short of engaging in hostilities against both sides and began to withdraw its forces from China. This also was due, at least in some measure, to the continuing clamor to "bring the boys home" sooner rather than later. The turn of VMSB-343 to return home came in May, when all the dive-bombers were transferred to Guam, where the squadron was deactivated shortly after its arrival there. The actual date of its deactivation was 10 June 1946. The squadron remained inactive until the end of the Korean War when it was reactivated and redesignated VMA-343. Initially, it was equipped with variants of the Douglas Skyraider.

The big Skyraider gave way to the North American FJ-series, the Fury. VMA-343 was among the Marine squadrons to operate the FJ-4 fighter-bomber version of the aircraft. It was scheduled to convert from the Fury to the Douglas Skyhawk in 1961 but was deactivated prior to the conversion. The squadron has remained inactive since that date.

The insignia of VMA-343 pictured is that worn by squadron members from the time of its reactivation following the Korean War until the time of its deactivation in 1961. The symbology of the red dragon and the eight ball has not been uncovered at the time this was written. It may be that the dragon was symbolic of VMSB-343's service in China, and units involved in this duty were frequently behind the proverbial "8-ball," but this is pure speculation.

The gorilla insignia of VMSB-343 was supplied by Mr. E.S. Holmberg for this work.

via Holmberg

MARINE SCOUT-BOMBING SQUADRON 344

Author's Collection

VMSB-344 was activated on 1 January 1944 at MCAS, Cherry Point, under the command of Major Norman E. Denning. It was one of the last Marine scout bombing squadrons to be activated during World War II and also could claim the somewhat dubious distinction of having been the only one to be equipped with the controversial Curtiss SB2C Helldiver throughout its service. Nicknamed the "Big-Tailed Beast," the SB2C, the last aircraft to bear the distinguished marque of this manufacturer, should have been a winner from the very beginning. Designed to replace the tried and true Dauntless, the Helldiver was bigger, faster, more heavily armed, and was capable of carrying a bomb load almost twice that of the SBD over greater distances. The design also sported folding wings, a feature the Dauntless lacked. However, the primary requisite for any carrier-based aircraft is structural strength, and in this vital area, the SB2C came in a distant second to the rugged little "Slow but Deadly," as the SBD was known.

A host of structural problems plagued the SB2C from the beginning. Tail hooks frequently pulled free of the airframe upon engagement of an arresting wire, a circumstance that led immediately to a serious situation should any aircraft be spotted forward of the landing area of the flight deck, which was usually the case during recovery. Upon a hard landing, hardly a rarity in carrier operations, the engine mounts were known to fail, which frequently led to the complete separation of the power plant from the airframe. But, most serious of all was the tendency of the "Beast" to shed its wings upon recovery if dived at too great a speed – hardly a laudable characteristic for an aircraft whose primary mode of attack was a near-vertical, seventy-degree dive! Problems with the "Beast" were so numerous, in fact, that several high-ranking

naval officers went so far as to recommend the cancellation of all planned production of the SB2C in favor of continuing with production of the proven but obsolescent SBD. However, by this time, the SB2C had acquired a momentum all its own. In addition to Curtiss, two other manufacturers, Brewster Aeronautical Corporation and Canadian Car and Foundry in Montreal, had been contracted to produce the aircraft. In addition, materials that would have been required to continue to build the SBD had been diverted to other, higher priority production, and to redirect them to Douglas, the manufacturer of the SBD, would have caused difficulties with other projects. Eventually, most of the problems with the SB2C were more or less corrected, but it remained limited with regard to diving speed throughout its service life. Also, the required strengthening added weight to the airframe and led to a reduction in both the speed and range of the Helldiver.

Regardless of the problems with the SB2C, VMSB-344 carried on with its training and was transferred from Cherry Point to nearby Greenville. On 20 August, it was ordered to the auxiliary airfield at Newport, Arkansas where, on 31 August, Major Denning was detached, and Major Jack Cosley assumed command on 1 September.

As a result of the lack of worthwhile employment for many of the Marine tactical squadrons already in the Pacific, VMSB-344 was ordered deactivated on 10 October 1944, a fate it shared with several Marine scout bombing squadrons at various fields in Arkansas at the time.

The insignia of VMSB-344 is an example of the only design attributed to the squadron during its service, and it was drawn by the artists of the Walt Disney Studios.

MARINE BOMBING SQUADRON 413
THE NIGHT HECKLERS, THE SHAMROCKS
THE FLYING NIGHTMARES

Author's Collection

Author's Collection

Marine Bombing Squadron 413 was activated on 1 March 1943 at MCAS, Cherry Point, under the command of Major Robert B. Cox. It had the distinction of being the first medium bomber squadron in the Marine Corps and was equipped with the Navy's version of the North American B-25 Mitchell, the PBJ in the Navy's aircraft designation system. The acquisition of the B-25 and the activation of squadrons equipped with it represented a departure from the norm as far as the Marine Corps' traditional employment of air power was concerned. Although the horizontal bombing missions executed by the Northern Bombing Group during World War I were the first combat missions flown by Marine aviation, the years between the two world wars saw the Marines employ single-engine dive-bombing aircraft almost exclusively as their "bombing" aircraft. This was in accordance with the stated mission of Marine aviation, the direct support of the Marine on the ground, and for this mission the dive-bomber was a far more suitable and accurate bombing platform. This concentration on dive-bombing made the B-25 and the squadrons equipped with it something of an anomaly in the Marine Corps. Also, a secondary mission of Marine aviation is to supplement

the Navy's carrier-based aviation assets, something that a twin-engine medium bomber was incapable of doing. Those factors may have been the major reasons for the rapid deactivation of the VMB squadrons after the end of World War II.

In the extremely budget-conscious world of the post-war American military, it should be remembered that a pair of F4U Corsairs was capable of carrying an identical bomb load, get to the target much faster and double as a superb fighter, all the while requiring only two aviators as opposed to ten or twelve. The only tactical advantage held by the PBJ was range with a full bomb load. Although the phrase "cost effectiveness" was little used at the time, this comparison certainly qualifies as an example of it.

The remainder of 1943 was spent at Cherry Point, as VMB-413 was molded into an effective fighting unit from a mere collection of men and machines, an endeavor that was hampered by the periodic transfer of trained crews to newly activated bombing squadrons. At times, it seemed the squadron's progress could be measured as "one step forward and two steps back," but this was the price to be paid for being a pioneer. Lieutenant Colonel Ronald D. Salmon assumed command of the squadron on 1 July and continued preparations for the squadron's eventual entry into combat. In early December, the squadron was alerted to prepare for movement to the West Coast, and shortly thereafter, it departed Cherry Point for NAS, North Island in San Diego, California. After a brief stay there over the holidays and to take care of some last minute items, VMB-413 departed the West Coast on 3 January 1944 aboard the escort carrier USS *Kalinin Bay* (CVE-68). Its destination was the South Pacific.

[Less than ten months after her service as an aircraft transport for VMB-413, *Kalinin Bay* would occupy a place of high honor in the history of the United States Navy and a Presidential Unit Citation for her part in the Battle off Samar on 24 October 1944 when a small force of escort carriers and their screening destroyers and destroyer escorts turned back an attack by much of the remaining surface strength of the Imperial Japanese Navy aimed at the destruction of the U. S. amphibious forces supporting the assault on Leyte in the central Philippines.]

One Tough Cookie!
USS Kalinin Bay (CVE-68) under way with a few aircraft tied down on her flight deck.
Note the erect crash barrier across her flight deck abreast the after end of her island. The
contents of the crates on deck and their contents are unknown. [U.S. Navy Photo]

The squadron's participation in these daylight strikes continued for something on the order of a week before VMB-413 switched its operational environment. During its training it had specialized in night missions, called "hecklers," designed to deprive the defenders of much-needed rest and weaken their ability to resist the main daylight strikes. It was in these night missions that the PBJs in the hands of the Marines came into their own. In the heckler mission, it was the norm for the attacking aircraft to spend considerable time in the target area. With two aviators in the cockpit to share the workload and a large fuel load allowed the PBJs to spend sufficient time over the target to be extremely effective in their role as night hunters. There were more than sufficient squadrons on hand to continue to pound the Japanese garrisons in the northern Solomons and on New Britain and New Ireland, and it was believed that the positive effects of attacking around the clock would be well worth the additional effort involved.

VMB-413 arrived at Espiritu Santo in the New Hebrides on 27 January where it remained until 7 March, and while there, Lieutenant Colonel Andrew B. Galatian, Jr. assumed command of VMB-413 on 6 February. Lieutenant Colonel Salmon was awarded the Distinguished Flying Cross for his overall performance while in command of the squadron for its pioneering work in the Marines' horizontal bombing effort, as would Lieutenant Colonel Galatin. The squadron then moved forward to Sterling Island in the Treasury group. After a brief period to get acquainted with its new surroundings, VMB-413 began to fly strike missions against Japanese positions at Rabaul and the surrounding area. The squadron's first mission was a strike against enemy supply concentrations southeast of the main installations centered around Rabaul. The target area was small, measuring approximately 500 x 150 yards. The bombing accuracy was nothing short of spectacular, with 82 of 84 bombs striking squarely in the target area for a hit rate of 97.6%. On its second mission the next day, VMB-413 had something of an off day when an accuracy of "only" 85.4% of bombs placed within the target area was recorded but improved the next mission when 90% accuracy was achieved. These first three missions demonstrated that the Marines had learned their lessons well with regard to horizontal bombing.

Homeward Bound
These four aircraft of VMB-413 were photographed on the homeward leg of the squadron's first combat mission
against Japanese installations in the Rabaul area of New Britain on 15 March 1944. [USMC Photo]

These New Regulations are Getting a Little Bit out of Hand!
The crew of one of the squadron's PBJ-1Ds was photographed posed for a publicity shot at VMB-413's base on Stirling Island. While the purpose of the long sheet of paper is not known, several details of the –D version of the PBJ are interesting, such as the multiple exhaust stubs on the engine cowling and the retracted radar dome that can just be discerned in the shallow notch in the lower fuselage just forward of the open access hatch in the belly of the aircraft.
[USMC Photo]

These night strikes introduced a new enemy to the Marines. The weather, particularly at night, in this part of the world during the Southern Hemisphere's fall was marked by immense, extremely violent thunderstorms that often completely blanketed very large areas. During this period of aviation development prior to the introduction of many of the communication and navigational devices that are considered routine today, the weather often posed a more serious threat to life and limb than did the Japanese. Indeed, VMB-413 would experience more losses due to weather than to enemy action. After having been fortunate enough to have not suffered any combat losses during its initial daylight strikes, the rapid upsurge of casualties hit the squadron hard, so hard, in fact, that they led Lt.Col. Galatin to poll his squadron on the question of whether or not the night missions should be continued. Doubtlessly, the colonel was gratified when the question was greeted with polite derision, and the squadron carried on its night attacks. Still plagued by the storms, it is likely that a few came to regret their earlier bravado as their B-25s bounced around like ping pong balls in the turbulent black skies. Later, it was estimated that at least half of the squadron's losses were wholly attributable to weather. As was typical, the Marines carried on in face of the weather and the Japanese could do to the contrary, and VMB-413 was engaged in this duty until May, when it was ordered to Espiritu Santo once again. No doubt, both VMB-413 and the Japanese were glad when the squadron arrived in the rear area.

It remained in the New Hebrides until July and was then ordered forward to Munda on New Georgia. After its arrival at Munda, it commenced its night missions again. The squadron's targets this time were the bypassed Japanese garrisons in the area of Kahili on Bougainville and the island of Choiseul in the Northern Solomons. Along with some swipes at Rabaul, this remained the squadron's area of operations.

Lieutenant Colonel Stewart W. Ralston assumed command of VMB-413 on 13 August and led the squadron until 7 November when Lieutenant Colonel Roswell B. Burchard, Jr, suc-

ceeded him. The New Year brought with it a new commander when Lieutenant Colonel Robert B. Cox assumed command on 1 January 1945 and led the squadron until 17 August when he turned VMB-413 over to Major Arthur C. Lowell. During these changes, the squadron continued to fly missions against the Japanese in the area until the war ended.

Shortly after the Japanese surrender, Major Norman R. Nickerson assumed command when he relieved Major Lowell on 14 September 1945, and VMB-413 returned to the U.S. where it was deactivated on 30 November 1945. During its slightly more than 31 months' service, the squadron lost seven aircraft, two operational losses and five in combat, and suffering a total of 40 casualties. Its first loss occurred on 22 January 1944 and cost the lives of six members of the squadron. Its worst month in combat was March 1944 during which an even dozen men were lost.

In the wake of the mass deactivations that took place following World War II, eventually some sense of sanity prevailed, and a considerable number squadrons that saw service during the war were reactivated as a component of the Organized Reserves, a post-war creation that would, over the years, play an ever more important role in our nation's defense establishment. Such was the case with VMB-413. It was reactivated in 1946 and redesignated a fighter squadron, VMF-413. Assigned to NAS, Dallas, it served alongside VMF-111 and VMF-112. As the vast numbers of aircraft produced during World War II reached the end of their service lives and made their way to museum exhibits or the scrap yard, the Reserves were among the first to feel the pinch of this lack of flyable aircraft, and the "Weekend Warriors" were forced to share a pool of aircraft that was assigned to the squadrons' station. In the case of VMF-413, they shared aircraft with VMF-111 and -112. but as an example of the state of the reserve force at the time, it did not have its own aircraft assigned. Instead, the three squadrons shared whatever was available on their training weekend. When one considers the significance of the description of "Weekend Warrior," if each squadron spent one weekend per month training, three of the four weekends in any given month

The Marine Attack Squadrons 165

Weekend Warrior
A Chance Vought F8U-1 Crusader of the Marine Reserves. The first model of this
superlative "Gunfighter" was the type flown by VMF-413. [USMC Photo]

meant the pool aircraft were flying, leaving precious little time for maintenance. This does not take into consideration the fact that there was a Navy Reserve squadron at NAS, Dallas, at the time drawing upon the same F-8 Crusaders. VMF-413 was deactivated in 1963 and has remained inactive since that date.

Two versions of the squadron's insignia are depicted. The one on the left is an original example and is in mint condition. The one shown on the right is a modern reproduction, and both are virtually identical in design, the black numeral 13 on a green, four-leaf clover. It is the only design verified to have been worn by VMB-413 during its service. The combination of the clover-

leaf and the number represents a rather imaginative but not very subtle way of skirting the prohibition against insignia that display the squadron's numerical designation. The first examples of this insignia were silk screened on aircraft canvas, and later versions were embroidered on gauze-backed green wool. The insignia pictured on the left is an example of the latter. Lieutenant Robert Krider drew the original insignia design.

It is likely that the same insignia was worn during the squadron's almost two decades of service in the Reserves since there was nothing in the design that indicated its previous incarnation as a bombing squadron.

MARINE BOMBING SQUADRON 423
THE SEAHORSES

Author's Collection

The Marines' first medium bombing squadron, VMB-413, was activated on 1 March 1943, and as is the case with virtually all pioneers, this squadron spent its first months in existence serving to prove the concept of a medium bomber force in the Corps. From today's viewpoint, the exact reason or reasons for the activation of these squadrons in the first place have been obscured by the mists of time. It was suggested prior to the attack on Pearl Harbor that the Marines establish such a force for night heckler or intruder missions. In fact, the Marines' VMB squadrons flew more missions in the heckler role than they did in the medium altitude horizontal daylight bombing role. Perhaps the existence of these squadrons is attributable to an excess inventory of the B-25 Mitchell medium bombers on the part of the Army Air Forces and the willingness of the Marines to try virtually anything at least once. But, regardless of the exact reasons, a total of eleven PBJ-equipped Marine squadrons would be activated during the war. [Editor's Note: PBJ was the Navy's designation for the North American B-25 Mitchell medium bomber which eventually would see service in a majority of the medium bombardment squadrons of the Army Air Forces.]

After VMB-413 successfully proved the concept of medium bombardment squadrons for the Marines, three more bombing squadrons were activated in the fall of 1943. Among these was VMB-423, which was activated on 15 September 1943 at MCAS, Cherry Point, North Carolina under the command of

Lieutenant Colonel John L. Winston. Many members of the initial cadre of VMB-423 and the other two squadrons activated on that date were transferred from VMB-413 to these new squadrons to provide these new units some measure of relatively experienced personnel.

In October, VMB-423 was transferred from Cherry Point to nearby MCAS, Edenton, where it began training in earnest, and less than a month after its arrival at Edenton, VMB-423 experienced its first losses when four of its members were killed in the crash of one of its PBJ-1Ds. After a brief period of leave for the Christmas season, the squadron was on the move again. The PBJs were loaded with the squadron's belongings, ground crews and other support personnel and headed west. On 3 January 1944, the squadron arrived at its new home, MCAS, El Centro, in the vast California desert. This arid location was practically devoid of human habitation and offered wide expanses of excellent open desert for bombing ranges. Unfortunately, VMB-423 suffered a second loss when one of its aircraft crashed in the desert with the loss of the entire crew. Even today, El Centro is the air station at which the majority of live-ordnance exercises are conducted by Marine squadrons.

While the squadron's flight echelon continued to blow large holes in the desert, its ground echelon was alerted for movement to the South Pacific. After loading its equipment, the ground echelon boarded USS *Hammondsport* (AKV-2) and sailed for the South Pacific, arriving at Espiritu Santo on 11 March. A month later, the flight echelon arrived in the New Hebrides along with its aircraft after sailing aboard USS *Prince William* (CVE-31). It sailed after experiencing some interesting adventures regarding the "midnight requisition" of the items considered necessary for the squadron's existence in a combat zone. After two months on Espiritu Santo, the squadron's flight and ground echelons were divided, with the flight echelon moving forward to Stirling Island south of Bougainville and the ground echelon remaining on Espiritu pending transfer to another location. When the squadron arrived at its new base, it relieved VMB-413, which was temporarily withdrawn from combat. After five weeks of operations from Stirling, the flight echelon was ordered to Green Island, which lies almost due east from Rabaul across the southern extremity of New Ireland. There it was reunited with its ground echelon.

After setting up shop at its new location, the reunited squadron spent the next year adding the weight of its bombs to the tons of ordnance dumped on the unfortunate heads of the many bypassed enemy garrisons on the islands of the Bismarks and the northern Solomons. The squadron's primary targets, however, were on the islands of New Britain and New Ireland. While engaged in one of these missions on 9 June, the PBJ flown by Lieutenant William H. Hopper was on the receiving end of a rather unpleasant surprise. The last sighting of an airborne Japanese aircraft at Rabaul had occurred four months earlier, but the Lieutenant's aircraft suddenly found itself under attack by a pair of Nakajima Ki-43 Oscar fighters. The combative lieutenant elected to fight it out with the enemy. He repeatedly turned into the enemy aircraft and maneuvered to bring his heaviest armament to bear. Finally, the enemy fighters broke off their attacks, perhaps in search of an easier target. Hopper was awarded the Distinguished Flying Cross for this engagement as well as his overall performance while serving with the squadron.

There are Pretty Ships and then there are ...
USS Hammondsport (AKV-2) rests at anchor looking somewhat the worse for wear. Most of the aircraft visible appear to be SB2C Helldivers. [U.S. Navy Photo]

[A Japanese Army aircraft, the Ki-43 was a dogfighter supreme, so nimble it could even turn inside the vaunted Zero, but this extreme maneuverability came at a price. As was the case with most Japanese aircraft, it had been designed with no armor or self-sealing fuel tanks in order to save weight, which made it fatally vulnerable to enemy fire. Furthermore, the Oscar was lightly armed, mounting only a pair of machine guns in the engine cowling, a considerable handicap for an interceptor.]

The unsuspected appearance of the Oscars was somewhat perplexing. Literally for months, strikes against Rabaul had been flown without the sighting of a single enemy aircraft. Had the Japanese succeeded in sneaking aerial reinforcements into the bypassed base? If so, from where had these aircraft come? In fact, it seems the industrious enemy had succeeded in piecing together some five to seven fighters from the myriad of wrecks that littered the many airfields in the Rabaul area. Despite their diligence and labor, the American fighters in the area quickly destroyed this scratch interceptor force. Another interesting note in the squadron's history concerns the collections taken up by

The Century Mark
It requires a great deal of hard work to keep a combat aircraft flying in any environment, especially in a forward combat area. Pictured here are the ground crewmen assigned to aircraft No.38 of VMB-423, which had just completed its 100th combat mission as indicated by the mission marks on the fuselage side below the open cockpit window. The Marines are: front row (l to r) Cpl. Ray Lawrence, Cpl. George Wadle and Sgt. Joe Cope; middle row (l to r) Cpl. Robert Deemer and PFC Charles Dillow; top row (l to r) Sgt. Robert Lee, Crew Chief S/Sgt. Leon Peterson and Cpl. Fred Jaroslowsky. [USMC Photo]

the schoolchildren of Oklahoma City. The 35,000 children who took part in this fund drive accumulated sufficient money to purchase a PBJ, and each of the children signed a scroll describing their support of the war effort. One of the crews of VMB-423 was composed of natives of the state of Oklahoma. The all-Okie crew and aircraft dropped the scroll, along with its bomb load, on Rapopo airfield at Rabaul on 27 May. In addition to the missions flown against Rabaul, the squadron was also tasked with furnishing air support to the Australian troops that had assumed responsibility for the perimeter on Bougainville. Their efforts on behalf of the Aussies were heartily commended by those troops, and the squadron received an official letter of commendation from Lieutenant General Stan E. Savage, commander of the Second Australian Corps.

On 19 July, Lieutenant Colonel Norman J. Anderson, who would eventually fly more PBJ combat missions than any other Marine, a total of 107, assumed command of the squadron.

As the months wore on, the crews of VMB-423 and the other squadrons involved in hammering the bypassed Japanese garrisons came to know their targets as well as they knew their own homes. In an attempt to relieve the boredom, the crews were rotated to Sydney, Australia, for short periods of leave, five at a time, while the remainder, no doubt, counted the hours until the return of those lucky ones so their opportunity would come soon.

By mid-June, the squadron's base of operations was shifted to Emirau, but the seemingly endless series of attacks against the impotent pockets of enemy resistance continued without interruption. Finally, on 10 August 1945, the squadron left the Bismarks-Solomons area behind and started northward to the Philippines. The move was completed on 16 August, the day after the shooting stopped. Also, on that same day, Lieutenant Colonel Louis L. Frank assumed command of VMB-423. Almost immediately after the Japanese surrender, VMB-423 left the South Pacific behind and returned to MCAS, Miramar. Almost as soon as the echoes of the last shots of the war faded, the PBJ-equipped squadrons, with the exception of VMB-612, began to be deactivated. The turn of VMB-423 came quickly, and it was deactivated at Miramar on 30 November 1945 and has remained inactive since that date.

During its service, VMB-423 suffered the loss of ten aircraft, three in combat and seven, more than any other VMB squadron, operationally. Lost with the ten PBJs were thirty-six members of the squadron.

The squadron insignia in the plate is a reproduction made for a reunion of the squadron. It is an exact duplicate of the original in design and details with the exception that the originals did not carry the squadron designation for security reasons. The background color of the originals was a blue disk. Two different versions of this insignia exist. The first version was embroidered on wool, and these examples were made in Australia during a period of R & R. The second version of this insignia was a decal applied to a leather disk. This design received official approval in 1943.

This design of VMB-423's insignia was drawn by Corporal Willie T. Phillips, a gunner in one of the squadron's aircraft who was killed in action on 23 December 1944, the last member of the squadron to be lost.

MARINE BOMBING SQUADRON 433

THE FORK-TAILED DEVILS

A Gift For Our Japanese Friends
A 500lb. general-purpose bomb suspended from the shackles in the bomb bay of one of the squadron's PBJs carries a message chalked on it by the ground crew, a fairly common practice among allied airmen. [USMC Photo]

VMB-433 was activated at MCAS, Cherry Point, North Carolina, on 15 September 1943 under the command of Major John G. Adams. The new squadron commenced its training cycle and alternated between Cherry Point and Camp Lejune for the remainder of the year. One of a relatively small number of medium bombing squadrons activated by the Marine Corps, its North American PBJ-1 Mitchell bombers spent many hours aloft over the training targets located in eastern North Carolina. The Marine Corps was learning anew the new tactic of the delivery of two-ton bomb loads from medium altitude horizontal bomb runs.

Immediately after the holidays of 1943, VMB-433 was alerted to prepare for movement to the West Coast to continue its training in preparation for its eventual deployment into a combat zone. The move from North Carolina to California was completed by 27 January 1944, and the squadron continued its training under the direction of Marine Fleet Air, West Coast

[MarFAirWest], the parent organization of all Marine aviation replacement and training activities in California. The squadron spent four months operating from MCAS, El Centro, in the California desert as it put the finishing touches on its bombing skills. Finally, it was alerted for movement to the South Pacific.

The ground echelon of VMB-433 sailed from San Diego on 26 May, and the flight echelon shipped out the following day. The squadron's first stop was MCAS, Ewa, Territory of Hawaii, on 1 June, but its stay there was brief. Six weeks into its short stop in Hawaii, VMB-433 moved westward again and arrived at its first active combat base in the Green Islands on 14 July 1944 with brief intermediate stops at the islands of Palmyra, Canton, Funafuti, and Espiritu Santo. After a short period of refresher training, the squadron flew its first combat missions as a part of the mass of Allied air power that continued to pound the bypassed Japanese forces at Rabaul on New

One Less Target
The hulk of one of the squadron's victims is pictured beached in the surf. Careful examination of the photo reveals massive damage to the hull amidships on the port side where the hull plating us bent upward from the turn of her bilge to the main deck. Apparently it suffered a direct hit from a bomb after she was beached. Had she been in deep water when she was hit, she surely rolled over to port and gone down like the proverbial stone. [USMC Photo]

Britain, New Ireland and the other nearby islands. By now, the once-mighty fortress had been reached to near impotence and served the Emperor only to absorb tons of bombs that would otherwise have been dropped on other, more active installations. Japanese aircraft had been almost entirely driven from the skies of New Britain and New Ireland in February, and the garrisons bypassed in order to save time and Allied lives. The defenders were cut off, receiving only an occasional visit by a submarine to bring in meager shipments of dwindling supplies of ammunition and to evacuate primarily aviation personnel vitally needed at other locations within the crumbling Empire. Rabaul and the surrounding areas were never directly assaulted by the Allied forces, and the thousands of Japanese troops in the Bismarks were slowly reduced to a primitive, day-to-day existence on near-starvation rations and with ever decreasing food and medical stores in the face of the air attacks that continued until the Japanese surrender.

In August, VMB-433 moved from the Green Islands to Emirau and continued to fly missions against the enemy to the south for the remainder of the war. Lieutenant Colonel Winton H. Miller assumed command on 23 April 1945 and was followed a month later by Major Boyd O. Whitney, who relieved Lieutenant Colonel Miller on 24 May. Major Andrew G. Smith, Jr.,

assumed command on 17 July 1945 and remained in command of VMB-433 during the remainder of its active service. With the Japanese surrender, all of the Marine bombing squadrons save one were ordered to return to the United States. All were deactivated within a few weeks of their reaching the U.S. The turn of VMB-433 came on 30 November 1945, and the squadron has remained inactive since that date.

During its more than twenty-six months of service, the squadron lost three aircraft, one operationally and two in combat. Its combat losses occurred on 2 September 1944 and 27 February 1945, and these accounted for twelve of the squadron's seventeen casualties.

Regarding the insignia of VMB-433, the example pictured is painted on leather. The design was drawn by Lieutenant Malcomb McGuchin and received approval by the Headquarters, Marine Corps in 1944. Original examples consisted of a decal applied to a leather disk.

A somewhat curious aspect of the design concerns the mount of the demon in the insignia. The beast is riding an aerial torpedo, a weapon that apparently was never employed by VMB-433. There is no explanation for the inclusion of the torpedo in the insignia design, but the PBJ was capable of carrying the weapon with special rigging.

MARINE BOMBING SQUADRON 443
THE WILDCATS

via Holmberg

On 15 September 1943, First Lieutenant Robert C. McConnell, the squadron's first commanding officer, read the orders activating VMB-443 at MCAS, Cherry Point, North Carolina. Far too junior to command a squadron, the Lieutenant was succeeded the following day by Major Alton D. Gould. VMB-443 was one of three VMB squadrons activated on the same date and, like the others, received a draft from VMB-413 as a part of its initial cadre. On 13 October, Lieutenant Colonel Dwight M. Guillotte succeeded Major Gould in command of the squadron, and a week later, VMB-443 moved from Cherry Point to Peters Point Field to continue its training. In mid-January 1944, the squadron's aircraft, flight crews, and a portion of its ground crews were ordered to NAS, Boca Chica, Florida for training in torpedo tactics. The torpedo was a much more effective anti-

shipping weapon than bombs delivered from normal bombing altitudes. A rapidly maneuvering ship at sea was a notoriously difficult target for a horizontal bomber. They were capable of literally turning out of harm's way in the time required for a bomb to fall from its release altitude to the target. The Army Air Forces dropped hundreds of tons of bombs and claimed a large percentage of hits on various warships and merchantmen during the first year of the war. However, the usual victims of these bombs consisted of any marine life unfortunate enough to be in the general vicinity of the bombs' point of impact. The Japanese ship that suffered so much as damage to its paintwork was rare indeed, not to mention, quite unlucky. Eventually, the Army Air Forces in the South Pacific hit upon a tactic that was even more effective than the torpedo against Japanese shipping in the area.

Major Paul I. "Pappy" Gunn of the Army Air Force is generally credited with the development of what came to be known as "skip bombing." by twin-engine medium bombers. This type of attack involved a high-speed approach at almost right angles to the target's course. Bomb release was at mast-top height short of the target. As a result, the bombs, generally 500-pounders, would skip across the surface of the sea, much like the way a flat rock tends to skip when thrown parallel to the water's surface and into the target. To reduce the vulnerability of the attacking aircraft to the ship's guns, the attack aircraft, usually various models of the B-25 Mitchell bomber, were field-modified to carry the heaviest possible battery of forward-firing .50-caliber machine guns. Major Gunn was able to cram four such guns into the nose of the aircraft and a like number on the fuselage sides. These guns and those of the upper turret totaled ten weapons, and this battery was murderously effective against small, unarmored vessels even without the use of bombs. Against larger ships, it was usually capable of overwhelming all but the most stout-hearted gun crews. Major Gunn was not a trained engineer, and it is said that when questioned about the effect of the heavy gun battery on the center of gravity of the aircraft, Gunn was reported to have replied, "We threw it out to save weight!" [Author's Note: It must be admitted that the engineers in the North American factory were able to improve on the Major's efforts. The last production models of the type specifically constructed for ground attack carried no fewer than eighteen .50-caliber guns!]

Luxury it Ain't!
MS Brastagi, a Dutch merchantman that was chartered by the Navy as a transport is the ship that carried the squadron's ground echelon to the New Hebrides is shown pier side at an unidentified location. This photo after she was chartered. Note the three-inch gun forward and the life rafts alongside the superstructure and the ship's rail to port. [U.S. Navy Photo]

Gunn was a retired enlisted Naval Aviation Pilot who lived in the Philippines, where he ran a small air freight service. When the Japanese conquered the islands, Gunn's family was interred in the infamous Santo Tomas Prison, and as a result, Gunn hated the Japanese with a deep, uncompromising hatred and believed the fastest way to free his family was to kill as many Japanese as quickly as possible. He felt his gunship modifications were a good means to that end.

If any doubts remained about the low-level tactics after the initial skip bombing attacks, the murderous effectiveness of the tactic was proven in the Battle of the Bismark Sea in March 1943. The Japanese sent a convoy of eight transports and an escort of eight destroyers from Rabaul to reinforce their garrison in the Salamaua area of New Guinea. Sighted by an Australian reconnaissance aircraft, the Fifth Air Force was determined to stop the convoy. The battle opened on 2 March and involved every type of aircraft from fighters to heavy bombers, but the low-flying medium bombers made most of the successful attacks. When the slaughter was over, all eight transports and four of the destroyers had been sent to the bottom. The remaining destroyers fled back to Rabaul. The troops that survived the sinking of their transports were left adrift in the waters of the Bismark Sea, and very few of those survived.

In view of this, one must wonder if the Marines seriously considered the employment of their PBJs in torpedo attacks, but nonetheless, the flight echelon of VMB-443 remained at Boca Chica for more than a month working on their torpedo tactics and techniques. In February, the squadron was ordered to the West Coast, arriving at MCAS, El Centro, later that same month. After satisfying three months in the California desert perfecting their bombing skills, VMB-443 began to depart the United States for the southwest Pacific. [The author can attest to the satisfaction one gets from training with things that do, in fact, go "boom."] The ground echelon sailed from San Diego aboard MS *Brastagi* on 18 May and arrived at Espiritu Santo mid-June. From the New Hebrides, it moved to Emirau a month later. The flight echelon arrived on Emirau on 15 August, and after a short time to become acquainted with its new surroundings, the squadron began to fly missions against enemy garrisons in the Bismarks, and Rabaul was a frequent destination.

VMB-443 continued to take part in the neutralization of the Bismarks until August of 1945, when it moved northward to the Philippines. Its arrival there coincided with the cessation of hostilities against Japan, and Major Earl E. Anderson assumed command of the squadron on 16 August. Like the other Marine medium bomber squadrons, VMB-443 returned to the United States and was deactivated 30 November 1945. It has remained inactive since that time. The squadron lost two aircraft operationally and two in combat and suffered twenty-one casualties during its service.

The insignia shown is an original example and is in excellent condition considering its age. The design and the brown border are machine embroidered on the orange twill background. The entire insignia is backed with cotton gauze. It is one of the first batch made for the squadron in the United States prior to its departure for the South Pacific. Later examples of the insignia are identical in color and in detail but were embroidered on a wool background during a period of R&R in Australia. The design received official approval of Headquarters, Marine Corps, in 1944.

It should be noted that some reproductions were produced for a recent squadron reunion. These are identical in design but are somewhat smaller than this example and have a ribbon at the bottom that carries the squadron designation.

The artist who drew the design is Donald Graser.

Running them Up!
One of the squadron's glass-nosed PBJs receives some last minute maintenance from a member of its ground crew as it runs up its engines. Although the location is not identified, it is likely that it was at Boca Chica judging by the near-mint condition of the aircraft and the utility poles in the background. Note the raised rectangular plate on the fuselage side below the co-pilot's partially open window. This is part of the cockpit armor installed in the B-25/PBJ aircraft. [USMC Photo]

MARINE TORPEDO BOMBER SQUADRON 453

The squadron was activated as Marine Bombing Squadron 453 on 25 June 1944 at MCAS, Cherry Point, North Carolina, under the command of Major John W. Stevens II, but bombing squadron command was a lieutenant colonel's billet. As a result, Major Stevens led the squadron for six weeks until he was succeeded by Lieutenant Colonel Joseph R. Little, Jr., on 31 July 1944.

By this time, VMTB-453 was activated, Marine aviation in the Pacific was mired deeply in the morale-killing routine of inactivity. There were many well-trained, experienced squadrons throughout the theater for which there was little in the way of useful employment. The Solomons Campaign had reached its successful conclusion in February, and most of the squadrons of the island garrisons of the Central Pacific were Army Air Forces units. Also, several of the Marines' PBJ-equipped medium bombing squadrons had been deployed to the Pacific several months earlier. As a result, the pace of life for many of the recently activated squadrons, including VMB-453, was slow indeed. This situation continued throughout the fall and into the winter of 1944. On 14 November, Lieutenant Colonel Little was ordered to other duty, and Major Donald G.H. Jacobs assumed command the following day. As 1944 became 1945, it became clear that the days of VMB-453 were numbered, and the squadron was deactivated on 20 February 1945.

The squadron was not inactive for long, however. On 1 July 1945, the squadron was reactivated at MCAS, El Toro, California and redesignated VMTB-453. Major George D. Wolverton commanded the new torpedo squadron from the date of its activation.

VMTB-453 was ordered to carrier qualifications training in anticipation for its eventual assignment to one of the escort carriers manned by all-Marine air groups to provide dedicated close air support for the invasion of the Japanese home islands that were planned for execution beginning in November, 1945. VMTB-453 was in training when the Japanese agreed to the Allies' surrender terms in the wake of the employment of the atomic bombs.

Its future combat career as a carrier squadron stillborn, VMTB-453 remained at El Toro, a component of MAG-46, until it was ordered deactivated on 20 March 1946, and has remained inactive since that date.

There is no surviving record of any insignia of either VMB or VMTB-453.

MARINE TORPEDO BOMBER SQUADRON 454
THE HELLDIVERS

via Holmberg

The squadron was activated as Marine Scout Bombing Squadron 454 at MCAS, El Toro, California, on 1 March 1944, and Major James H. Clark assumed the duty as the squadron's commanding officer on that date. VMSB-454 was brought up to full strength in terms of personnel and commenced training with its Curtiss SB2C-1A Helldiver dive-bombers. Training proceeded throughout the spring and summer of 1944, but before the squadron was deployed, it was redesignated a torpedo squadron, VMTB-454, on 14 October 1944.

Several factors combined to bring the change in the squadron's mission. First the heyday of the pure dive-bomber in the Marine Corps had been during the Solomons Campaign from 20 August 1942 until the withdrawal of the survivors of the defending Japanese aircraft from Rabaul in February 1944. Only a relatively small number of dive bomber squadrons were destined to see service in the Philippines, and these already were in the Pacific. Also, the Marines' stalwart SBD Dauntless production had ceased in July 1944. So for a time, all the Marine scout bomber squadrons remaining in the United States were in imminent danger of deactivation. This was prevented, however, by the Marines' successful campaign to have some of its squadrons assigned to escort carriers. Beginning early in 1944, the upper echelons of command in the Marine Corps foresaw the coming of the situation in which Marine aviation found itself in the latter months of the year. A considerable number of well-equipped, superbly trained squadrons were languishing in quiet rear areas where, in fact, they were making little contribution to the overall allied war effort aside from pounding weak, bypassed Japanese garrisons in both the south and central Pacific. The solution to this state of affairs was to send these squadrons to sea. Also, it was universally accepted that World War II could be brought to a successful conclusion only by the direct amphibious assault and conquest of the Japanese home islands. Should these assaults, planned for the fall of 1945, take place, none doubted the fighting would be protracted and bloody. It was estimated that Allied casualties would run into the tens of thousands, with a million dead and wounded among the Japanese. Based on experience gained at considerable cost during the long advance across Pacific Basin, it was clear to those tasked with development the assault plans that among the prime requirements for success would be close air support delivered accurately and in a timely manner. This was a skill developed to its zenith within the limits of existing technology by the Marine Corps.

The closest American airfields to the southernmost of the Japanese Home Islands, Kyushu, lay some 350 miles away on Okinawa. Clearly, to depend on land-based air power to supply the required support would lead to unacceptable delays between the initial call for support and the first weapons on target. The alternative would be to resort to standing patrols above the battle area, but the distance from base to target would allow for little "loiter time" in the target area and reduced ordnance loads.

The obvious solution to this dilemma was carrier-based aviation, but the Navy was loathe to tie its carriers to what amounted to virtually a fixed position for the duration of an amphibious assault and thereby exposing them to the dangers of air and submarine attack. Also, as the fighting in the latter months of the Philippines campaign and off Okinawa would prove, the threat posed by the kamikaze would require more and more fighters to be assigned to the carriers' air groups. The ready-made solution to this problem was the escort carrier, and the surplus of Marine squadrons enabled air groups to be put together quickly. Thus, the large carriers of the Fast Carrier Force would assume a near-strategic role in the months ahead with their strikes against the Japanese Home Islands. The Marines' unquestioned expertise at close air support mission and the escort carrier, while not exactly a match made in heaven, proved to be a natural combination.

In view of what was to come, it must be remembered that these grim estimates and the planning for the invasions were carried on without knowledge of the development of atomic weapons or the evolving plans for their eventual employment

This assignment of a considerable number of Marine squadrons to the escort carriers was one of the major factors driving the re-equipment of VMSB-454 with the Avenger series. The SBD lacked folding wings, a requirement for operations from the CVEs, and the massive SB2C was too heavy with too fast a landing speed. While the Avenger was the largest, heaviest aircraft to regularly operate from carriers during World War II, it was a very forgiving, docile aircraft with a low enough landing speed to pose far fewer potential problems when operating from a CVE. Also, the TBF/TBM was designed as a torpedo aircraft, but it carried a bomb load equivalent to the SB2C.

As a result, VMTB-454 was redesignated VMTB(CVS)-454 on 5 November 1944 and began preparations for carrier training shortly thereafter. The squadron was ordered from El Toro to MCAS, Mojave, for ordnance training with its newly acquired TBM-3E Avengers. After five months of rearranging portions of the topography of the California desert, the squadron was ordered to MCAS, Santa Barbara, for carrier qualifications in June 1945. It boarded *USS Puget Sound* (CVE-113) on 17 July after its initial field carrier landing practice ashore.

The squadron spent the remainder of July aboard the CVE and returned to Santa Barbara in early August. As the war in the Pacific came to a close, VMTB-454 was aboard USS *Point Cruz* (CVE-119), where it was paired with VMF-217. As of 1 January 1946, the squadron was still aboard the escort carrier, but it returned to Santa Barbara later in the month and was deactivated there on 28 January 1946. It has remained inactive since that date.

The insignia of VMSB/VMTB-454 was designed by the Walt Disney Studios and original examples of the insignia were issued in two lots. The first issue was embroidered on a wool background, and the second issue was silk-screened on leatherette disks.

The insignia in the accompanying plate is an embroidered example of the first group made and was provided by Mr. Eugene Holmberg for inclusion in this book.

Baby Flat Top
USS Puget Sound (CVE-113) was photographed as she rode at anchor at an unidentified location. Most of her aircraft spotted on her flight deck are TBM Avengers. She is painted in the overall blue camouflage scheme designed to make it more difficult to spot her from the air. [U.S. Navy Photo]

MARINE TORPEDO BOMBER SQUADRON 473

Marine Bombing Squadron 473 was activated on 25 July 1944 at MCAS, Cherry Point, North Carolina. One of the last of the Marines' medium bombing squadrons to be activated, its commanding officer was Major William M. Frash. On 15 December 1944, the squadron was transferred from Cherry Point to the auxiliary airfield at Kinston to continue its training. However, by this period of the war, interest in and useful employment for the medium bombing mission in Marine Corps aviation had begun to wane, and VMB-473 was deactivated on 15 March 1945.

Concurrent with the demise of horizontal bombing within the Marine Corps was the rise of interest in the assignment of Marine squadrons to aircraft carriers. The early months of 1945 would witness the assignment of several VMF squadrons to the air groups of the Navy's Fast Carrier Force, and the fruition of a plan to supply all-Marine air groups to several escort carriers dedicated to the vital task of close air support of ground troops.

Initially the requisite carrier training was carried out under the auspices of the Navy's training program. However, due to the ongoing requirement for additional Navy squadrons and air groups as well as individual replacements for losses and for rotation of experienced personnel to stateside duty, it soon became clear that the Marines would have to establish their own carrier training and qualification program. This point was further driven home by the unacceptably high rate of operational losses experienced by the first Marine fighter squadrons deployed aboard the Fast Carriers in early 1945. A given aviator might be very proficient and experienced in the operation of his assigned aircraft, but carrier flight operations are a world unto them selves, the most hostile environment ever devised by man in which to operate aircraft and remains so to this day. As a result, several recently deactivated Marine squadrons were given a second lease on life to serve as dedicated carrier training squadrons. Such was the case with regard to the former VMB-473. It was reactivated on 1 August 1945 at MCAS, El Centro, California, and redesignated VMTB-473 under the command of Captain Charlton A. Main.

After the war's end, the squadron was transferred from MAG-35 at El Centro to MAG-46 at MCAS, El Toro, and it continued to serve as a carrier training squadron until its second and, thus far, final deactivation on 20 March 1946.

There is no surviving record of any insignia for either VMB- or VMTB-473.

MARINE SCOUT BOMBING SQUADRON 474

On 10 April 1944, the existing Bomber Training Unit, under the control of Marine Base Defense Air Group 46, at MCAS, El Toro, California, was disbanded. VMSB-474 was one of the squadrons activated on that same date to take over the functions of the former unit, and Major Richard L. Blain assumed command of the new squadron.

Activated as a replacement training squadron to supply aircrews to the existing scout bombing squadrons deployed in the Pacific theater, VMSB-474 operated a mixture of various models of both the SBD Dauntless and SB2C Helldiver aircraft flown by those squadrons. It continued to serve in this role until near the end of hostilities against Japan, but as the war drew to a close, the days of the scout-bomber in the Marine Corps rapidly came to an end. Technology spelled the end of the pure scout bomber. The Corsair proved capable of carrying an equal or greater bomb load and delivering it with almost equal accuracy to that of a dive bomber, and the Avenger was more versatile with its ability to carry torpedoes and mines in addition to a one-ton bomb load. Also, it had greater range as a scout.

As a result, VMSB-474 was deactivated just after the actual surrender by the Japanese. The end came for the squadron on 10 September 1945, and the squadron has remained inactive since that date.

Following Major Blain in command of the squadron were: Major Glenn L. Todd, from 12 July 1944 through 31 March 1945; Major Walter J. Carr, Jr., from 1 April through 29 June; Captain Henry D. Noetzel, from 30 June through 6 August, and Captain John F. Adams, Jr., 7 August through 10 September 1945.

There is no record of any insignia having been adopted by VMSB-474.

MARINE BOMBING SQUADRON 483

The last of the Marines' bombing squadrons to be equipped and trained to serve in the horizontal, medium bombing role, VMB-483 was activated at MCAS, Cherry Point, North Carolina, on 26 August 1944 under the command of Major Louis L. Frank. In December 1944, the squadron was transferred from Cherry Point to MCAAF, Kinston, for further training, and Major Duncan E. Slade assumed command on 5 January 1945.

By this, the last Christmas season of World War II, however, it was clear that there were already more Marine bombing squadrons deployed in the Pacific theater than could be employed effectively. As the forces under General MacArthur and those led by Admiral Nimitz converged on the Philippines in late 1944 and effectively became one massive drive toward the Japanese Homeland, it was clear that the horizontal bombing mission would be fulfilled by Army Air Forces squadrons. The personnel assigned to the VMB squadrons could be more effectively used in other roles, and, as a consequence, VMB-483 was ordered deactivated on 15 March 1945. It has remained among the inactive squadrons of the Marine Corps since that date.

There is no surviving record of any insignia of VMB-483 having been adopted or approved during its brief service.

MARINE SCOUT-BOMBING SQUADRON 484

VMSB-484 was the second of the two scout bombing squadrons to be activated on 10 April 1944, when the Bomber Training Unit of Marine Base Defense Air Group 46 at MCAS, El Toro, California, was disbanded on that date. The first commanding officer of the new squadron was Major William W. Wood. The mission of VMSB-484 was that of a training squadron to supply replacement aircrews to the Marine scout bombing squadrons already deployed to various locations throughout the Pacific Theater. Equipped with various models of both the SBD Dauntless and the SB2C Helldiver, the activation of the squadron had little immediate effect on the day-to-day conduct of its assigned missions that virtually were unchanged from those prior to 10 April 1944.

By the date of the activation of VMSB-484, the mission of the scout-bomber in the Marine Corps was well on its way to going the way of the dinosaurs. The mighty F4U Corsair proved to be the virtual equal of the pure dive-bomber in bombing accuracy and was capable of carrying a greater ordnance load at higher speeds. Once freed of its ton or more of bombs, rockets, and napalm, the F4U reverted to the outstanding fighter it had been from the beginning.

The big Grumman/Eastern Aircraft TBF/TBM Avenger claimed the remainder of the scout-bomber mission as its own. Capable of carrying a heavy load of a wider variety of ordnance than either the SBD or the SB2C, the Avenger enjoyed a greater range than the dive-bombers when employed in the scouting role.

Further, production of the SBD came to an end in July 1944, and the SB2C was plagued by a host of troubles from its beginning. At one time, serious consideration was given to cancellation of the entire production of the aircraft due the number of problems with the design and the time required to correct them.

No Marine scout bombing squadrons would see service from the escort carriers manned by all-Marine air groups in the closing months of the war, and only a relatively small number would see service in the Philippines Campaign, beginning in January 1945. Despite the small number of Marine scout-bomber squadrons to serve in the Archipelago, however, these would write the final chapters in the story of the Marine scout-bomber in sterling terms of accurate bombing and the saving of many American lives among the ground troops who benefited from their support. The numbers of glowing words of praise received from Army commands during the campaign brought down the curtain on the service of the Marine scout-bombing squadrons in grand style.

As World War II entered its final stages, the days of the dive-bomber were coming to a close, and VMSB-484 was deactivated on 10 September 1945. During its service, the following officers followed Major Wood in command of the squadron: Major George E. Koutelas, from 20 March through 25 April 1945; Major George W. Wolverton, from 26 April through 30 June 1945; Captain Robert Floeck, 1 through 23 July 1945 and Captain Carl F Eakin, Jr., 24 July through 10 September 1945.

There is no record of any insignia for VMSB-484.

MARINE ATTACK SQUADRON 513
THE FLYING NIGHTMARES

Author's Collection

Marine Fighting Squadron 513 was activated on 15 February 1944 at MCAAF, Oak Grove, North Carolina, under the command of Major Thomas O. Bales. The squadron was initially a component of MAG-51 and spent the early months of its existence training in the employment of the 11.75-inch "Tiny Tim" rocket in preparation for its eventual deployment to the European Theater. Once there, the group was to employ the massive rocket as its primary weapon in the arsenal of their Corsairs against the German V-1 rocket sites. On 11 July 1944, MAG-51 and its component squadrons were alerted to be ready to deploy to Europe six days later. The group's forward echelon was flown to Norfolk while VMF-513 and VMF-514 hurriedly completed their training with the Tiny Tim, but as it has been related elsewhere, this deployment of Marine squadrons to Europe, Project *Danny,* was canceled on 30 July, for reasons more political than military. The cancellation of *Danny* left the Marine Corps with an entire air group, superbly trained and equipped with the latest in aircraft and equipment that was suddenly shorn of its mission.

In the Pacific, the long succession of amphibious assaults up the ladder of the Solomons had come to a successful conclusion early in 1944. A cordon of Allied bases and airfields from which the once mighty base had been strangled into passivity ringed the Japanese bastion of Rabaul. The second major objective of the Solomons campaign, the creation of a sinkhole into which Japan would pour much of its ability to make war, had likewise been accomplished. The waters and the jungles of the Solomons and the Bismarks had been turned into a graveyard of Japanese imperial ambitions. From Iron Bottom Sound in the south where the wrecks of 24 Japanese men-of-war, including

two battleships, lay in the cold, black depths of the waters off the island of Guadalcanal, to Rabaul's Simpson Harbor in the north, the Imperial Japanese Navy had been bled white. Likewise, its air arm had been crippled beyond recovery. Thousands of Japanese aircraft had been destroyed in the air and on the ground, but, while the aircraft could be replaced for the most part, their crack aircrews could not. And while it was known that the Allied fighter squadrons in the Solomons, most of which were Marine squadrons, had extracted a tremendous toll from the ranks of the veteran Japanese airmen, the full extent of damage would not be demonstrated conclusively until the Battle of the Philippine Sea in June 1944. In a single day of the most concentrated fighter-versus-fighter combat in the history of aerial warfare, almost 400 of the Emperor's aircraft were destroyed in exchange for a relative handful of American losses. While this massive execution was at the hands of the Navy fighter squadrons embarked aboard the ships of the Fast Carrier Force, their Marine cousins many miles to the southwest had laid much of the groundwork for this victory to the south in the Solomons.

As a result, Marine Corps aviation was trapped in the doldrums, to a large extent a victim of its own success. It had been excluded from Europe, and it had been, if possible, almost too successful in the Pacific. There was little in the way of active Japanese opposition to the continuous missions flown against bypassed enemy garrisons in the Solomons and the central Pacific. The flight decks of the Fast Carrier Force were home to a growing host of Navy squadrons, and the air campaigns in the southwest Pacific were almost exclusively the property of the Army Air Forces. For a time, many Marine squadrons, both overseas and in the United States, were left with little meaningful employment.

In the wake of the cancellation of Project *Danny*, VMF-513 was ordered to MCAF, Walnut Ridge, Arkansas, on 14 September 1944. On 4 December, it was transferred to MCAS, Mojave, and effective the same date, the squadron was redesignated as a carrier squadron, VMF(CVS)-513. In preparation for the eventual invasion of the Japanese home islands, several of the previously under-employed Marine squadrons were redesignated as such and ordered to carrier training. It was planned to form carrier air groups composed entirely of Marine squadrons and send them into battle aboard escort carriers, where they would engage in the Marine specialty of close air support for the assault troops on the ground. VMF(CVS)-513 was teamed with VMTB-234 to form MCVG-3 and was assigned to USS *Vella Gulf* (CVE-111) of the *Commencement Bay* class.

In early June 1945, the squadron was ordered to San Diego, where it joined its parent carrier, and the CVE departed the United States on 17 June for the Western Pacific. *Vella Gulf* arrived at Pearl Harbor on 25 June, and MCVG-3 was temporarily detached from the carrier and ordered to MCAS, Ewa, where the Marines continued flight operations until their carrier was ready for sea again.

Author's Collection

Vella Gulf sailed from Pearl Harbor in early July, and the Corsairs and Hellcat night fighters of VMF-513 and the Avengers of VMTB-234 flew aboard shortly after the carrier cleared the harbor. [It should be noted that virtually no Marine squadrons aside from the fighting squadrons assigned to the escort carriers carried more than one type of first-line aircraft in its complement. This was due to the recognition that night fighters were a tactical necessity, but CVEs lacked the deck and hanger space to embark a separate night squadron. The obvious answer was to include the specialized aircraft in the day fighter squadron.] As July drew to a close, the carrier arrived at Saipan where, during its few days in the Marianas, VMF-513 flew its only combat missions of World War II when the aircraft of MCVG-3 launched a short series of strikes against bypassed Japanese garrisons in the islands. These relatively easy targets were frequently visited by the new air groups of carriers on their way to more active areas of combat. These strikes served a dual purpose. They added to the continuing discomfort of the enemy. Further, they allowed the often-inexperienced aircrews a chance to get acquainted with the idea of firing live ordnance against targets that could, and frequently did, shoot back. For many months, it had been the policy of the carrier command to "blood" new air groups against enemy garrisons that populated many of the islands throughout the Pacific.

After a short stay in the Marianas, *Vella Gulf* sailed for Okinawa. Its stay in the Ryukyus was a short two-day's duration before it was ordered to Guam, where it arrived on 15 August. By this date, the cities of Hiroshima and Nagasaki had been incinerated beneath the terrible, towering mushrooms that heralded the beginning of the nuclear age, and faced with the certainty of sudden, total destruction at the hands of their enemies, Japan finally accepted the Allies' terms and surrendered unconditionally. The formal instrument of surrender was signed aboard USS *Missouri* (BB-63) on 2 September 1945 as she lay at anchor in Tokyo Bay in the shadow of Mount Fujiyama.

As was the fate of many of the squadrons activated during World War II, VMF-513 was deactivated in the months immediately following the war's end. In the case of VMF-513, however, it was not condemned to languish on the inactive list for long. The squadron was reactivated on 1 August 1947 at MCAS, Cherry Point and redesignated a night fighter squadron, VMF(N)-513, on that date. Immediately after its reactivation, the squadron received its aircraft, the F4U-5N, the latest night fighter version of the familiar Corsair, and began to train in its new role.

In addition to its Corsairs, VMF(N)-513 was among the first Marine squadrons to receive the Grumman F7F-3N Tigercat. The penultimate design in Grumman's superb line of piston-engine "Cats," the F7F was a refinement of two earlier experimental designs. A typical Grumman product, it was big, fast and rugged, but it was also radical in that it was a twin-engine design and featured a tricycle landing gear. While in a carrier air wing of today, all the fixed-wing aircraft are twin-engine, the Tigercat must be considered in the context of the times. A mere five years before the first flight of the XF7F-1 prototype, the standard United States Navy carrier-based fighter, also a Grumman product, the F3F-3, was a single-engine biplane, weighing less than 5,000 pounds and capable of barely 250mph. Powered by a pair of 2,100hp Pratt & Whitney engines, the F7F-3 had a larger wingspan than any other aircraft to routinely operate from a carrier to

Night Hunter
An F4U-5N Corsair night fighter of VMF(N)-513 pictured on a Korean airfield fully armed and ready for its next sortie. Note the curved shape protruding from the fuselage just aft of the open cowl flaps. This is an exhaust shield to protect the pilot's night-vision, a matter of no small importance when one considers the terrain over which the squadron operated during night ground attack sorties. [USMC photo]

date and weighed more than eight tons empty. It was capable of speeds up to 450 M.P.H., and its service ceiling was in excess of 42,000 ft. In short, it was the last word in heavy fighters in the mid-1940s. The ample size, speed and firepower of the Tigercat also made it a natural for employment as a night fighter. With its excess of power and adequate space in the fuselage, it was easy to fit the aircraft with an airborne radar set and a radar operator's station. [The first Marine squadrons to be equipped with the day fighter version of F7F were on their way to Okinawa when the atom bombs fell on Japan.]

VMF(N)-513 was still operating from Cherry Point when war again flared in the Far East. The North Koreans invaded their neighbors to the south during the early morning hours of 25 June 1950 in an attempt to unify the peninsula under Communist control. Acting in concert with the United Nations, the United States was determined to halt the Communist expansion and began to rush men and material to Korea and to Japan. As a result, VMF(N)-513 was ordered depart Cherry Point immediately for the West Coast. Upon their arrival in California, the squadron's personnel were loaded aboard the transport *General A.E. Anderson* and sailed for Japan on 14 July 1950, where it arrived on 31 July and debarked to prepare to enter combat. VMF(N)-513 would spend the next three years alternating between Korean and Japanese bases as it flew combat missions against the North Koreans and Chinese Communists.

On 1 August, the squadron, a component of MAG-33, moved to Itazuki Air Force Base, and upon arrival there, it was assigned to the 5th Air Force for air defense duties. At the time, no one knew the eventual extent of the fighting, and the Air Force lacked sufficient resources to cover all the United States installations in Japan from the threat of enemy attack should the Communists elect to widen the war. At the time, this fear was widely held and largely stemmed from the mistaken belief that communism was monolithic and that all communist nations followed marching orders originating in the Kremlin. While the Soviet Communists were the bloc's unquestioned leaders, others in the bloc more often looked to their own concerns before they worried all that much about following the Soviet's lead.

Shortly after the squadron's arrival in Japan, the U.N. [primarily United States] forces had been forced to withdraw under heavy North Korean pressure into the area around the South Korean port of Pusan, where they were determined to mount a successful defense until the arrival of sufficient forces to switch over to the offense. American air power hammered the advancing North Korean forces day and night and extracted a fearful

Jet Hunter
Although it is of rather poor quality, this photo of one of the squadron's F3D Skyknights is interesting for the details it captured. The squadron's WF tail code is painted in dull red on the overall dark blue finish of the aircraft and the folded wing, under-wing drop tanks and the pierced steel plank (PSP) parking area offer a cleared picture of the conditions of operations in Korea.

toll in men, equipment and supplies from the ranks of the enemy. Fortunately for the U.N. cause, the threat of air attack against Japan failed to materialize, and when the North Koreans launched a major attack against the Pusan perimeter on 1 September, the F4U-5N Corsairs of VMF(N)-513 began to fly night interdiction strikes alongside the Air Force's B-26s. By 15 September, VMF(N)-513 had flown 343 sorties against the enemy.

MacArthur's amphibious masterstroke, the landing of the First Marine Division at Inchon on South Korea's west coast near the capital city of Seoul, went ashore on 15 September. Dubbed Operation *Chromite*, the landing succeeded beyond the planners' most optimistic predictions. Kimpo airfield, near Seoul, fell to the 5th Marine Regiment two days later, and Marine aircraft began to arrive there almost immediately after its capture. Their initial combat missions from Kimpo were flown on 20 September. The next day, MAG-33, which still included VMF(N)-513, and MAG-12 exchanged squadrons to align them with their new responsibilities as the American advance continued. On the night of 23 September, the F7F-3N flown by Major E. A. Van Gundy with Master Sergeant T. H. Ullom as his radar operator scored the squadron's first kill of the Korean War when they destroyed a North Korean PO-2 intruder near Seoul. Despite its being an obsolete wood and canvas biplane, the PO-2 was a notoriously difficult prey for the American night fighters. Its aeronautically primitive wood and fabric structure provided a poor radar target. This, coupled with its slow speed and maneuverability, made it extremely difficult to counter. Employed primarily as a night heckler to rob those on the ground of much needed sleep, the old aircraft was very successful. On the flip side, however, if one of the interceptors succeeded in getting a PO-2 in its sights, the old airplane was almost certainly doomed to a swift and likely fiery demise.

On 27 September, the Joint Chiefs of Staff authorized MacArthur to cross the 38th parallel in order to destroy the North Korean Peoples' Army and to unite all of Korea under the banner of the South. As part of the plan to accomplish this objective, the First Marine Division was to land near the port of Wonsan on North Korea's east coast and cut the enemy's line of retreat through that area. After a lengthy delay caused by extensive mine fields in the waters near the port, the Marines went ashore on 24 October, but not before Wonsan had been captured by South Korean troops advancing along the coast. The first Marine squadrons arrived at the airfield at Wonsan on 13 October, and VMF(N)-513 arrived shortly thereafter. The facilities were, to say the least, spartan, and due the lack of runway lighting, the squadron was committed to normal daylight missions. During this period, the squadron flew a mixture of day and night fighter versions of the Corsair, the F4U-4 and the F4U-5N, respectively, and the F7F-3N Tigercat. [The squadron's F7F-3Ns did not relocate to Wonsan, but continued to fly their assigned night intruder and defense missions from the K-1 airfield at Pusan, in South Korea.] The lights had been installed by late October, and VMF(N)-513's Corsairs returned to their nocturnal interdiction missions. However, it is not clear if the squadron continued to operate its F4U-4s after it began its night operations again.

Despite the urging of the Tenth Corps commander, the First Marine Division continued to advance cautiously into the mountains of North Korea. Rather than a headlong attack, which would fragment the division in the extremely rugged terrain of

Haze Gray and Under Way
This undated photo shows the USS General A.E. Anderson (AP-111) passing under the Golden Gate Bridge into San Francisco Bay. [U.S. Navy Photo]

the area, the division's commander, Major General O.P. Smith, kept his forces concentrated and left a series of fortified positions in the wake of his advance. The wisdom of General Smith's methods was to be proven fully in the coming weeks. In response to the U.N. advance across the 38th parallel that divided the two Koreas, the Communist Chinese began to send large forces into North Korea. By confining their movements to the hours of darkness, they managed to avoid detection despite extensive aerial reconnaissance by the U.N. command. They struck the advancing U.N. columns in a quick series of savage attacks then seemed to disappear. The reason for the seeming withdrawal of the Chinese remains a mystery to this day, but perhaps the first attacks were meant as a warning to the U.N. command of what lay in store should it continue its northward drive. If this was the case, the warning went unheeded, and the Chinese struck in overwhelming force in late-November. In the west, many units simply disappeared amid a sea of swarming Chinese infantry.

In the east, the Chinese attempted to trap the Marines in the mountains near the Chosin Reservoir. The first Chinese assaults against the division were driven back at tremendous cost to the attackers, but, despite their initial success, the Marines were in mortal danger as the enemy attempted to drive a wedge between them and the sea. General Smith's division then began its famous "attack in the other direction." When some questioned General Smith about his division conducting the first retreat in the history of the Marine Corps, his rather pithy reply was that since his troops were surrounded, the movement could not be called a retreat. It was, in fact, an attack along a different axis of advance. Regardless of whether the movement was an attack or a retreat, the Chinese soon realized this "paper tiger," as they often referred to the United States and its forces, had extremely sharp claws and teeth and was well-schooled in the use of both. This marked the first exposure of the Chinese Communist forces to a modern, well-equipped force that was prepared to receive their attacks and whose morale was unbroken. The tremendous firepower the Marines were able to bring to bear on their attackers must have come as a shock, but the Chinese persisted, and the toll in blood must have been almost beyond comprehension.

Under a continuous blanket of air cover from the aircraft overhead, the division retraced its steps amid the murderous terrain and subzero temperatures. The Chinese dogged every step and contested every yard of the Marines' march. Virtually every Navy and Marine squadron then in Korea contributed to the air support effort on behalf of the division, with the night-flying Corsairs of VMF(N)-513 providing much of that delivered during the hours of darkness and poor visibility. The combination of the bitter winter weather, the firepower of the division and the aircraft inflicted horrendous casualties on the enemy and rendered many of the Chinese units involved in these actions unfit for further combat for many months to come.

While the Corsairs of VMF(N)-513 clawed at the Chinese forces attempting to destroy the First Marine Division in the north, the elements of the squadron equipped with the F7F-3N continued their nightly "road work" the length and breadth of the territory under communist control in the Korean Peninsula. Truck convoys, trains, supply depots and troop concentrations were hunted and attacked without respite. Many of these missions were flown in conjunction with a Navy "Firefly" aircraft

Author's Collection

that dropped flares to light the area while the Tigercats carried out their attacks. [Editor's Note: These "Fireflies" were usually Navy Convair PB4Y-2 Privateers, an improved model of the famous Consolidated B-24 Liberator long-range bombers of World War II that were flown by the Navy's patrol squadrons.] These missions were among the most hazardous flown by the squadron during its service in Korea. The flickering light from the flares played havoc with the night vision of the Tigercat pilots and seriously impaired their depth perception, hardly a cheerful prospect when executing radical maneuvers at high speed and low altitudes in aircraft burdened with heavy loads of fuel and munitions. Also, their targets usually were to be found deep in the narrow, winding valleys that made up much of the terrain, especially in North Korea, and the enemy's habit of stringing cables from mountain to mountain above these valleys to ensnare aircraft sometimes was added to this witch's brew. Combined with weather that was often near or slightly below normal operational minimums, these missions would have been, at best, extremely dangerous even without the sometimes heavy volumes of small arms fire the enemy directed at their attackers. Despite the difficulties involved, the squadron's aircraft extracted a heavy toll from the enemy, although not without losses in men and aircraft.

The Chinese advance forced the withdrawal of the aircraft based at Wonsan, and, on 1 December 1950, VMF(N)-513's Corsairs were relocated to the airfield at Yonpo near the port of Hungnam out of the reach of the enemy. From their new base, the squadron continued its attacks against the Chinese. By 11 December, the First Marine Division had succeeded in breaking out of the trap and began to arrive inside the perimeter at Hungnam. Behind them was a Chinese field army in tattered ruin, gutted by a combination of intact American morale and firepower and the appalling cold. The last elements of the Division boarded the ships lying in the harbor and were withdrawn from North Korea on Christmas Eve.

Continued enemy pressure forced the eventual evacuation of most U.N. aircraft to bases in Japan, and after two weeks at Yonpo, the squadron left Korea for Itami, Japan, on 15 December. The move caused only a short pause in the squadron's tempo of missions over Korea, and as soon as it completed the forced relocation, the squadron once again began to hammer the Chinese in a successful attempt to prevent an overwhelming assault against the perimeter protecting the vital port as preparations for the evacuation of the Marines from Hungnam continued.

The Chinese advance continued in the west, and the South Korean capital once again fell into the hands of the enemy on 5 January 1951, but shortly after that date, the Communist offensive was checked by a combination of factors. They had suffered terrible casualties at the hands of the U.N. forces on the ground and from their air support. With every step the Chinese marched southward, their supply lines lengthened by the same distance, and their primitive supply organizations, already heavily battered by air attack, were unable to sustain the advance. As the enemy's supply lines lengthened, those of the U.N. forces shortened, and the Korean Peninsula is at its most narrow in the area of Seoul, allowing an almost continuous line of defenses to be put into place. Also, U.N. air power was at its most effective in the more open terrain in the area.

Going Hunting
Under the watchful eye of its crew chief, an F7F-3N Tigercat of VMF(N)-513 begins to taxi in prepara-
tion for its next sortie into the gathering Korean night. The external carriage of three auxiliary fuel tanks
and five-inch rockets indicates a long night of anti-heckler patrol lies ahead. [USMC photo]

While engaged against the enemy offensive, the U.N. forces had also been building their strength for their eventual counterattacks, and the U.N. went over to the offensive in mid-February. Two series of attacks, Operations *Killer* and *Ripper*, were launched in succession, but aside from the recapture of Seoul, the territorial objectives of these offensives were strictly limited. In addition to driving the Chinese from South Korean soil and re-establishing the battle lines along or slightly to the north of the 38th Parallel, the U.N. forces sought to inflict the maximum number of casualties possible on the enemy. The intended success of these operations was twofold. First, it would instill a renewed sense of confidence in U.N. forces that had been badly shaken by the Chinese attacks the previous November. Second, the attacks would serve to convince the enemy, North Korean, Communist Chinese and Russian alike, that, regardless of their best efforts, the U.N. would never be driven from South Korea by force of arms.

These attacks were set-piece battles in the truest sense. Rather than sweeping, cavalry style maneuvers, each assault was preceded by heavy air attacks against supplies, reinforcements and defensive positions along with massive artillery barrages. The infantry then attacked with strong armored support with aircraft and artillery on call to reduce any surviving enemy strongpoints that lay in their path. The night-flying intruders of VMF(N)-513 were heavily committed to these support and interdiction missions and were very instrumental in the success of the U.N. offensives. Seoul was recaptured by 15 March 1951, and the enemy was driven back above the 38th parallel across almost the entire breadth of the Korean Peninsula, suffering uncounted thousands of casualties in the process. Some enemy units in the path of the operations simply ceased to exist while others were reduced to bloody fragments. [Editor's Note: It is of interest to note that objections were raised by some so-called "neutral" or "non-aligned" nations, both within the United Nations and elsewhere, to the use of the names "Killer" and "Ripper" for these attacks on the grounds the names indicated a desire on the part of the U.N. command to "kill" the enemy! In due time, the U.N. command was instructed to use what today would be termed more "politically correct" terminology for future operations. In view of the current state of world affairs, this offers another excellent example of the fact that history often repeats itself, as well as leaving some among us to shake our heads in wonder at the thought processes of some of our fellow men.]

Author's Collection

The bloody defeat inflicted on the enemy by *Killer* and *Ripper* convinced the Chinese of the futility of attempting to force a U.N. withdrawal from Korea on the field of battle. But, perhaps an even more important effect was the restoration of the confidence of the U.N. forces in their ability to meet the enemy in battle and destroy him. Gone was the cocky, somewhat careless "home by Christmas" attitude on the part of the Americans displayed prior to the Chinese intervention in the fall and early winter of 1950. It had been replaced with a grim self-confidence and determination on the part of the United States 8th Army, the hard core of the U.N. command, that they would be in Korea for as long as required and convinced them that they were better soldiers than their enemies. It has been said that the 8th Army emerged from the purgatory of the winter battles confident, tested and battle hardened and that no better American army had ever taken the field. With the realization of their inability to force a military decision and probably more than a little Soviet pressure, the Chinese and North Koreans then began an attempt to win at

the conference table what they could not win on the battlefield. The peace talks that would eventually end the fighting after more than 24 months of frustration and additional bloodshed opened on 10 July 1951, and in the ensuing political chess game, the armies in the field were reduced to hardly more than pawns as the truce talks ground onward toward their inevitable conclusion.

For VMF(N)-513, the Korean War settled into somewhat of a routine, if placing one's life in mortal jeapordy on a regular basis can ever be described as "routine." In early-1951, the other Marine night fighter squadron in the theater, VMF(N)-542, was withdrawn to the United States to be reequipped with the latest night fighter to enter Navy and Marine service, jet-powered the Douglas F3D Skyknight When VMF(N)-542 departed Korea, it turned its aircraft and many of its squadron personnel over to VMF(N)-513. These additional aircraft and personnel allowed VMF(N)-513 to fly almost as many missions as both of the separate squadrons had flown previously. To illustrate the squadron's tempo of operations, during the ninety days beginning 1 April 1951, it averaged eighteen missions per night, attacked an estimated 11,890 enemy vehicles and claimed the destruction of 1,420. During the next fifteen months and two changes of bases, the squadron's operations remained near this level, subject to aircraft serviceability rates.

In June 1952, VMF(N)-542 returned to Korea, bringing the F3D-2 Skyknight into combat for the first time. Prior to month's end, however, VMF(N)-542 was, in effect, absorbed by VMF(N)-513 which took control of the F3Ds, as well as the Tigercats that -542 brought to Korea. On 12 June, Lieutenant Colonel Peter B. Lambrect, the former commanding officer of VMF(N)-542, assumed command of VMF(N)-513. Unfortunately, Lambrect was lost in action a week later, and command of the squadron passed to Lieutenant Colonel Jack C. Scott, who would receive the Distinguished Flying Cross for heroism while serving with the squadron.

Despite the Skyknight's arrival, VMF(N)-513 continued to fly the F7F-3N in combat for several months. Even though the experienced F3D air and ground crews inherited from

A Revolution in Close Air Support
One of the squadron's first-generation AV-8A Harriers waits for the fuses to be inserted into its load of Mk.82 500lb. bombs before its next flight. [USMC photo]

"And Away We Go!"
The nose wheel of this AV-8C of VMA-513 has just lifted off the flight deck of an
Amphibious Transport Dock, an LPD, of the Austin-class on 1 April 1982 during
the acceptability trials of the Harrier aboard LPDs. [DoD Photo]

VMF(N)-542 gave VMF(N)-513 a leg up with the new aircraft, the process of transitioning to an entirely new aircraft and from props to jets as well, in the midst of combat operations proved somewhat protracted. This situation was not aided by a shortage of parts and inadequate radio and radar spares for the new aircraft, but the squadron was declared operational in the F3D-2 on 1 November 1952. Their new aircraft allowed the squadron to shift its operations from primarily those of night interdiction to the escort of the Air Force's night bombing missions. Earlier in the conflict, the losses inflicted on the B-29s by MiG-15 jet interceptors forced the big bombers to shift from day to night operations, but the MiGs soon adapted to the new tactics and were making life miserable for the bombers again. The big Skyknight soon proved itself to be the best of the first generation of American jet night fighters, and the Air Force requested the Marines' help, somewhat reluctantly no doubt.

The black-painted F3D-2s were so successful at the task of bomber escort that not a single B-29 was lost to MiGs while escorted by a Skyknight. On the other hand, VMF(N)-513 proved quite adept at killing MiGs. Six of the squadron's eleven kills in Korea were against the enemy interceptors while escorting the bombers during a period of less than five months. The last two fell to the cannon of the Skyknight flown by the squadron's commanding officer, Lieutenant Colonel Robert F. Conley.

The enemy soon realized the mortal danger the Skyknights posed to their night-flying MiGs, and, in an attempt to turn the tables on the Americans, they began to hunt the F3Ds, aided by their ground control radar sites, the only option open to the MiGs. A favorite tactic of the MiGs, which lacked radar, was to attempt to "bait" one of the Marine fighters by sending one of their aircraft into the area near the American bombers in order to attract the attention of the escorting American fighter. As the F3D took the bait and began to stalk the lone MiG, known as a "rabbit," additional enemy aircraft would attempt to get into position to bring the Skyknight under attack while its attention was on the "rabbit". As they closed on the F3D, they would attempt to spot the bright trail of flames from its engines, which stood out like twin beacons against the night sky.

Their tactics were sound, but the MiGs did not take into account the presence of American ground control radars and of a tail warning radar set aboard the American aircraft. The friendly ground control sites would warn the F3D of the presence of the hunting enemy aircraft as soon as they were detected, and after several near misses by MiGs, the Skyknight crews learned to watch their tail warning sets closely. When the ambushing MiGs were "painted" by these radars, the American would attempt to close rapidly on the "rabbit" and kill it before its companions could come to its aid, but if the bait's companions were in position to launch their attack before the F3D could take the lone MiG under fire, the Skyknight's crew would turn its attention to the approaching MiGs. They would "play dumb" and continue to allow the enemy to close. Just before the enemy reached firing positions, the American pilot would "chop" his throttles causing the engines to "swallow" the bright exhaust flames. They would then haul their big, but surprisingly nimble, fighter up and over in a split-S maneuver designed to bring the F3D into a position behind the pursuing MiGs. Such tactics required good timing and often resulted in the combatants blindly groping for each other in the dark skies. On other occasions, startled by the sudden disappearance of their intended prey, the confused enemy often would hesitate long enough for the American aircraft to launch a successful attack. Soon, however, the MiGs learned to depart the area with all due haste when they lost contact with the American aircraft that had been, until only moments earlier, their intended victim. Hesitation on their part could prove fatal.

Despite their success in the bomber escort business, the squadron kept its hand in the night interdiction game as well. In late March 1953, VMF(N)-513 launched the first in a series of pre-dawn bombing attacks against enemy artillery positions along the battle lines, and the F3D proved itself to be a competent bombing aircraft in its own right.

By the early summer of 1953, the squadron received a dozen additional F3Ds, bringing its total to twenty-four, and the last of the F7F-3Ns were retired. Also, as the Korean War entered its final months, an attempt was made to give combat experience to as many aircrews as possible. To this end, VMF(N)-513 was augmented by four aircraft and crews of the Navy's VC-4 of USS *Lake Champlain* (CVA-39). Unfortunately, even as the war neared its conclusion, the squadron lost two aircraft and crews on combat missions to unknown causes, one Marine crew and its aircraft, and one aircraft and crew from VC-4.

After the signing of the armistice ending the fighting, VMF(N)-513 remained in Korea until the fall of 1953 and then was withdrawn to Japan. It was later returned to the United States and to a more peaceful routine of squadron deployments. In 1955, the squadron was again deployed to Japan for a three-year tour at NAS, Atsugi, which lies on the Kanto Plain on the main island of Honshu.

Its tour completed, the squadron returned to MCAS, El Toro and was redesignated VMF(AW)-513 on 26 July 1958. Upon its redesignation, it was assigned to IIId MAW's MAG-15 as its all-weather fighter squadron, and it immediately began to exchange its F3Ds for the Douglas F4D-1 Skyray. The change of designation and aircraft was accomplished quickly but was accompanied by some sadness. The new F4D-1 was a single-seat aircraft, and the services of the squadron's enlisted radar operators were no longer needed after more than a decade of sterling work. [Among these men was Warrant Officer Eugene Holmberg who contributed numerous insignia to this work.]

At the time of its introduction, the F4D-1 was the latest word in interceptor aircraft, and it set several performance records shortly after it entered service, most notably the record for time-to-climb, a welcome capability for an interceptor. However, the decade of the 1950s perhaps was unsurpassed for its rapid pace of aeronautical development. Almost before a squadron had time to become thoroughly acquainted with a new air-

Parade Formation
Two of a division of four of the squadron's latest generation AV-8B Night Attack Harriers pass overhead for the camera's lens. [via webshots]

craft, it would be superseded by a more advanced model or by an entirely new design. VMF(AW)-513 was one of last Marine squadrons to receive the radical, manta-shaped Douglas aircraft and was declared operational with it early in 1959. The next eighteen months were spent in training and in a series of short deployments in the United States

The squadron's only extended deployment with the Skyray began on 16 October 1961 when its personnel boarded USS *Noble* (APA-218) for transport to Japan. It arrived at NAS, Atsugi, on 4 November and spent the next year operating from Japan in a series of short deployments to other bases throughout the Western Pacific. On 1 November 1962, VMF(AW)-513 was relieved of duty at Atsugi and was redesignated VMFA-513 on the same date. The squadron then returned to El Toro and began its transition to the mighty McDonnell F-4B Phantom in January 1963. It was the third Marine squadron to receive this remarkable workhorse of an aircraft, and by November of 1964, the squadron completed its work-up period in its new mount and was ready for extended deployment and was ordered to NAS, Atsugi. After seven months in Japan, VMFA-513 was on the move once again, this time to Da Nang in South Vietnam.

It arrived in South Vietnam in May 1965 and relieved the first Marine Phantom squadron to be deployed to that war-torn country, the "Gray Ghosts" of VMFA-531. While "in country," the squadron flew virtually all of its missions in support of the "Mud Marines" in the I Corps area in the northern part of the country. Its stay in Southeast Asia was a relatively brief one of six months, and it departed Vietnam in October 1965 to return to the United States.

Author's Collection

When the squadron returned to the United States, it was to a new base on the other side of the continent. Instead of the familiar surroundings of El Toro, VMFA-513 was stationed at MCAS, Cherry Point. After a short period to become accustomed to its new surroundings, the squadron entered a normal rotational schedule of unit deployments, followed by a stay at Cherry Point before deploying again.

This relatively routine existence continued for most of the next five years until the squadron was reduced to cadre status in June 1970 in preparation to be reequipped with revolutionary AV-8A Harrier V/STOL attack aircraft.

The squadron stood up again on 16 April 1971, and effective on that date, it was redesignated as an attack squadron, VMA-513, under the command of Lieutenant Colonel C.M. Baker. Its new home was MCAS, Beaufort, South Carolina. The "Flying Nightmares" were the first Marine squadron to be equipped with the Harrier and with the new aircraft came a quantum leap forward in capability. The ability of the Harrier to operate in the vertical takeoff and landing mode while carrying a useful war load allows the aircraft to be based much closer to the battlefield, just beyond enemy artillery range and to do so from virtually any short stretch of road, forest clearing or virtually any relatively level patch of ground larger than the aircraft itself. This serves to greatly decrease the time required to reach the battle area and this reduced transit time of the aircraft from its base to the battlefield works as a "force multiplier." This allows a smaller number of Harriers to fly the same number of sorties as a larger number of conventional aircraft.

Their conversion to the new aircraft completed successfully, the squadron deployed to the Med for six-months aboard USS *Guam* (LPH-9). One of the highlights from this cruise was an opportunity to conduct operations with Harriers of the Spanish Navy. When the deployment was completed, the "Nightmares" were transferred from Beaufort to MCAS, Cherry Point, in January 1976. At Cherry Point, they became a component of MAG-32. Shortly thereafter, VMA-513 was deployed to MCAS, Iwakuni.

After its return from Japan, the squadron again changed its home station when it was transferred to MAG-13 at MCAS, Yuma, in 1984. During this period, the squadron received the latest model of the Harrier in United States service, the AV-8C, a modification of the original model, which it continued to operate until it stood down in August 1986 in preparation to be reequipped with the AV-8B Harrier II. The last of the squadron's C-models were transferred into storage in February 1987, but conversion training to the new aircraft had begun the previous month under the auspices of VMAT-203 at Cherry Point.

Its conversion training completed, the squadron returned to a new home at Yuma, Arizona, and a normal rotational deployment schedule. This routine continued until its 1990 deployment

A Ride to Japan
USS Noble (APA-218) posed for this portrait off her
home port of San Diego in 1956. [U.S. Navy Photo]

to the Far East, which began in November. Iraq had invaded the Kingdom of Kuwait on 2 August, and Operation *Desert Shield* was ordered as a response to the Iraqi aggression. In December 1990, the decision was made to add Marine Harriers to the buildup of Coalition forces in Southwestern Asia.

Among the Marine Harriers deployed to Saudi Arabia was a four-aircraft detachment from VMA-513, Det. B, from MCAS, Iwakuni. Initially based at Sheikh Isa, the AV-8Bs were moved to Al Jubial Air Base in December, where preparations continued for the eventual forceful ejection of Iraqi forces from Kuwait. At the commencement of Operation *Desert Storm* on 17 January 1991, the Harriers began pounding Iraqi positions in Kuwait in preparation for the inevitable ground offensive that would drive the Iraqi army from Kuwait and/or destroy it in place. The massive Coalition attack opened on 24 February and lasted 100 hours. During the offensive, the aircraft of VMA-513 logged 103 combat sorties while engaged in close air support of the advancing troops, primarily the First and Second Marine Divisions during their drive on Kuwait City.

The squadron's detachment suffered no losses during its deployment and returned to MCAS, Iwakuni in March 1991. The deployment of four complete Harrier squadrons plus the detachment from the "Nightmares" caused the squadron's normal six-month deployment to be extended to eleven months. The entire squadron returned to Yuma from Japan in October 1991.

Author's Collection

In the wake of the attacks of September 11, 2001, a detachment of the squadron deployed to Bagram Air Base, Afghanistan, in support of Operation *Enduring Freedom.* The detachment remained in combat for a year and supported troops of more than twenty Coalition nations that made up Combined Joint Task Force 180. During this intense operational period, the half-dozen aircraft of VMA-513 amassed 1,250 combat sorties totaling 3,763.6 flight hours and thankfully suffered no losses.

Concurrent with the detachment operating in Afghanistan, another six aircraft detachment twice deployed aboard ship in support of Operation *Iraqi Freedom* in Iraq and Operation *Enduring Freedom.*

In early 2005, aviators from both VMA-513 and -311 combined to support a deployment of the 31st M.E.U.(SOC) in Japan. In mid-year, the squadron's aircraft received a software upgrade that allowed them to generate the very precise targeting coordinates required to employ the JDAM, Joint Direct Attack Munitions. This very accurate weapon is a powerful new arrow in the quiver of Marine airpower, and it was employed with considerable success during its next deployment to Iraq during which the Nightmares flew 1,310 combat sorties for a total of 4,520 hours in support of I Marine Expeditionary Force.

In February 2006, VMA-513 again deployed to Al Asad Airbase, Iraq, to provide air support for Marine ground units engaged there. During this period in Southwest Asia, the squadron flew 4,519 combat hours with a sortie completion rate of 95%. It also initiated the JDAM into combat when it employed the GBU-38,500lb. version of the JDAM against hostile strongpoints.

In April 2007, another six-aircraft detachment deployed in support of the 13th Marine Expeditionary Unit (Special Operations Capable) while a further detachment deployed with the 31st M.E.U. once again. It was during this latter deployment that the squadron set another first in the annals of Marine aviation when it was the first to operate from a foreign warship, HMS *Illustrious.*

These operations are ongoing, and as this was being written, VMA-513 continues its operations in support of United States objectives around the world.

Regarding the insignia worn by VMF-513 and its lineal successors during their half-century plus of service to this nation, ten examples are depicted. The first pair are examples of the current squadron insignia, and both represent the classic insignia design that has served the squadron since it was reactivated and redesignated a night fighter squadron, even though it continues to feature the figure of the owl in the day/night sky. The one on left is done in desert colors, while the one on the right is a full-color example. Both were obtained from the squadron's coffee mess and follow the current trend in Marine squadron insignia. Slightly smaller than its predecessors, its wear is limited to aviator's flight suits as opposed to the earlier, larger designs that were worn frequently on the Navy-issue brown leather G-1 flight jackets.

The third example is an insignia design the squadron elected to substitute for the old one in the wake of its service in Operation *Desert Storm.* All was proceeding well until the commanding officer voted to keep the old insignia, and it should be kept in mind that, in the military version of democracy, the commanding officer's vote accounts for 51% of the electorate. As a result of this vote, the old design was retained, and the new one became a footnote in the history of VMA-513.

The fourth insignia is an example of the squadron's flight suit shoulder rectangle.

The third pair represent examples of the squadron's insignia worn from November 1962 until it stood down as a fighter/attack squadron in June 1970 and is slightly larger than the current design.

The much larger VMF(AW)-513 design was worn between 26 July 1958 and November 1962.

The eighth is the insignia worn by VMF(N)-513. As can be readily seen, the squadron's insignia has been virtually unchanged from 1947 until early 2000, a somewhat unusual example of longevity among squadron insignia.

The ninth insignia is that of VMF-513 during its service in World War II. The design originated at the Disney Studios and is a reproduction and is identical to that pictured in the December 1994 National Geographic Magazine supplement devoted to the insignia of the United States armed forces during World War II. It should be noted that some examples of the squadron's insignia of that period are somewhat smaller in size but identical in design to that shown.

The final insignia of VMA-513 depicted is an example of a commemorative insignia that celebrates the squadron's fifty-plus year record of service from installations in Japan during deployments and combat in the Far East.

A Real Butt Buster
Four of the six aircraft of VMA-513 that deployed in support of Operation Enduring Freedom were photographed while refueling from a KC-10A Extender tanker aircraft of the U.S. Air Force during their flight to Afghanistan. [USMC Photo via the VMA-513 Website]

Nightmare 07
Aircraft 07 of VMA-513 poses for the camera while its pilot prepares to enter the cockpit on the ramp at MCAS, Yuma. This angle clearly demonstrates the excellent visibility afforded by the large bubble canopy of the AV-8B. The hump just forward of the windscreen houses the laser designator and the clear lens in the extreme nose of the aircraft is a part of the ARBS (Angle Rate Bombing System). [USMC Photo, via Webshots]

It Sure Beats Walking
Sgt. Ellison of VMA-513 is pictured beside one of the squadron's Harriers along with a favored means of transportation around Al Asad airfield in Iraq. [USMC Photo via the VMA-513 Website]

MARINE ATTACK SQUADRON 542
THE TIGERS,
A.K.A., THE FLYING TIGERS

Author's Collection

Marine Night Fighting Squadron 542 [VMF(N)-542] was activated on 6 March 1944 at MCAS, Cherry Point under the command of Major William C. Kellum. After spending the first six months of its service training on the East Coast, the squadron was ordered to San Diego in preparation for further movement westward and was assigned to Marine Base Defense Air Group 45 upon arrival in California. It remained on the West Coast only briefly before its flight and ground echelons were separated for transfer to the South Pacific. On 29 August, the flight echelon and its aircraft were loaded aboard the aircraft ferry USS *Kitty Hawk* (APV-1) and departed for the island of Manus in the Admiralties, and after three weeks at sea, they arrived at their destination on 18 September. A week later, it was transferred to the island of Pityilu to await the availability of an airfield in the newly captured atoll of Ulithi.

Meanwhile, the ground echelon had a few additional days to enjoy San Diego before boarding the transport S.S. *Dashing Wave* on 9 September. A month later, it moved ashore on Falalop Island on the eastern side of Ulithi Atoll, where Army engineers had begun construction of an airstrip. The completion of the airfield was turned over to the Navy's Seabees, who finished the work on a 3,500-foot airstrip three weeks later. The F6F-3N Hellcats of VMF(N)-542 arrived at the new field on 29 October and began to fly their defensive combat air patrols the following night. The huge anchorage of Ulithi was quickly converted into an advanced base for the fleet, and at times, it held as many as 500 ships, warships from the mightiest battleships and carriers to destroyer escorts and all types of auxiliaries needed to support the massive trans-Pacific drive that would culminate in

Tokyo Bay is just under a year. Despite the nearness of Ulithi to the enemy bases on the bypassed island of Yap, it was nearly five months before the Japanese attempted to attack this most lucrative of potential targets, and as a result, VMF(N)-542 spent many quiet, i.e. boring, hours orbiting above the anchored ships and waiting for the enemy.

By February 1945, preparations were underway for the squadron's next move, this time to the Philippines. The forward echelon departed for Leyte on 15 February, while the flight and ground echelons remained at Ulithi in preparation for the assault against Okinawa. For the Philippines campaign, operational control of the squadron was shifted from MAG-45 to MAG-31, but the squadron's tour in these islands was destined to be of short duration. All of the squadron's contact with the enemy would be during the final amphibious operations of World War II, the capture of the Ryukus, the gateway to the Japanese home islands. Had the war run its expected course, these islands would have been the springboard for the invasion of Japan.

The assault against Okinawa, the primary objective of the campaign in the island chain, was dubbed Operation *Iceberg* and began on Easter Sunday, 1 April 1945. The northern half of the island was quickly overrun by the assault troops, and the all-important airfields that lay in that part of Okinawa were hurriedly repaired to receive the hundreds of aircraft waiting to come ashore. MAG-31 was to be based at Yontan, and the squadron was ferried to within range of the base aboard the escort carrier USS *Sitkoh Bay* (CVE-86) on 7 April and its aircraft were in the process of being catapulted aloft when a kamikaze attacked the CVE. Luckily, five Corsairs from VMF-311 were in a position to intercept the

One Ugly Boat!
This 1942 vintage photo depicts USS Kitty Hawk (APV-1) under way at near her top speed. Note the TBF Avenger on deck on the port side and the open hanger amidships. [U.S. Navy Photo]

attacker which cartwheeled into the sea only fifty yards from the little carrier. After a collective exhaled breath, all hands returned to the task of getting the squadrons' aircraft airborne.

By the time of their arrival at Yontan on the island's West Coast, the night fighters were needed badly. Okinawa lay within easy reach of the southernmost of the Japanese Home Islands, which lay only some 350 miles to the north, and both day and night conventional and suicide attacks were proving as deadly as they were frequent. VMF(N)-542 was the first operational night fighter squadron to arrive on the scene, and it was forced to scrounge for an existence until its ground echelon arrived on 1 May. Despite its somewhat hand-to-mouth existence, the squadron notched its first kill during the evening of 16 April 1945. Lieutenants Arthur J. Arceneaux and William W. Campbell were vectored toward what proved to be a pair of single-engine enemy aircraft forty-five miles west of "Point Bolo" off the island's west coast. Aceneaux claimed a Navy Zero, and Campbell claimed an Army Nakajima Ki-84 Frank fighter within seconds of each other at 1845. The pair was awarded Distinguished Flying Crosses for their kills, and by month's end, the squadron added three more victory symbols to its scoreboard.

By the latter part of May, enemy activity in the night skies had begun to lessen somewhat, and VMF(N)-542 added night heckler missions to its mission schedule. Armed with bombs and rockets in addition to their normal load of machine gun ammunition, VMF(N)-542 looked for targets of opportunity within the continually shrinking portion of the island still held by the Japanese. Despite their successes, however, it was not all one-sided. After splashing a bogie during the night of 16 May, Lieutenant Campbell failed to return from the sortie. Exactly four weeks previously, he had scored one of the squadron's first victories. The reason for Campbell's loss remains unexplained, but it is likely he was hit by return fire from his victim, although this was

Author's Collection

never confirmed. The last radio transmission received from the lieutenant was heard as he commenced his final attack, and no friendly eyes witnessed his final action.

On 23 May, Major Kellum was relieved of command of VMF(N)-542 and ordered to staff duty. He was replaced by Major Robert B. Porter, who, while relatively new to night fighters, had recorded three kills during a 1943 tour in the Solomons with VMF-121. Porter assumed command of the squadron on 24 May and flew his first patrol at Okinawa that same evening. The patrol was uneventful, but the hours following it were anything but uneventful. In an effort to destroy American air power at Yontan, the Japanese resorted to a variation of one of their traditional suicide attacks. Five Japanese Army Mitsubishi Ki-21 Sally bombers loaded with special assault troops were to crash-land on the airfield. Once on the ground, the troops' mission was to destroy as many aircraft and as much equipment while inflicting a maximum number of casualties among the squadrons' personnel as they could before they met their inevitable fate. Four of the attacking aircraft were quickly claimed by the heavy concentration of anti-aircraft guns around the field, but the fifth, despite heavy damage from the guns, crash-landed on the runway at 2230. In the action that followed, the Japanese succeeded in destroying a few aircraft and setting fire to a fuel dump holding 70,000 gallons of aviation fuel, but the arrival of Marine infantry and armor quickly put an end to the raid. To Major Porter, it seemed almost as if the enemy had staged this show to welcome him to the island!

The first days of June were quiet, but Lieutenant William E. Smith killed a twin-engine fighter early in the morning of the 3rd, earning a Distinguished Flying Cross, and Lieutenant Fred Hilliard scored the squadron's only day kill the following afternoon. Hilliard's kill was confirmed by radar, and he reported contact with another enemy aircraft moments later. Nothing further was heard from Hilliard, and despite a thorough search of the area, no trace of the lieutenant or his aircraft was ever found.

Author's Collection

Major Porter extracted revenge for Hilliard's loss on 15 June during a five-hour "nightcap," or night combat air patrol. At 2100, he was vectored to a contact that proved to be a Kawasaki Ki-45 Nick twin-engine Army fighter. It quickly fell to the major's night-stalking Hellcat, and at 2230, the same controller vectored him to another unidentified contact. Slowly decreasing the range until he could visually identify his quarry, Porter soon recognized the portly fuselage of a Mitsubishi G4M Betty bomber in the moonless sky. Closing to point-blank range, Porter triggered a short burst, and the hapless Betty's fuel tanks exploded in a bright orange glare. Porter's two victories marked the first occasion on which a pilot of -542 had scored multiple victories on the same sortie. Later, it was discovered that Porter had expended only 700 rounds of ammunition for two kills, less than half the average per kill. Porter later attributed his frugality to the fact that his personal F6F-5N, called "Black Death," carried a pair of 20mm cannon in place of two of the usual six .50-caliber machine guns. The hitting power of a 20mm round was many times that of a .50-caliber round, and its killing power was further enhanced by the small explosive charge it carried. The month of June saw five Japanese aircraft fall to the guns of Porter and the other pilots of VMF(N)-542.

As the fighting on the island painfully drew to a conclusion, the level of enemy aerial activity dropped accordingly as the enemy began to husband his remaining strength to defend the Home Islands against the Allied assault that all believed to be inevitable. July produced few kills for any of the Marine night fighter squadrons on Okinawa, and August produced fewer still. However, it was appropriate that since VMF(N)-542 had opened the scoring for the night fighters, they closed it as well. At 0308 on 8 August, Lieutenant William E. Jennings destroyed a Japanese Army fighter for the squadron's eighteenth and last kill of the campaign. It was also the 69th and last kill for the Marine night fighter squadrons of the Tactical Air Force. A week later, the Japanese agreed to allied terms for surrender, and the shooting stopped. On 31 August, Major Porter relinquished command of the squadron to Major Kellum, who was released from staff duty with the hostilities virtually at an end. Porter was awarded the Distinguished Flying Cross upon his departure from the squadron. In addition to its eighteen kills, VMF(N)-542 was awarded the Presidential Unit Citation for its service in the Okinawa-Ryukyus campaign during the period 7 April through 14 July 1945. During the Okinawa campaign, Major Porter and Captain Wallace E. Sigler attained the unofficial title of ace.

After the end of the war in the Pacific, VMF(N)-542 was ordered to the United States. Upon arrival back on U.S. soil, the squadron was teamed with VMF(N)-534 under MAG-31 as the night fighter squadrons assigned to Marine Air West Coast.

After the end of World War II, the Navy and Marine Corps began to replace both the day and night fighter versions of Grumman's F6F Hellcat with almost indecent haste. Obviously, the tremendous numbers of fighter aircraft of all types in service at the war's end had much to do with the replacement of the Hellcat, but even more important was the pace of aeronautical development, largely driven by the war. When it flew its first combat missions in the fall of 1943, the F6F was the world's best carrier fighter, and only four years later, it was obsolescent. The Hellcats were either transferred to the various reserve units around the country or scrapped. The Marines' night fighting

Author's Collection

via Holmberg

Hellcats were replaced with another Grumman product, the big, powerful F7F Tigercat series. Marine night fighter squadrons equipped with the first night version of the new fighter, the F7F-2N, were in the process of moving westward across the Pacific to take part in the invasion of the Japanese home islands when the enemy surrendered. For VMF(N)-542, the big twin-engine 'Cat arrived in 1947, when the squadron's F6F-5N Night Hellcats were replaced with the second night fighter model of the Tigercat series, the F7F-3N. With its tremendous speed and heavy firepower, as well as a second crewman to operate the increasingly sophisticated radar of the time, the F7F-3N was an excellent night fighter, and it served the squadrons equipped with it very well until they were, in turn, replaced with jet-propelled night/all-weather fighter aircraft.

By the late 1940s, the Truman administration reduced the U.S. armed forces to their lowest levels in a decade, and VMF(N)-542 and others, while they remained active units, were operating barely above the cadre level. This depressing state of affairs continued until war exploded on the Korean Peninsula in June 1950. Many squadrons, including VMF(N)-542, were badly in need of hasty augmentation by recalled Reservists and additional aircraft before they could be dispatched into combat. The squadron quickly received more personnel and Tigercats, and after a short training period, it departed El Toro for San Diego, where its personnel and aircraft were loaded aboard USS *Cape Esperance* (CVE-88), which sailed for Japan on 26 August 1950. The CVE arrived at its destination on 11 September, and VMF(N)-542 and its aircraft were off-loaded and assigned to control of the 5th Air Force for local air defense against a possible North Korean attack against American installations in Japan. While the squadron was employed in flying local air defense patrols and standing cockpit alerts from their temporary base at Itazuke, the Marines went ashore at Inchon on 15 September, and the tide of the fighting began to change dramatically in favor of the U.N. forces. The airfield at Kimpo, near the South Korean capital of Seoul was captured on 17 September, and the first American aircraft arrived there the next day.

VMF(N)-542 moved from Itazuke to Kimpo on 19 September and immediately began to add its weight to the preponderance of U.N. air power that was pounding the enemy. Under heavy attack on its front by the 8th Army and ROK units from the perim-

A Well-worn Cat
The ground crew of a Grumman F7F-3N Tigercat of VMF(N)-542 getting a thorough going over on a Korean airfield after its return from a mission. Note the rather battered condition of the fighter's nose, and the attention being paid to the starboard prop and wing leading edge. It is likely the dents and scrapes were the results of debris from the explosion of one its victims on the previous night's sortie. [USMC photo]

Severe Clear
An F3D-2M Skyknight of VMF(AW)-542 is pictured carrying a full load of the first generation Sparrow air-to-air missiles. The gull gray color scheme of the aircraft dates this photo in the period between September 1955 and May 1958, when is surrendered the Skyknight in favor of the F4D Skyray. [USMC Photo]

eter around Pusan and from the Marines and ROKs in their rear around Seoul as well as attempting to conduct operations in the face of the virtually unchallenged air supremacy enjoyed by the U.N. forces, the battered, weakened North Korean forces finally broke and streamed north in headlong retreat. Many enemy units simply disappeared as their retreat became a rout, and the huge number of casualties inflicted by the aircraft that scourged their ranks day and night never will be accurately tallied. In addition to their air defense duties against the night heckler missions of the enemy, the two Marine night fighter units in Korea, VMF(N)-542 and -513, ranged nearly the full length and breadth of the peninsula by night in search of targets for their cannon, bombs, and rockets. Aided by the "Firefly" flare aircraft, these two squadrons added their part of the growing masses of blackened wreckage and bodies the fleeing enemy left in his wake.

The rapidity with which the North Korean army broke and fled in the face of the landing at Inchon and the advance from the Pusan pocket led to the development of a "home by Christmas" attitude on the part of the Americans. However, this happy state of mind came to a crashing end in the wake of the massive Chinese intervention. During the heavy combat of late November and December as the First Marine Division successfully broke out of the Chinese trap in the mountains in the area of the Chosin Reservoir in North Korea and fought its way to the sea, the night flying Tigercats and Corsairs of VMF(N)-542 played their part as the dreaded "blue airplanes" battered the enemy wherever they were found to aid their fellow Marines on the ground. As the U.N. forces fell back before the tides of Chinese, VMF(N)-542 was withdrawn from Korea to Itami Air Base in Japan. Once there, it continued to operate from Japan until March 1951, when it turned its aircraft and many of its personnel over to the "Flying Nightmares" of VMF(N)-513 and departed Japan to return to El Toro on 24 March.

Somewhat in the dark regarding their sudden departure from the Far East, it was not until the squadron arrived at El Toro that they learned they were to be reequipped with the latest Navy/Marine night fighter and the squadron's first jet aircraft, the big Douglas F3D-1 Skyknight. The first production examples of the new aircraft had flown thirteen months earlier, and the Navy's VC-3 became the first operational squadron to receive the Skyknight, The Navy squadron began to receive the F3D-1 in December 1950, and VMF(N)-542 was the first Marine squadron to get the new fighter. Due to its recent combat experience in Korea, the squadron was tasked with turning the new aircraft into a viable weapon for the Marine Corps. The first of the improved F3D-2 models with engines 34% more powerful and a radar capable of target acquisition range almost 50% beyond that of the -1 arrived within a few months, and training with this later version of the F3D began in earnest in preparation for the squadron's return to combat in Korea.

After almost fourteen months training with their new aircraft, the squadron departed the U.S. bound once again for Korea. Its aircraft complement was a mixture of the new F3D-2s and the familiar F7F-3Ns. Under the command of Lieutenant Colonel Peter D. Lambrecht, the squadron's jets departed for Korea on 27 May 1952 and arrived in Japan on 18 June, after stops at NAS, Moffett Field, and Atsugi, Japan. The remainder of the squadron and its Tigercats, departed for the Far East from San Diego via NAS, North Island. Upon their arrival in Korea, the assets of VMF(N)-542 were once again absorbed by VMF(N)-513, and Lieutenant Colonel Lambrecht assumed command of the "Flying Nightmares." Unfortunately, Lambrecht was lost on his first mission over Korea. [Although the reason for Lambrecht's loss has never been determined, it is believed that he undertook one or more strafing runs against enemy ground targets and either fell victim to ground fire or stalled and crashed while maneuvering to bring his guns to bear on the enemy.] Aviators have a long-standing rule regarding attacks against ground targets with alerted defenders that one violates at their considerable peril that goes something like, "One pass and haul ass!"

Meanwhile, some of VMF(N)-542's personnel returned to El Toro, where the squadron again was brought up to full strength in aircraft and personnel, and it assumed the duty of the Marines' training squadron for the Skyknight. Later, it was the first Marine squadron to receive the F3D-2M missile-capable model of the aircraft armed with the first versions of the Navy-developed Sparrow air-to-air guided missile. The squadron continued in its training role throughout the remainder of the Korean conflict and did not return to the combat zone.

On 1 September 1955, the squadron was redesignated VMF(AW)-542, and was reassigned to MAG-33 of the IIId MAW on 1 August 1957. On 12 May 1958, it received the first of its new Douglas F4D-1 Skyray interceptors and was reassigned to MAG-15. For the next year, VMF(AW)-542 remained at El Toro as it trained in its new aircraft. As it again neared operational status, it was ordered aboard USS *Bon Homme Richard* (CVA-31) for carrier qualifications. Without doubt, the initial "traps" by the squadron's "Fords" caused some raised eyebrows among those watching who were not familiar with the landing characteristics of the aircraft. Invariably, it would come aboard in a somewhat drunken attitude with the port wing low due to the aerodynamics of the airframe and control surfaces.

Its carrier qualifications successfully behind it, the squadron deployed to NAS, Atsugi, on 20 August 1959, where it relieved the "Black Knights" of VMF(AW)-314. The squadron operated from Atsugi for the remainder of the year before it deployed from Japan to NAS, Cubi Point, in the Philippines from January until May 1960. While operating from Cubi Point, it took part in Operation *Blue Star*, a joint U.S.-Nationalist Chinese amphibious exercise and operated from Taiwanese bases for two weeks. On 2 November 1960, VMF(AW)-542 was relieved at Atsugi by VMF(AW)-314 and returned to El Toro. For the next two years, the squadron operated from El Toro in a series of routine exercises, training missions, and short deployments to other bases within the U.S. before its next overseas deployment. During this deployment, the squadron operated from Taiwan and Okinawa for short periods before returning to the U.S. in the fall of 1962.

By this time, the days of the all-weather squadron designation and of the F4D-1 in Marine Corps service were numbered. VMF(AW)-542 was redesignated VMFA-542 on 2 November 1962 and, as such, was the first of the Marines' all-weather fighter squadrons to be redesignated a fighter-attack squadron. It received the first examples of its new aircraft, the mighty McDonnell F-4B Phantom II, on that same date. As the squadron's SkyRays were gradually replaced with Phantoms, it began to work up to a combat ready status in its new aircraft, and as a fighter-attack squadron, VMFA-542 began to add close air support to its repertoire for the first time in its history.

On 30 October 1961, the squadron left its aircraft at El Toro and boarded transport aircraft for their flight to Japan, where they once again relieved the "Black Knights" at NAS, Atsugi, upon their arrival on 1 November. As the squadron built its expertise in its new aircraft and missions, more and more time and space in the news media was being devoted to word of a new war in Asia. Civil wars had flared once again in Laos and Cambodia, and hardly a day passed without word of an increasing American commitment to the government of South Vietnam in its struggle against a Communist-led insurgency. Finally, in the wake of the so-called Tonkin Gulf Incident, U.S. combat troops

via Holmberg

were ordered into the country, and the Marines landed at Da Nang to protect the large air base there as the U.S. committed increasing numbers of aircraft into the country. Soon the role of the Marines was expanded from that of protecting the base to that of offensive sweeps against the enemy. Before many months passed, the number of aircraft based at Da Nang exceeded its capacity, and a new base was constructed at Chu Lai.

In April 1965, the squadron was ordered to Japan as an intermediate step toward its eventual commitment to the war in Vietnam. Orders arrived in July, and the squadron moved into combat for its third war in less than twenty years. When VMFA-542 deployed to Vietnam it initially was based at Da Nang but was soon ordered to the new facility at Chu Lai. In August, the squadron was heavily committed to support of the 7th Marines in Operation *Starlite*, the first major American ground operation of the war. It continued its mission of support of the various operations conducted in the Marines' operational area in northern South Vietnam for the remainder of its initial tour in country, which lasted until early December when it was withdrawn to Iwakuni, Japan. It would return to the war zone approximately ten months later.

A Load of Snakes
This pair of F-4B Phantoms of VMFA-542 were photographed en route to a target in South Vietnam. They are armed with a heavy load of Mk.82 500lb. "Snake Eye" retarded-fall bombs. The "snake eye" was a standard Mk.82 bomb fitted with folding petal-like tail fins that deployed upon release to retard the weapons' fall long enough to allow *the aircraft that released them to clear its blast and fragmentation pattern before it detonated. This weapon was particularly favored for close air support missions and was often combined with napalm canisters in the so-called "snake and nape" configuration, making for a particularly deadly consequence for those on the receiving end. [USMC photo]*

During its service in Southeast Asia, a majority of the squadron's missions were flown in support of Marine ground units and other Free World Forces operating in the northern areas of South Vietnam and were divided between scheduled strikes in support of numerous operations involving large numbers of friendly ground forces and quick reaction strikes flown to give support to units that found themselves unexpectedly engaged in close-range combat. These were usually characterized as "hot pad" missions. The "duty squadron" would have a pair of fully fueled and armed aircraft on a five-minute alert status. Their crews spent their "watch" either in the cockpit or in very close proximity to the ready aircraft. Upon receipt of a call for support, the aircraft were "scrambled" and were on their way to the fight within mere minutes. Details of the mission were usually received by radio as the aircraft were en route, and they would contact the unit requesting support to mark the location of the friendly troops and mark the areas to be hit. One of the aircraft would then make a bombing run with the friendly ground forces calling any corrections required. These strikes saved many lives and often inflicted severe casualties on the enemy, but they could be extremely hazardous to the aircraft involved. In additions to the usual hazard of enemy ground fire, these missions were flown around the clock and often in weather that, under normal conditions, would have kept the aircraft safely on the ground. Unless one has experienced it, it is difficult to imagine the feelings of those in the cockpit as they maneuvered their heavily laden aircraft at high speeds and low altitudes under the pale, flickering light of flares and low clouds and rain and often in the face of heavy ground fire as well. More than a few aircraft were lost on these extremely hazardous missions, but it was a rare occasion when the pilots did not respond to a request for support from their fellow Marines on the ground.

In addition to its air support role, VMFA-542 also flew a number of strike missions into North Vietnam across the DMZ as far north as the area around Vinh. This area was always heavily defended, and the squadron suffered some losses at the hands of the defenders. In addition, several other aircraft were damaged by the concentrations of AAA and SAMs. Other missions were flown against the Ho Chi Minh trail in northern Laos, another heavily defended hot spot. This area received an increased amount of attention from American strike aircraft after the ridiculous, politically driven bombing halt that was unilaterally declared in November 1968. Throughout its service in Southeast Asia, the squadron's operational tempo was very high as illustrated by the fact that, between May 1968 and January 1970, the squadron expended more than 20,000 tons of ordnance against targets.

For the next four years, VMFA-542 alternated between tours in Vietnam, four in all, and short breaks from the rigors of combat in Japan. This continued until the U.S. commitment began to be drawn down in 1969. VMFA-542 flew its last mission of the war on 13 January 1970, a night interdiction attack over Laos. On 30 January, the squadron left Vietnam behind for the last time and returned to El Toro by the way of stops at Cubi Point in the Philippines, Guam, Wake, and Hawaii.

Shortly after its arrival in California, VMFA-542 was reduced to cadre status. During the month of April, its strength totaled one officer. It was deactivated there on 30 June 1970.

The squadron was reactivated on 12 January 1972 at MCAS, Beaufort, South Carolina, and redesignated VMA-542 on that date and was the second Marine attack squadron equipped with the remarkable AV-8A Harrier V/STOL aircraft to be assigned to MAG-32. It continued to serve with MAG-32 at Beaufort until June 1974, when it was transferred to MCAS, Cherry Point, and became a component of MAG-20. In January 1976, -542 again was transferred to MAG-32. It took to its new aircraft and the attack mission like the proverbial duck to water and was recognized as Marine Attack Squadron of the Year for fiscal years 1978 and 1979. Also, during "surge" operations in May 1979, the squadron

Author's Collection

via Holmberg

completed 42 sorties in a two-hour period and expended no fewer than 162 250lb. Mk.81 "Snakeye" bombs and in so doing broke the Israeli world record of seven minutes by averaging 6.4 minutes per aircraft for recovery, refuel, rearm, and takeoff.

The squadron continued to operate these British-built initial versions of the Harrier until 1986, when they were replaced with the new AV-8B Harrier II. The new Harrier, from McDonnell-Douglas, while bearing an extremely close external resemblance to the older models, but with its new wing, more powerful engine, and upgraded avionics, it offers a considerable step forward in capability compared to the first Harriers. The squadron completed its transition to its new aircraft in May 1986.

VMA-542 was one of the squadrons deployed to southwest Asia in response to the Iraqi invasion of the Kingdom of Kuwait in August 1990. Upon its arrival there, it came under the operational control of MAG-13. The squadron departed Cherry Point for Sheikh Isa in Saudi Arabia but was moved to Al Jubial Air Base shortly thereafter, when that facility was upgraded to support V/STOL operations.

With the commencement of Operation *Desert Storm*, the squadron flew missions into Kuwait in preparation for the eventual

ground offensive that was to drive the Iraqis from the occupied kingdom. With the commencement of the aerial phase of *Desert Storm*, the squadron shouldered its share of the load, striking targets throughout southern Iraq, and two days before the massive ground offensive was launched, VMA-542 set records for the conflict by flying 58 sorties per day as it hammered the enemy fortifications in the area to be attacked by the 1st and 2nd Marine Divisions. During the 42-day war in Southwest Asia, the squadron flew more than 1,000 sorties totaling more than 1,200 hours of combat and expended more than 1,000 tons of ordnance on Iraqi targets.

VMA-542 had the unhappy distinction of being the only Marine squadron to lose two aircraft in action during the Gulf War. The first loss occurred on 23 February 1991, and unfortunately, the pilot, Captain James E. Wilbourne, was lost with his aircraft. As air operations continued against all types of Iraqi targets, the ground offensive was launched on 24 February, and the Harriers of VMA-542 and the other Marine squadrons supported the spectacular drive of the Marine ground forces northward toward Kuwait City. The squadron's second loss was on 25 February, when the Harrier flown by Captain Scott Walsh was claimed by the enemy air defenses. Happily, Captain Walsh ejected safely and was rescued. During *Desert Storm*, the Tigers compiled an enviable record. They flew more sorties, delivered more ordnance and accumulated more combat hours than any other Harrier unit in the theater.

The squadron returned to Cherry Point in April 1991, and after its post-deployment stand down, VMA-542 faced a new challenge when it was selected to introduce the newest version of the Harrier, the radar-equipped night attack Harrier II Plus, to the fleet in 1993. When its training period ended, the squadron again entered the normal unit deployment rotation cycle showing off the capabilities of its new aircraft.

The squadron next saw combat in 1999 when it completed thirty-eight combat sorties over Kosovo while deployed in support of 26th MEU aboard USS *Nassau* (LHD-5). It returned to the troubled skies above the new Balkan nation in 2000 while aboard USS *Wasp* (LHD-1). After its return from this second Balkan deployment, the squadron, along with Test & Evaluation Squadron 9 (VX-9), participated in the evaluation of the "Litening II" targeting pod. The tests were successful, and the new system was subsequently adopted. When it was incorporated into the Harrier's electronics suite, it turned the aircraft into one of the most accurate bombing platforms in the world.

September 11, 2001 found a detachment from the squadron working up aboard *Wasp* in preparation for deployment in support of 22nd MEU. Subsequently, the detachment and the MEU deployed aboard *Wasp* in support of Operation *Enduring Freedom* over Afghanistan and returned home in September 2002.

In January 2003, less than four months after its return from its previous deployment, VMA-542 found itself at war in Iraq for the second time. Preparations for the deployment left precious little time to enjoy the holidays with families and friends before the Tigers boarded USS *Bataan* (LHD-5) and sailed for the Persian Gulf. This marked the first time that an entire squadron of sixteen AV-8B aircraft deployed aboard an LHD-class ship. Prior to the commencement of Operation *Iraqi Freedom*, the squadron participated in Operation *Southern Watch* to deny external resupply of the Iraqi forces.

Operation *Iraqi Freedom* commenced on 19 March 2003, and at the Operation's forefront was the I MEF. In the air above the advancing Marines were the Harriers of VMA-542. Utilizing the refueling capabilities of Marine KC-130s, the aircraft struck distant targets deep in the enemy's rear as the advance approached Baghdad. These strikes marked the debut of the previously mentioned Litening II targeting pod in combat with the Marines, and its capabilities proved to be all the testing had promised and more.

After I MEF advanced over the border and deeper into Iraq, the lack of aerial tanker resources led the Marines to establish a Forward Operating Base, an FOB, at the abandoned Iraqi airfield at An Numaniyah. The FOB served as a refueling stop on the way to targets, such as those in the Tikrit area, more than 400 miles away from *Bataan*. First use of the FOB came during the night of 8 April, marking the first touchdown of tactical aircraft on Iraqi soil. If any was needed, the FOB as a waypoint en route to distant targets provided a perfect validation of the decision to adopt the Harrier in the first place.

By mid-April, the mechanized steamroller that was I MEF crushed the Iraqi opposition that lay in their path and entered Baghdad, the pace of strikes slowed to virtually nothing and then came to a complete halt. By the end of these strikes, VMA-

A Traveling Tiger
An AV-8B Harrier II of VMA-542 is preparing for takeoff carrying a full load of long-range under-wing fuel tanks. [via Webshots]

So This is what they Mean by Haze Gray!?
An AV-8B Harrier II of VMA-542 commences its takeoff run on the rain slickened deck of USS Bataan (LHD-5) on a cloudy, rainy day. The lack of under-wing ordnance indicates that this is a training sortie. [U.S. Navy Photo]

542 had accumulated 1,000 hours of combat over more than 600 sorties during which the squadron expended more than 170,000 pounds of ordnance and was awarded the Presidential Unit Citation for its participation in Operation *Iraqi Freedom.*

2004 proved to be another busy year for the squadron when it supplied a detachment of six aircraft to the Fighting Griffins of HMM-266 (Rein). The squadron boarded *Wasp* and sailed for the northern Indian Ocean in support of operations against the Taliban in Afghanistan. In May, the remainder of VMA-542 received a warning order for deployment to Al Asad Airbase in Iraq. This marked the first time a Marine squadron based on the East Coast was simultaneously deployed for combat operations into two active theaters.

The seagoing detachment of the squadron arrived in theater on 11 April 2004 and immediately commenced combat operations in support of Task Force Linebacker when it moved ashore to Kandahar Airbase, which lies 3,300 feet above sea level. Originally home to most of the MiG-21 fighter interceptors of the old Soviet-backed Afghan regime, much of the 10,000 foot runway had been either destroyed outright or mined, rendering much of the facility unusable for conventional aircraft but more than adequate for the Harriers of the detachment. During slightly more than three months of operations from Kandahar, the squadron's half-dozen Harriers employed GBU-12 laser-guided weapons, iron bombs, five-inch air-to-ground rockets and 25mm cannon fire in support of ground forces that included Marines, Army Special Forces and the Afghan National Army. During this period of intense operations, six aircraft completed more than 1,100 combat sorties with only four aborts.

While the squadron's detachment was busily engaged in Afghanistan, ten of its Harriers deployed to Iraq on 13 May by a trans-Atlantic flight. After brief stops for rest and to refuel, the Marines were engaged in supporting Operation *Iraqi Freedom II* by 20 May. In the face of rapidly spreading insurgent violence,

VMA-542 responded with 2,171 combat sorties totaling 3,952.3 hours within six months, primarily engaged in armed recce, convoy escort and close air support missions. During this span of operations, the squadron's strength was augmented to 22 aircraft. By November, while insurgent attacks had risen throughout the country, the city of Fallujah had been clearly recognized as the epicenter of the violence, and plans were put into place to pacify the area. With the coming of daylight on 7 November marked the start of an eight day campaign aimed at breaking the back of the insurgency in and around the city, and VMA-542 found itself at the forefront of the offensive that would span the next eight days. By 15 November, the level of violence had diminished appreciably, a circumstance no doubt aided to a large degree by the more than ten tons of ordnance and several hundred rounds of 25mm ammunition delivered by the Harriers of the "Tigers."

Shortly after the completion of the offensive in Fallujah, the squadron rotated home to Cherry Point for some well-deserved rest and repair of body and spirit, but the respite was not to last, for slightly more than eighteen months after return to North Carolina, VMA-542 found itself serving in the Middle East once again. In August and September 2006, a detachment of the squadron was attached to the "Blue Knights" of HMM-365 in support of 24th MEU for the evacuation of non-combatants from Lebanon. With the evacuation successfully completed, operations shifted from the Med to the Indian Ocean off the coast of Pakistan in support of Operation *Mountain Fury 2006.* During this portion of its busy 2006 deployment, the squadron became the first to employ the Joint Direct Attack Munition (JDAM) during operations from an LHD-class ship. The JDAM is a kit that, when attached to a "dumb bomb" of 500, 1,000 or 2,000-pounds, turns it into an extremely accurate precision guided weapon, adding considerable flexibility to potential weapons loads aboard a wide range of aircraft. Upon completion of its commitment to *Mountain Fury*, the squadron shifted its

Home Again
The Harrier assigned to the commanding officer of VMA-542 was photographed from the cockpit of another aircraft shortly after its return from another sortie during Operation Iraqi Freedom II. The barren background clearly illustrates the stark terrain of much of Southwest Asia. [USMC Photo]

area of operations westward into the waters of the Persian Gulf from which VMA-542 completed forty-two sorties in support of British forces engaged in Operation *Medusa*. The squadron was detached from HMM-365, and it then returned to Cherry Point. [Concurrent with the detachment of the VMA-542 contingent, HMM-365 dropped "REINFORCED" from its designation.]

The squadron spent less than a year at home before a detachment joined HMM-365 again and deployed to Iraq for the fifth time in the history of VMA-542. It was in Southwest Asia from September 2007 until its return in April 2008.

This break was from the stress of combat both welcome and short before workup for the next deployment began in the fall of 2008, and this one would bring a new experience to the squadron. In the spring of 2009, a detachment of VMA-542 was attached to the "Thunder Chickens" of VMM-263 in support of 22nd MEU, marking the first shipboard deployment of the remarkable MV-22 Osprey. The tilt-rotor Osprey is the replacement for the tried and true, but aging, CH-46 Sea Knight, a.k.a. the Frog, and its expanded performance envelope considerably expands the war-fighting capabilities of the Marines.

In July of the following year, the squadron deployed a detachment of eight aircraft and 170 Marines from Cherry Point to MCAF, Iwakuni in support of 31st MEU (SOC). After a month at Iwakuni, the detachment moved south to Okinawa where it boarded USS *Essex* (LHD-2). After a busy deployment of exercises and dodging typhoons in the western Pacific, the detachment returned to Cherry Point in January 2011.

While one detachment was in the Pacific, a second Det. of VMA-542 joined VMM-266 (REIN) and boarded USS *Kearsarge* (LHD-3) in support of the upcoming deployment of 26th MEU. From September 2010 until February 2011, the squadron was a part of Central Command's theater reserve and was busy training and keeping its aircraft in top operating condition. In early March, the ship and its embarked Marines transited the storied Suez Canal and headed west through the southern Mediterranean to the "shores of Tripoli," where it joined the force positioned to enforce U.N. Resolution 1973 to protect civilians during the Libyan civil war. Its mission quickly changed from peacekeeping to active combat with the commencement of Operation *Odyssey Dawn* on 19 March 2011. The first strikes were flown the following day with attacks near the city of Benghazi. These missions continued for the next two weeks, during which the squadron delivered more than 39 tons of ordnance.

On 21 March, an F-15E Strike Eagle of the U.S. Air Force crashed in the Libyan Desert due to equipment malfunction. Both pilots ejected safely after they notified higher echelons of command, which, in turn, alerted the appropriate combat SAR assets. Approximately ninety minutes after receiving notification of the loss of the F-15, a pair of the squadron's AV-8Bs were orbiting above the downed aircrew and conversing with them over the radio. Twelve minutes after their arrival over the site, the Harriers destroyed a pair of Libyan army vehicles that were threatening the American airmen.

"Kinetic" operations over Libya continued until 4 April, and during its participation in Operation *Unified Protector,* the squadron's Det. A flew 86 sorties for a total of 220 flight hours. They employed 80 laser guided weapons and were credited with the destruction or immobilization of 72 targets. The vast majority of these sorties were armed reconnaissance missions between

the hours of 2200 and 0600. [The author realizes that in today's highly charged political environment nothing can be stated in simple, black and white terms. Instead, it must be "jargonized" in the latest carefully sanitized, politically correct terms, but those requirements aside, "kinetic," really?]

Their commitment to the U.N. Libyan operations completed, Det. A returned to Cherry Point on 12 May 2011 completing a deployment lasting 258 days, 239 of which were spent at sea. The aviators added 1,093.8 flight hours to their logbooks.

On 29 September 2011, another Det. A was activated in preparation for deployment in support of 24th MEU at sea, and the remainder of the squadron began preparations for deployment to Japan in support of 31st MEU, continuing the proud tradition of service to country and Corps established by Marine Attack Squadron 542.

The first two insignia in the plates are examples of the current design worn by VMA-542 at the present time and represent the many squadron insignia that are made in desert and camouflage colors. They are identical in detail and size to the officially approved insignia of VMA-542. The third is the squadron's current official, full-color insignia, and the fourth is an example of the flight suit shoulder "bullet" for the AV-8B Harrier II. The next insignia is an example of the squadron's that commemorates VMA-542's service in Operations *Desert Shield* and *Desert Storm*.

A Great Day to be at Sea
This beautiful overhead shot of USS Kearsarge (LHD-3) was taken just after she completed a ninety-degree course change to port. Careful examination of the details in the shot reveals MV-22 Ospreys with their wings folded resting on the forward starboard corner of the flight deck, SH-60 Sea Hawk helicopters just forward of the island and a pair of SH-60s along the port side. Another MV-22 is on the port side aft, just forward of the port elevator. The AV-8Bs of VMA-542 are on the after end of the flight deck. [U.S. Navy Photo]

The next series of four insignia are examples of designs worn by VMFA-542 during the decade between November 1960 and its deactivation on 30 June 1970. As can be seen, the first two of these are virtually identical to the current official insignia with the exception of the designation in the ribbon at the bottom. The first of these four, the one with the medium gray background, dates from the years 1967 through mid-1970. The second one with the lighter gray background was worn between 1965 and 1967. Number three is an example of the first insignia design of VMFA-542 and was worn between 1963 and 1965. The fourth of these insignia, the "Commando Bolt" insignia is an unofficial design favored by those who took part in the strikes into Laos.

The insignia of VMF(AW)-542 is featured in the next illustration. This example is a reproduction but is virtually identical to actual examples of the insignia worn between 1 September 1955 and 2 November 1962. Alongside this insignia is an example of the "cruise" or deployment patch from the squadron's time in the Far East during 1959/1960 and features the manta-like planform of the Douglas F4D Skyray.

The example of the insignia of VMF(N)-542 is a reproduction of the squadron's World War II insignia. Originally designed by the Disney Studios, it received official approval in 1943 and was worn virtually unchanged between the squadron's activation and 1 September 1955.

via Holmberg

Ready To Go
This pair of Harriers prepare for a rolling take-off from USS Kearsarge (LHD-3) during the squadron's 2010 deployment. They are armed with Mk.82 500lb. "dumb" bombs on their inboard weapons pylons. [U.S. Navy Photo]

MARINE ATTACK SQUADRON 611
THE BLACK SEAHORSE (WORLD WAR II)

via Holmberg

The lineal predecessor of the latter day attack squadron, Marine Bombing Squadron 611 was activated on 1 October 1943 at MCAS, Cherry Point, North Carolina, under the interim command of Captain Prescott D. "Peck" Fagan. Fagan led the squadron for six weeks pending the arrival of Lieutenant Colonel George A. Sarles, formally of VMSB-151, on 16 November. It was one of four medium bombing squadrons activated on the same date as components of Marine Aircraft Group 61, the parent group for all the Marine PBJ-equipped squadrons. In late December, the squadron moved from Cherry Point to the much less crowded surroundings of Page Field at Parris Island, South Carolina. The group and its component squadrons spent the majority of the next year in training at locations up and down the East Coast. As the squadrons approached an acceptable level of readiness for deployment, they and their parent group were alerted for transfer to the West Coast.

MAG-61 departed Page Field for Miramar on 1 April 1944 and was followed immediately by its squadrons. The desert areas of Southern California east of San Diego offered far more opportunities for the employment of live ordnance in training than did the more crowded areas on the East Coast. After spending most of the summer putting the finishing touches on its training, the flight echelon of VMB-611 sailed from San Diego aboard USS *Manila Bay* (CVE-61) on 24 August 1944 for the South Pacific, via MCAS, Ewa, Territory of Hawaii. The squadron's ground echelon sailed for Hawaii on 23 September 1944 also bound for the South Pacific via Hawaii. It arrived in Pearl Harbor after a

voyage of nine days, and after a week at NAS, Pearl Harbor, located on Ford Island, it also sailed for the South Pacific.

While the squadron's aircraft and the bulk of its flight echelon sailed aboard the CVE, its ground echelon and the remainder of the flight echelon boarded SS *Zoella Lykes*, a civilian cargo ship chartered by the navy as a troop transport and set sail for Pearl Harbor, arriving there in the first week of October. These chartered ships retained their merchant marine crews, which could, on occasion, cause more than a few headaches, and this would certainly prove to be "one of those occasions." It seems that *Zoella Lykes* was scheduled to participate in the planned invasion of the island of Yap in the Palau group and had, in fact, received orders to that effect. However, as it transpired, this assault was cancelled. For reasons unrecorded, the *Zoella Lykes*'s captain was unhappy with this turn of events, and he joined a convoy leaving Pearl Harbor on 10 October. After the convoy left Pearl Harbor, the captain parted ways with the convoy and proceeded literally to wander the vast reaches of the Pacific for more than two months. All the while, the embarked Marines likely wondered if they were destined to spend their remaining periods of service as unwilling passengers aboard this 1944 version of the Flying Dutchman. During these two months, despite considerable effort on his part, Colonel Sarles was left to ponder the fate of many members of his squadron. Indeed, he wondered if perhaps *Zoella Lykes* had fallen victim to Japanese submarine or air attack. [Fortunately, despite a sizeable submarine force as far as numbers were concerned, the Imperial Japanese Navy never made a concerted effort to launch an undersea offensive against Allied merchant shipping in spite of the fact they were fully aware of the staggering losses inflicted by the German U-boats. In view of the vast distances involved in the Pacific, had the Japanese done so, it would have made victory much more difficult for the allies and undoubtedly prolonged the war by many months.]

Finally, in mid-December, word reached Colonel Sarles that *Zoella Lykes* had anchored in Ulithi Atoll in the Carolines, and he immediately made arrangements to fly to Ulithi to retrieve the missing members of the squadron's flight echelon. Unfortunately, due to space limitations, the ground echelon was destined to remain aboard the wandering cargo ship.

In early December, the short-handed squadron had commenced operations from Emirau. From there, night heckling missions and strikes were flown against bypassed Japanese garrisons in the Northern Solomons and the Bismark Archipelago, with especial attention being given to the areas encompassing Vanakanau and Tobera. Combat operations of any type are never easy, and for VMB-611, they were made doubly difficult by the missing ground echelon. The flight crews were forced to perform much of their own maintenance work with whatever assistance that could be had from the ground echelons of VMB-413 and -423 when their workload permitted.

VMB-611 was not destined to spend many weeks on Emirau, however. By the time the squadron flew its first combat mission, the movement of Marine squadrons to the Philippines had begun, and VMB-611 would see considerable service there. The first component of the squadron departed Emirau and arrived on the island of Mindoro in the central Philippines on 25 February 1945. There, it passed time awaiting its orders to the large southern island of Mindanao, where the squadron was scheduled to serve in support of the

Direct Route to the South Pacific
This photo of USS Manila Bay (CVE-61) was taken just after she sailed from the West Coast bound
for Pearl Harbor. The PBJs of VMB-611 occupy her entire flight deck. [U.S. Navy Photo]

operations of the United States Sixth Army. After a stay on Mindoro of slightly less than three weeks, the ground echelon arrived at Moret Field at Zamboanga on the western tip of Mindanao on 17 March 1945. Upon arrival, VMB-611, minus its flight echelon, was attached to MAG-32 for administrative purposes.

Ironically, the first element of VMB-611 to arrive on Mindanao was the long-lost orphans of the ground echelon. It seems that *Zoella Lykes* had continued her wandering ways, moving from port to port in the liberated areas of the Philippines. Finally, on 24 February 1945, they managed to part ways with their erstwhile hosts and get ashore. They arrived at Zamboanga by LST on 17 March, and almost before they were able to get their meager gear ashore and make camp in a nearby coconut grove, they set to work at preparing Moret Field for PBJ operations. This required ten days of hard labor, something these Marines had done very little of during their extended stay aboard *Zoella Lykes*.

The flight echelon of VMB-611 continued to fly a reduced schedule of missions against the enemy in the Bismarks, through the latter part of March. It was then ordered to cease operations in preparation for its move to Mindanao. It departed shortly thereafter and arrived in the Philippines on 30 March, where it was reunited with its long-lost and nearly forgotten ground echelon. It then began preparations to commence operations from Moret Field, which was named in honor of Lieutenant Colonel Paul A. Moret, who had been the first commanding officer of VMSB-131 and was killed in the crash of a transport aircraft on New Caledonia while serving in a staff position. The arrival of VMB-611 on Mindanao added

a new dimension to the repertoire of operations of the Marine squadrons there. During its operations from Emirau, the squadron had employed its radar-equipped PBJs mainly in night, low-level attacks on enemy targets afloat and ashore. Relatively fast [for a twin-engine medium bomber], heavily armed and carrying a bomb load of 3,000 pounds, the PBJ also possessed sufficient range to allow it to carry out missions throughout the southern Philippines, the Sulu Archipelago and Borneo. No doubt, the arrival of VMB-611 proved a nasty shock to the enemy, whose ocean-going shipping had been driven from the waters of the Philippines and who had been forced to rely on small craft for the movement of troops and supplies by night. These had been largely immune from attack until the arrival of the PBJs. Prior to the arrival of the Marine Mitchells, the aircraft equipped with surface-search radar of sufficient resolution to accurately locate these small craft were not equipped to mount effective attacks against them. Even relatively small boats at sea could be detected quite easily by the radar sets aboard the Marine aircraft, and, shorn of their cloak of darkness, the enemy was hunted around the clock. The sudden, unexpected attack by a PBJ in the inky darkness must have proven a mortal surprise to the Japanese aboard the intended victim of the attacking aircraft. Often, the first indication of an attack would be the flash and whoosh of a 5-inch High-Velocity Aircraft Rocket or streams of tracers from the heavy battery of .50-caliber machine guns carried by the PBJ, either eight or fourteen guns, depending upon the aircraft model. These weapons could reduce these unarmored targets to a drifting mass of bloody splinters in a matter of moments.

The Long Way Around
SS Zoella Lykes as she appeared in the post-World War II colors of the Lykes Lines. Entering service in 1940, she was scrapped in 1973, and it is doubtful that any tears were shed over her fate among the Marines who endured months of what amounted to virtual incarceration aboard her in late-1944 and early-1945 [Unattributed photo via the mercantilemarine.org website]

On the Prowl
One of the squadron's PBJ-1Ds is pictured in flight. Note that its ventral radar dome is in the fully stowed position, which very likely indicates this flight was not a combat sortie. Also note the apparent absence of anyone in the nose position. [USMC Photo]

Also, their ample fuel load allowed them to hunt a specific area for several hours or to range far and wide in search of the enemy.

Concurrent with these missions hunting small craft at sea, the squadron mounted attacks against Japanese installations in the nearby Sulu Archipelago located some eighty-five miles from the southwestern tip of Mindanao.

Colonel Sarles led the first strike against the Sulus on the night of 31 March 1945 against the island of Bongao. Attacking at low altitude, four PBJs struck troop concentrations and artillery emplacements while they navigated by radar, but the attack was deemed to be unsatisfactory. The following day, a medium altitude daylight attack was sent against the same targets, and the outcome was much better with excellent coverage to the target areas noted. This day attack was followed up that same night with another attempt under the cover of darkness. This time the attacking aircraft alternated releasing one million candlepower parachute flares to illuminate the targets and followed up with bombs.

After the Marines finished their attacks, the island was on the receiving end of a heavy naval bombardment, and as a result of the efforts of VMB-611 and the navy's gunnery, Australian troops executed a casualty-free amphibious assault on 2 April. After the Aussies went ashore, VMB-611 made a close air support strike to break up some enemy strongpoints that were contesting the Australian advance.

As soon as the assault force was firmly ashore on Bongao, VMB-611 turned its attention to Jolo, the largest of the islands in the Sulu group. Again, the primary targets were enemy artillery emplacements positioned where they would be able to contest the landing. These targets received a thorough working over prior to the assault on 5 April.

Three days later, VMB-611 demonstrated its medium altitude horizontal bombing ability in a rather spectacular fashion in what would prove to be its final mission against the Japanese in the Sulus. The enemy was deeply entrenched on the slopes of Mt. Daho, in position to threaten the entire advance. Of particu-lar interest was a large bunker near the summit, which, in addition to being the enemy's command bunker, was well positioned to cover other defensive positions and sweep ravines with fire that would provide cover to the attackers. Bombing from several thousand feet, the summit of Mt. Daho was smothered with 1,000lb. bombs, with one scoring a direct hit on the command bunker and thoroughly wrecking it as well as its inhabitants. This devastating attack was followed up as soon as the smoke and dust cleared by a dive bombing strike just ahead of a low-level run by the medium bombers using five-inch rockets.

Their work in the Sulus completed, VMB-611 turned its attention to the enemy on Mindanao once again. In a variation on the usual repertoire of bomb and rocket strikes, the squadron was tasked with support of a force of Filipino guerillas led by a former Australian P.O.W., Major Rex Blow, in its attempt to capture Malabang Airfield. They seized the airfield, but their hold on it was rather tenuous by several Japanese positions just across a nearby river. Lt.Col. Sarles led a force of a half-dozen of the squadron's PBJs, and two of these, including that flown by Sarles landed on the airfield, where the colonel and Major Blow conferred on how best to support the guerilla force. Blow was to act as a forward air controller and talk the Marines on to their targets by radio. Sweeping low across the river, the PBJs released their weapons, depth charges. The tremendous concussion created by their detonation leveled virtually all the vegetation, not to mention Japanese, within their blast radius – a rather novel use of these weapons.

VMB-611 was then ordered to concentrate its efforts against the Japanese in the Bukidnon Valley in north central Mindanao. Near the northern end of the valley lay Del Monte airfield, the primary American airfield south of Luzon prior to the island's capture by the Japanese in 1942. Although no Japanese aircraft remained there, Del Monte and several other airfields nearby were heavily defended by a concentration of heavy and light anti-aircraft batteries. The squadron spent ten days pounding the Japanese in valley. These attacks served a dual purpose. The first, obviously, was the destruction of the enemy anti-aircraft emplacements, and the second was to create a diversion for the pending amphibious attack at Macajalar Bay. At first, these attacks were met with a storm of anti-aircraft fire, which claimed the PBJ flown by Lieutenant Charles Good. The aircraft crashed and caught fire, but fortunately the crash was near positions held by friendly forces who rescued the entire crew, although unfortunately one man died of wounds inflicted by enemy fire.

Despite the squadron's losses, its efforts were successful. When the landing came on 17 April, the Japanese were taken completely by surprise, and VMB-611 enjoyed a brief lull in its operational tempo. It was during this period of relative quiet that the squadron was visited by several members of a USO troupe, including the comedian Joe E. Brown, who accompanied Colonel Sarles on a reconnaissance mission over Japanese-held territory.

The lull was brief, and the squadron was soon back in action, launching a series of strikes against the Japanese throughout its area of operations. However, despite the effectiveness of these low-level attacks, they brought additional hazards to the aircraft involved. This was especially true when missions were flown against land targets. Large areas of the Philippines and the Japanese-held islands to the west were uncharted with regard to, for example, the height of various topographical features of the terrain. The relative freedom from enemy anti-aircraft fire was offset by the hazards imposed by the terrain. Tragically, this fact was brought home by the loss of Lieutenant Colonel Sarles on a mission on 30 May against the enemy in Davao area of Mindanao. Major Robert R. Davis assumed

command of VMB-611 the following day. Sarles was posthumously awarded the Distinguished Flying Cross for his leadership of the squadron. A second aircraft lost an engine in flight over Moro Gulf and was forced to ditch. Fortunately, Lieutenant Wray E. Bennet and his entire crew were promptly rescued by friendly natives.

The squadron continued operations against the enemy on Mindanao through out the remainder of hostilities and was awarded the Navy Unit Commendation for its services during the period from 16 March through 30 June 1945. The squadron suffered the loss of two aircraft to operational causes and six in combat. Lost with these aircraft were a total of eleven officers and twenty-three aircrewmen.

On 27 August 1945, VMB-611 was ordered southward from Mindanao to Peleliu while the other squadrons of MAG-32 were ordered in the opposite direction, northward to Tsingtao, China, where it arrived and commenced operations as part of the occupation forces on 16 October.

VMB-611 was deactivated on 30 November 1945, but it received a second lease on life as a Reserve squadron. Assigned to NAS, Glenview, Illinois, it was reactivated as an attack squadron, VMA-611. It continued to serve until it was deactivated for a second and final time in one of the periodic reductions that took place among the Reserves in the latter years of the 1950s and early-1960s.

The first insignia shown, that of VMA-611, was worn by the squadron during its years of service as a Reserve squadron, and the insignia of VMB-611, the bomb-squirting seltzer bottle, was a result of a concept originating from the mind of the squadron's first commanding officer, "Peck" Fagan and the artist George Connell.

via Holmberg

Let's Go for a Ride
Lieutenant Colonel G.A. Sarles, the commanding officer of VMB-611 assists the comedian Joe E. Brown adjust his Mae West life preserver prior to Brown's flight on Sarles' aircraft on a reconnaissance mission on Mindanao. Note the "hose nose" housing for the radar scanner and the painted over Plexiglas panels in the nose of the aircraft above Brown's left shoulder. [USMC Photo]

MARINE BOMBING SQUADRON 612
CRAM'S RAMS

via Holmberg

VMB-612 was activated on 1 October 1943 at MCAS, Cherry Point, under the command of Captain James W. Cunningham. Six weeks later, Lieutenant Colonel Jack R. Cram, a winner of the Navy Cross for his exploits at Guadalcanal, assumed command. [See the section on VMA-231 for details on the action for which Cram received the award.] Another of the Marines' relatively small number of PBJ-equipped medium bomber squadrons, it was directed to begin training in low-level night radar bombing and torpedo missions shortly after its activation. This training commenced in January 1944, and for the next six months, the squadron alternated between Boca Chica, Florida, and MCAS, New River, North Carolina, as it polished its skills in this difficult and demanding method of attack. In July, the squadron was ordered to the West Coast as the first stop on its way to its ultimate destination, the central Pacific. The squadron's time in the Southern California sun was short, and on 24 August, after embarking all sixteen of the squadron's PBJs and the flight echelon aboard USS *Natoma Bay* (CVE-62), the squadron left the United States behind. The little carrier cleared Point Loma at the entrance to San Diego harbor and pointed her bow southwestward toward Hawaii. After a week at sea, *Natoma Bay* tied up alongside a pier at the air station on Ford Island in Pearl Harbor and off-loaded the PBJs. They were then fueled and flown to MCAS, Ewa, only a short flight from Pearl Harbor, where they remained for nearly a month before heading west again. After intermediate stops at Johnston Island, and Majuro and Eniwetok in the Marshalls, VMB-612 took up residence on Saipan, where its aircraft and flight crews arrived on 28 October. Interestingly, when the squadron departed Eniwetok, only

Lt. Col. Cram knew their ultimate destination, but at least one flight crew received a bit of a shock when, as they were actually opening the sealed packet of orders that would direct them to Saipan, they heard the Japanese radio propagandist Tokyo Rose welcome VMB-612 to the Pacific and mentioned Lt. Col. Cram by name!

While the flight echelon was aboard the CVE and ashore at Ewa, the ground echelon sailed for the Pacific aboard S.S. *Island Mail*, a bulk cargo vessel chartered by the Navy as a transport. She anchored off Saipan on 25 October, and VMB-612 moved ashore. Initially, the squadron had been intended for service in the Philippines, but General MacArthur declined the services of Marine aviation in general and VMB-612 in particular. [This decision was made prior to the recognition of the inability of the Army Air Forces to provide the required air support during the drive to liberate the Islands.]

In the wake of the Marines' exclusion from the Philippine Campaign, some wondered where and how to best employ the squadron. The only Japanese forces that remained in the Marianas were scattered, bypassed garrisons that hardly presented suitable targets for a squadron that had received many months of training in night, radar directed anti-shipping strikes. After a week, the staff of MAG-21, VMB-612's parent air group, hit upon the idea of sending the squadron in search of enemy shipping in the waters around the Volcano and Bonin Islands. The area around these two island groups promised to be a target-rich environment in view of the many ships that regularly made runs between the islands and Japan proper. These island groups included Iwo Jima, where the Japanese were feverishly working to complete their defenses that would spill so much American blood three months hence, and successful attacks in these areas would serve to slow the flow of supplies to the defenders and to further reduce the already severely depleted Japanese merchant marine.

Iwo Jima was 630 miles from Saipan and only slightly more than that from the Japanese home islands, and Chichi Jima, another island where considerable numbers of Japanese ships likely could be found, lay 120 miles beyond Iwo from Saipan. In order to reach their targets at this range, the PBJs were stripped of virtually all their machine guns and their turrets to reduce weight and to increase their strike range. Even the four .50-caliber guns mounted on the fuselage sides and used in low-level strafing attacks were removed. Lt. Col. Cram carried out the squadron's first combat sortie on 13 November when he went hunting enemy shipping in the vicinity of the Bonin and Volcano Islands. Upon his return, he claimed a Japanese freighter and a submarine sunk as a result of his low-level rocket attacks. While he received credit for both claims, the examination of existing captured Japanese records after the war fail to note the loss of any submarine in that area on that date.

[Japanese records on items such as this are far from complete for a whole host of possible reasons. Sloppy record keeping could be the cause or any particular record may have been destroyed, either intentionally to keep information from falling into Allied hands or in one of the many American air attacks against Japanese naval installations throughout the Pacific and especially those in the Home Islands in the latter months of the war. Submarines are also notorious for not reporting their position on a timely basis for any number of reasons, not the least

Another Day of Pacific Sunshine
The PBJ-1Ds of VMB-612 are securely tied down on the flight deck of USS Natoma Bay
(CVE-62) during the squadron's transit from San Diego to Hawaii. [USMC Photo]

of which is to lessen the possibility of their transmissions being tracked via radio direction finding equipment and subjected to attack as a result. The German U-Boat commander, Admiral Karl Doenitz, required frequent position and operational reports from his boats at sea, and this led directly to many of them being lost as the Allied navies dispatched ships and aircraft to hunt the submarines whose positions were revealed by radio direction finding. It is also quite possible that Lt. Col. Cram attacked a reef in the darkness under less than ideal visibility. Waves breaking over a reef or any low-lying bit of land bear a striking resemblance to the wake of a ship when seen at night from the air. Also, despite the fact that the aircraft carried automatic cameras to document their attacks, they frequently failed to function properly. This inability to verify the success or failure of their attacks led to a great sense of frustration among almost all airmen engaged in night operations.]

Cram was back at work in the Bonins during the night of 16/17 November when he attacked a small convoy at sea. He was credited with three hits, but once again, there was no photographic evidence available. This night also saw the squadron's first operational loss when the PBJ flown by Lieutenant Samuel

C. Balthrop was forced to ditch due to fuel exhaustion. Four members of the six-man crew were rescued by a destroyer the next day, but unfortunately, no sign of the other two men was found. Some missions were flown against targets up to 900 miles from Saipan, which required the aircraft to remain in the air for twelve hours, so fuel starvation would likely prove to be a contributing factor in many of the squadron's losses, but the exact cause of some will never be known.

When the cause of the loss of Balthrop's aircraft was reported, and a number of carefully monitored tests were conducted to determine and record fuel consumption under what were considered to be normal operational conditions. This proved to be higher than anticipated. They also carefully calculated the effects of engine wear on fuel consumption, and strict attention was paid to engine changes when they reached their time limits. However, more than one member of the squadron actually preferred to fly aircraft with older, 500-hour engines installed based on the theory that, "You knew what the old one was going to do."

Armed with eight five-inch rockets and 500lb. bombs, the PBJ-1Ds and the twenty-seven crews of VMB-612 launched nightly strikes against their distant enemy. On some nights,

Getting Ready
The ground crew of this PBJ-1D of VMB-612 is hard at work preparing their aircraft for another sortie against the Japanese. Note the installation of the nose mounted radar scanner bullet. If the reader looks closely, the ribs of the original Plexiglas nose canopy can be seen. When the radar was installed, the need for the usual bombardier was eliminated, and the glass panels were painted over in the same gloss sea blue as the remainder of the aircraft. Also note the power cart under the starboard wing. [USMC photo]

numerous worthwhile targets were located and attacked, but others yielded nothing more than several hours of boredom. During the night of 26 November, a five aircraft strike was mounted against the area in the Bonins called "Dunker's Derby." The hunting was poor, and one of the PBJs simply disappeared without a trace. The last radio contact with the aircraft of First Lieutenant Edward Madvay came at 0230, and nothing, not even a piece of wreckage or an oil slick, was seen or heard again, and Japanese records were mum of the loss as well. A like fate befell the aircraft of First Lieutenant Cleo J. Falgout on the night of 30 November. On the plus side of the ledger on the same night as Falgout's loss, after finding no suitable shipping in its assigned area, Lieutenant Bill Allen loosed his load of rockets into what appeared to be a worthwhile target on the island of Haha Jima. The rockets' impact was followed in short order by a spectacular series of explosions and what appeared to be an ammunition dump going up in flames. Although the squadron was in action for less than the entire month, it logged thirty-five missions, 159 sorties and 706 flight hours in addition to the claims and losses noted.

During November, despite relatively frequent contact with the enemy, no hits were scored against enemy vessels aside from those claimed by Lt.Col. Cram during VMB-612's maiden sortie, but, after overcoming the shock prevalent when one is shot at in anger for the first time, things began to improve. By the end of the squadron's tour on Saipan, three enemy ships had been claimed as probably sunk and twenty-seven damaged. [Japanese records do not confirm the claims of the ships sunk, but, when examined in detail after the war, their records-keeping proved spotty, at best.] These claims were made against the loss of three PBJs, along with five officers and eight men.

In addition to the usual dangers of their night missions, life on Saipan could occasionally prove to be hazardous to life and limb. The Japanese knew that the giant B-29's based in the Marianas posed a mortal threat to the Home Islands and attempted to raid the American bases there when possible. An example of this came at noon on 27 November. As luck would have it, the timing of the raid came at the time of the daily test of the air raid siren, and as a result, most paid little attention to the warning until the anti-aircraft batteries on a nearby hill opened fire with a vengeance. As shrapnel from the detonating rounds began to rain down on those watching, the Americans scattered to any location that offered any promise of protection from the combination of Japanese bombs and American anti-aircraft fire. Unfortunately, several American aircraft were airborne at the time, and the gunners claimed at least one friendly aircraft, and another, a light observation plane, ditched offshore rather than continue to risk the barrage.

Major Lawrence F. Fox assumed command of VMB-612 on 15 February 1945 as the squadron continued operations from Saipan, but on 10 April 1945, VMB-612 moved forward to the base on its former target, Iwo Jima. From there, the squadron flew missions against the Japanese mainland. Still specializing in night attacks, enemy shipping and harbors were visited regularly by the squadron's aircraft. In April 1945, the first examples of the big 11.75-in. "Tiny Tim" rocket were received, and the squadron began the development of the proper tactics for its employment.

The Navy's early 1944 requirement for a stand-off anti-ship weapon led to the rocket's development as a joint project of CalTech University and the Naval Ordnance Test Station at Inyokern, deep in the California desert, and was a monument to American ingenuity and improvisation. The rather odd dimension

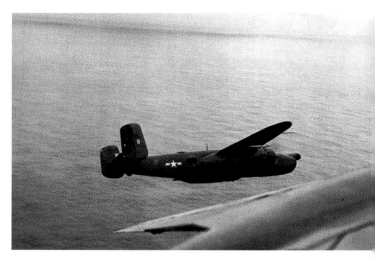

Beginning the Attack Run
A pair of VMB-612 PBJs are shown as they commence a turn into their attacks against a target on the haze coast of Japan. [USMC Photo]

came to pass due to the fact that 11¾ inches was the diameter of the standard 500lb. semi-armor piercing bomb, the warhead, and the standard steel oil well pipe that was utilized for the rocket's casing. The result was, for the time, a huge rocket-propelled weapon with a length of ten feet, three inches and weighed almost 1,300lbs. with a range of 1,640 yards. The rocket motor was rated of 3,000lbs. of thrust and burned for one second, boosting the 150lb. high explosive warhead to 550mph. This speed bestowed the ability to penetrate several inches of armor on the "Tiny Tim."

Despite its considerable promise, however, the big rocket was not without its problems, the most serious of which was its accuracy or lack thereof. One of the reasons for the lack of accuracy stemmed from the size of the weapon itself. Its size and weight demanded a large rocket motor to impart sufficient velocity upon launch to obtain the desired range. In turn, this led to the flame and heat generated by the motor's ignition caused damage to the metal skin of the aircraft in the area around the rocket's attachment point. Several methods were attempted to alleviate this problem and the one that seemed to offer the most promise was to attach a lanyard from the rack carrying the rocket to the motor's igniter. Upon launch, the rocket fell free of its rack about three feet. At this point, the lanyard pulled free and triggered the igniter, and the rocket went merrily on its path of mayhem and destruction to the enemy. This was all well and good as long as the aircraft was perfectly aligned in its flight path with no sideslip or any other such deviation and that there was no air turbulence around the aircraft that could cause the rocket to "wobble" prior to motor ignition. It must be remembered that this was before the present days of guided weapons, and the rocket or any other ballistic weapon was going to go where it was pointed at the instant of its launch.

During this period, Lieutenant Colonel Cram returned to the squadron and assumed command once again on 2 May. The Colonel was an enthusiastic advocate of the Tiny Tim and was eager to use it against the Japanese shipping that was the squadron's primary target. But, no amount of enthusiasm could overcome its relative inaccuracy. Another potential problem with the weapon that the author has been unable to find any recorded comments regard-

ing, but surely must have been a significant obstacle to its successful employment in night attacks, was the extremely bright flare of the rocket motor on launch. Whereas the five-inch H.V.A.R.s had been a part of the squadron's weapons arsenal from the beginning, these had a motor much smaller than that of the Tiny Tim and were launched from racks beneath the PBJs' wings offset from the aircraft centerline. The Tiny Tim, on the other hand, was carried on racks mounted under the fuselage directly on the centerline. The tremendous glare of the motor as it accelerated away from the launching aircraft was directly in the line of sight of the pilot and copilot and must have been somewhat detrimental to their night vision, to say the least, hardly an ideal happenstance when performing combat maneuvers at low altitudes.

On 29 July, the squadron, now a component of MAG-22, moved from Iwo Jima to Chimu airfield on Okinawa, where it continued strikes against Kyushu until word was received of the Japanese surrender. During these final days of World War II, Major Lawrence Fox, who had been awarded the Distinguished Flying Cross for his service with the squadron, again assumed command of the squadron upon Lieutenant Colonel Cram's transfer on 1 September.

MAG-22 began to move forward from Okinawa to Japan on 20 September. This movement was done entirely by air utilizing the aircraft of the group's two transport squadrons, VMR-353 and VMR-952, and the PBJs of VMB-612 were also pressed into hauling personnel and cargo. The three squadrons moved all of the group's personnel and 275 tons of equipment 600 miles to its new base at Omura on Kyushu with no loss or damage to either personnel or equipment. Initially, VMB-612's living conditions were the worst they had experienced since they left Hawaii a year earlier. Shortly after the squadron's arrival in Japan, a major typhoon swept the area destroying or damaging much of what they had so successfully transported from Okinawa, and they were reduced to subsisting on that detested staple of the front line ground troops, K-rations. In November, the group shifted from Omura to Sasebo, and shortly thereafter, it was ordered back to the U.S. VMB-612 was deactivated on 15 March 1946. The squadron has remained on the inactive list since that date.

Final Preparations
In this posed publicity shot, Lt.Col. Cram in the pilot's seat and his copilot are pictured preparing to take off for another mission. [USMC Photo]

Author's Collection

For its service in the central Pacific during the period 1 November 1944 through 31 May 1945, VMB-612 was awarded the Navy Unit Commendation, and it suffered the loss of eleven aircraft, four to operational accidents and seven in combat. Also lost were thirty-nine members of the squadron to all causes.

The first insignia of VMB-612 shown is one of the silk-screened "PX patches" that were sold as souvenirs in base exchanges. The remaining two insignia are embroidered, and unfortunately, neither is completely accurate, but, of the two, the second of these is the better. i.e. more accurate one. In the lower-most part of the design is a row of machine gun ammunition, which should be divided into groups of six, one and two rounds as is clearly evident in the first example. This violated the prohibition against the display of the squadron's designation in its insignia while in a

combat zone, but while clearly a violation of regulations, it is not overt. This may have allowed the design to slide past any officers that may have been of a mind to enforce insignia regulations, but more likely it was due to an effort to get on with the war rather to enforce such prohibitions. A member of the squadron, Gunnery Sergeant Morton Mandel, originated this design.

Regarding the second version, the significance of the owl is not known, but it would be appropriate for a squadron that hunted almost entirely by night.

Prior to the adoption of the insignia shown, an earlier, proposed design consisting of a leaping black panther on a clock face with bombs to represent the hours. Lightning bolts that pointed to six o'clock and twelve minutes past the hour represented the hands of the clock.

The Sunday Punch of VMB-612
This PBJ-1J carries a pair of 11.75-inch "Tiny Tim" rockets on a belly rack under the bomb bay. Note the complex web of braces used to support the rockets and their racks. With its large warhead, the big rocket packed sufficient punch to sink almost any Japanese merchant ship, *but its somewhat spotty accuracy rendered it something less than the ideal anti-shipping weapon. Records indicate that approximately ten of the squadron's aircraft were modified to carry the "Tiny Tim." [U.S. Navy Photo]*

MARINE BOMBING SQUADRON 613

Author's Collection

The Flying Cannon
This excellent photograph of a PBJ-1H as it banks into a gentle turn to starboard reveals most of the details of this model of the aircraft. The dark half-circle on the lower nose is a shadow in the opening through which the muzzle of the 75mm gun protruded. Although the original photo caption states this PBJ-1H was assigned to VMB-613, the paint scheme makes it more likely that it was, in fact, assigned to a Navy patrol squadron operating in the Atlantic. [U.S. Navy Photo]

Marine Bombing Squadron 613 was activated on 1 October 1943 at MCAS, Cherry Point, North Carolina, the third of four such squadrons to be activated there on that same day. Its first commanding officer was Captain Robert C. Woten. Too junior to command an organization such as a medium bombing squadron, Woten led VMB-613 for six weeks pending the arrival of Major Harry F. Baker, Jr., on 17 November.

The squadron was the first of the Marines' bombing squadrons to be equipped with the factory-built "attack" versions of the PBJ, the H-model. Earlier, Army Air Forces squadrons in combat in New Guinea had modified their standard B-25s, mainly C and D models, to serve as potent low-level "strafers." These alterations were strictly non-regulation field modifications that consisted of removing the bombsight and bombardier's station from the nose of the aircraft and rigging a battery of fixed, forward-firing .50-caliber machine guns in place of the removed equipment which was deemed unnecessary in low-level attacks. Additional guns were hung on the fuselage sides below the cockpit in self-contained "packages." These modifications turned the B-25 into an extremely destructive low-level attack aircraft. Major Paul I. "Pappy" Gunn of the Army Air Forces, one of the more colorful characters who populated the U.S. war effort in the Pacific, is generally credited with having been the moving force behind these unofficial conversions. According to legend, a squadron engineering officer saw one of the modified aircraft and questioned Gunn regarding the effect of so much additional weight in the nose of the aircraft on its center of gravity. Gunn is said to have replied, "We threw it [the center of gravity] out to save weight!"

Prior to the Japanese attack on Pearl Harbor, Gunn, a retired enlisted Naval Aviation Pilot, had run a small air freight service in the Philippines. When the Japanese attacked the islands in the early months of the war, Gunn offered his services to the defenders. After the fall of the Philippines to the enemy, his wife and children had been interred in the infamous Santo Tomas prison in Manila, and as a result, Gunn hated the enemy with a rich and powerful zeal and wanted nothing more than to do whatever was necessary to bring the war to an early end. He believed the proper way to accomplish that was to kill as many Japanese in as short a time as possible, and these heavily modified B-25s used in low-level attack was the best means to accomplish that goal available at the time.

These modified aircraft were employed in low-level attacks against Japanese airfields and shipping. Their forward-firing guns were capable of overwhelming even the most determined gun crews who attempted to face the attacking aircraft. The rain of heavy slugs from the guns and the fragmentation bombs that dangled from small parachutes in the wake of the B-25s literally tore hundreds of enemy aircraft and troops to shreds. Many ships had their sides blown out by the 500-pound bombs that the aircraft released in their high-speed, low-level attacks to literally "skip" across the surface of the sea and into their intended victims. Small wooden "coasters," which were used to move large numbers of troops and many tons of supplies throughout the South Pacific, literally were reduced to bloody splinters in short order by the concentrated fire of these gun batteries.

As good as these field modifications proved to be, the engineers who designed the aircraft improved upon them. Later, factory-produced "gunship" versions of the B-25/PBJ series carried as many as fourteen forward-firing guns in the solid-nose version of the –J model. While VMB-613 would eventually receive this version of the aircraft, the first model received by the squadron was the PBJ-1H. It carried four machine guns

Hawaii Bound
USS Tulagi (CVE-72) was photographed from one of her escorts shortly after departing San Diego bound for Hawaii. The PBJ-1Hs of VMB-613 are secured to her flight deck. [U.S. Navy Photo]

in the nose, a pair on either side of the forward fuselage, and the dorsal gun turret was moved forward to a point just behind the cockpit to enable its pair of guns to be added to the fire of the eight fixed guns. However, the feature that drew the most attention to the aircraft was a large, circular opening in the lower left portion of the fuselage nose. Peering in sinister repose from within this opening was the muzzle of a 75mm field piece. A modification of the Army's lightweight pack howitzer, this weapon added considerably to the already heavy punch of the aircraft in a low-level attack. As potent as the howitzer was conceptually, it proved somewhat less effective than was hoped in practice. The weapon was loaded manually, and as a result, its rate of fire was such that only one or, at the most, two rounds could be fired during an attack run. Also, it was difficult to aim with any accuracy while jinking to avoid anti-aircraft fire. On the other hand the gout of flame from the gun's muzzle must have had a considerable psychological impact on those on the receiving end. But, in fact, many crews chose to remove the weapon to lighten the aircraft or to add additional machine guns in place of the cannon.

In February 1944, the squadron was transferred from Cherry Point to NAS, Boca Chica, Florida, where it would train for an additional mission, anti-submarine patrol. The move was led by the squadron's new commanding officer, Major George W. Nevils, who assumed command on 26 February. While looking for submarines was not among the most exciting of missions, no doubt few complained about the prospect of quitting the damp chill of a North Carolina winter for the warmth of the Florida sun. After spending almost a month in sunny Florida, the squadron returned to Cherry Point on 22 March and remained there until August, when it was transferred to Newport, Arkansas. Located at the upper point of a rough triangle composed of Newport in the north, Little Rock in the west and Memphis, Tennessee, in the east, the base there served as a frequent stopover point for Marine squadrons awaiting deployment.

The squadron's flight echelon departed the hills of Arkansas on 21 October for the flight to San Diego with stops at El Paso, Texas, and MCAS, El Centro, California. It arrived at NAS, North Island, in San Diego on 22 October. Several last-minute modifications to the squadron's aircraft and on 30 October, it embarked on *USS Tulagi* (CVE-72) for the first leg of its deployment to the Pacific theater. It experienced a bit of excitement when the convoy began to maneuver evasively to avoid a Japanese submarine that had been reported in the vicinity of its planned course. The sub was sidestepped successfully, and the rest of the voyage was routine. After its arrival in Hawaii, the squadron parted company with the carrier and was transferred to MCAS, Ewa, on 4 November.

The ground echelon of VMB-613 sailed from San Diego aboard the chartered Army transport USAT *George W. Julian* on the morning of 22 November bound for Hawaii. Immediately after its departure, it began to encounter problems. First, *Julian* encountered an area of rough weather, and more than a few of the Marines spent several hours in the head. Secondly, the Army served only two meals while at sea. The Officer-in-Charge of the Marines won the day when he offered to have the squadron's mess personnel "join the Army" for the rest of the cruise to allow three meals to be served to all hands. No doubt, the Army enjoyed the Marines' presence as a result. The transport reached Hawaii and joined the rest of the squadron there on 3 December but sailed for Kwajalein in the Marshalls a week later. The squadron was reunited on Kwajalein on 23 December. The Christmas season was spent in relative quiet allowing it to become accustomed to its new surroundings, and it commenced operations against the bypassed Japanese garrisons in the Marshalls in early January 1945. On 11 January 1945, a portion of the squadron was detached and ordered to nearby Eniwetok for anti-submarine patrol duties, but it rejoined the rest of the squadron on Kwajalein on 13 March.

VMB-613 remained in the Marshalls flying strikes against the enemy for the remainder of the war. Despite the fact that the Marshalls represented a relatively quiet rear area by the time of

The Army Goes to Sea
USAT George W. Julian was the Army-chartered transport that carried the ground
echelon of VMB-613 to war. [Smithsonian Historical Division Photo]

their arrival of VMB-613, even these "easy" missions were not without their cost. Two of the squadron's PBJs were lost, one to operational causes and one in combat, with the loss of two officers and six aircrew. With the Japanese surrender, VMB-613 was ordered back to U.S. soil immediately and was deactivated on 21 October 1945. It has remained among the ranks of inactive squadrons since that date.

The actual, unofficial insignia is the one pictured and that was displayed on buildings, signs, and the like in the squadron's area. It consisted of a disk-shaped background on which was centered a winged globe and anchor. These were superimposed on the handles of three maces, the heads of which pointed to the ten-, twelve- and two o'clock positions of the round background. Protruding from the center of the globe was the barrel of a 75mm gun carried by the squadron's aircraft, and inside the muzzle of the gun was a white skull. However, it is not clear if any insignia were ever produced from this design.

The officially approved design of VMB-613 was of a winged bulldog which represents Marine aviation, and the machine gun and bomb are representative of the primary weapons employed in combat by the squadron's PBJs. However, it seems that, despite its official approval, this design was never actually used by the squadron.

The Disney Studios drew a design for VMB-613, but it was never used. This design depicted a bumblebee struggling to tip a heavy black bomb off a large white cloud. Unfortunately, the only example of this proposed insignia in the author's possession is a black-and-white illustration of rather poor quality. This design was adopted later by the Navy's Patrol Bombing Squadron 139 (VPB-139) in November 1944.

MARINE BOMBING SQUADRON 614
THE RUPTURED DUCKS

via Holmberg

VMB-614 was the fourth and last of the Marine Bombing Squadrons to be activated at MCAS, Cherry Point, on 1 October 1943. Its first commanding officer was Captain Roger M. Bowman, who was succeeded by Major John G. Walsh, Jr., on 17 November 1943. Bowman was promoted to Major and remained with the squadron in the billet of Operations Officer.

Its early months of service were in parallel with those of its sister squadron, VMB-613, with service at Cherry Point, NAS, Boca Chica and Newport, Arkansas. It spent many busy days and nights in training, setting a record for Marine PBJ squadrons by logging 1041.8 flight hours for the month of January 1944. February continued as had the previous month with the squadron flying around the clock, and it was during one of these night training exercises that tragedy struck. During the night of 23/24 February, the Cherry Point area came under a blanket of heavy clouds and rain. Flight operations were cancelled and all aircraft aloft were recalled. A pair of the squadron's PBJs were returning to base when they collided. The wreckage of the two PBJs fell into the Neuse River near New Bern, North Carolina. All ten crewmen died in the collision.

On 18 March 1944, VMB-614 was ordered to NAAS, Boca Chica, Florida minus its aircraft. Using a motley collection of cast-off PBJs that had been left behind by other squadrons, VMB-614 began training to employ the PBJ as a torpedo bomber and set a record for its number of successful torpedo runs. A highlight of their time in Florida was the occasional liberty run across the Florida Straits to Havana, Cuba. Known at the time as the "Paris of the Western World," many liberty hours were spent in the city's gambling halls and "other" places of entertainment.

After a month in Florida, the squadron returned to Cherry Point, and the return flight was an eventful one for several squadron members as a number of aircraft were forced to make unscheduled stops due to mechanical problems. It was so bad that during one enforced stop at an Army Air Force field, the

PBJ in question was condemned as unfit for flight, but it was patched up and made it home to the Point.

Shortly after its return to North Carolina, fifteen of the squadrons' well-trained crews from VMB-614 were transferred to squadrons overseas as replacements for crews lost in combat. New crewmen reported and training continued as the new men were integrated into the fabric of the squadron.

On 2 August 1944, the squadron was ordered from Cherry Point to the Marine Corps Air Facility at Newport, Arkansas, the "stand-by" post for squadrons about to be transferred to the Pacific. However, unlike its sister squadrons, VMB-614 remained at Newport long after VMB-613 and others departed for service in the central and western Pacific. During its extended stay in the Ozarks, Major Harold L. Luntz relieved then Lieutenant Colonel Walsh on 9 November 1944. Major George F. Mackey succeeded him, in turn, on 29 November. The squadron remained at Newport until mid-1945.

Finally, VMB-614 was alerted of its pending transfer to the Pacific, and it departed Newport for NAS, Alameda, California. After a brief stay in the San Francisco Bay area, the squadron's flight echelon sailed for Hawaii on 25 July 1945. It arrived and was transferred to nearby MCAS, Ewa, on 1 August. By this date, it was clear to all that World War II had entered its final stages, which were expected to reach their culmination with amphibious assaults against the Japanese home islands. None were aware that the terrible specter of atomic warfare would be revealed for all to see in the shadow of the mushroom-shaped cloud that would rise above the ashes of Hiroshima less than a week later. As preparations continued for the atomic raids from the Marianas, the squadron spent its time at Ewa making final preparations for its transfer to Midway, which took place within a few days.

As the squadron's flight echelon made its way across the Pacific from Alameda, its ground echelon sailed from San Diego in early August. The squadron was reunited and commenced operations from Midway by 31 August. Although the Japanese would formally surrender to the Allies in two days, all hands were on alert for any last-minute attacks by enemy forces that refused to accept the decision to surrender. However, despite its vigil, the squadron did not encounter the enemy. The Rising Sun of Imperial Japan had set in the waters west of Midway in the wake of the crushing defeat of June 1942. The squadron departed Midway within a few weeks and was deactivated on 28 December 1945. It has remained inactive since that date.

The example of the insignia of VMB-614 is a drawing that resides in the author's collection. A member of the squadron, Lieutenant Walter Dean, is credited with the design and represents the only insignia ever approved by the Headquarters, Marine Corps, for VMB-614.

Coming Home to Roost
This PBJ-1J of VMB-614 was photographed just before it touched down at an unidentified location and date. This photo is of interest because of the overall gloss sea blue color scheme, which dates the photo as likely from early 1945. Also, note the installation of the radar scanner in a pod on the starboard wingtip as opposed to the more common nose and belly locations. [U.S.M.C. Photo]

MARINE TORPEDO BOMBER SQUADRON 621

via Holmberg

The squadron was activated as Marine Bombing Squadron 621, VMB-621, at MCAS, Cherry Point, North Carolina, on 10 April 1944, under the command of Major Robert J. Klitgaard, who was succeeded by Lieutenant Colonel Donald E. Huey on 24 May. The squadron received its full complement of personnel and aircraft and commenced its training in the delivery of explosive ordnance from horizontal, medium-altitude bombing runs, as well as in low-level, high-speed strafing attacks. These tactics maximized the capabilities of the versatile PBJ gunships. The squadron's training proceeded into the winter of 1944, and Lieutenant Colonel Huey was transferred to other duties on 19 November. Major George F. Mackey led the squadron for a week until Major Klitgaard began his second tour at the helm of VMB-621 on 29 November.

As the final days of 1944 slipped from the calendar, it became clear the Marines had activated more bombing squadrons than could be employed usefully in the Pacific. As a result of this realization, several VMB squadrons were redesignated torpedo squadrons, and among these was VMB-621. It was redesignated VMTB-621 on 31 January 1945, and Major Klitgaard was detached the following day. Lieutenant Joseph F. King assumed command on 2 February.

The center of Marine torpedo bombing activities was at MCAS, Santa Barbara, California, and VMTB-621 was alerted

of its pending transfer from Cherry Point to California in early February. It arrived at Santa Barbara on 15 February, and Lieutenant Thomas L. Kizer, Jr., assumed temporary command from Lieutenant King on 26 February, pending the arrival of Major Allan H. Ringblom on 26 March. As the squadron's command arrangements were straightened out, VMTB-621 received its complement of TBM-3Es and went about the business of learning the tasks involved in close air support, and while it was not emphasized to the extent of the close air support mission, time was spent as well in torpedo tactics. As part of the program to supply Marine air groups to several escort carriers for employment in the planned amphibious assaults against the Japanese home islands, the squadron spent a portion of its time at Santa Barbara undergoing carrier qualification training.

As the war drew near its inevitable end, VMTB-621 was ordered to MCAS, Ewa, Territory of Hawaii. The squadron loaded its aircraft, personnel, and baggage aboard *USS Card* (CVE-11) and sailed from San Diego in mid-August. It arrived in Pearl Harbor and was transferred to Ewa on 27 August 1945.

After the Japanese surrender, VMTB-621 remained at Ewa and was deactivated on 10 March 1946 and has remained inactive since that date.

The insignia design shown is that worn by VMB-621, its vulture and skull representing the effect of an attack by the squadron.

Another insignia design is attributed to the squadron after its redesignation as a torpedo squadron. It was of an axe-wielding turkey riding a falling torpedo. The turkey represents the affectionate nickname bestowed on the TBF/TBM. The axe is emblematic of the duty of the squadron to attack the enemy, while the torpedo indicates the squadron's designation and mission. However, the torpedo would likely have never been employed had the squadron entered combat. Unfortunately, research to date has not found an illustration of this insignia.

Sub Hunter and Taxi
The USS Card (CVE-11) is shown as she appeared earlier in her career. Her earlier service was spent in the Atlantic hunting German U-boats, but was transferred to the Pacific in the wake of the German surrender. [U.S. Navy Photo]

MARINE TORPEDO BOMBER SQUADRON 622

via Holmberg

The squadron was activated on 10 May 1944 at MCAS, Cherry Point, North Carolina, and designated Marine Bombing Squadron 622, VMB-622, under the command of Major Russell A. Bowen. Equipped with the factory-built gunship versions of the PBJ, the -H and -J models, the squadron was transferred from Cherry Point to the Air Facility at Newport, Arkansas, on 10 September 1944, to continue its operational training.

A month after its arrival in Arkansas, Major Bowen left the squadron, and Major Pat W. Densman assumed command on 19 October, only to be replaced by Major David C. Wolfe on 4 November. After less than two weeks, Major Finlay T. Clarke, Jr., assumed command on 17 November 1944. During this period of virtually rotating commanding officers, VMB-622 completed its operational training and was ordered to MCAS, Mojave, California, for weapons training. It arrived in the vast California desert on 14 February 1945, now under the command of Lieutenant Edward L. Ogden since 7 February 1945. Two weeks later, Lieutenant Robert N. Jackson assumed command, effective 24 February.

By this period of the war, it had been realized that the Marines had an excess of bombing squadrons, half of which would never see combat. General MacArthur's long drive northward from New Guinea and the Navy/Marine island-hopping campaign across the vastness of the central Pacific under Admiral Nimitz converged in the Philippines in October 1944. This, coupled with the final decision to abandon the on-again, off-again plan for an amphibious assault on mainland China, meant, for all practical purposes, the end of the Marines' medium bombing program. This had come about only due to an excess of the B-25/PBJ aircraft in the inventory of the Army Air Forces and the Marines' willingness to try anything once.

The end result of all this with regard to VMB-622 was that the squadron was redesignated VMTB-622 on 15 May 1945 and assigned to carrier training. The PBJ-1H and -1J gave way to the TBM-3E Avenger, and many of the squadron's personnel were transferred as replacements for the deployed VMB squadrons. New personnel qualified in the TBM replaced those lost as replacements, and training commenced under the auspices of the Torpedo Bomber Training Unit and the Anti-Submarine Warfare School in San Diego. Major William W. Wood assumed command on 25 March 1945, and the squadron's training in its new role continued.

After completion of torpedo and anti-submarine training, the squadron commenced its carrier qualifications. After many hours of "bounce practice," as the Field Carrier Landing Practice was known, the squadron was ordered aboard *USS Wake Island* (CVE-65) for the real thing. VMTB-622 was engaged in its qualifications when the Japanese surrendered.

With the end of the war, VMTB-622 was transferred to MAG-46 at MCAS, El Toro, California, and continued to serve there until it was deactivated on 31 January 1946, thus bringing the squadron's days of service to an end.

The insignia in the plate is that of VMTB-622. The design of Donald Duck astride an Avenger and hurling bombs and rockets at an unseen enemy was designed by the Disney Studios and received official blessing in August 1945. Original examples of this insignia were embroidered on a twill backing.

There is no record of any insignia, either official or unofficial, for VMB-622.

MARINE TORPEDO BOMBER SQUADRON 623

Author's Collection

via Holmberg

The lineal predecessor of VMTB-623, VMB-623, was activated on 15 May 1944 at MCAS, Cherry Point, North Carolina. Its initial commanding officer was Major Lawrence F. Fox, who led the squadron for less than a month, and on 12 June, Major Carl J. Fleps assumed command.

The second Marine Bombing Squadron to be activated at Cherry Point in May 1944, the squadron proceeded with its training in preparation for its eventual deployment. Equipped with the PBJ-1H and -1J gunships, training was concentrated on the tactics of medium altitude horizontal bombing and low-level strafing and bombing. As its training continued, Major Fleps turned command of the squadron over to Major Henry N. Carrier, Jr., on 18 December 1944, and training continued until February of 1945, when VMB-623 received a new designation and a change of aircraft. Major Carrier was detached on 19 February 1945. The following day, VMB-623 was redesignated VMTB-623, and Lieutenant Sam H. Boren, Jr., assumed command. The squadron's PBJs gave way to TBM-1C and -3E Avengers, and Lieutenant James R. Stone, Jr., relieved Lieutenant Boren on 24 February and remained in command until the arrival of Major Eric D. Schwarz on 13 March.

Shortly thereafter, the new torpedo squadron was alerted to prepare for transfer from Cherry Point to the West Coast. The move was completed, and the squadron began training from its new home at MCAS, Santa Barbara, California, by mid-May, which was the home of the Marines' single-engine torpedo squadrons. VMTB-623 progressed through torpedo and anti-submarine training and proceeded to carrier training. Virtually every Marine squadron destined to serve aboard a carrier during World War II received their carrier qualification training at Santa Barbara.

Paired with the "Hellhawks" of VMF-213 to form Marine Carrier Air Group 9 [MCVG-9] eventual assignment to *USS Saidor* (CVE-117), VMTB-623 commenced its first carrier qualifications aboard *USS Makassar Strait* (CVE-91) mere days before the formal surrender of the Japanese. The qualifications

took place 29-31 August 1945 off San Diego. All went well until one of the squadron's TBMs ran out of fuel just short of the ramp. The Avenger settled gently into the carrier's wake and floated like a cork due to its empty fuel tanks. The pilot, who was the only crewman aboard, abandoned the slowly sinking aircraft and was rescued without even getting wet!

On 9 October, MCVG-9 was transferred from Santa Barbara to the air depot at Miramar for an overnight stay before boarding *USS Prince William* (CVE-31) for transportation to Hawaii. The squadron boarded the CVE the following morning and sailed that same afternoon. It arrived at the air station on Ford Island at Pearl Harbor on Sunday, 14 October, and was transported to MCAS, Ewa. The air group operated from the complex of air stations on Oahu and from *USS Tripoli* (CVE-64), *Commencement Bay* (CVE-105), and *Corregidor* (CVE-58) prior to joining its intended carrier *Saidor* in December.

It appeared that a long, happy relationship between the squadrons of MCVG-9 and its parent carrier had begun at last, but the war was over. America was in the process of rapidly demobilizing its recently victorious armed forces to levels that would fall below those of prior to 7 December 1941 within a few months. In early February, orders were received to deactivate MCVG-9 and its component squadrons. Mass personnel transfers began immediately, and VMTB-623 was deactivated at Ewa on 20 March 1946. The squadron has remained inactive since that date.

The first insignia is that of VMTB-623. Another of the insignia designs from the Disney Studios, this original example of the squadron's insignia is embroidered on a white wool background. Aside from some slight discoloration due to age, it is in remarkably good condition. Regarding the symbolism of the design, the turkey is representative of the nickname bestowed on the TBF/TBM aircraft series. The depiction of the comic turkey becoming airborne from a carrier deck is somewhat misleading. First, the noble turkey is incapable of flight. Second, despite the look of intense concentration and effort on the face of the bird belies the fact that the "Turkey" in question, the Avenger, was relatively easy to operate from a carrier, despite its being the largest, heaviest single-engine aircraft to fly from a carrier during World War II.

The second design is that approved for VMB-623. The figure of Satan hurling a flaming thunderbolt is representative of the death and destruction of which the PBJs were capable of bringing to the enemy. This design was drawn for VMB-623 by the well-known cartoonist Al Capp.

MARINE TORPEDO BOMBER SQUADRON 624

via Holmberg

The squadron was activated as VMB-624 on 20 June 1944 at MCAS, Cherry Point, North Carolina. Commanded for less than a week by Major Harry W. Taylor, Major Winton H. Miller assumed command on 26 June 1944, who led the squadron until he was detached on 16 November. Major Taylor again assumed command the following day and led the squadron for a month. Major Edward J. Doyle took command on 19 December, serving in this capacity until he was detached on 13 February 1945.

VMB-624 was the last Marine Bombing Squadron to be activated during World War II, and, fittingly, it served in this role for a shorter period of time than any of the others. On 15 February 1945, VMB-624 was redesignated VMTB-624 and transferred from Cherry Point to MCAS, Mojave, California. It was led to California by its interim commanding officer, Lieutenant Frank Onischuk, who remained in command until the arrival of Major Dayton Swickard on 13 March.

Its westward movement completed, the squadron received its TBM Avengers and commenced its training for its eventual carrier qualifications. VMTB-624 was to be paired with the "Bulldogs" of VMF-216 aboard *USS Rendova* (CVE-114). However, before the air group could see action, the Japanese surrendered, and World War II came to an end. The squadron did not board *Rendova* until after the end of hostilities because she was not placed in commission until 22 October 1945.

The day prior to the formal surrender, Captain J.B. Shirley assumed command of the squadron, and VMTB-624 continued to serve until it was ordered deactivated on 10 March 1946. The squadron has remained among the inactive since that date.

The cartoonist Al Capp designed an insignia for VMB-624 that depicted a female character from the comic strip "Alley Oop" standing on an airborne PBJ-1H. This design received official approval for use in 1944, but if any insignia were actually produced from the design, none appear to have surfaced in the hands of collectors.

There is no record of any insignia having been approved or having been worn unofficially by VMTB-624.

MARINE SCOUT BOMBING SQUADRON 931

via Holmberg

Smile for the Camera
This spotless SBD-5 posed for a publicity shot either during or just prior to its delivery flight to a squadron or an air depot. This is indicated by the presence of the temporary "ferry" number chalked on the engine cowling. Also, note the dummy bomb. [U.S. Navy Photo]

VMSB-931 was activated on 15 April 1944 at MCAS, Cherry Point, North Carolina. The squadron's first commanding officer was Captain James E. Campbell, who served in an interim capacity pending the arrival of Major John L. Dexter on 1 May.

Initially equipped with the final model of the Douglas Dauntless dive-bomber to be produced, the SBD-5, the squadron was transferred from Cherry Point to MCAS, Eagle Mountain Lake, near Ft. Worth, Texas, on 10 May. Operational training was carried out under a broiling Texas sun throughout the summer until VMSB-931 was redesignated a fighter-bomber squadron, VMBF-931, in October 1944. Shortly thereafter, Major Dexter was detached, and Lieutenant Roy E. Rigsby assumed command on 10 November.

In mid-November, the squadron left Eagle Mountain Lake behind and returned to North Carolina. It arrived at MCAAF, Oak Grove, on 18 November, and Major James T. McDaniel assumed command from Lieutenant Rigsby on that date. The squadron settled into its new surroundings and prepared to begin its training as a fighter-bomber squadron, but before the training was well underway, VMBF-931 was again redesignated to VMSB-931 again on 30 December 1944. So rapid were these designations that the squadron perhaps was one of the few fighter-bomber units to be equipped with dive-bombers. The squadron was re-equipped with the Curtiss SB2C-4E Helldiver and continued its operational training. Captain Robert W. Johannesen assumed command of VMSB-931 on 11 May 1945.

The squadron was destined never to see combat and remained at Oak Grove until after the Japanese surrender serving as a component squadron of MAG-34, and it was deactivated on 31 January 1946. It has remained inactive since that date.

The insignia of VMSB/VMBF-931 was designed by the popular cartoonist Milton Caniff and was approved by Headquarters, Marine Corps, shortly after the squadron was activated in 1944. While unconfirmed, it is unlikely any changes were made to the design during the squadron's brief service as a fighter-bomber squadron. It served in this role for less than six weeks, and the figure of a blue devil mounted on the winged stallion Pegasus and hurling a fireball would have been equally emblematic of both a VMSB and a VMBF squadron. Also, in spite of the fact that the inclusion of a unit designation was officially proscribed, the squadron number was not changed when it was redesignated a fighter-bomber unit. Original examples of the insignia are embroidered on a gold wool disk.

MARINE SCOUT BOMBING SQUADRON 932

via Holmberg

Marine Scout Bombing Squadron 932 was activated at MCAS, Cherry Point, North Carolina, on 15 May 1944, a month after its sister squadron, VMSB-931. Its first commanding officer was Major Fred J. Frazer. Equipped with the Douglas SBD-5 Dauntless, the squadron was ordered to MCAS, Eagle Mountain Lake, Texas, on 19 June 1944. In company with those of VMSB-931, the squadron's SBDs spent the summer boring holes in the brilliant summer skies of Texas until it was redesignated VMBF-932 on 16 October.

Shortly after the squadron's redesignation, it was alerted to prepare to return to North Carolina. Major Frazer was detached and ordered to other duty on 15 November 1944. Captain Albert L. Clark assumed command the following day and carried on with the preparations for the move eastward. The squadron departed Texas on 20 November and arrived at MCAAF, Oak Grove, two days later, where Major Jack W. Morrison assumed command on 22 November 1944.

The fighter-bomber career of the squadron was short, and it was redesignated VMSB-932 once again on 30 December. It was reequipped with the Curtiss SB2C-4E Helldiver and continued operations from Oak Grove as a component squadron of MAG-32.

Captain George T. Limpkin assumed command of VMSB-932 on 16 January 1945 and was succeeded by Captain Edward C. Willard on 12 March. VMSB-932 never served overseas. It remained at Oak Grove for the remainder of its active service and was deactivated there on 31 January 1946.

In another parallel with its sister squadron, Milton Caniff also created the insignia design of VMSB-932. The figure of the bulldog in the Marine campaign hat has been associated with the Marine Corps for many years, and the simple addition of the gold wings made the bulldog emblematic of an aviation unit. The nickname "TEUFELHUND" is a German word that is translated as "Devil Dog." It was bestowed on the Marines by their German opponents in combat in France in the First World War.

Original examples of the insignia were embroidered on a Navy blue wool disk.

MARINE SCOUT BOMBING SQUADRON 933

Marine Scout Bombing Squadron 933 was activated on 20 June 1944 at MCAS, Eagle Mountain Lake, Texas, under the command of Major Robert J. Bear. Equipped with the Douglas SBD-5 Dauntless, it had the distinction of being the first squadron activated at Eagle Mountain Lake to be equipped with powered aircraft. MCAS, Eagle Mountain Lake, had been activated on 1 December 1942 to serve as the home of the Marines' glider program, and Marine Glider Group 71 and one glider squadron, VML-711, were activated there. However, the Marines gave up on their glider program, and the base was turned over to the Navy on 30 June 1943. It reverted to Marine Corps control on 1 April 1944, and several different types of squadrons were based there during the remainder of World War II and in the months immediately following the Japanese surrender. In early January of 1946, the Marines' night fighter squadrons in the United States were concentrated there.

Regarding VMSB-933, the squadron remained in Texas until it was ordered to MCAAF, Atlantic Field, North Carolina, on 1 October. Shortly after the squadron arrived in North Carolina, Major Bear was detached, and Major Ernest R. Hemingway assumed command on 19 October. The squadron did not remain at Atlantic Field for an extended period and was ordered to the auxiliary field to Bogue, North Carolina, on 15 November 1944. It remained there throughout the remaining months of World War II. The squadron's post-war career was short, however, and VMSB-933 was among the first squadrons to fall victim to the axe of the massive post-war reductions of the armed forces. It was deactivated at Bogue on 10 September 1945. The squadron has remained among the ranks of inactive squadrons since that date.

The squadron's insignia was designed by the Walt Disney Studios and was approved shortly after the activation of VMSB-933. The design, with its comic figure of a centaur centered on a star and dressed in Western garb and carrying a bomb, is in keeping with the squadron's Texas roots and mission. However, the saguaro cactus in the design is misplaced. As a native of north Texas, the author can attest to the fact that the nearest native saguaro is several hundred miles to the west of Ft. Worth!

Unfortunately, while this design received official approval for use by the squadron shortly after its activation, it is not clear if any insignia were actually produced to this design. If so, they are rare items, indeed, and probably reside among the treasured possessions of former squadron members.

MARINE SCOUT BOMBING SQUADRON 934

VMSB-934 was activated at the auxiliary airfield at Bogue, North Carolina, on 15 July 1944 under the command of Major Floyd Cummings. It had the distinction, if one could call it that, of being equipped with the somewhat controversial Curtiss SB2C-4E Helldiver. It was one of a relative handful of Marine scout bomber squadrons to receive the "Beast" from the outset, and as soon as sufficient personnel and aircraft were on hand, the squadron commenced its training in preparation for its deployment into combat in the Pacific theater.

On 21 August, the squadron was transferred from Bogue to another auxiliary field at Atlantic, North Carolina, to continue its operational training. However, after a short stay at Atlantic, VMSB-934 returned to Bogue, and Major William A. Houston, Jr., assumed command of the squadron on 16 November. On 26 December, Major Edward R. Polgrean relieved Major Houston, who was transferred to other duty.

VMSB-934 was destined to remain in the United States for the remainder of its service. After the Japanese surrender on 2 September 1945, the United States began to reduce its armed forces at a pace that was little short of frantic. As a squadron that had seen no active service, VMSB-934 was a logical candidate for early demise, and it was deactivated at MCAAF, Bogue, on 15 October 1945. The squadron has remained inactive since that date.

It is likely that an insignia design was proposed for adoption by VMSB-934 during its fifteen months of service, but there is no record of the submission of any design for approval. Whatever design or designs that may have been considered by the squadron have been lost in the mists of the sixty-plus years since its activation.

MARINE SCOUT BOMBING SQUADRON 941

VMSB-941 was activated on 15 July 1944 at MCAAF, Bogue, North Carolina, and was commanded by Major Walton L. Turner. Major Turner led the squadron for nine weeks and was succeeded by Major James L. Fritsche on 24 September.

By this period of World War II, it was clear that the Marines had more squadrons in service than could ever be employed. The Marines effectively had been barred from service in the European theater, and, with the forging of the final links in the "ring around Rabaul" earlier in the year, the opportunities for useful employment for additional Marine scout bombing squadrons in the roles in which they had served in the Solomons clearly were limited.

Also, the air groups of the carriers of the Fast Carrier Force had an ample stock of bombing squadrons and would see the strength of these reduced within a few months due to the need to increase the complement of fighters aboard the carriers. As a result, the service life of VMSB-941 would be limited to only a few months, and the squadron was deactivated on 10 October 1944. It has remained inactive since that date.

Regarding any insignia adopted by VMSB-941, a member of the squadron, Staff Sergeant Curt Sarff developed a design, but apparently it was never submitted for approval and any records of the details of the design have not survived the passage of time.

MARINE SCOUT BOMBING SQUADRON 942

VMSB-942 was activated on 24 August 1944 at MCAAF, Bogue, North Carolina, and was commanded by Major Ernest R. Hemingway. It was destined to suffer the identical fate as its sister squadron, VMSB-941, and was deactivated on 10 October 1944. So brief was the squadron's service there is no record of aircraft assignment to it. VMSB-942 has remained among the ranks of inactive Marine squadrons since that date.

There is no surviving record on any insignia design either proposed or adopted by VMSB-942 during its brief service.

MARINE TORPEDO BOMBER SQUADRON 943

Initially designated Marine Scout Bombing Squadron 943, the squadron was activated on 1 July 1944 at MCAS, Santa Barbara, California, and was commanded by Captain W.H. Fuller. As was frequently the case, VMSB-943 underwent a series of command changes in the early weeks of its service. Captain Henry W. Hise succeeded Captain Fuller on 23 August. Two months later, Captain Floyd G. Phillips assumed command for all of two days and was followed by Major Harold B. Penne on 27 October.

Equipped from the outset with the Curtiss SB2C-4 Helldiver, the squadron went about initial operational training until its transfer on 27 October from Santa Barbara to the sprawling complex of MCAS, El Toro, some 100 miles to the southeast. Almost before the squadron was settled into its new surroundings, it was redesignated VMTB-943 on 20 November 1944.

The squadron exchanged its Helldivers for various models of the Avenger torpedo bomber, and the additional aircrewmen required by the new aircraft reported to VMTB-943. A week after the squadron's redesignation, Major Penne was detached and ordered to other duties, and Captain Floyd G. Phillips was designated the squadron's interim commanding officer once again on 29 November. Two days later, Major Allan H. Ringblom arrived and assumed command on 1 December 1944.

Shortly after its redesignation as a torpedo squadron, VMTB-943 assumed the duty as a replacement training squadron. Its duty was to furnish aircrews to the Marine torpedo squadrons already deployed in the Pacific as well as those about to be deployed aboard the escort carriers that would specialize in close air support for the amphibious assaults ahead. It continued to serve in this capacity for the remainder of World War II.

Major Ringblom was succeeded by Major Otis V. Calhoun on 2 March 1945 and led the squadron for two months until Major William M. Ritchey assumed command on 4 May. On 27 July 1945, Major Russell R. Riley relieved Major Ritchey and led the squadron for the remainder of its service.

After the Japanese surrender, VMTB-943 remained at El Toro, serving as a component squadron of MAG-46 until it suffered the fate common to all of the Marines' scout-bombing and torpedo squadrons and was deactivated on 31 January 1946. The squadron has seen no active service since that date.

Corporal Edwin J. Martin, Jr., designed the squadron's insignia. Apparently the idea of a central figure that represented the squadron's new aircraft and weapon appealed to Corporal Martin, and the turkey carrying a Mk. XIII torpedo was adopted. While "turkey" was the nickname of the Avenger, it should be recalled that the turkey is a flightless bird. Headquarters, Marine Corps, approved the design in August 1945. If any insignia were made to this design, research has failed to uncover an example.

There is no record of any insignia design for VMSB-943.

MARINE SCOUT BOMBING SQUADRON 944

VMSB-944 was activated on 10 April 1944 at MCAS, Cherry Point, North Carolina and was commanded by Major Paul L. Andre, Jr. On 1 June, Major Richard M. Caldwell assumed command following Major Andre's transfer.

On 15 June, VMSB-944 was ordered from Cherry Point to the auxiliary airfield at Camp Lejune, North Carolina, and remained there until it was deactivated on 10 October 1944 after just six month's service. It has remained among the inactive squadrons since that date.

There is no record of any insignia design submitted or approved for VMSB-944 during its brief service.

TORPEDO BOMBER TRAINING UNIT

Author's Collection

The sudden coming of World War II found the Marines without any torpedo bombing squadrons despite the almost universal preference of the torpedo as an anti-ship weapon. However, as more and more Marine squadrons, especially scout-bombing squadrons, were committed to grinding battles in the Solomons, first in defense of Guadalcanal and then in the accelerating offensive operations of early 1943, several Marine VMSB squadrons found themselves equipped with the Grumman TBF-1 Avenger torpedo bomber and serving as torpedo squadrons regardless of their mission designations on paper. Although it had not been anticipated the Marines at Guadalcanal found themselves at the tender mercies of the Imperial Japanese Navy, and, in theory at least, the torpedo was a more effective weapon against armored warships than the bomb.

Initially, the Marine Avenger squadrons received their torpedo training under the tutelage of the Navy. However, the Navy was in the midst of a massive expansion of its own. The attack on Pearl Harbor found the Navy's torpedo squadrons equipped with the antiquated Douglas TBD Devastator. While the TBD managed to escape serious losses in its initial combat exposures in the carrier raids in the early months of 1942 and at the Battle of the Coral Sea on 7-8 May, the TBD squadrons met their first serious fighter opposition at Midway on 4 June 1942. The results spelled the end of the Devastator among the first line squadrons of the fleet. Torpedo 8 was wiped out with only one aviator surviving the action, and the losses inflicted on the other two torpedo squadrons were only slightly less severe. Torpedo squadrons 3, 6, and 8 launched a total of forty-one aircraft against the Japanese fleet. Thirty-five were lost. Also, the TBD was in the process of replacement by the Grumman TBF Avenger by the time of Midway. As a result, the Navy had its plate full with the conversion of its surviving torpedo bomber crews to

the new aircraft and with the training of the host of new squadrons that were being established on almost a weekly basis.

The effect of this was that the training of the Marine torpedo squadrons was hurried and often on a "catch as catch can" basis. Many of the Marine aircrews that went into action from Henderson Field on Guadalcanal in late 1942 may never have dropped a torpedo equipped with a live warhead before their initiation into combat. Paradoxically, considering the wretched state of American torpedoes in general and the Mk. XIII aerial torpedo in particular, at the time, this may not have made all that much difference. While during the years prior to World War II, a great deal of faith had been placed in the effectiveness of the torpedo versus the bomb against armored ships. This was perhaps best stated by Britain's Royal Navy that "it was better to let water in at the bottom than air out of the top." However, the standard American aerial torpedo of the time, the Mk.XIII, was near to useless. It was slow and delicate. [It could be dropped at speeds of no greater than 100 knots at an altitude of no more than 100 feet.] It ran deeper than set and was equipped with an exploder that often failed to function. This is in sharp contrast to the Japanese aerial torpedo which was much more rugged and reliable and faster. It could be dropped at more than twice the speed from three times the altitude, and, much to the pain of the United States Navy, its larger warhead detonated when it found its target! These problems with the Mk XIII were corrected eventually, but by the time they were made good, torpedo actions for the Marines had dropped dramatically.

These problems aside, the Navy's rush to train its own torpedo squadrons led to the activation of the Marine Torpedo Bomber Training Unit at San Diego. This followed the Marines' reasoning that there is only one way to do anything, and that is the Marine way. The unit continued to train the VMTB squadrons until after the end of World War II when it was deactivated.

The example of the TBTU insignia in the plate was designed by the Walt Disney Studios, and its comic depiction of one of Donald Duck's nephews, Huey, Dewey, or Louie, perched on a torpedo with his diploma clutched in one hand and busily reading the torpedo manual is an excellent graphic representation of the feelings of many of the graduates after their hurried introduction into the world of torpedo tactics.

Opposite: Deckload Strike
Although this photograph was taken aboard a CVL in 1944, it is useful to show the details of the TBF/TBM Avenger that was the aircraft utilized by the TBTU. [U.S. Navy Photo]

SELECTED BIBLIOGRAPHY

BOOKS

Andrew, Colonel John R. "Rod", Jr.; *U.S. MARINES IN BATTLE, AN-NASIRIYAH, 23 MARCH – 2 APRIL 2003;* Washington, D.C.; Marine Corps Historical Center; 2009.

Bishop, Chris & Dorr, Robert F.Editors, *VIETNAM AIR WAR DEBRIEF;* London, England; Aerospace Publishing, Ltd.; 1996. Chronological account of the air war in Southeast Asia from 1945 through 1975. Lots of color & many first-person accounts.

Blakeney, Jane; *HEROES, U.S. MARINE CORPS 1861 – 1955 – ARMED FORCES AWARDS & FLAGS;* Washington, D.C.; Guthrie Lithograph Co., Inc.; 1957.

Boyce, Colonel J. Ward, U.S.A.F. (Ret.), Editor; *AMERICAN FIGHTER ACES ALBUM;* Mesa, AZ; American Fighter Aces Association; 1996. Alphatical listing of the 1,442 American fighter aces. Contains a brief biographical sketch, victories credited & awards earned. Has some errors but overall a good reference for the individuals.

Brown, Lieutenant Colonel Ronald J.; *U.S. MARINES IN THE PERSIAN GULF, 1990 – 1991, WITH MARINE FORCES ALOAT IN DESERT SHIELD AND DESERT STORM;* Washington, D.C.; Marine Corps Historical Center 1998.

Boggs, Major Charles W., Jr.; *MARINE AVIATION IN THE PHILIP-PINES*; Washington, DC; Historical Division, Headquarters Marine Corps; US Government Printing Office; Undated Excellent reference on the Marine air operations throughout the campaign.

Canzona, Captain Nicholas A U.S.M.C. & Montross, Lynn; *U.S. MARINE OPERATIONS IN KOREA, 1950 – 1953, Vol. III;* Washington, D.C.; United States Government Printing Office; 1957

Condon, Major General John P. & Mersky, Peter B.; *CORSAIRS TO PAN-THERS, U.S. MARINE AVIATION IN KOREA*; Washington, D.C.; Marine Corps Historical Center; 2002.

Cosmas, Graham A. & Murray, Lieutenant Colonel Terrence R.; *U.S. MARINES IN VIETNAM, VIETNAMIZATION AND REDEPLOYMENT, 1970 – 1971,* Washington, D.C.; Marine Corps Historical Center, 1986.

Doll, Thomas; *USN/USMC OVER KOREA*; Carrollton, TX; Squadron/Signal Publications, Inc.; 1988. General background on Korea and the call-up of Reserves.

—, Jackson, B.R. & Riley, W.A.; *NAVY AIR COLORS, Vols. 1 & 2*; Carrollton, TX; Squadron/Signal Publications; 1983 & 1985

Donald, David & Lake, John, Editors; *US NAVY & MARINE CORPS AIR POWER DIRECTORY*; London; Aerospace Publishing, Ltd.; 1992 Excellent reference covering wings, groups, squadrons, air stations, aircraft & weapons as of the date of publication.

Dorr, Robert F.; *DOUGLAS A-1 SKYRAIDER*; London; Osprey Publishing, Ltd.; 1989.

—, *GRUMMAN A-6 INTRUDER*; London; Osprey Publishing, Ltd.; 1987.

Drendel, Lou; *AIR WAR OVER SOUTHEAST ASIA, Vols. 1, 2, & 3*; Carrollton, TX; Squadron/Signal Publications; 1982, 1983 & 1984.

—; *USMC PHANTOMS IN COMBAT*; Carrollton, TX; Squadron/Signal Publications; 1990.

Dunham, Major George R & Quinlan, Lieutenant Colonel David A.; *U.A. MARINE IN VIETNAM, THE BITTER END, 1973 – 1975*; Washington, D.C.; Marine Corps Historical Center, 1990.

Elliott, Major John M., USMC (Ret.); *THE OFFICIAL MONOGRAM US NAVY & MARINE CORPS AIRCRAFT COLOR GUIDE*, Vols. 1, 2, 3 & 4; Sturbridge, MA; Monogram Aviation Publications; 1987, 1989, 1991 and 1993. While devoted primarily to aircraft colors and markings, the series contains data on activation & deactivation dates, limited color plates of insignia & many excellent photos accurately dated.

Francillon, Rene J.; *TONKIN GULF YACHT CLUB*; Annapolis, MD: Naval Institute Press; 1988. Listing of each combat deployment by carrier, aircraft type, squadron and dates. Losses and kills.

—; *VIETNAM, THE WAR IN THE AIR*; London; Aerospace Publishing, Ltd.; 1987

Frank, Richard B.; *GUADALCANAL*; New York, NY; Penguin Books; 1992. Limited data on Marine aviation activities.

Grosvenor, Gilbert, Editor; *INSIGNIA & DECORATIONS OF THE U.S. ARMED FORCES*; Washington, D.C.; The National Geographic Society; Revised 1 December 1944. While hard to find, this is an excellent reference on AAF, USN & USMC squadron insignia during that period of WW II. Has small, but legible, color reproductions of more than 250 Navy & Marine aviation unit insignia.

Hallion, Richard P.; *THE NAVAL AIR WAR IN KOREA*; New York, NY; Kensington Publishing Corp.; 1986

Hammel, Eric; *GUADALCANAL – STARVATION ISLAND*; New York, NY; Crown Publishers, Inc.; 1987.

Hata, Ikuhiko & Izawa, Yasuho, Transulated by Ghorman, Don Cyril; *JAPANESE NAVAL ACES & FIGHTER UNITS IN WORLD WAR II*; Annapolis, MD; Naval Institute Press, 1989 Costly but interesting view from the "other side of the hill."

Hicks, Major Norman W, U.S.M.C., Kuokka, Major Hubard D, U.S.M.C. & Montross, Lynn; *U.S. MARINE OPERATIONS IN KOREA, 1950-1953 Vol IV;* Washington, D.C.; United States Government Printing Office; 1962.

Jackson, R.B.; *DOUGLAS SKYRAIDER*; Fallbrook, CA; Aero Publishers, Inc.; 1969

Kasulka, Duane; *USN AIRCRAFT CARRIER UNITS, 1946 – 1973*, Vols. 1, 2 & 3; Carrollton, TX: Squadron/Signal Publications, Inc.; 1985 & 1988

Kilduff, Peter; *DOUGLAS A-4 SKYHAWK*; London; Osprey Publishing, Ltd.; 1983

Knott, Capt. Richard C., USN, Editor; *THE NAVAL AVIATION GUIDE*; Annapolis, MD: Naval Institute Press; 1985. Excellent source for listing of then-current squadrons, missions, etc. & general background on Naval Aviation.

Koalowski, Francis X. "Frank;" *U.S. MARINES IN BATTLE, AN-NAJAF ,* *AUGUST 2004;* Washington, D.C.; Marine Corps Historical Center, 2009.

Lake, John, Editor; *McDONNELL F-4 PHANTOM, SPIRIT IN THE SKIES*; London; Aerospace Publishing, Ltd.; 1992. Covers all operators of the F-4.

Love, Robert W., Jr., *HISTORY OF THE UNITED STATES NAVY, Vols. 1 & 2*; Harrisburg, PA; Stackpole Books; 1992.

Lowery, Colonel Nathan S.; *U.S. MARINES IN AFGHANISTAN, 2001 – 2002, FROM THE SEA;* Washington, D.C.; Marine Corps Historical Center, 2011.

Lundstrom, John B.; *THE FIRST TEAM AND THE GUADALCANAL CAM-PAIGN: NAVAL FIGHTER COMBAT FROM AUGUST TO NOVEMBER* 1942; Annapolis, MD; US Naval Institute Press; 1994. Excellent, detailed reference on the activities of the Marine squadrons during that critical period of WWII.

Mied, Lieutenant Colonel Pat, U.S.M.C. & Yingling, Major James W, U.S.M.C.; *U.S.MARINE OPERATIONS IN KOREA, 1950 – 1953, Vol V;* Washington, D.C.; United States Government Printing Office; 1972

Three volumes of the Marines' five volume official history of the Korean War.

Mersky, Peter B., *U.S. MARINE CORPS AVIATION 1912 TO THE PRES-ENT*; Baltimore, MD; Nautical & Aviation Publishing Co. of America; 1987. Good short history of Marine aviation.

—;*TIME OF THE ACES: MARINE PILOTS IN THE SOLOMONS, 1942 – 1944*; Washington, D.C., Marine Corps Historical Center; 1993.

— & Polmar, Norman; *THE NAVAL AIR WAR IN VIETNAM*; Baltimore, MD; Nautical & Aviation Publishing Co.; 1981.

Miller, Thomas G., Jr.; *CACTUS AIR FORCE*; New York, NY; Harper & Row; 1969. May have been the best reference on the subject until the publication of Lundstrom's work & covers more than fighter squadrons.

Morse, Stan, General Editor; *GULF AIR WAR DEBRIEF*; London; Aerospace Publishing, Ltd.; 1991. Lists orders of battle, missions, losses for the Gulf War.

Musciano, Walter A., *SAGA OF THE BENT-WING BIRDS*; New York, NY; AEROFILE, Inc.

Nelson, Derek & Parsons, Dave; *OFFICIAL & UNOFFICIAL U.S. NAVAL AIR PATCHES*; Osceola, WI: Motor Books International; 1990

Pawlowski, Gareth L.; *FLAT-TOPS AND FLEDGLINGS*; New York, NY; Castle Books; 1971

Rawls, Walton; *DISNEY DONS DOG TAGS – THE BEST OF DISNEY MILITARY INSIGNIA FROM WORLD WAR II*; New York, NY; The Abbeville Publishing Group; 1992

Scutts, Jerry; *MARINE MITCHELS;* St. Paul, Minnesota, Phalanx Publishing Co., Ldt., 1993. Excellent, brief monograph of the Marines' VMB squadrons of WWII.

Sherrod, Robert L.; *HISTORY OF MARINE CORPS AVIATION IN WW II*; Baltimore, MD; Nautical & Aviation Publications of America; 1987. Excellent, detailed historical record.

Shulimson, Jack; *U.S. MARINES IN VIETNAM: AN EXPANDING WAR, 1966;* Washington, D.C.; Marine Corps Historical Center 1982.

—, Blasiol, Lieutenant Colonel Leonard A, Smith, Charles R., & Dawson, Captain David A.;*U.S. MARINES IN VIETNAM, THE DEFINING YEAR, 1968*; Washington, D.C.; Marine Corps Historical Center, 1997.

—& Joshnson, Major Charles C; *U.S. MARINES IN VIETNAM: THE LANDING AND THE BUILDUP, 1965*; Washington, D.C.; Marine Corps Historical Center; 1978.

Smith, Charles R.; *U.S. MARINES IN VIETNAM, HIGH MOBILITY & STANDDOWN, 1969;* Washington, D.C.; Marine Corps Historical Center, 1998.

Sterns, Lieutenant Colonel LeRoy D.; *U.S. MARINES IN THE PERSIAN GULF, 1990-1991; THE 3D MARINE AIRCRAFT WING IN DESERT SHIELD AND DESERT STORM;* Washington, D.C.; Marine Corps Historical Center, 1999.

Styling, Mark; *CORSAIR ACES OF WORLD WAR II*; London; Osprey Publishing; 1995.

Telfer, Major Gary L., Rogers, Lieutenant Colonel Lane & Fleming, V. Keith, Jr.; *U.S. MARINES IN VIETNAM; FIGHTING THE NORTH VIETNAMESE, 1967*; Washington, D.C.; Marine Corps Historical Center, 1984.

Thomas, Geoff; *U.S. NAVY CARRIER AIRCRAFT COLOURS*; New Malden, Surrey, Great Britain; Air Research Publications; 1989. Don't be misled by the title. It lists air group composition and orders of battle for each major carrier campaign of WW II in the Pacific.

Tillman, Barrett; *AVENGER AT WAR*; Annapolis, MD; Naval Institute Press; 1970.

—; *CORSAIR – THE F4U IN WORLD WAR II*; Annapolis, MD; Naval Institute Press, 1979.

—; *DAUNTLESS – THE SBD IN WORLD WAR II*; Annapolis, MD; Naval Institute Press, ????.

—; *HELLCAT – THE F6F IN WORLD WAR II*; Annapolis, MD; Naval Institute Press, 1979.

—; *WILDCAT – THE F4F IN WORLD WAR II, Second Edition*; Annapolis, MD; Naval Insititute Press; 1990. This is an excellent series of works by Tillman and are much more operational histories than technical histories. The volume on the HELLCAT is the best source used for the activities of Marine night fighter squadrons.

—; *WILDCAT ACES OF WORLD WAR II*; London, Osprey Publishing; 1995

Westermeyer, Paul W.; *U.S. MARINES IN BATTLE, AL-KHAFJI, 28 2JANUARY – 1 FEBRUARY 1991;* Washington, D.C.; Marine Corps Historical Center, 2008.

White, Alexander S.; *DAUNTLESS MARINE, JOSEPH SAILER, JR., DIVE BOMBING ACE OF GUADALCANAL*; Fairfax Station, VA; White Knight Press; 1996. Bioggraphy of the first commanding officer of VMSB-132 & posthumous Navy Cross winner.

Various Aircraft Monographs by several authors from Squadron/Signal, Osprey, etc. Among works of this type, the "Naval Aircraft Series" by Steve Ginter is highly recommended.

PERIODICALS

The Hook,
Various Articles, The Tailhook Association. Each issue features information on squadron histories, activation/deactivation, recent deployments, etc. In short, a gold mine of information.

Wings of Gold,
Various Articles, The official publication of the Association of Naval Aviation Good information source on naval aviation, past and present.

Naval Aviation News,
"Tracing Squadron Lineage, Part 1" & part 2; Naval Historical Center; Jan./Feb. 1987 & Mar./Apr. 1987. Excellent Source for Current Naval Aviation; Periodically has articles on insignia, & the older editions are a gold mine of information on insignia & lineage.

Naval Institute Proceedings;
"The Navy Did Its Part"; Palmer, M.A.; Naval Institute; May 1991. Listing of the Navy Squadrons Participating in Desert Storm.

World Air Power Journal,
Various articles on individual aircraft types & current events in aviation; published quarterly.

Wings of Fame,
From the same publisher as *World Air Power Journal*, but its focus is on historical events and aircraft, as opposed to the former's focus on current events & aircraft.

As a general comment, the importance of the internet in any research/reference endeavor cannot be overstated. All the active squadrons in service today have an official website, and while some are more up to date and helpful than others, these are an excellent source of information. In spite of their usefulness, it must remembered that the maintenance of updating of a squadron's website is a responsibility of its Public Affairs Officer, and the PAO is a military officer, not a professional historian. Therefore, while current information, e.g., a squadron's deployments in the global war on terror, are likely quite accurate, information from previous wars should be crosschecked with other sources.

Regarding various online reference sites, such as the online encyclopedia *Wikipedia*, it must be kept in mind that they do not employ a professional research and writing staff. Instead, they rely on the submissions of others, and as a rule, these submissions are not fact-checked, so these sources should be crosschecked. This comment should not be construed as a negative comment regarding sites such as *Wikipedia*. It is simply a statement of fact that should be kept in mind.

Several sites devoted to various security and military information are easily found on the web. Again, however, a note of caution is appropriate. Some of these are free and others offer more information for subscribers, but a careful comparison of the entries in some of these sites with the individual units' sites will reveal that these are often word-for-word "lifts" from the official unit sites.

There are also lists of all of the currently active squadrons in the Marine Corps available on the web and a list of inactive Marine squadrons, as well. The latter is not totally complete as it does not list units such as Headquarters and Maintenance Squadrons, etc. However, the listings present are, for the most part, accurate.

The sites that offer photographs of many subjects included in this work are almost too numerous to count. These are a mix of those in the public domain, such as those from the military services and the Department of Defense, and others are copyrighted. These must be checked thoroughly before use.

The web is also an excellent source of historical information for inactive units. Virtually all squadrons have a website in one form or another. Some contain scarcely more than an outline of the unit's history, while others will have a history that is comparable to anything that might be produced by the Marines' History and Museums Division, which is another excellent source of information.